COMPETITION AND THE ENTERPRISE ACT 2002

Two week loan

Please return on or before the last
date stamped below.
Charges are made for late return.

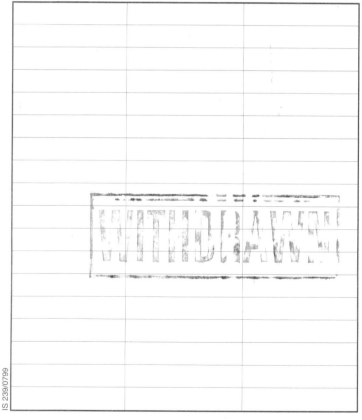

INFORMATION SERVICES PO BOX 430, CARDIFF CF10 3XT

COMPETITION AND THE ENTERPRISE ACT 2002

Mark Furse, BA (Economics and Law), LLM, PhD
Consultant and Senior Lecturer, Nicolas Copernicus University, Torun

JORDANS

2003

Published by
Jordan Publishing Limited
21 St Thomas Street
Bristol BS1 6JS

British Library Cataloguing-in-Publication Data
A catalogue record for this book is available from the British Library.

ISBN 0 85308 809 8

Typeset by Jordan Publishing Limited
Printed by MPG Books Ltd, Bodmin, Cornwall

Preface

The Enterprise Act 2002 marks a significant further change to the competition law regime in the UK, almost completing the process begun with the Competition Act 1998 (some minor matters remain to be resolved in the anticipated Communications Act). This text is intended to be an accessible guide to the competition provisions of the Act, and assumes some familiarity with the competition regimes of the UK, which the Act both supplements and changes, and of the EC, alongside which the Act is to operate. However, given that the Act, if successful, will widen the scope for the reliance on competition law by those injured by illegal anti-competitive conduct, I have included at the outset a brief general discussion of the regime prior to the Act's entry into force. Readers will also be aware that throughout 2002 there were intense discussions as to the reform of EC competition law. In this book I have only been able to anticipate these based on the available documentation at the time of the book being written, and it is likely that there will be some changes still to emerge as the proposals are finalised – the CBI has been robust in querying the wisdom of making fundamental changes to the UK competition system at a time when there was such uncertainty about the EC reforms.

This is the first book of this nature I have written, and I have found it an interesting challenge to have to analyse an Act in the absence of any significant published commentary on the new law. I have relied heavily on the available resources – in particular the debates on the passage of the Act as reported in *Hansard*, the invaluable DTI *Explanatory Notes*, responses to the Bill from interested bodies, and preliminary guidance prepared by the Office of Fair Trading and the Competition Commission. This is particularly the case in relation to super-complaints dealt with in Chapter 6. Within only a few months of this book being published readers will have the opportunity to avail themselves of a large amount of material relating to the Act. My hope is that this will complement and supplement this book, rather than contradict it.

Although I have dealt here with a great many of the competition provisions of the Enterprise Act 2002, I have not provided a commentary to all of them. In particular I have not dealt with a number of provisions of the Schedules, which are self-explanatory, and which are of course set out in the text of the Act reproduced at the end of the book.

It is customary to acknowledge the support of one's employers in the preface of a book such as this. I should, therefore, give credit to Graham and Sara Springett, licensees of the Ebrington Arms, an exceptionally well-run traditional Cotswold pub, where I have been working during the period of writing (and I must confess that when I am not working there I may often be found on the other side of the bar). When this book is published, I shall be teaching at Nicolas Copernicus University, Torun, Poland, but hope to re-enter UK academia full time later in the year, and would welcome any expressions of interest. I have, in the interim, found the experience of working behind a bar most refreshing. However, I have yet to persuade the regulars of the full merits and excitement of competition law, a subject which continues to grip me. I would also like to thank Danny Clarke for keeping me fit in body as well as mind. Students of the University of Nancy 2, where I spent some time in late autumn 2002 as a Visiting Professor working through the intricacies of the Enterprise Bill (as it then was), asked some of the right questions and helped to clarify some of the more awkward provisions of the legislation.

I am also grateful to Brenda Sufrin, Reader in Law at Bristol University, with whom I co-authored an article on market investigation references (dealt with in Chapter 4). Her ideas have necessarily influenced this chapter for the better. The editorial team at Jordans have been professional and helpful as always. Any and all errors or omissions in this text are my sole responsibility. Should any reader wish to bring my attention to any matters which they feel have been overlooked, or underdeveloped, I may be contacted directly at: mark@mfcompetitionlaw.com

The law in this book is intended to be up to date as at the date on which the Act received Royal Assent, although in certain respects I have been able to incorporate material published up to 4 January 2003.

Mark Furse
Ebrington, The Cotswolds
January 2003

Contents

Chapter Three – MERGER CONTROL

Chapter Four – MARKET INVESTIGATIONS

Table of Cases

References are to paragraph numbers.

Table of Statutes

Table of Statutory Instruments

References are to paragraph numbers.

Table of European Materials

References are to paragraph numbers.

Table of Guidance and Other Materials

References are to paragraph numbers.

Command papers

Competition and Enterprise Act 2002: Draft Guidance and Explanatory Notes

Competition Act 1998: Guidance

Other Guidance

Overseas Guidance

United States

Table of Abbreviations

The Act	Enterprise Act 2002
CA	Consumers' Association
CA 1998	Competition Act 1998
CAT	Competition Appeals Tribunal
CBI	Confederation of British Industy
CC	Competition Commission
CC *Market Investigation References*	CC *Market Investigation References: Competition Commission Guidelines* (Consultation Document) (Sept 2002)
CC *Mergers*	CC *Merger References: Competition Commission Guidelines* (Consultation Document) (Sept 2002)
CCAT	Competition Commission Appeals Tribunal
CDDA 1986	Company Directors Disqualification Act 1986
CDO	competition disqualification order
CS	Competition Service
the Director	the Director General of Fair Trading
DTI	Department of Trade and Industry
ECHR	European Convention on the Protection of Human Rights and Fundamental Freedoms 1950
ECJ	European Court of Justice
EC Merger Control Regulation	Regulation 4064/89 on the Control of Concentrations Between Undertakings
FTA 1973	Fair Trading Act 1973
HHI	Herfindahl–Hirschman Index
MMC	Monopolies and Mergers Commission
NCA	National Competition Authority
NCC	National Consumers' Council
OFCOM	Office of Communications

OFT	Office of Fair Trading
OFT *Market Investigation References*	OFT *Market Investigation References* (July 2002)
OFT *Mergers*	OFT *Mergers: Substantive Assessment* (Oct 2002)
RIPA 2000	Regulation of Investigatory Powers Act 2000
SFO	Serious Fraud Office
SLC	substantial lessening of competition
SSNIP	small but significant non-transitory increase in price
WIA 1991	Water Industry Act 1991

Chapter One

THE COMPETITION PROVISIONS OF THE ENTERPRISE ACT 2002

INTRODUCTION

1.1   The Enterprise Act 2002 ('the Act') received Royal Assent on 7 November 2002. The Act updates the mergers and monopolies regimes enshrined within the Fair Trading Act 1973 (FTA 1973), reforms the institutional structure of the domestic competition law regime, introduces a stand-alone criminal offence in relation to certain cartel conduct, and enhances the role of private litigation. As such, it completes the reform of domestic competition law that began with the Competition Act 1998. As well as its relationship to the other domestic law of competition, the Act should be seen also in the context of its relationship with EC competition law, enshrined in Arts 81 and 82 EC,[1] and the procedures relating to the application of that law, which were, at the time of the passage of the Act, subject to a substantial reform process. In particular, this reform radically alters the relationship between EC and domestic competition law, clearly delineating the boundaries within which each can be applied.[2]

1.2   This chapter will set out the background of the Act, its broad structure, and the framework within which it operates. The following chapters will deal in more detail with each of the specific parts of the Act that relate to competition law, as well as discussing any guidance and clarification produced at the time of writing.

---

[1]   Articles of the EC Treaty are referred to throughout as Art XX EC.

[2]   Political agreement was reached on the reform proposals at the end of November 2002, and Council Regulation (EC) 1/2003 was enacted in December 2002 (see **1.32**).

THE DOMESTIC COMPETITION LAW REGIME

The Competition Act 1998[1]

1.3   The Competition Act 1998 (CA 1998) received Royal Assent on 9 November 1998, and its core provisions began to bite on 1 March 2000 ('the starting date'). The CA 1998 was intended clearly to replace a diverse and idiosyncratic system of public regulation of competition law with one modelled explicitly on the competition law of the EC. Thus, s 2 of the CA 1998 introduced the Chapter I Prohibition, a prohibition on anti-competitive agreements, which is the domestic mirror of Art 81 EC. Similarly, s 18 introduced the Chapter II Prohibition, the equivalent of Art 82 EC. Section 60 provided that the provisions of the CA 1998 were, so far as possible and in the absence of any 'relevant differences', to be interpreted in a manner which was consistent with EC law. In addition, private remedies were, indirectly, provided for. Since the starting date, there have been a number of decisions taken by the Director General of Fair Trading ('the Director'), and a small number of private actions, seeking both damages and injunctive relief, have been reported.[2]

1.4   The CA 1998 replaced various statutes. The law relating to illegal agreements had previously been enshrined in the Restrictive Trade Practices Acts 1976 and 1977 (the provisions of which may continue to be applied in private actions to agreements falling within the terms of the Acts entered into while they still had effect), and the Resale Prices Act 1976, which had introduced a prohibition on horizontal resale price maintenance. The Competition Act 1980 had related to unilateral courses of conduct, but was in practice little used. None of these statutes provided a quick route to a private action by a party injured by another's anti-competitive conduct.

---

[1]   There are a number of books dealing with the provisions of the CA 1998. These include Frazer, T and Hornsby, S *The Competition Act 1998: A Practical Guide* (Bristol, Jordan Publishing, 1999); Freeman, P and Whish, R *A Guide to the Competition Act 1998* (London, Butterworths, 1999); Rodger, BJ and MacCulloch, A (eds) *The UK Competition Act: A New Era for UK Competition Law* (Oxford, Hart Publishing, 2000); Flynn, J and Stratford, J *Competition: Understanding the 1998 Act* (Bembridge, Palladian Law Publishing, 1999); Livingston, D *The Competition Act 1998: A Practical Guide* (London, Sweet & Maxwell, 2001); Coleman, M and Grenfell, M *The Competition Act 1998: Law and Practice* (Oxford, OUP, 1999).

[2]   It appears that one effect of the CA 1998 has been increasingly to 'legalise' the process of competition law. The Under-Secretary of State commented at an early stage of the proceedings relating to the Act that: 'Those who run both competition authorities – the OFT and the Commission – say that legal resources are being deployed increasingly on the other side of investigations. It is a trend, but it is not under their control' (*Hansard*, Standing Committee B, 16 April 2002, col 47).

1.5   The enforcement of the CA 1998 will not be discussed in this book in any great detail, although specific cases will be referred to as necessary.[1] However, some general comments as to the vigour with which the CA 1998 is being enforced may shed some light on the state of competition law activity in the UK. The two prohibitions of the CA 1998 fully entered into force on 1 March 2000 and, by the end of the first two years, the position was described by the Director of Competition Enforcement in the Office of Fair Trading (OFT) in the following terms:

> 'In the year to March 2002 we issued nine published decisions. Three were infringement decisions with fines, 2 exemptions and 4 non-infringement decisions. We issued three unpublished s 47 decisions saying why we would not vary or withdraw an existing published decision. Three section 25 notices on proposed interim measures were issued. One was resolved by informal assurances and one by agreement between the parties. No interim measure directions were made. We have also handled four appeals to the CCAT.'[2]

1.6   It is not the purpose of the Act to make fundamental changes to the relatively new law of the CA 1998. However, a number of changes are made in the light of the experience gained under the operation of the CA 1998. These relate primarily to procedural matters. Other changes to the CA 1998 are necessitated as a consequence of more fundamental changes introduced by the Act, such as the criminalisation of cartel conduct, and the reshaping of some of the institutions.

The Fair Trading Act 1973 – monopolies and mergers

1.7   At the same time, the CA 1998 left in place the provisions of the Fair Trading Act 1973 (FTA 1973), a substantial piece of legislation which made provision for monopolies and mergers investigations.[3] At the heart of the FTA 1973 lay the 'public interest' test, against which conduct and mergers were to be evaluated. Thus, in relation to monopolies, for example, the Competition Commission (CC) could be asked to determine whether 'facts found by the Commission in pursuance of their investigations … operate, or may be expected to operate, against the public interest' (s 54(3)). The meaning of 'public interest' was explained further in s 84:

---

[1]   For a discussion of the early case-law, see Rodger, BJ 'Early Steps to a Mature Competition Law System: Case Law Developments in the First 18 Months of the Competition Act 1998' [2002] ECLR 52. The OFT maintains a register of the publicly notified cases, which may be accessed at *http://www.oft.gov.uk/business/competition+act/decisions/index.htm*.

[2]   Bloom, M 'Key Challenges in Public Enforcement', a speech to the British Institute of International and Comparative Law, 17 May 2002, OFT website.

[3]   The leading commentary on the FTA 1973, although it is now dated, is Cunningham, JP *The Fair Trading Act 1973* (London, Sweet & Maxwell, 1974). Further substantial discussion may be found in Livingston, D *Competition Law and Practice* (London, FT Law and Tax, 1995).

'(1) In determining for any purposes to which this section applies whether any particular matter operates, or may be expected to operate, against the public interest, the Commission shall take into account all matters which appear to them in the particular circumstances to be relevant and, among other things, shall have regard to the desirability –

(a)   of maintaining and promoting effective competition between persons supplying goods and services in the United Kingdom;

(b)   of promoting the interests of consumers, purchasers and other users of goods and services in the United Kingdom in respect of the prices charged for them and in respect of their quality and the variety of goods and services supplied;

(c)   of promoting, through competition, the reduction of costs and the development and use of new techniques and new products, and of facilitating the entry of new competitors into existing markets;

(d)   of maintaining and promoting the balanced distribution of industry and employment in the United Kingdom; and

(e)   of maintaining and promoting competitive activity in markets outside the United Kingdom on the part of producers of goods, and of suppliers of goods and services, in the United Kingdom.'

1.8   The lack of precision enshrined in this 'test' was criticised repeatedly. In 1995, the House of Commons Trade and Industry Committee reported that:

'The DGFT defined the public interest as "consumer well-being" but admitted that "I do not think anybody could possibly pretend that they could sit down and do some sums and have an answer they can defend against all comers at the end of the day". The Chairman of the MMC said that it was impossible to define the public interest in a general context, and the Minister simply referred to the criteria set out in the Act.'[1]

1.9   The core area to which the FTA 1973 applied was the control of monopoly conduct. The Monopolies and Mergers Commission (MMC) (which became the CC under the CA 1998) could be required to 'investigate and report on … (a) … the existence, or possible existence, of a monopoly situation' (s 5(1)), following a reference made by the Director. Monopoly situations were defined in s 6 in relation to the supply of goods, and in s 7 in relation to the supply of services. Sections 6 and 7 provided that a 'monopoly situation' may exist in situations in which 25% or more of the goods or services of a particular description were supplied by, or to, one and the same person in the UK. Such a situation was referred to as a 'scale monopoly'. In addition, provision was made for the examination of 'complex monopolies', as the power to investigate was also given where the 25% was supplied by or to 'members of one and the same group consisting of two or more … persons'. In s 6, it was provided that the two or more persons:

'are any two or more persons, not being a group of interconnected bodies corporate, who whether voluntarily or not, and whether by agreement or not, so conduct their respective affairs as in any way to prevent, restrict or distort competition in connection with the

---

[1]   HC249, 1995 *Trade and Industry Committee Fifth Report: UK Policy on Monopolies* (London, HMSO), point 20.

production or supply of goods of that description, whether or not they themselves are affected by the competition and whether the competition is between persons interested as producers or suppliers or between persons interested as customers of producers or suppliers.'

1.10   The procedure to be applied in relation to monopoly investigations was somewhat cumbersome. The Director was given the power, in s 44, to gather information 'for the purpose of assisting him in determining whether to make a monopoly reference'. Where the Director intended to make use of this power, he had first to submit a copy of the reference to the Secretary of State, who had the power to direct the CC not to proceed with the reference (s 50(6)). The CC would produce its report, and make any recommendations that it felt were appropriate. This report would be sent to the Minister and the Director. The final power to make any orders in relation to conduct was held by the Minister, or undertakings might be negotiated, at the request of the Minister, by the Director with the companies concerned.

1.11   The breach of any order would not give rise to criminal liability, but third parties were, at this stage, able to bring civil proceedings in respect of a breach, and the Crown could seek an injunction or 'any other appropriate relief' (s 93).

1.12   The CA 1998 made some amendments to the investigatory powers available to the Director, and reconstituted the old MMC but, apart from that, the monopoly provisions of the FTA 1973 were left undisturbed. The retention of the scale monopoly provisions was unexpected, and attracted some criticism.[1] The case put forward by the Department of Trade and Industry (DTI) was that:

'A prohibition approach is, however, less able to deal with the situation where, for example, an individual abuse has been tackled, but where there is a prospect that other abuses by the dominant company may continue in the future. In such a situation, structural remedies to reduce the dominant position of the firm concerned may be more appropriate than relying on the prohibition alone to deter future abuse. Taking action to reduce market power in this way would be possible under the scale monopoly provisions of the [FTA 1973], but is not readily achievable under a prohibition based approach. There is accordingly an argument that the scale monopoly provisions of the FTA should be retained for use in these limited circumstances.'[2]

1.13   The case for the retention of the complex monopoly provisions, however, was much stronger. In particular, the experience with Art 82 EC at the EC level had shown that it was very difficult to apply Art 82 EC to

---

[1]   See, for example, Scholes, J 'The UK Draft Competition Bill: Comments Raised on Observations of the Competition Law Association' (1998) ECLR 32.

[2]   DTI *A Prohibition Approach to Anti-competitive Agreements and Abuse of Dominant Position: Draft Bill* (London, HMSO, 1997), para 6.22.

situations of 'collective dominance' (also referred to as 'joint dominance' or 'oligopolistic dominance').[1] Even in situations where it was possible to do so, the case-law suggested that markets involving a maximum of three, or at most four, firms might be caught,[2] whereas the experience in the UK of complex monopoly investigations under the FTA 1973 showed that it was possible to apply the provisions to markets constituting tens, or even hundreds, of firms,[3] where their parallel conduct, which would not amount to an 'agreement' or 'concerted practice' within the meaning of Art 81 EC, or the Chapter I Prohibition, nevertheless had a detrimental impact on the public interest. The move from these monopoly inquiries to 'market investigations' is discussed further in Chapter 4.

1.14   The provisions in the FTA 1973 relating to mergers were less obviously in need of reform than those relating to monopolies. However, the involvement of the relevant Secretary of State drew charges of political involvement in the competition law system in two respects. The first was that the Secretary of State was responsible for the decision, acting on the advice of the Director (although there was no obligation to follow this advice), to refer a merger. The second was that he was responsible for any decision, acting on the advice of the CC, to permit or prohibit a merger or permit it with undertakings or divestiture.

1.15   The main changes made to the merger regime by the Act are the removal, save in exceptional cases, of the role of the Minister, and the alteration of the test of a merger's acceptability from that of the 'public interest' test, to that of a 'substantial lessening of competition' (SLC) test. These developments are explained in more detail in Chapter 3.

Special sector legislation

1.16   In addition to the general competition legislation of the FTA 1973 and the CA 1998, there is a substantial amount of legislation relating to the control of 'special sectors' – such as water, rail, gas, electricity, postal services, and television broadcasting. There are also situations in which the special sector regulators have 'concurrent' powers with the Director to apply the CA 1998 to their relevant sector. The Act does not make substantial changes to this body of rules. Newspaper mergers falling at present within the special procedure of

---

[1]   The leading case on collective dominance is now *Airtours plc v Commission of the European Communities* Case T-342/99 [2002] 5 CMLR 317, [2002] UKCLR 642. See also *Compagnie Maritime Belge SA v Commission* joined cases C-395/96P and C-396/96P [2000] 4 CMLR 1076.

[2]   See, for example, *Price Waterhouse/Coopers & Lybrand* (Commission Decision 1999/152) (1999) OJ L50/27.

[3]   As in *Domestic Electrical Goods: A Report on the Supply in the UK of Televisions, Video Cassette Recorders, Hi-fi Systems and Camcorders* (London, HMSO, 1997), Cm 3675.

s 58(1) of the FTA 1973 are exempted from the effect of the Act,[1] and the provisions of the Water Industry Act 1991 relating to mergers are amended by the Act. Elsewhere, consequential amendments which flow from the changes introduced to the competition procedures and institutions by the Act are made as necessary. These are dealt with as appropriate within this book.

The institutions

1.17   The CA 1998 made substantial adjustments to the institutional structure as it had previously stood. In particular, the Restrictive Practices Court was abolished, once it had heard a final case relating to the resale prices of over-the-counter medicaments. The central figure in the enforcement of the CA 1998 is the Director, who is supported by the OFT. The Director has the power to make decisions to the effect that the prohibitions of that Act have been infringed, and may impose a penalty in relation to such infringements. In addition, under ss 32 and 33, the Director may make 'directions' in relation to agreements and to conduct. Decisions of the Director could be appealed to the Competition Commission Appeals Tribunal (CCAT) (s 46), and from there to the Court of Appeal or other appropriate court on matters of law (s 49). The Director is required to issue guidance relating to the application of the CA 1998, and a number of 'technical guidelines' have been published. The Director also has responsibility under the FTA 1973 for initiating monopoly inquiries, for negotiating undertakings in lieu of such inquiries, and following inquiries where requested to do so by the Secretary of State, and finally for monitoring the adherence to any undertakings or orders entered into or made. The Director is also required to give advice as to whether any particular merger should be referred to the CC.

1.18   The old MMC was reconstituted as the CC, which was divided into two parts: the investigatory arm, responsible for monopolies and mergers inquiries (which also exercised some specific powers in relation to special sector legislation); and the CCAT, headed by a President. While it was originally intended that the membership of the two parts should not overlap, in fact there have been some instances in which an overlap has occurred.

1.19   The Secretary of State for Trade and Industry has a less substantial role under the CA 1998 than that enjoyed under the FTA 1973 (outlined above). The key role of the Secretary of State under the CA 1998 is that of making delegated legislation relating to matters such as exclusions from the prohibitions. Although, in relation to the FTA 1973, as we have seen, the role

---

[1]   Although these are to be dealt with in the legislation relating to the general communications industry currently under preparation – see **1.63–1.64**.

of the Secretary of State was a substantial one, in practice the aim of the Government was to reduce this role as far as possible. In particular, it was announced that the Minister would publish and follow the advice of the Director in relation to mergers, save in the most exceptional circumstances.[1]

1.20 The Act has made some significant changes to the institutional framework operating in the UK and has streamlined some of the procedures. These changes are set out in Parts 1 and 2 of the Act, and are further reflected in later substantive provisions (such as those relating to cartel offences, dealt with in Chapter 5). The general changes are addressed in Chapter 2. In particular, one of the key thrusts underpinning the Act has been that of the removal of the day-to-day enforcement of competition law in the UK from the political arena, and the role of the Secretary of State has been further cut back.

Third-party involvement in the system

Civil actions

1.21 The role of third parties in any competition law system is a crucial one. In the US, in particular, third-party civil actions play a key role in the enforcement process, and the provision of the treble-damages suit in the Clayton Act is expressly designed to encourage this. Further impetus comes from the contingency fee system, and the possibility of class-actions. It is almost inevitable that successful government intervention is followed up by private suits.[2] In the EC, the Commission has tried to encourage private actions,[3] albeit with only limited success. However, there are clearly cultural difficulties in encouraging greater private engagement in the competition law system. In April 2001, the DTI conducted a survey of 100 competition experts from around the world. One conclusion drawn was that 'only 10% of British respondents thought that competition policy was important to the UK public. This compared with 83% in the USA'.[4]

1.22 In the UK, the CA 1998 did not make explicit reference to a right to damages or other remedies flowing from breaches of the Act, but it was explained during the passage of the Bill that:

> '... third parties have a right of private action. Our clear intention in framing this Bill is that third parties may seek injunctions or damages in the courts if they have been adversely affected by the action of undertakings in breach of the prohibitions. This is an

---

[1] The so-called 'Tebbit Doctrine'.
[2] See generally Jones, CA *Private Enforcement of Antitrust Law in the EU, UK and USA* (Oxford, OUP, 1999).
[3] For example, via the *Notice on Cooperation between National Courts and the Commission* (1993) OJ C39/6.
[4] *Peer Review of the UK Competition Policy Regime, www.dti.gov.uk.*

important element of the regime. There is no need to make explicit provision in the Bill to achieve that result. Third party rights of action under the domestic regime are to be the same as those under articles [81 EC and 82 EC].'[1]

Thus, it is explained in the OFT technical guideline, *Enforcement*, that:

'Third parties who consider that they have suffered loss as a result of any unlawful agreement or conduct have a claim for damages in the courts. Section 60 provides for the United Kingdom authorities to handle cases in such a way as to ensure consistency with Community law, and expressly refers to decisions of the European Court and the European Commission as to the civil liability of an undertaking for harm caused by its infringement of Community law.'[2]

1.23 There have not, however, been a great number of reported cases brought on the basis of the prohibitions in the CA 1998, and none has yet been reported in which damages have been awarded. Injunctions have been sought on a number of occasions. The first such case was *Claritas (UK) Ltd v The Post Office and Postal Preference Service Ltd*,[3] in which the claimant sought to prevent the Post Office allegedly abusing a dominant position in the market for mail deliveries to collect information about mail-order customers by sending a mail shot which made extensive use of the 'Royal Mail' logo. The injunction was denied on the grounds that the Post Office was not dominant in the market in which the alleged abuse took place.[4] Injunctions have also been denied in the cases of *Getmapping plc v Ordnance Survey*[5] and *Suretrack Rail Services Ltd v Infraco JNP Ltd*.[6] However, in *Network Multimedia Television Ltd (t/a Silicon.Com) v Jobserve Ltd*,[7] the claimant was successful in obtaining an injunction, on the basis of the Chapter II Prohibition, restraining the defendant from refusing to allow third parties to advertise vacancies on the allegedly dominant defendant's website if they also advertised on the claimant's website. All of these cases concerned interim injunctions, and, at the time of writing, no cases have been completed in which a claimant has been successful in obtaining a remedy under either of the prohibitions of the CA 1998. However, in the case of *Hendry and others v The World Professional Billiards and Snooker Association Ltd*,[8] the claimants were partially successful in having some of the rules of the WPBSA declared as being in breach of the Chapter I

---

[1]   *Hansard* (HL) 25 November 1997, col 995.
[2]   Paragraph 5.1. See also CA 1998, s 60(6)(b).
[3]   [2001] UKCLR 2.
[4]   However, the OFT, in its decision in *Consignia plc and Postal Preference Service Ltd* CA98/4/2001 [2001] UKCLR 846, took the view that the combination of factors in the case were such that they 'provided reasonable grounds for suspecting that there were sufficiently close associative links between the ordinary mail market and the consumer lifestyle market to merit an investigation of Consignia's conduct on that market' (para 17), although it went on to find that there had in fact been no abuse perpetrated.
[5]   [2002] EWHC 1089, [2002] UKCLR 410.
[6]   [2002] EWHC 1316, [2002] All ER (D) 261 (Jun).
[7]   [2001] UKCLR 814, upheld on appeal as *Jobserve Ltd v Network Multimedia Television Ltd* [2002] UKCLR 184.
[8]   [2001] UKCLR 5.

Prohibition. Damages were not awarded, and the bulk of the claims brought were dismissed.[1]

1.24   One of the more contentious issues relating to the application of EC competition law has been that of the so-called 'euro-defence'. This refers to the situation in which a defendant to an action – usually, but not necessarily, a contractual one – argues that the contract in question, or other obligation, is invalidated by the application of competition law. These defences are often viewed in a dim light, particularly given the inability of the domestic courts to rule on arguments regarding the third paragraph of Art 81, under which exemptions may be granted by the EC Commission in respect of certain conduct falling within Art 81(1) (this point is considered further below). In the UK, this defence may now reasonably be termed the 'competition defence'. It was raised in the case of *Intel Corpn v VIA Technologies Inc and others*,[2] where Collins LJ noted that, for the purpose of the action, '"Euro-defences" are not in a special category, and indeed I accept … that the expression must not be treated as a pejorative term'. In the context of the interlocutory proceedings taking place, the judge also accepted that:

> 'the ease with which a defence based on article 81 or 82 may be generated on the basis of vague or imprecise allegations makes it necessary to scrutinise them with care in order to avoid defences with no merit at all going to a lengthy trial with expert economic evidence.'[3]

It is clear that the UK courts are likely to continue to treat 'competition defences' with a degree of scepticism, although, in the light of the case-law of the European Court of Justice (ECJ), care must be taken not to quickly reject valid claims.[4]

1.25   The second reported case arising under the CA 1998 shed some light on the approach that the courts might take in cases which were also being considered by the OFT. The two procedures are separate under the Act, and there is nothing to prevent a party from both complaining to the OFT, and, at the same time, bringing a private action. Such a situation arose in *Synstar Computer Services (UK) Ltd v ICL (Sorbus) Ltd and International Computers Ltd.*[5] Here, the court was asked to deal with an allegation of an abuse perpetrated in the 'after-sales' market in relation to certain computer systems. This is an area which raises some difficult questions of fact, albeit that these have been

---

[1]   See Furse, M 'Competition Law and the Courts' (2002) NLJ 1567–1568.

[2]   [2002] EWHC 1159, [2002] UKCLR 576.

[3]   At [90].

[4]   See, eg *Eco Swiss China Time Ltd v Benetton International NV* Case C-126/97 [2000] 5 CMLR 816 at para 36.

[5]   [2001] UKCLR 585.

somewhat clarified by the EC Commission.[1] At the time of the hearing, before Lightman J, a decision in respect of the complaint lodged with the OFT was expected imminently, and there were indications that if this went against the claimant, an appeal was likely, and an appeal was certain if the complaint was decided in the claimant's favour. The judge considered the issue of whether proceedings should be stayed, following the principles enunciated in a number of cases by the ECJ, which suggested, *inter alia*, that stays should be granted in order to prevent inconsistent decisions from being reached. The case was therefore stayed, pending the outcome of the administrative procedure. In the event, the OFT found that there was no dominance in the alleged market.[2] In the earlier *Post Office* case,[3] there was no reference in the judgment to the involvement of the OFT.

1.26 The experience to date suggests that the civil courts are not being actively used on a wide scale as a forum for the resolution of disputes relating to competition law. In its *Notice on Cooperation between National Courts and the Commission*,[4] the Commission points out that there are strong advantages to bringing claims before a court rather than before an administrative body. In particular, the administrative body is unable to award damages or costs, and courts can order interim measures.[5] Further, the courts can craft a remedy addressed to the particular needs of the claimant, whereas the administrative body is obliged to consider the position in general. On the other hand, making a complaint to the OFT has very low cost implications, and it is the OFT which, if motivated to pursue the complaint, bears the responsibility and costs of establishing the infringement. Complaints may be made anonymously, and the message that emanates from the OFT is 'don't notify, *do complain*'. It is clear, however, that one of the thrusts of the Act is to engage private parties more actively in the enforcement of competition law, in particular by greatly enhancing the procedures under which damages may be claimed following an adverse decision by the Director.[6]

Complaints

1.27 Under the terms of the CA 1998, any person may make a complaint to the OFT in respect of alleged breaches of the prohibitions. Following EC law, the Director is not obliged to pursue a complaint.[7] If he does not do so, however, the rejection of the complaint must be in the form of a decision such

---

[1] These are set out in the note on the *Pelikan/Kyocera* complaint, in the *25th Annual Report on Competition Policy* (Com (96) 126 final) at points 86 and 87.

[2] *ICL/Synstar* CA98/6/2001, [2001] UKCLR 902.

[3] See **1.23**.

[4] (1993) OJ C39/6.

[5] Although the Director also has the power to do so under s 35 of the CA 1998.

[6] See **6.19–6.36**.

[7] *Automec srl v EC Commission* Case T-24/90 [1992] 5 CMLR 431.

that it may be capable of appeal to the CCAT.[1] Any person who is not one to whom a decision is addressed 'may apply to the Director asking him to withdraw or vary a decision' (CA 1998, s 47(1)).[2]

1.28   A large number of complaints had been made by the end of 2001, under the CA 98. However, many of these were not well directed or cogently argued. The *Annual Report 2001* of the OFT reveals that, in 2001, 1298 complaint cases were opened. Only 63 of these (4.8%) gave the OFT 'reasonable grounds to suspect an infringement of the Act had taken place, leading to a formal s 25 investigation'. At the end of 2001, some 44 cases were under active investigation, but it was estimated that only about 25% of these would lead to formal decisions being taken. More generally, the OFT commented that:

> 'Complaints came from a variety of markets and covered a wide range of practices and behaviour, from refusal to supply to alleged cartels. There were a surprisingly large number of complaints relating to resale price maintenance.
>
> Of the complaints received from businesses, by far the largest proportion came from small and medium-sized enterprises – a group specifically targeted in our business education program.'

However, the OFT was clearly concerned about the quality of complaints. In a speech made in May 2002,[3] Margaret Bloom, the Director of Competition Enforcement, commented that 'while the increase in numbers [of complaints] was a most gratifying response to our campaign "Complain; don't notify", the quality was much less so'. As noted above, some 95% of complaints do not satisfy the threshold required by s 25 of the CA 98 for the launch of an investigation. Only 10% of complaints from large firms met the threshold, and only 1% of complaints from individuals satisfied the criteria.[4] Ms Bloom's general comments regarding the role of the complainant are instructive:

---

[1]   See *Bettercare Group Ltd supported by the Registered Homes Confederation of Northern Ireland Ltd, Bedfordshire Care Group v The Director General of Fair Trading* [2002] CompAR 226. In this case, the OFT contested a challenge to a decision made by it on the grounds that, in fact, no formal decision capable of being challenged had been made. A complaint had been rejected by way of a series of letters between a staff member and the complainant. The CCAT held that this correspondence constituted a decision, and should be published as such. The response of the OFT has been to indicate that, in future, 'it is likely that the OFT will adopt a larger number of non-infringement decisions. These will probably be less detailed in their reasoning than those to date. They may well be cases where reasonable grounds to suspect an infringement were not established at any stage. They are likely to include some cases where the investigation is not public knowledge' (Bloom, M 'Key Challenges in Public Enforcement', a speech to the British Institute of International and Comparative Law, 17 May 2002, OFT website). See also the judgment of the CCAT in *Freeserve.Com Plc v Director General of Telecommunications, supported by BT Group Plc* [2002] CAT 8.

[2]   Provisions relating to third-party appeals are made in the Competition Act 1998 (Director's rules) Order 2000, SI 2000/293, art 28.

[3]   'Key Challenges in Public Enforcement', a speech to the British Institute of International and Comparative Law, 17 May 2002, OFT website.

[4]   This is perhaps not a surprising figure. Research into MMC investigations undertaken by the author showed that a great many of the public comments to inquiries were ill directed, dealing with general consumer complaints rather than specific competition concerns.

'Typical complaints, that may satisfy s 25, are refusal to supply, resale price maintenance, price discrimination, predation and exploitation. For some of these, the complaints are self-enforcing – a most effective form of enforcement. While we are investigating a refusal to supply, for example, the complainant may subsequently inform us that the complainee has started to supply because he has informed them of our investigation. Normally we take no further action as a matter of administrative priority. Some complainants try to secure as much publicity as possible from the media in the hope of pressurizing the complainee – and also the OFT. Such publicity has no effect on our priorities.'

1.29 No changes are made to these basic procedures relating to third-party involvement in the system by the Act, but they are supplemented by the making of express provision for 'super-complaints' (s 11). These are discussed further in Chapter 6. Super-complainants are 'designated consumer bodies', and the first complaint recognised by the OFT as a super-complaint was made in October 2001, when the Consumers' Association (CA) made a complaint relating to practices in the private dentistry market. The OFT launched a comprehensive investigation after establishing that the CA's case merited further consideration and research. This particular investigation used the powers provided in FTA 1973, s 2. In its *Annual Report 2001*, the OFT indicated that this investigation was to:

'examine the market including how NHS and private dental services work together, the incentives for dentists to treat patients under the NHS or privately, and the constraints on new services. It will also study the expectations and rights of consumers and the quality of information available to them.'

It was anticipated that the investigation would be concluded by the end of 2002. However, under these arrangements, there would be no power for the OFT to impose remedies were it to find that the market was not working in the public interest. Rather, the OFT would be required to make a reference to the CC under the FTA monopoly provisions discussed above.[1] Third-party appeals against OFT decisions are facilitated by amendments to the CA 1998 made by the Act, and these are considered in Chapter 6.

THE RELATIONSHIP BETWEEN THE EC COMPETITION LAW REGIME AND THE DOMESTIC REGIME

1.30 At the time that the Act was introduced, Arts 81 EC and 82 EC were directly effective, with the vital exception of the third paragraph of Art 81(3). These two Articles provide the broad framework for the application of

---

[1] The approach to this investigation was discussed in Committee (*Hansard*, Standing Committee B, col 81).

competition law in the EC, and are reflected in ss 2 and 18, respectively, of the CA 1998.

Article 81 EC

1.31 Article 81(1) prohibits:

'all agreements between undertakings, decisions by associations of undertakings and concerted practices which may affect trade between Member States and which have as their object or effect the prevention, restriction or distortion of competition within the common market ...'.

The second paragraph of Art 81 declares that agreements or contracts which fall within Art 81(1) 'shall be automatically void'. The third paragraph makes provision for the granting of exemptions from the illegality of Art 81(1) in respect of any agreement, etc:

'which contributes to improving the production or distribution of goods or to promoting technical or economic progress, while allowing consumers a fair share of the resulting benefit, and which does not:

(a) impose on the undertakings concerned restrictions which are not indispensable to the attainment of these objectives;

(b) afford such undertakings the possibility of eliminating competition in respect of a substantial part of the products in question.'

At the time of the introduction of the Act, this third paragraph was not capable of application before the national courts, in the absence of any decision taken by the EC Commission relating to its application. The EC Commission was given a monopoly on the application of this Article, and, once any decision was made, this was binding on national courts in the event of any dispute.

1.32 In 1999, the Commission initiated a reform programme in relation to the application of competition law, which, when brought into force, will have far-reaching implications. Its proposals were outlined in the *White Paper on Modernisation of the Rules Implementing Articles [81] and [82]*.[1] A key feature of this reform is that Art 81(3) is to be given direct effect such that it may be invoked before a national court. The exemption process will be replaced by one of 'legal exception', and the Commission will lose its monopoly in this respect, although it retains a pre-eminent role in shaping the guidelines and principles, and intervening in key cases. The legislation necessary to complete this process

---

[1] (1999) OJ C132/1.

was enacted at the end of 2002.[1] The new Regulation will not enter force until 1 May 2004.

1.33 The principle underlying this change is to reduce the workload of the Commission, and to allow it to be more pro-active, rather than having to use its resources to respond to applications for exemptions in respect of agreements which are, for the most part, benign. Instead of the Commission making the assessment of an agreement's overall acceptability, it is now for the companies who are party to the agreements to make this judgment, which may then be reviewed by national courts or national authorities in the event that any dispute arises.

1.34 In addition to individual exemptions being available, a number of block exemption regulations also exist, which bring together the principles established over a number of individual cases in specific areas.[2] Some revisions to the procedures under which certain of these regulations may be applied will be necessitated by the reform process. This is particularly so in the case of Regulation 240/96, relating to technology transfer agreements. As a consequence, some changes will also be necessary to domestic procedures, and one of the intentions behind the Act has been to allow the flexibility to make these changes in the most efficacious way possible.

Article 82 EC

1.35 Article 82 EC, which prohibits the abuse of a dominant position in the common market or a substantial part of it in so far as it may affect trade between Member States, has always been directly effective in its entirety. In addition, it applies in far fewer cases than does Art 81 EC, and there is no exemption process, such that the application of the Article raises far fewer procedural problems. Any problems relating to its application are usually matters of factual analysis. The reform process being undertaken at Community level will not explicitly affect the application of the substantive

---

[1] Council Regulation (EC) 1/2003 on the implementation of the rules on competition laid down in Articles 81 and 82 of the Treaty (2003) OJ L1/1. This Regulation is likely to be referred to for some time as 'the new Regulation 17'.

[2] The main block exemption Regulations at the time of writing are: Regulation 2790/99 on the application of Art 81(3) of the Treaty to categories of vertical agreements and concerted practices (1999) OJ L336/21; Regulation 2658/2000 on the application of Art 81(3) of the Treaty to categories of specialisation agreements (2000) OJ L304/3; Regulation 2659/2000 on the application of Art 81(3) of the Treaty to categories of research and development agreements (2000) OJ L304/7; Regulation 1475/95 on the application of Art 81(3) of the Treaty to certain categories of motor vehicle distribution and servicing agreements (1995) OJ L145/25 (this is currently being revised, and a new Regulation is expected in 2003); and Regulation 240/96 on the application of Art 81(3) of the Treaty to certain categories of technology transfer agreements (1996) OJ L31/2.

rules of Art 82, although the general procedural reforms (discussed below) will impinge on the way in which the Article is applied by authorities.

Procedural law and the Member States

1.36 Since 1963, the procedures relating to the application of Arts 81 and 82 EC have been set out primarily in Regulation 17. This set out the relationship between the competencies of the EC Commission and the Member States in the application of the law. In particular, it gave the Commission the power to take adverse decisions, bringing infringements to an end, the concomitant power to impose penalties on those breaching the substantive rules, and the necessary investigatory powers to pursue infringements. A new 'Regulation 17' has now been published, and this makes some substantial changes to the division of powers, as well as updating various investigatory and enforcement procedures. In particular, this has far-reaching implications for the relationship between national and EC competition laws, which will impact significantly on the way in which competition law may be invoked in the UK,[1] although, as noted above, these changes will not be implemented until 1 May 2004 – a timetable intended to accommodate the anticipated enlargement of the EC.

National law and EC competition law

The supremacy of EC law and concurrent jurisdiction

1.37 The fundamental and constant fact governing the relationship between national law and EC law is that the latter is, in the event of any conflict, supreme. This principle is enshrined in Art 10 EC,[2] and has been asserted by the ECJ in a number of judgments.[3] In relation to competition law, Arts 81 and 82 EC draw a clear demarcation between those cases in which EC law may be invoked, and those in which it cannot. In both cases, the test is that of whether there is an effect on 'trade between member states'. In the absence of

---

[1]   See **1.42–1.49**.

[2]   Article 10 provides that:

'Member states shall take all appropriate measures, whether general or particular, to ensure fulfilment of the obligations arising out of this Treaty or resulting from action taken by the institutions of the Community. They shall facilitate the achievement of the Community's tasks.

They shall abstain from any measure which could jeopardise the attainment of the objectives of this Treaty.'

[3]   See, in particular, *Costa v ENEL* Case 6/64 [1964] CMLR 425, and *R v Secretary of State for Transport, ex p Factortame Ltd (Factortame II)* [1989] 3 CMLR 1.

such an effect, EC law is impotent.[1] These provisions do not directly address the question of when national laws may be applied.

1.38 It is clear from the broad supremacy principle that Member States cannot apply national competition laws in any way that obstructs, directly or indirectly, the operation of EC competition law. By itself, however, this principle does not eliminate the possibility that national competition laws may be applied alongside EC law, perhaps to the same cases, with different results being achieved. In the leading case of *Walt Wilhelm v Bundeskartellamt*,[2] the ECJ accepted the possibility that this situation could arise, but held that 'parallel application of the national system should be allowed only in so far as it does not impinge upon the uniform application, throughout the Common Market, of the Community rules'.[3] In particular, national authorities or courts would be acting within their powers were they to:

> 'intervene against an agreement, in application of their national law, even when the examination of the position of that agreement with regard to the Community rules is pending before the Commission, subject, however, to the proviso that such application of the national law may not prejudice the full and uniform application of the Community law.'[4]

1.39 A similar position was reached in the case of *GB-INNO-BM NV v Vereniging van de Kleinhandelaars in Tabak*,[5] in which the Court held that the:

> 'Treaty imposes a duty on member states not to adopt or maintain in force any measure which could deprive [art 82] of its effectiveness [… and] member states may not enact measures enabling private undertakings to escape from the constraints imposed by [Art 81 EC].'[6]

The leeway that this left to Member States to apply their own competition laws led to some uncertainty as to, for example, the position that would arise were an agreement to be subject to an exemption at Community law, but fall foul of a prohibition at the national level.[7] These issues were of particular concern to the MMC when it investigated the market for new cars, and it was faced with the problem that the structure of the sales distribution networks and agreements was conditioned in part by the operation of the relevant EC block

---

[1] Although the test of this is a broad one: 'it must be possible to foresee with a sufficient degree of probability on the basis of a set of objective factors of law or of fact that the agreement in question may have an influence, direct or indirect, actual or potential, on the pattern of trade between the member states' (*Société Technique Minière v Maschinenbau Ulm* Case 56/65 [1966] ECR 235 at 249; [1966] CMLR 357 at 375).

[2] Case 14/68 [1966] CMLR 100.

[3] At para 6.

[4] At para 7.

[5] Case 13/77 [1978] 1 CMLR 283.

[6] At paras 31 and 33.

[7] See, for example, Galinsky R 'The Resolution of Conflicts Between UK and Community Competition Law' (1994) ECLR 16.

exemption Regulation.[1] It was generally considered that there was no prohibition on a Member State examining a practice already considered under Community law, and there was a recognition too that Member States' systems, and the Community system might pursue different economic, social, and political objectives.

1.40　　In the UK, the introduction of the CA 1998 went some way towards demarcating the relationship between the two systems. In particular, in relation to the Chapter I Prohibition, express provision was made in the CA 1998 to the effect that an exemption at the EC level would have effect in the UK.[2] In addition, the effect of s 60 was such as to ensure that there would be only limited deviation from EC practice in the UK, and then only in circumstances in which the CA 1998 was either explicit on its terms, or in which there were relevant differences. Section 60, which is of fundamental importance to the application of the CA 1998, is in the following terms:

'**60　Principles to be applied in determining questions**

(1) The purpose of this section is to ensure that so far as is possible (having regard to any relevant differences between the provisions concerned), questions arising under this Part in relation to competition within the United Kingdom are dealt with in a manner which is consistent with the treatment of corresponding questions arising in Community law in relation to competition within the Community.

(2) At any time when the court determines a question arising under this Part, it must act (so far as is compatible with the provisions of this Part and whether or not it would otherwise be required to do so) with a view to securing that there is no inconsistency between –

    (a)　the principles applied, and decision reached, by the court in determining that question; and

    (b)　the principles laid down by the Treaty and the European Court, and any relevant decision of that Court, as applicable at that time in determining any corresponding question arising in Community law.

---

[1]　See *New Cars: A Report on the Supply of New Motor Cars within the UK* (HMSO, 2000), Cm 4660. The relevant EC block exemption Regulation is Regulation 1475/95 on the application of Art 81(3) of the Treaty to certain categories of motor vehicle distribution and servicing agreements (1995) OJ L145/25. This Regulation is to be replaced shortly.

[2]　Section 10 of the CA 1998 is in the following terms:

'(1) An agreement is exempt from the Chapter I Prohibition if it is exempt from the Community prohibition –

    (a)　by virtue of a Regulation,

    (b)　because it has been given an exemption by the Commission, or

    (c)　because it has been notified to the Commission under the appropriate opposition or objection procedure and–

        (i)　the time for opposing, or objecting to, the agreement has expired and the Commission has not opposed it; or

        (ii)　the Commission has opposed, or objected to, the agreement but has withdrawn its opposition or objection.

(2) An agreement is exempt from the Chapter I Prohibition if it does not affect trade between member states but otherwise falls within a category of agreement which is exempt from the Community prohibition by virtue of a Regulation.'

(3)   The court must, in addition, have regard to any relevant decision or statement of the Commission.

(4)   Subsections (2) and (3) also apply to –

    (a)   the Director; and

    (b)   any person acting on behalf of the Director, in connection with any matter arising under this Part.

(5)   In subsections (2) and (3), "court" means any court or tribunal.

(6)   In subsections (2)(b) and (3), "decision" includes a decision as to –

    (a)   the interpretation of any provision of Community law;

    (b)   the civil liability of an undertaking for harm caused by its infringement of Community law.'

1.41   The position under the CA 1998 would be that the UK authorities were able to examine a practice which had also been examined at the level of the EC, but would be expected to reach a similar conclusion, unless there was a 'relevant difference'. This was consistent with the position set out by the sponsoring minister of the CA 1998 in the parliamentary debates:

'I cannot over-emphasise that the purpose of the Bill is to ensure as far as possible a consistency with the EC approach and thereby to ease the burdens for business.'[1]

The FTA 1973 could be applied to conduct that would also fall within the scope of EC competition law, as was the case in the new cars investigation,[2] and indeed the majority of recent reports related to situations in which, within the definition supplied in *Société Technique Minière*,[3] there would be an effect on trade between Member States.

Reform and the 'new Article 3'

1.42   With the new procedural Regulation, however, fundamental changes are made to this relationship. Article 3 of Regulation 1/2003 is, in part, in the following terms:

'1. Where the competition authorities of the Member States or national courts apply national competition law to agreements, decisions by associations of undertakings or concerted practices within the meaning of Article 81(1) of the Treaty which may affect trade between Member States within the meaning of that provision, they shall also apply Article 81 of the Treaty to such agreements, decisions or concerted practices. Where the competition authorities of the Member States or national courts apply national competition law to any abuse prohibited by Article 82 of the Treaty, they shall also apply Article 82 of the Treaty.'[4]

---

[1]   Lord Haskel, *Hansard* (HL) 17 November 1997, col 417.

[2]   See **1.39**.

[3]   See **1.37**.

[4]   Council Regulation (EC) 1/2003 on the implementation of the rules on competition laid down in Articles 81 and 82 of the Treaty (2003) OJ L1/1.

This position is somewhat different from that set out in the original proposal, which would have required the exclusive application of EC law wherever it was capable of being applied. In practice, however, the principle of supremacy of EC law, and the obligation not to frustrate its operation, may ensure that in practice there is little practical difference between the two approaches. In its accompanying memorandum to the original proposal, the Commission set out the arguments supporting this position:

'This Article stipulates that where an agreement or practice is capable of affecting trade between member states only Community competition law applies. National competition authorities, being empowered to apply Articles 81 and 82 in their entirety, will thus apply Community law in all cases affecting trade between member states.

... The primary principle resolves clear conflicts in favour of Community law. It does not, however, effectively prevent inconsistencies and differences in the treatment of agreements and practices between member states, even if such agreements and practices affect trade between member states.

At the present stage of development of the Community it is essential to ensure that there is a level playing field throughout the European Union, allowing companies to reap the full benefits of the single market. As is evident from the very content of Article 81(3), many agreements have desirable effects on economic welfare. It is inconsistent with the notion of a single market that agreements and practices capable of affecting cross-border trade should be subject to different standards and that an agreement which would be considered to be innocuous or beneficial under Community law can be prohibited under national competition law. To address this problem effectively it is necessary to adopt the solution alluded to by the Court of Justice in *Walt Wilhelm*, namely to regulate the relationship between national law and Community competition law as provided for in Article 83(2)(e) of the EC Treaty.

Article 3 ensures that agreements and practices capable of affecting cross-border trade are scrutinised under a single set of rules, thereby promoting a level playing field throughout the Community, and removing the costs attached to the parallel application of Community law and national laws for both competition authorities and business. The provision does not limit the scope for action of national competition authorities, which will be able to apply Community law. Experience gained at national level will contribute to the development of Community competition policy within the network.

The Article also ensures that all cases concerning agreements and practices affecting trade between member states become subject to the mechanisms of co-operation inside the network of competition authorities. It is a fundamental aim of the proposed Regulation that the Commission and the national authorities should form a network of competition authorities that co-operate closely in the application of Articles 81 and 82. The network will incorporate mechanisms that seek to ensure the consistency of Community competition law is preserved.

The proposal eliminates the risk that the proper functioning of the network might be affected by the concurrent application of Community competition law and national competition law. The objective is to ensure an efficient allocation of cases, generally to a single authority, which is considered the best placed to act. This objective would be hampered if national authorities were bound to continue dealing with the case under their own competition law. In several member states the competition authority that has received a complaint based on national law is obliged to adopt a formal reasoned decision. These parallel proceedings should be avoided.'

1.43 The far-reaching consequences of this move cannot be overstated.[1] In essence, in any case, where there is an effect on trade between Member States, national competition law cannot be applied in a way which is inconsistent with the application of EC law, and EC law must be applied alongside, or in the alternative to, national law. Consider, for example, the cases in which an adverse decision has been reached by the Director under the CA 1998 to date. As of 25 November 2002, the following adverse decisions had been taken:

– *Napp Pharmaceutical Holdings Ltd*[2]
– *Predation by Aberdeen Journals Ltd*[3]
– *Market Sharing by Arriva Plc and First Group plc*[4]
– *Price Fixing Agreements Involving John Bruce (UK) Ltd, Fleet Parts Ltd and Truck and Trailer Components.*[5]

On reading the evidence put forward in the decisions, it is likely that in at least *Napp* and *John Bruce* EC law would have had to be applied.

1.44 From a domestic perspective, the situation in relation to monopoly inquiries under the FTA 1973 would be similarly complicated. Since mid-1999, the following six investigations have been completed:

– *A report on the supply in Great Britain of raw cows' milk*[6]
– *The supply of impulse ice cream: A report on the supply of ice cream purchased for immediate consumption*[7]
– *New cars: A report on the supply of new motor cars in the UK*[8]
– *Supermarkets: A report on the supply of groceries from multiple stores in the UK*[9]

---

[1] The overall impact of the EC modernisation process on the application of competition law in the UK was pointed to by the Confederation of British Industry (CBI) in its response to the Enterprise Bill, which suggested, amongst other things, that it was unfortunate that substantial reforms to the UK system were proceeding before it had become clear what the full impact of EC modernisation would be. See, for example, *Hansard*, Standing Committee B, cols 140–141, where it was argued by Mr Waterson that it was 'slightly eccentric of this country to be ploughing its own furrow, not only so soon after the previous legislation, but when we are expecting EU reforms and a new European system. It would be sensible to allow that system to be introduced and bedded down and to see how it works in practice before we move ahead'.

[2] CA98/2/2001, [2001] UKCLR 597; on appeal *Napp Pharmaceuticals Holdings Ltd v The Director General of Fair Trading* [2002] CompAR 13.

[3] CA98/5/2001, [2001] UKCLR 856 – this Decision was subsequently remitted to the OFT by the CCAT, and was then reissued as Decision CA98/14/2002, [2002] UKCLR 740.

[4] CA98/9/2002, [2002] UKCLR 322.

[5] CA98/12/2002, [2002] UKCLR 435.

[6] July 1999, Cm 4286.

[7] January 2000, Cm 4510.

[8] April 2000, Cm 4660.

[9] October 2000, Cm 4842.

–   *Scottish milk: A report on the supply of fresh processed milk to middle-ground retailers in Scotland*[1]
–   *The Supply of Banking Services by Clearing Banks to Small and Medium-Sized Enterprises within the UK.*[2]

Of these, it was noted in the reports on milk that there was no 'international trade', and hence it is unlikely that the EC would be able to exert jurisdiction. In respect of the other four reports, an argument could be made with varying strengths that trade between Member States was relevant. Clearly, this would be the case in relation to the supply of new cars, and impulse ice cream. The argument would be weaker, although sustainable, in relation to banking services and supermarket supplies. This does not mean in these cases, however, that the new Regulation would have precluded these investigations, or any successors under the market investigation provisions of the Act (see Chapter 4).

1.45 Because the new Art 3 of the procedural Regulation refers to situations in which Arts 81 and/or 82 EC apply (in order to eliminate the problems of conflicts in the law), there will remain situations in which market investigations may proceed, even where the market concerned is one in which there is trade between the Member States. As has been noted above,[3] there is a lacuna in the operation of Community competition law, which does not extend to wide oligopolies in the absence of agreements or a concerted practice. The strength of the monopoly provisions of the FTA 1973, and their successors in the Act, is that they may be applied to situations in which individual companies are doing nothing wrong, but where, collectively, the aggregated result of their conduct in the market is such as to damage competition. Investigations in this area may not necessarily relate to situations in which the matters under question lie 'within the meaning of Article 81(1)' or 'to any abuse prohibited by Article 82'.

1.46 Further consequences flow from the change. National competition authorities are expected to play a role in determining cases falling within their geographic competence. The proposal 'is based on the premise that national competition authorities will apply Articles 81 and 82 in accordance with their respective national procedural rules'.[4] The OFT will therefore be placed in the position of determining whether to consider a case which it may be interested in pursuing under the terms of the CA 1998, or under Arts 81 and 82 EC. In this context, the reference in s 60 of the CA 1998 to 'relevant differences' may create some problems. It might be, for example, that a case in which there was

---

[1]   December 2000, Cm 5002.
[2]   March 2002, Cm 5319.
[3]   See **1.12**.
[4]   Explanatory memorandum to the draft Regulation [2000] 5 CMLR 1148 at 1160.

an effect on trade between Member States, and which was therefore dealt with under the EC provisions, would be resolved in a different way from one in which there was no effect on trade between Member States, all else being the same. In particular, it is often noted that EC competition law does not serve exclusively the goals of industrial economics. In the *Metro* case, the ECJ held that:

> 'the requirement contained in Articles 3 and 81 EC that competition shall not be distorted implies the existence on the market of workable competition, ie, the degree of competition necessary to ensure the observance of the basic requirements and attainment of the objectives of the Treaty, in particular the creation of a single market achieving conditions similar to those of a domestic market.'[1]

This single market objective is not one that need be pursued within a domestic economy, and thus constitutes a 'relevant difference' for the purpose of s 60 of the CA 1998.

1.47 It is to be hoped, however, that the possibility of divergence between the treatment of cases will be avoided, although for this to happen some modifications in the policy approach of the OFT, particularly to vertical restraints, will be necessary.

1.48 The new Art 3 may also impact on the powers of concurrent regulators to deal with situations in which, at present, they have jurisdiction under industry-specific legislation. The current thinking, however, is that most of these specific powers may still be invoked, as they do not relate to situations in which either Art 81 EC or Art 82 EC could be invoked.

1.49 Concern has also been raised about the relationship of the operation of the EC regime with the new cartel offence (see generally Chapter 5). However, it appears to be the case that there is no inherent conflict between the two systems. The cartel offence is one that is committed by individuals, not by undertakings. It is also a stand-alone offence, not related directly to either Art 81 EC or the Chapter I Prohibition. As noted by the Under-Secretary of State, it is 'separate from, but compatible with, the EC civil regime'.[2] The Confederation of British Industry (CBI), however, was firmly of the view that:

> 'Decentralisation can only work if all Member States "sing from the same hymn sheet". Unfortunately, even before the Commission's reforms are in place, one large Member State has – in full knowledge of Modernisation and despite paying lip service to the need for consistent application of the rules – gone off on a tangent by doing its own thing ... for the UK to adopt a criminal regime may significantly reduce the willingness of NCAs in other Member States to pass information within the network to the UK for fear that their citizens may be prosecuted. ... given that the Commission will not be able to guarantee immunity from prosecution in the UK, for the UK to adopt a criminal system

---

[1] *Metro-SB-Grossmarkte GmbH & Co KG v Commission* Case 26/76 [1978] 2 CMLR 1 at 2.
[2] See **1.13**.

> could seriously reduce the likelihood that individuals involved in cartels affecting the UK would want to come forward for leniency. … given that the EU's regime is civil, not criminal, companies which are found by the Commission to have infringed Article 81 will be subject to a civil administrative fine. On the other hand, individuals in the UK involved in breaching Article 81 could find themselves subject to criminal proceedings and imprisonment. We believe this to be inherently unfair.'[1]

However, even following modernisation, there will be no requirement for absolute uniformity in the competition laws adopted by Member States, and there is reason to believe that the CBI may be somewhat overstating the case for the opposition. The UK will not be alone in applying criminal sanctions to anti-competitive conduct.[2]

Merger control

1.50   The position in relation to merger control has always been different from that of the application of Arts 81 and 82 EC. Once the EC Merger Regulation was enacted,[3] exclusive competence was given to the EC Commission[4] to examine mergers with a 'Community dimension', as defined in the Regulation. There are only three circumstances in which mergers with a Community dimension may fall within the jurisdiction of the Member States. The first is where a Member State makes a request to the Commission to have a merger referred back to it. This procedure may be invoked where:

> '(a)   concentration threatens to create or to strengthen a dominant position as a result of which effective competition will be significantly impeded on a market within that member state, which presents all the characteristics of a distinct market, or
>
> (b)   a concentration affects competition on a market within that member state, which presents all the characteristics of a distinct market and which does not constitute a substantial part of the common market.'[5]

There have been only a small number of cases in which the UK has invoked this procedure. A second exception is found in Art 21, which recognises certain limited 'legitimate interests' of the Member States. The three interests specifically referred to in this context are public security, the plurality of the media, and prudential rules. A third exception is found in Art 298 EC, which relates to measures that may be taken in respect of 'trade in arms, munitions and war material'.[6]

---

[1]   Quoted in *Hansard*, Standing Committee B, col 151.

[2]   *Inter alia*, Ireland, France, Germany and Austria impose some criminal sanctions, although these are not often brought into play.

[3]   Regulation 4064/89 on the Control of Concentrations Between Undertakings (1989) OJ L395/1, reprinted with corrections at (1990) OJ L257/13, as amended.

[4]   Article 21(1) of the Regulation.

[5]   Article 9(2) of the Regulation.

[6]   Procedures to deal with these situations are included in ss 67–68 of the Act (see **3.70**).

1.51   Merger control has been widely perceived as being a matter of some national sensitivity, and there were difficulties in obtaining the necessary agreement to the enactment of the EC Merger Regulation. Merger procedures in the Member States remain diverse, and the approach under the FTA 1973 was a distinctive one. There is no attempt in the Act to approximate the new domestic regime to that of the EC, although in one area this may happen.

1.52   In the EC Merger Regulation, the test of a merger's acceptance is that of whether it tends to 'create or strengthen a dominant position as a result of which effective competition would be significantly impeded'.[1] In the Act, the old 'public interest' test of the FTA 1973 has been replaced with that of whether the merger will lead to a substantial lessening of competition ('the SLC test' – see generally Chapter 3). Late in 2001, the EC Commission began a process of consultation in relation to reform of the EC Merger Regulation.[2] This was designed in part to allow discussion as to whether the EC regime should be aligned more closely with that of the US. The Commission invited comment as to the merits of the SLC test, noting that the introduction of this test into the EC system would:

> 'facilitate merging parties' global assessment of possible competition issues arising from contemplated transactions, by obviating the current need to argue their case according to differently formulated tests. This would in turn provide competition agencies with a better basis on which to build effective co-operation in cases that are notified in several jurisdictions.'[3]

It is possible then that the dual combination of the Act and EC reform will result in the merger regimes of the UK and the EC being in closer alignment than to date.

THE WHITE PAPER

1.53   In July 2001, the DTI published its White Paper, *A World Class Competition Regime*,[4] setting out its plans for further reform of the domestic competition law regime. In the foreword, Patricia Hewitt, Secretary of State for Trade and Industry, summed up the position in the following terms:

> 'In this White Paper, I am setting out my proposals for the reform of competition law. Competition and enterprise will be strengthened. The Office of Fair Trading, enhanced by a strategic board, with increased powers and more resources, will have duties to promote competition in the economy. Ministers will be taken out of the vast majority of

---

[1]   Article 2(2) of the Regulation.

[2]   *Green Paper on the Review of Council Regulation (EEC) No 4064/89* COM(2001) 745/6 final, 11 December 2001.

[3]   At para 160.

[4]   Cm 5233.

monopoly and merger cases, and decisions on day to day cases will be taken by the Competition Commission against a competition-based test. This will increase business certainty. We are giving the Office of Fair Trading a formal role to advise where regulations may have an impact on competition issues and we propose to introduce strong deterrents to anti-competitive behaviour by introducing a new criminal offence for those engaged in cartels. Through measures such as the introduction of the super-complaint, where named consumer bodies can raise important market issues with the Office of Fair Trading, we are putting consumers at the heart of competition policy.'

1.54 Unfortunately, the impression created by the White Paper is that of a document produced in somewhat of a rush, as it is a little thin on substance, given the importance and scale of the reforms put forward in it. The key points set out in the White Paper, and supporting evidence, are brought forward in the following chapters, where appropriate.

1.55 The key themes that emerge in the White Paper are that competition decisions should be taken independently of the political process, that there be 'a strong deterrent effect', and that there be 'real redress for third parties'. The former goes strongly to the heart of the FTA 1973, and the ministerial involvement in its application discussed above. The latter two hint at deficiencies in the regime created by the CA 1998.

Responses to the consultation exercise

1.56 A large number of parties submitted responses to the Competition White Paper and, broadly, most welcomed its provisions, although there was criticism of the detail, and the CBI raised general concerns as to whether it was appropriate to reform the UK regime substantially when it was not yet clear what final shape the EC reforms would take.

1.57 Not surprisingly, the CC welcomed the proposed changes.[1] It drew particular attention to the new independence from day-to-day political oversight in the decision-making process.

1.58 The CA and the National Consumer Council also welcomed the changes. Both bodies welcomed the introduction of the super-complaint procedure and the CA, in particular, found the possibility of representative actions 'exciting'.[2]

1.59 For industry, the British Chambers of Commerce 'warmly welcomed' the publication of the Bill, commenting that:

---

[1] CC Press Release 21/02, 26 March 2002.

[2] The CA has issued a series of briefing papers on various aspects of the Enterprise Bill (*www.which.net/ campaigns*).

'Any observer of the USA cannot help but be struck by the almost missionary zeal that goes into protecting competition in that country. If we want to emulate the US economy's dynamism and entrepreneurial spirit, we must aim for a far more proactive competition regime in the UK, which encourages consumers, businesses and the OFT to root out anti-competitive practices.

There is nothing more frustrating as an entrepreneur than finding you are unable to compete because other businesses have cheated and we therefore wholeheartedly support what the Government is trying to achieve via this Bill.'[1]

The CBI, on the other hand, was less than enthusiastic in its welcome of the Bill – a 'curate's egg' – and could not see how its provisions 'will actually boost enterprise'. Its response was summarised in its press release:

'We are in favour of mergers being decided on established competition law principles, rather than on a vague public interest test, and they should be free of Ministerial intervention. We also support a new corporate structure for the OFT. A major concern is the definition of the criminal offence which we believe is vague and uncertain. We are also concerned about the powers of surveillance and prosecution proposed for the OFT. Other concerns are the appeal process on merger decisions, the wide sanction of disqualification for company directors, the outdated threshold tests for mergers, overseas disclosures and representative actions by consumer groups.'

Amongst other points, the CBI took the view that the CA 1998 had been substantially successful in addressing the problems of the adequacy of the UK competition law regime, other than in relation to merger control.[2]

THE ENTERPRISE BILL

1.60   The Enterprise Bill was first brought forward on 26 March 2002. A list of the relevant references for the debates is given in the footnote reference accompanying this text.[3] Where these debates shed light on the Act's provisions, they are referred to throughout the book, as appropriate. Due to the strict timetable set by the Government for the passage of the Bill, not all of

---

[1]   CC Press Release 21/02, 26 March 2002.

[2]   See CBI 'Enterprise and Productivity: The Government's Strategy for the Next Parliament' (CBI preliminary discussion paper, 29 June 2001).

[3]   At committee stage in the Commons (Standing Committee B House of Commons, *Hansard* 13 June 2002, cols 1033–1109, 17 June 2002, cols 22–125; House of Lords, first reading *Hansard* (HL) 19 June 2002, col 741; second reading *Hansard* (HL) 2 July 2002, cols 138–190; House of Lords Committee, *Hansard* (HL) 16 July 2002, cols 1095–1101, 1119–1166, 1187–1222, 18 July, cols 1427–1467, 1488–1543, 16 July, cols 1095–1101, 1119–1166, 1187–1222, 22 July, cols 1322–1379, 29 July, cols 738–745, 763–805, 30 July, cols 821–852; House of Lords Report Stage, *Hansard* (HL) 15 October, cols 702–716, 732–753, 782–848, 21 October, cols 1070–1086, 1098–1143, 1160–1210; House of Lords Third Reading *Hansard* (HL) 28 October, cols 12–19, 34–86; House of Commons consideration of Lords amendments *Hansard* 30 October, cols 899–971; House of Lords Consideration of Commons Amendments and Reasons *Hansard* (HL) 4 November, cols 530–549; House of Commons Lords message considered *Hansard* 5 November, cols 245–254; House of Lords Consideration of Commons Amendments *Hansard* (HL) 6 November, cols 856–861.

its provisions were examined in Committee, and there was opposition criticism of the lack of adequate time for scrutiny of what was a very technical Bill. There was also criticism of the huge number of Government amendments brought forward at various points, which suggested that there were matters which were insufficiently thought out at the time that the Bill was introduced in Parliament. Those who have followed the passage of the legislation may well be tempted to agree with the Opposition spokesman, Andrew Robathan, who pointed out, almost at the end of the Parliamentary process, that 'the Bill has had nearly 750 amendments, largely from the Government, and nine new clauses. That is no way to prepare legislation. It was badly thought out and badly prepared'.[1]

1.61   The Act received Royal Assent on 7 November 2002. It will not enter into force in one tranche, and, at the time of writing, the best information was that the main provisions would enter into force in the summer of 2003, with some of the amendments to the CA 1998 and institutional arrangements taking effect more quickly.

1.62   Under the terms of the Act, the OFT and CC are required to publish guidance on a wide range of matters. At the time of writing, the following draft guidance was available and is relied on, as appropriate, throughout this book:

—   OFT *Market Investigation References*
—   OFT *The Cartel Offence: No-action Letters for Individuals*
—   OFT *Super-complaints: Guidance for Designated Consumer Bodies*
—   OFT *Competition Disqualification Orders*
—   OFT *Mergers: Substantive Assessment*
—   CC *General Advice and Information Guidance*
—   CC *Statement of Policy on Penalties*
—   CC *Market Investigation Reference: Competition Commission Guidelines*
—   CC *Merger References: Competition Commission Guidelines*
—   CC *Competition Commission Rules of Procedure.*

Extensive reference is also made to the DTI *Explanatory Notes* to the Bill – which are also now available in a final version to accompany the Act.

THE COMMUNICATIONS BILL

1.63   At the same time as the Enterprise Bill was progressing through Parliament, plans were under way for a major piece of legislation dealing with the regulation of communications, and the role of the Office of

---

[1]   *Hansard*, 5 November 2002, cols 245–246.

Communications (OFCOM) in that process. The new law, when introduced, will have a significant impact on certain competition aspects of the relevant industries. In particular, the rules on media ownership are to be simplified and liberalised, and provisions relating to mergers in the industry will be found in the new Communications Act, and not the Enterprise Act 2002.

1.64 Part V of the Communications Bill, published by the DTI on 19 November 2002,[1] deals with the competition functions of OFCOM. These extend to matters relating to the provision of electronic communications networks, electronic communications services, and broadcasting and related matters. The Bill also extends to newspaper mergers (discussed in Chapter 3). OFCOM is given concurrent jurisdiction with the OFT and other regulators under the CA 1998 in relation to the application of the Chapter I and II Prohibitions to the specified industries. It is also given power in relation to market investigation references (see Chapter 4).

COMMENCEMENT

1.65 The Secretary of State is to make orders relating to the commencement of the provisions of the Act, and different provisions may enter into force at different times. The Opposition moved an amendment, later withdrawn, to delay commencement until 1 March 2005, on the grounds that the 1998 regime had not yet bedded down.[2] It is anticipated that the main provisions will come into force in the summer of 2003, and the date of 1 May has been touted, although this is not yet certain.

---

[1]   Information relating to the Bill may be found at *www.communicationsbill.gov.uk*.
[2]   *Hansard*, Standing Committee B, col 706.

Chapter Two

THE NEW INSTITUTIONAL ARRANGEMENTS

INTRODUCTION

2.1   The CA 1998 made substantial reforms to the older institutional structure, abolishing the Restrictive Practices Court, and replacing the Monopolies and Mergers Commission (MMC) with the new Competition Commission (CC), which also incorporates the Competition Commission Appeals Tribunal (CCAT). The status of the Office of Fair Trading (OFT) was left more or less as it was, although new powers were conferred upon it.[1] The role of the Secretary of State, influential in mergers and monopolies references, was also left unaffected, and some new powers were granted in relation to the CA 1998, such as the power to make certain orders, putting flesh on the bones of parts of that Act.

2.2   The new Act makes more substantial reforms to the basic tripartite relationship, significantly changing the constitution of the OFT, separating out the CCAT, which becomes the Competition Appeals Tribunal (CAT), from the CC, and eliminating much of the role of the Secretary of State, save in all but the most exceptional circumstances, which are dealt with, as appropriate, in the chapters relating to mergers and market investigation references. At the same time, a new 'Competition Service' (CS) was created to assist and support the work of the CAT. The Consumer Protection Advisory Committee, which had a small role to play in relation to the operation of the FTA 1973, was abolished, and those parts of the FTA 1973 relating to it were repealed.

2.3   While the powers of the institutions are dealt with in relation to the specific substantive provisions of the Act throughout this book, in this

---

[1]   Technically, the OFT was 'not a statutory body, but simply the administrative support that has grown up around the DGFT to support him or her in the exercise of his or her statutory functions' (*Explanatory Notes*, para 20) (the DTI has prepared *Explanatory Notes* to the Bill and Act at each stage of its progress. All references in this text are to the version of the notes dated 19 June 2002. A final version is available on the DTI website).

chapter, the broad structure of the changes, and the wider, less specific, roles of the institutions will be dealt with. These are set out in the Act in Part 1 (ss 1–8) in relation to the OFT, in Part 2 (ss 12–21) in relation to the role of the CAT, and in Part 5 (ss 185–187), which deals with the role of the CS.

2.4 Some very broad statements relating to 'Strong, Proactive and Independent Competition Authorities' are set out in Part 4 of the White Paper. The uncontroversial starting point is that 'the Government wishes to see truly independent competition authorities which work proactively to root out instances of anti-competitive behaviour'.[1]

2.5 Three clear themes emerge from the White Paper. The first is that the competition authorities should be largely seen to be independent from the politics of the day, hence the reduction in the role of the Secretary of State. The second is that those appointed to the authorities should be appointed on the basis of their expertise in relation to competition or, where relevant, consumer protection. In the latter regard, the approach to be taken was spelled out in para 4.32:

> 'Historically, our competition authorities have been staffed largely from the pool of generalist civil servants. Staff became increasingly expert in competition over time but it was unusual to recruit people on the basis of specific competition expertise. Such expertise (particularly in staff who are qualified economists, lawyers and financial analysts) is vital in assessing mergers, when investigating whether agreements are anti-competitive and whether a dominant company has abused its position. Competition analysis also underpins the diagnoses of where competitive pressures may be muted. But in many other countries – including Italy, the US, Germany and France – the norm is for staff enforcing competition law to be recruited on the basis of their expertise in the subject. The UK has to do likewise.'

2.6 The third theme relates to the new pro-active stance to be adopted by, in particular, the OFT to competition issues. In addition to its role in market investigation references, dealt with in Chapter 4, the OFT, and other sector regulators, will be expected to 'advise where laws and regulations create barriers to entry and competition or channel markets in a particular direction, thereby holding back innovation and progress'.[2]

---

[1] Page 13.

[2] See **4.15**. In this respect, the experience of Australia may be pertinent. There, a National Competition Council was created as part of the country's National Competition Policy to review and reform anti-competitive laws and regulations. A large number of diverse Acts have been analysed as part of that process (over 2000 laws were identified as potentially affecting competition), and various steps have been taken to reform them where it has been found to be appropriate to do so. See Fels, A 'Australia's Comprehensive Review of Anti-competitive Laws' in Amato, G and Laudati, LL (eds) *The Anti-competitive Impact of Regulation* (Cheltenham, Edward Elgar, 2001).

THE OFFICE OF FAIR TRADING

2.7   The provisions relating to the OFT, which is in effect established anew by the Act, are set out in ss 1–8, and in Sch 1. Section 1 of the Act puts the OFT on a firm statutory footing, and s 2 abolishes the office of the Director General of Fair Trading ('the Director'), whose functions, property, rights and liabilities are transferred to the OFT.[1] The effect is that the OFT becomes a Non-ministerial Government Department, is a Crown body, and its staff are civil servants.

2.8   The OFT has a duty to publish both an Annual Report[2] and an Annual Plan.[3]

2.9   The general functions of the OFT, set out in ss 5–8, are to be: the acquisition of information; the provision of information to the public; the provision of information and advice to ministers; and promoting good consumer practice. In relation to the acquisition of information, for example, the OFT has the power to 'carry out, commission or support (financially or otherwise) research' (s 5(3)). This is for the purpose of ensuring that it has sufficient information to take informed decisions. It may also carry out educational functions to inform the public of 'the ways in which competition may benefit consumers', or may support such activities (s 6).

2.10   More detailed rules relating to the constitution of the new OFT are set out in Sch 1, of which para 1 provides that the OFT itself 'shall consist of a chairman, and no fewer than four other members appointed by the Secretary of State' – the figure of five to seven members has been touted. The Chairman is, for the time being, also the Chief Executive, a matter which was subject to fierce debate, and on which the Government was pushed to the limit by the House of Lords, which felt it was inappropriate to combine both roles in a single appointment. From the ending of the transitional period, express provision is made for the two roles to be separated. The terms of appointment are to be determined by the Minister, but shall not exceed five years, although

---

[1]   Any legislative reference to the Director which remains in force after the Enterprise Act 2000 has been brought into effect is to be read as a reference to the OFT.

[2]   Annual reports published by the Director have been a useful source of information relating to the enforcement of competition laws, and the priorities of the Director.

[3]   Amendments to the Act that would have imposed a number of formal obligations on the OFT in relation to the reports were rejected at Committee stage. The Under-Secretary of State pointed out: 'As with the current DGFT, the chairman of the board will be the accounting officer and, therefore, accountable to Parliament for how the OFT's resources are used. He may be summoned by parliamentary Committees, and the OFT will have to agree a service delivery agreement with the Treasury for it to obtain resources in the first place' (*Hansard*, Standing Committee B, 16 April 2002, col 50).

this may be renewable.[1] Once the Chairman and other members are appointed, they may be removed by the Minister only on grounds of 'incapacity or misbehaviour'. John Vickers, the last person to hold the post of Director, will be appointed the first Chairman. Members of the Board will be appointed under the *Nolan* procedures, with an open competition, and the first advertisements for the posts appeared in the press in autumn 2002.

2.11   The OFT is to appoint such staff as it requires, and will, in effect, continue the service of existing staff members, although it has already been indicated that further recruitment in addition to that already undertaken in response to the CA 1998 will be carried out.

2.12   Internal rules of procedure, including matters such as setting a quorum, are to be determined by the OFT.

THE COMPETITION APPEALS TRIBUNAL

The Competition Appeals Tribunal

2.13   The new CAT takes over the functions of the CCAT, and is, in addition, given new functions to hear appeals relating to merger investigations, market investigation references, and third-party actions. These specific functions are dealt with, as appropriate, in the relevant chapters below. The CAT is to be completely independent of the CC.

2.14   The provisions relating to the CAT, and the supporting CS, are to be found in ss 12–16 and in Schs 2–5. The CAT is created by s 12, and is to consist of a President appointed by the Lord Chancellor, and further members. In the first instance, the President will be the existing President of the CCAT, Sir Christopher Bellamy. Members may be either appointed to form a panel of Chairmen, or appointed as ordinary members. The terms of appointment in both cases shall not exceed eight years. A Registrar will be appointed by the Secretary of State. The Lord Chancellor will be responsible for the appointment of the President and the panel of Chairmen, whereas, previously, all appointments were made by the Secretary of State. Ordinary members will continue to be appointed by the Secretary of State. Appointments will be made on a part-time basis, and ordinary members will be able to continue with their 'day jobs'.

---

[1]   The members are to be part-time appointments.

2.15 More detailed rules relating to the appointments to the CAT are set out in Sch 2.

2.16 In any particular proceeding before the Tribunal, it shall consist of a Chairman, who must be either the President or a member of the panel of Chairmen, and two other members. Decisions are to be made by majority vote, in any case where there is not unanimous agreement (s 14).

2.17 Tribunal rules may be made in accordance with Sch 4. Paragraph 1 provides that any decision of the Tribunal must state the reasons for that decision, and whether it was unanimous or taken by a majority. When the decision is presented, any information which, if disclosed, would harm 'legitimate business interests' may be excluded.

2.18 Decisions of the CAT may be enforced by the High Court in England and Wales (Sch 4, para 2), or may be recorded for execution in the Books of Council and Session in Scotland (Sch 4, para 3). In Northern Ireland, decisions may be enforced with the leave of the High Court in Northern Ireland (Sch 4, para 5).

2.19 Part 2 of Sch 4 makes provision for the Tribunal Rules which may be adopted by the Tribunal. The matters covered include, *inter alia*: the institution of proceedings (including the setting of time-limits for actions to be commenced, and the power to reject proceedings in certain cases); the possibility of holding pre-hearing reviews; the conduct of the hearing; quorum of the Tribunal; fees to be chargeable 'in respect of specified costs of proceedings'; and interim orders.

The Competition Service

2.20 The function of the new CS is 'to fund, and provide support services to' the CAT (s 13).[1] Schedule 3 puts a little more detail on the bare bones of s 13. The CS is to consist of the President and the Registrar of the CAT, and at least one appointed member, who shall be appointed by the Secretary of State in consultation with the President of the CAT. The members of the CS shall designate one of them to be the Chairman of the CS. The CS has the power to appoint the staff that it needs to fulfil its functions, and the CS has the 'power to do anything which is calculated to facilitate, or is conducive or incidental to, the performance of its functions' (Sch 3, para 10). Part 2 of Sch 3 allows for the transfer of property, rights and liabilities from the CC to the CS in

---

[1] 'Support services' includes 'the provision of staff, accommodation and equipment and any other services which facilitate the carrying out by the Tribunal of its functions' (s 13(3)).

accordance with a scheme made by the Secretary of State. In effect, the CS performs the service currently provided by the CC to the CCAT, but secures the complete independence of the CAT.

THE COMPETITION COMMISSION

2.21   Changes to the role and constitution of the CC are made consequent to the other institutional changes, and the changes to some of the substantive procedures with which it is involved.[1] These are set out in ss 185–187, and Sch 11, which makes amendments to CA 1998, Sch 7. In particular, rules of procedure are to be made in respect of the various reference groups, ie merger reference groups, market reference groups, and special reference groups. In September 2002, the CC published its consultation document *Competition Commission Rules of Procedure* (the *Draft Rules*), setting out its rules applicable to all references made to the CC under the relevant enactments.[2]

2.22   Part II of the *Draft Rules* relates to the appointment of groups to deal with references made. Each group must consist of at least three persons, one of whom may, but need not necessarily be, the Chairman of the CC. The Chairman of the CC or, in his or her absence, a Deputy Chairman, may attend meetings of any group and offer advice, which the group is bound to have regard to. However, the Chairman or the deputy may not vote unless they are serving on the relevant group.

2.23   Groups must comply with the statutory timetables applicable to the reference for which they have been constituted, and, as soon as is practicable after their appointment, must draw up an administrative timetable for the reference.[3] In drawing up the timetable, regard shall be had to the views of any of the main parties to the reference.

---

[1]   For a broad discussion of the role of the CC in the new structure, see the CC's publication *General Advice and Information Guidance: Consultation Document*, September 2002.

[2]   The FTA 1973 and the CA 1980 (to the extent to which they remain applicable), the Telecommunications Act 1984, the Airports Act 1986, the Gas Act 1986, the Electricity Act 1989, the Broadcasting Act 1990, the Water Industry Act 1991, the Electricity (Northern Ireland) Order 1992, the Railways Act 1993, the Airports (Northern Ireland) Order 1994, the Gas (Northern Ireland) Order 1996, the Postal Services Act 2000, the Transport Act 2000, the Financial Services and Markets Act 2000, and the Enterprise Act 2002.

[3]   Paragraph 5.3 of the *Draft Rules* sets out the main stages of any reference, although noting that these need not necessarily take place within the order in which they are set out: (a) gathering information, (b) issuing questionnaires, (c) hearing of witnesses, (d) verifying information, (e) providing a statement of issues, (f) considering responses to a statement of issues, (g) notifying and publishing provisional findings, (h) considering possible remedies, (i) considering exclusions from disclosure, and (j) publishing reports.

2.24 It is for the group to determine whether any of the hearings are to be held in public. In taking such a decision, the group is to have regard to: (a) the views of the main and third parties; (b) the need for confidentiality; (c) the extent to which this may inhibit persons giving evidence; (d) the extent to which parties may be encouraged to give evidence by virtue of the hearing being held in public; (e) the proper conduct of the reference; (f) the timetable; (g) the resource implications; and (h) the transport implications of the location of the hearing. Where hearings are held in public, the group may determine that those in attendance have the right to be heard, or to cross-examine witnesses, or to participate otherwise.

2.25 Any of the investigation powers conferred on the CC in relation to references may be exercised by the group, and it may impose penalties in accordance with the relevant guidance[1] where relevant parties do not comply with the obligations imposed on them.

2.26 Groups will make provisional findings on references, which will be given by way of notices (which will also be published on the CC website) to the relevant parties, who will be able to make written representations in relation to these findings. There is no obligation to allow the main parties to make oral submissions at this stage. The group will also consult the main parties if it considers it appropriate to do so when considering what remedies might be advanced to address the problems identified, although it is not obliged to hold a remedies hearing.

2.27 Final findings will be made once the group has considered any submissions made in response to its interim findings notice. At this time, reports shall be published as required by the Act. It is the responsibility of the group to decide what material to exclude in the light of s 239 of the Act.

2.28 The group also has responsibility for considering whether an undertaking or order should be accepted or made under ss 82 and 83 (in relation to merger references) or ss 159 and 160 (in relation to market investigation references).

---

[1] See CC *Statement of Policy on Penalties*. The penalties that may be imposed are considered in Chapters 3 and 4, where appropriate.

Chapter Three

MERGER CONTROL

INTRODUCTION

3.1   The reform of merger control set out in the Act is almost a total rewrite of the provisions of the FTA 1973, although the bones of the old regime are clearly visible.[1] As indicated in the White Paper:

> 'Government policy in recent years has been to take merger decisions primarily on competition grounds. Practice has also been for the Government to follow the advice of the competition authorities in most cases. The reform proposals build on these developments. They have two central elements. Firstly, decisions on the vast majority of mergers will be transferred from Ministers to the OFT and the Competition Commission. Secondly, the test against which mergers are assessed will be changed from a broad-based '"public interest" test to a new competition-based test. The Government is also committed to procedural and other improvements, such as the introduction of maximum statutory timetables for investigations, and building more transparency into the process.'[2]

It was accepted in Committee that 'the principles involved in changes to the [merger regime] are broadly supported by the whole gamut of organisations, and by Opposition members'.[3]

3.2   The key questions to be asked of any merger regime are:

–   What are the thresholds at which it operates?
–   What are the procedural requirements, and, in particular, is notification compulsory?
–   What is the substantive test by which the merger will be evaluated?

---

[1]   The provisions of the FTA 1973 relating to newspaper mergers, under which a substantial number of reports have been made, will not be affected by the Act.

[2]   Paragraph 5.2. The reform process began well before the White Paper was published. In August 1999, the Government published *Mergers: A Consultation Document on Proposals for Reform* and, in October 2000, published *Mergers: The Response to the Consultation on Proposals for Reform*.

[3]   *Hansard*, Standing Committee B, col 253.

n the UK, the effect of the Act is to make substantial alterations to all of these aspects. Particular focus will be laid on the fact that the test of a merger's acceptance now becomes that of whether it substantially lessens competition (the substantial lessening of competition (SLC) test) – a change described as 'one of the cornerstones of the new merger regime'.[1] For the Government, the introduction of this new test would 'ensure that the new regime is predictable, transparent and streamlined'.[2] It is likely that there will be no more referrals to the Competition Commission (CC) under the new system than there were under the FTA 1973 procedures.[3] It is also the case that 'in practice, competition has been the principal factor in UK merger policy for many years … legislating for a competition test is not likely to make a large difference to the way in which mergers are regulated'.[4]

3.3   Part 3 of the Act, which contains the provisions relating to mergers is, at over 100 sections, the largest part of the Act and is largely self-contained. It is divided into five chapters: duty to make references (ss 22–41); public interest cases (ss 42–58); other special cases (ss 59–70); enforcement (ss 71–95); and supplementary (ss 96–130). At the time of writing, the Office of Fair Trading (OFT) and the CC had both released their draft guidance in respect of mergers, and extensive reference to this is made in this chapter.[5]

EC merger control

3.4   It has already been noted in Chapter 1 that the EC is in the process of consulting on its merger regime, with the intention that there be substantial reform. *Inter alia*, it is intended to simplify and lower the thresholds at which the EC regime will be applicable, and the Commission has indicated a preparedness to move to the SLC test.[6] At the time of writing, the relevant legislation is Regulation 4064/89 on the Control of Concentrations Between Undertakings ('the EC Merger Regulation').[7]

---

1   *Hansard*, 13 June 2002, col 109.

2   *Hansard*, Standing Committee B, col 258.

3   *Hansard*, Standing Committee B, col 259.

4   *Hansard*, Standing Committee B, col 296.

5   See OFT *Mergers: Substantive Assessment* (OFT 506, October 2002), hereinafter 'OFT *Mergers*', and CC *Merger References: Competition Commission Guidelines* (September 2002), hereinafter 'CC *Mergers*'. The CC *Statement of Policy on Penalties* is also relevant in relation to the investigation of merger references by the CC. For a general, if brief, discussion of the new merger regime, see Begent, C 'Mergers Under the Enterprise Bill' [2002] Comp Law 278.

6   See the *Green Paper on the Review of Council Regulation (EEC) No 4064/89* COM (2001) 745/6 final, 11 December 2001. The EC Commission website contains the relevant documentation, including responses to the reform proposals at *http://europa.eu.int/comm/competition/mergers/review*.

7   Reprinted in a corrected version at (1990) OJ L257/13, amended by Regulation 1310/97 (1997) OJ L180/1.

3.5   Under the EC Merger Regulation, the EC Commission has exclusive competence[1] to examine mergers where the thresholds set out in Art 1(2) and (3) are met.[2] There are, however, three exceptions to this general rule. The first of these is provided for in Art 9(2), under which Member States may in some cases request that mergers be referred back to them for their own assessment.[3] The second flows from Art 21, which provides an exception in cases where 'legitimate interests' of the Member States are affected. The relevant interests are those of public security, the plurality of the media, and prudential rules. The third exception arises not from the Regulation, but from the more general law of the Treaty. Article 298 EC provides that Member States may take necessary measures relating to their security, including the production of or trade in arms.

3.6   Member States may also request that the Commission examines a merger which falls within the competence of that State and lacks a Community dimension.[4]

3.7   The test by which a merger is evaluated is that of whether the concentration 'creates or strengthens a dominant position as a result of which competition would be significantly impeded in the common market or in a substantial part of it' (Art 2(3)). Where mergers do not fall within the thresholds set out in the EC Merger Regulation, Member States remain free to apply their own national rules to them.[5] There are no procedural requirements imposed on Member States in relation to merger control by the application of EC law.

---

[1]   Article 21(2).

[2]   These thresholds are a combination of absolute turnover requirements, a Community-wide turnover, and a turnover spread across more than one Member State.

[3]   This arises where:

'(a) a concentration threatens to create or strengthen a dominant position as a result of which effective competition will be significantly impeded on a market within that Member State, which presents all the characteristics of a distinct market, or

(b) a concentration affects competition on a market within that Member State, which presents all the characteristics of a distinct market and which does not constitute a substantial part of the common market.'

This provision is sometimes referred to as 'the German clause'.

[4]   Article 22, also referred to as 'the Dutch clause'. This clause is very rarely invoked, and was originally intended to apply to those Member States having no, or only poorly developed, merger regimes. However, in 2002, the Department of Trade and Industry (DTI) requested the Commission to examine the UK aspects of the merger between GE Engine Services and Unison Industries (DTI Press Release P/2002/134, 28 February 2002). Section 21(3)(e) of the Act makes explicit reference to the possibility of the invocation of Art 22.

[5]   Although note that, by virtue of Art 22, a Member State may request that the Commission examine a merger which falls below the thresholds.

THE DUTY TO MAKE REFERENCES

Notification and references

3.8   There is no requirement in the UK merger regime compulsorily to notify mergers.[1] However, in certain circumstances, completed mergers must be referred to the CC by the OFT.[2] This is the case where 'a relevant merger situation has been created' (see **3.12–3.23**) and this has resulted, or may be expected to result, in a substantial lessening of competition within any market in the UK[3] for goods or services[4] (s 21(1)) (the OFT's approach to the assessment of the substantial lessening of competition is dealt with at **3.25–3.45**). It will be noted that this introduces a key distinction between the Act and the FTA 1973, in that it is the OFT, rather than the Minister, who is to make the reference.[5] The OFT's guidance, *Mergers: Substantive Assessment*, deals with the situations in which the OFT is likely to make a merger reference, and its powers to accept undertakings in lieu of making a reference.

3.9   There are, however, important exceptions to this general rule. The first two of these require the OFT to make an assessment of the merger's importance and impact. Thus, no reference need be made where the markets concerned are of insufficient importance to justify the reference (s 22(2)(a)). The OFT has indicated that 'this exception is likely to apply only very rarely'.[6] More importantly, perhaps, s 22(2)(b) provides that a reference need not be made where, in the view of the OFT:

> 'any relevant customer benefits in relation to the creation of the relevant merger situation concerned outweigh the substantial lessening of competition concerned and any adverse effects of the substantial lessening of competition concerned.'[7]

For this exception to apply, the OFT must believe that the benefits alleged will materialise within a reasonable period of time, and that they would not arise but for the merger. It is not necessary that the benefits claimed arise in the same market as the identified SLC takes place. However, the OFT's 'normal

---

[1]   This was also the case in respect to the FTA 1973, although it has been noted that: 'In practice however, most major mergers under the UK system are cleared before they are implemented, even without the threat of fines. The financial risks of forced divestment are enough to ensure prior consultation with competition authorities in virtually every important case.' (Livingston, D *Competition Law and Practice* (London, FT Law and Tax, 1995), para 42.01.)

[2]   These two parts of the procedure are likely to become known as the stage one (OFT) and stage two (CC) proceedings.

[3]   Throughout this Part of the Act, a reference to the UK includes any part of the UK, and extends to markets which operate in the UK as well as in other countries (s 22(6)).

[4]   The meaning of 'supply of services' is considered in full in s 128.

[5]   Although the practice has been, in more recent times, for the advice of the Director General of Fair Trading to be published and followed by the Minister.

[6]   OFT *Mergers*, para 7.5. There are some circumstances in which mergers in very small markets might still warrant references being made (ibid, para 7.6).

[7]   'Relevant customer benefits' are defined in s 30.

expectation is that these customer benefits will arise in the market where the competition concerns have been identified. To show that benefits in one market outweigh a [SLC] in another will require a very high standard of proof'.[1]

3.10 Further exceptions are provided for in s 22(3). These are generally of a technical nature, or relate to situations in which the OFT is considering whether to accept undertakings in lieu of making a reference (see **3.75–3.76**), or public-interest notices are in force (see **3.57–3.61**).

3.11 The OFT will offer informal advice or confidential guidance to parties where a merger is being contemplated that may fall within the relevant thresholds.[2]

Relevant merger situations

3.12 The sections relating to the definition of a relevant merger situation are somewhat long. The primary requirements are that:

–   two or more enterprises[3] cease to be distinct; *and*
–   the value of the turnover in the UK of the enterprise being taken over exceeds £70m; *or*
–   in relation to the supply of goods or services of any description, at least one-quarter of all the goods or services of that description which are supplied in the UK are supplied by or to one and the same person (s 23(1), (2), (3) and (4)).

'Cease to be distinct'

3.13 Enterprises 'cease to be distinct' where 'they are brought under common ownership or common control' (s 26(1)). The provisions in this respect are based almost exactly on s 65 of the FTA 1973, with a minor modification allowing for the effect of the operation of the CA 1998. The effect of s 26(2)–(4) is the same as that of s 65(2)–(4) of the FTA 1973. Three levels of control may be discerned: material influence over policy; control over policy; and a controlling interest in the relevant enterprise. One effect of this is that enterprises may cease to be distinct when there is a change in the level of control. Section 26(4)(a), for example, would cover the situation in which there was a change from 'material influence' to 'control'. It has been pointed out

---

[1]   OFT *Mergers*, para 7.9.
[2]   See also *Hansard*, Standing Committee B, col 260.
[3]   'Enterprise' is defined in s 129. It is pointed out in the *Explanatory Notes* that 'the definition includes "part of the activities of a business" as it is sometimes an operating division of a company that is acquired rather than the whole of the company' (para 106).

that this means that it might be possible to refer a merger which proceeds over time at any one of three points.[1] However, s 29[2] provides that in situations where control is obtained by 'a series of transactions', these may be treated as having occurred simultaneously on the date on which the last of them occurred, thus obviating the need to examine the transactions individually, consolidating the examination of all into a single reference. This applies only over any two-year period.

3.14 Section 27 deals with the time when enterprises cease to become distinct, and reproduces s 66 of the FTA 1973. The effect of the section is to allow the authorities to treat any incremental changes in control achieved through a series of transactions ('successive events') as having all taken effect on the date of the last transaction, and there is no need to determine which precise transaction led to the increase in control necessary to qualify as a merger situation. The difference between this section and s 29 is that s 27 applies to what might be deemed a single transaction, whereas s 29 applies to a series of discrete transactions, albeit one having the same effect as the single transaction broken up over time to which s 27 applies.

3.15 There are various ways in which 'common control' may be found to exist. Section 26(2) thus provides that enterprises may be treated as being under common control if they are:

(a)   enterprises of interconnected bodies corporate;[3]
(b)   enterprises carried on by two or more bodies corporate, of which one and the same person has control; and
(c)   an enterprise carried on by a body corporate and an enterprise carried on by a person or group of persons having control of that body corporate.

3.16 A controlling interest in an enterprise will normally be found to exist where the shareholding reaches the point where more than 50% of the voting rights have been acquired. Control over policy has not often been considered in previous reports of the Monopolies and Mergers Commission (MMC) and the CC. The question is one of fact, and the most important single factor is probably the ability of the shareholder (who will have a minority holding, albeit possibly the largest single holding) to appoint directors to the board.

---

[1]   For full discussions of the merger regime of the FTA 1973, see *Butterworths Competition Law Service*, Division VII, and Livingston, D *Competition Law and Practice* (London, FT Law and Tax, 1995), Chapters 33 and 37.

[2]   Section 29 reproduces s 66A of the FTA 1973.

[3]   'Interconnected bodies corporate' is defined in s 129(2) to apply to situations in which '(a) one of them is a body corporate of which the other body is a subsidiary; or (b) both of them are subsidiaries of one and the same body corporate'.

There is no single shareholding percentage at which it is possible to say with confidence that control over policy will be established.

3.17 The ability materially to influence policy is also a matter which is not capable of being reduced to any precise rules. In its guide to mergers under the FTA 1973, the OFT indicated that:

> 'In assessing whether a particular size of shareholding enables the holder materially to influence the policy of the company concerned, account has to be taken of factors such as the distribution of the remaining shareholdings; whether the holder has board representation or any agreements with the company enabling him to influence policy; as well as any special provisions in the constitution of the company such as restrictions on voting rights.
>
> A shareholding of more than 25%, which generally enables the holder to block special resolutions, is likely to be regarded as conferring the ability materially to influence policy even if all the remaining shares are held by one person. Any shareholding greater than 15% is liable to be examined by the Office to see whether or not the holder may be able materially to influence the policy of the company concerned, although a holding of less than 15% might also attract scrutiny in exceptional circumstances. Equally, there are no precise criteria for determining when a shareholding gives the holder de facto control over the policy of the company concerned; a view has to be taken case by case in the light of the particular circumstances.'[1]

There are a number of reports in which a shareholding of more than, but close to, 20% has been found to confer the ability materially to influence policy.[2] A material influence over policy might also flow, not from ownership, but from contractual arrangements, or from the possession of certain protective rights.

Control acquired by stages

3.18 It is possible, as suggested in **3.13**, for more than one merger situation to flow from the same set of factual circumstances. This might be the case, for example, where a shareholding which confers the ability materially to influence a company's policy increases to one which gives *de facto* control over the company. Equally, there could be a move from *de facto* control to a controlling interest (once a controlling interest has been acquired, further increases in a holding would not constitute new merger situations). However, it is clearly inappropriate to examine each of these situations as a separate merger demanding a reference, save in the most exceptional of circumstances. As

---

[1] OFT *Mergers: A Guide to Procedures under the Fair Trading Act 1973*, paras 5 and 6.

[2] See, for example, *Government of Kuwait/BP* (Cm 477, 1988), and *British Airways/Sabena* (Cm 1155, 1990). In *Stora Kopparbergs Bergslags AB/Swedish Match NV/The Gillette Company* (Cm 1473, 1991), for example, Gillette had taken a 22% holding of the equity of Swedish Match NV in the form of non-voting convertible loan stock, and also held certain pre-emption rights. The MMC concluded in part that: 'in our view a prudent Wilkinson Sword management would be bound constantly to take into account the fact that Gillette was a major shareholder in its parent company, Swedish Match NV, was its parent company's largest creditor and had important rights in relation to significant decisions affecting the future of the company, notwithstanding the limits to Gillette's rights' (para 1.6).

indicated, as long as these situations occur within the same two-year period, the transactions are to be treated as having occurred simultaneously, obviating the need for more than one reference to be made.

Turnover exceeds £70m

3.19 The turnover test, set out in s 23(1)(b), and expanded on in s 28, replaces the asset test of the FTA 1973.[1] The figure is a compromise between the Government, which had insisted on a figure of £45m up to Third Reading, and the Lords, which was insisting on a figure of £100m. £70m is the figure suggested originally by the Confederation of British Industry (CBI). The effect of the move from £45m to £70m is estimated to be that 50% fewer mergers would be caught by the provisions.[2] The value of the turnover, which must be turnover in the UK, of the enterprise being taken over is to be determined in accordance with such rules as are made by the Secretary of State.[3] The OFT is to keep the threshold under review, and may advise the Secretary of State from time to time as to whether the figure remains appropriate.

25% of relevant goods or services

3.20 The share-of-supply test is taken directly from the FTA 1973. A relevant merger situation is created where the merger creates or enhances[4] a share of the market, however defined, of 25% or above. Section 23 allows the person making the reference to determine what the reference framework in terms of the relevant goods or services is, as well as the appropriate benchmark by which the 25% figure is determined.[5] It is to be hoped that, in practice, a more robust approach is taken, for the requirements of the Act bear only a slight relationship to any accepted economic definition of relevant

---

[1] The Government argued that the £45m figure would equate roughly to £70m assets – one of the tests set out in the FTA 1973 – and would, therefore, catch as many mergers as under the FTA regime. See Lord Sainsbury *Hansard* (HL), 18 July 2002, col 1454:

> 'The £45 million figure was derived from data research we undertook in my department. Briefly, the figure is based on an analysis of the assets and turnover levels of 110,000 UK companies. Our intention was to find a figure that we believed would account for roughly the same number of companies as is currently the case under the assets test.'

Further research showed that the number of UK companies with assets of £70m or more was 7473, and the total number with a turnover of more than £45m was 7057 (*Hansard* (HL), 15 October 2002, col 792).

[2] There were 5350 companies on the Fame database which had a UK turnover of more than £70m in 2000–2001 (*Hansard*, 30 October 2002, col 937).

[3] At the time of writing, no such rules have been made.

[4] Ie the 'merger must result in an increment to the share of supply or consumption and the resulting share must be at least 25%' (OFT *Mergers*, para 2.2), and 'where an enterprise already supplies or acquires 25% of particular goods or services, the test is satisfied so long as its share is increased as a result of the merger. It does not matter how small an increase that may be' (ibid, para 2.18).

[5] Section 23(5), for example, permits this to be determined by 'value, cost, price, quantity, capacity, number of workers employed or some other criterion, of whatever nature'.

markets or harm. In the EC, the Commission's analysis proceeds on the basis of its *Notice on the Definition of the Relevant Market for the Purposes of Community Competition Law*.[1] This puts the hypothetical monopolist test[2] at the heart of market definition. The approach has been followed in the context of the application of the CA 1998 by the OFT.[3] Simply to define a market by reference to a vague product or service description, as would be possible on the face of the Act, does not assist in determining whether there are any competitive problems arising from a merger.[4] However, the OFT has indicated that it:

> 'will have regard to the narrowest reasonable description of a set of goods or services to determine whether the share of supply test is met. This practice is intended to make it easier for companies and their advisers to determine whether the Act applies to a particular merger situation.'[5]

Although this is likely to provide only cold comfort to industry, the OFT is still required to consider whether there may be a SLC as a result of the merger before a reference is made, and, at this point, a more sensitive analysis of the competitive situation will be made (see **3.31–3.45**).[6]

Time-limits

3.21   Section 24 reproduces the time-limits of the FTA 1973[7] in relation to relevant merger situations. References must be made to the CC within four months of their completion, or within four months of the notice of material facts being made public or given to the OFT, where this is later. 'Made public' is defined as being 'so publicised as to be generally known or readily ascertainable' (s 24(3)). The presumption is that in these cases, even if the merger has not been notified to the OFT, it should be presumed to have been aware of it. There has been no reported case in which the issue of 'being made public' was a key factor, and it has been suggested that 'the filing of documents at Companies House should be sufficient to place the information in the public domain and make it readily ascertainable'.[8] Section 31 gives the

---

[1]   (1997) OJ C372/5.

[2]   Known more formally as the SSNIP test, where SSNIP stands for a small but significant non-transitory (ie permanent) increase in price (see further, **4.47**).

[3]   Technical guideline *Market Definition* [2000] UKCLR 61.

[4]   In the case of *Aberdeen Journals Ltd v The Director General of Fair Trading* [2002] CompAR 167, the CCAT was trenchant in its criticism of a Decision finding a breach of the Chapter II Prohibition of the CA 1998 (*Predation by Aberdeen Journals* CA98/5/2001, [2001] UKCLR 856). Although the argument there related to unilateral conduct, the general points regarding the importance of market definition, and the rigour with which it must be approached, are of more general application.

[5]   OFT *Mergers*, para 2.19.

[6]   Section 123 gives the Secretary of State the power to alter the share-of-supply test by making an Order to that effect.

[7]   As amended by the Deregulation and Contracting Out Act 1994.

[8]   Livingston, D, *Competition Law and Practice* (London, FT Law and Tax, 1995), para 33.52.

OFT the power to request information in relation to mergers from any person carrying on an enterprise which has ceased to be distinct.

3.22   The time-limits provided for may be extended by a further 20 days by agreement between the OFT and the relevant parties, or by notice by the OFT where it has not been given requested information, where undertakings are being sought, or where the UK has made a request to the EC Commission under Art 22(3) of the EC Merger Regulation (see **3.6**).

Anticipated mergers

3.23   In addition to being able to make references in cases where a relevant merger situation has arisen, the OFT may also make references in respect of anticipated mergers (s 33). In recent years, the majority of references have been in relation to anticipated mergers (see **3.8**). Exactly the same provisions are made in respect of such references as apply to consummated mergers, subject only to the prospective, rather than retrospective, nature of the proceedings and analysis, and the substantive test is the same. Where a reference has been made in relation to a contemplated merger which has subsequently been abandoned, the CC may cancel the reference.[1] The CC may also vary a reference that has been made in relation to a completed merger into one in relation to an anticipated merger, and vice versa, where the facts justify this (s 37(2)).

Determination of references

3.24   It is for the CC to determine the effect of a merger on a reference to it. The CC is required, by s 35, to determine (a) whether a relevant merger situation has been created, and:

> '(b) if so, whether the creation of that situation has resulted, or may be expected to result, in a substantial lessening of competition within any markets in the United Kingdom for goods or services.'

Where this is found to be the case, there is deemed to be an 'anti-competitive outcome' (s 35(2)). It is this change in the substantive test which is the most fundamental alteration to the merger regime brought about by the Act.[2] The

---

[1]   This addresses an anomaly in the FTA 1973, under which the MMC did not have the power to abandon a reference. This was highlighted in the three-page report on *NTL Communications Corp/Newcastle United plc* (1999), Cm 4411, accurately described by Frazer as 'a pointless waste of time made necessary only by the absence of any provision in the Fair Trading Act 1973 for the laying aside of a merger reference' ([1999] UKCLR 253).

[2]   In the *Explanatory Notes*, it is noted that 'the term "substantial lessening of competition" is not defined in the Bill. However, it is intended that advice and information on the operation of the competition test will be provided by the CC (and the OFT)' (para 125). Draft guidance to this effect has now been published, and is drawn on in this chapter.

OFT can also frame references so as to consider only whether the jurisdictional test has been met, and not to consider the substantive competitive effects of the merger (s 35(6) or (7)). It is extremely unlikely that such limited references will ever be made.

'Substantial lessening of competition'

3.25 It has already been noted that the EC Commission has indicated that it is considering adopting the SLC test (see **1.52**). This is likely to emerge as the predominant international standard in the assessment of mergers, although this does not mean that every relevant authority will reach the same conclusions in respect of mergers.

3.26 In the *Explanatory Notes*, the SLC test is explained in brief at para 126:

'Similar language is used in the legislation controlling mergers in a number of other major jurisdictions including the US, Canada, Australia and New Zealand. The concept is an economic one, best understood by reference to the question of whether a merger will increase or facilitate the exercise of market power (whether unilateral, or through co-ordinated behaviour), leading to reduced output, higher prices, less innovation or lower quality of choice. A number of matters may be potentially relevant to the assessment of whether a merger will result in a substantial lessening of competition. These matters include, but are not limited to:

- market shares and concentration;
- extent of effective competition before and after the merger;
- efficiency and financial performance of firms in the market;
- barriers to entry and expansion in the relevant market;
- availability of substitute products and the scope for supply- or demand-substitution;
- extent of change and innovation in a market;
- whether in the absence of the merger one of the firms would fail and, if so, whether its failure would cause the assets of that firm to exit the market;
- the conduct of customers or of suppliers to those in the market.'[1]

---

[1] It should be recognised that these are complex issues. The leading US text on merger control, ABA Section of Antitrust Law *Mergers and Acquisitions: Understanding the Antitrust Issues* (Chicago, ABA, 2000), does not have a section on the SLC test, but some 300 pages are devoted to various elements of the analysis, all of which relate to the application of the SLC test in practice. The SLC test is also employed by, *inter alia*, Canada, Australia, New Zealand, France and Germany. Ireland is also in the process of moving to the SLC test, and has brought forward legislation to this effect. The approach in Spain also produces a result which is very similar in practice.

3.27 While some scepticism has been expressed about the move from the dominance test to the SLC test suggested by the EC Commission,[1] there appears to be an emerging consensus that there would be benefits. A broad analysis of the way in which the test might work was set out in the *Response of the Irish Delegation to the Merger Green Paper*.[2]

3.28 In the UK, it is not a matter of the SLC test replacing a dominance test, but rather of an exclusively competition test replacing the vague 'public interest' test of the FTA 1973. The question to be addressed in this context is that of how the SLC test might be expected to work in practice, and whether it will result in a significantly different approach from that at present. It is likely, in fact, that the effect of the test in the UK will be less noticeable than in the EC. The OFT for example, argues that:

> 'the change to the [SLC] test is expected to make little difference to how mergers are assessed. For some years, the effect of a merger on competition has been the primary consideration in decisions on whether to refer a merger to the CC, and in the CC's conclusions on mergers referred to it. Consequently, the [DGFT's] published advice on reference decisions, and the CC's reports on merger references, under the FTA regime provide useful insights into how the new test is likely to be applied.'[3]

The move to the SLC test was broadly welcomed, with the greater part of those responding favouring the change. However, the CBI expressed some concern about the adoption of a substantive test that was different from that applied by the EC authorities,[4] and some other concerns were raised in respect of this relationship at Committee stage. It was suggested, for example, that divergent tests could result in the situation where companies would attempt to structure mergers so as to fall within the EC regime rather than the UK regime.[5] Although the 'public interest' test is unlikely to be mourned, there was

---

[1] See, eg RBB Economics 'SLC Versus Dominance – A Rose By Any Other Name?' (occasional newsletter):

> 'The key issue to investigate from an economic point of view in order to establish whether a move from the dominance test to the SLC test is necessary or whether the discussion is indeed only a matter of semantics is whether there are merger cases that would be considered to be problematic under the SLC test but that would not be captured under the dominance test. ...
>
> Since the dominance test can capture a wide variety of competition scenarios, sticking to the dominance test might be desirable in the sense that it requires explicit consideration of the competitive constraints prevailing in the industry and thus provides a useful check on the merger appraisal undertaken by the Commission. If one trusted the Commission to get its analysis right every time, there might be a case for adopting a SLC based test in the sense that it could avoid some unnecessary complexity in cases where market definition and market shares are least useful as a guide to the impact of a merger. The danger, however, is that the resulting increase in discretion could mean an unnecessary leap in the dark.'

[2] Published on the EC Commission's website at: *http://europa.eu.int/comm/competition/mergers/review/comments/ref111_ireland.pdf*.

[3] OFT *Mergers*, summary.

[4] On the other hand, given the fact that mergers are to be examined under *either* the EC *or* the UK regime, and *never* by both, there is perhaps a less forceful argument to be made in respect of this area than there is in relation to, say, the analysis of market conduct.

[5] *Hansard*, Standing Committee B, col 280.

one attempt in committee to reinstate it, as it allowed for consideration of wider social issues than the SLC test would permit.[1]

General concerns about mergers

3.29 The primary concern relating to mergers is that they may produce unilateral effects, which is to say the outcome of the elimination of a competitive restraint on each of the two parties. If this leads to the creation of any market power, which need not necessarily equate to dominance, the result will be an increase in prices, and a corresponding reduction in output. Where such effects will follow a merger, there may be said to be a SLC, such that the merger may be caught by the prohibition. This may be the case where market shares are lower than a dominance threshold (which would typically apply at market shares in excess of 40%). A further problem with mergers relates to the increased risk of horizontal, or oligopolistic, co-ordination ('co-ordinated anti-competitive effects'). In this respect, the position has been summarised in the US Department of Justice's *Horizontal Merger Guidelines*:

> 'A merger may diminish competition by enabling firms in the relevant market more likely, more successfully, or more completely to engage in coordinated interaction that harms consumers. Coordinated interaction is comprised of actions by a group of firms that are profitable for each of them only as a result of the accommodating reactions of the others. This behaviour includes tacit or express collusion, and may or may not be lawful in and of itself.'[2]

The possibility of post-merger collusion has often been considered in MMC/CC merger reports, and a significant risk that such collusion will follow may provide, at present, the grounds for the rejection of the merger.[3] However, as the Irish Delegation noted, clear guidance as to how the policy would operate in such cases will be needed:

> 'Many mergers in oligopolistic markets do not increase market power. Some mergers in oligopolistic markets are driven by intense price rivalry, which leads firms to seek efficiencies via merger, and these mergers may even enhance competition. For these reasons, and in order to enhance the legal predictability of the test, it would be extremely desirable that guidelines be introduced on how the competition test would apply.'

The economics of tacit collusion are considered further in the following chapter, as the theory is important in relation to market investigation references (see **4.67–4.70**). The arguments have been judicially revisited

---

[1] Mr Barnes *Hansard*, Standing Committee B, cols 267– 269. See also Mr Field, col 342. The TUC also expressed concern about the removal of Ministers from the decision-making process in merger control (see *Hansard*, 13 June 2002, col 1080).

[2] DoJ, 1992, para 2.1.

[3] In the EC, on the other hand, the analysis is far more difficult. Situations where mergers lead to the creation of a position of collective dominance may be prohibited, as was the case in the 2000 Decision in *Airtours/First Choice* (2000) OJ L93/1. Here, the Commission blocked a merger on the grounds that, post-merger, the market for short-haul foreign package holidays in the UK would tend to collective dominance. This Decision was then savaged by the Court of First Instance in *Airtours plc v EC Commission* Case T-342/99 [2002] 5 CMLR 317, [2002] UKCLR 642.

recently by the Court of First Instance, in the case of *Airtours plc v Commission* (see also **3.39**).[1]

3.30 Three types of mergers may be identified for the purpose of competition analysis, each of which raises slightly different concerns: horizontal mergers, vertical mergers, and conglomerate mergers. The approach of the OFT and the CC to these is considered below (at **3.38–3.45**).

The OFT and CC approaches to the SLC analysis

3.31 The OFT can make a reference to the CC only in situations in which there is 'at least a significant prospect that a merger may be expected to lessen competition substantially'.[2] For the CC, the application of the SLC test sits at the heart of its responsibility in relation to merger references. Accordingly, both the OFT and the CC are required to consider the SLC test, albeit to different ends. Both have published guidance relating to the application of the test, and much of the analysis will be the same. The CC's approach to the assessment of the SLC test is set out in Part 2 of its *Merger References* guidelines, and there is no obvious difference between the approach set out here, and that set out by the OFT, save that the language is sometimes different. However, there are some points on which the CC guidelines go further. For example, the treatment of market definition is more fully developed than is the case in the OFT guideline, although this is in part because the OFT has dealt with the issue of market definition in the relevant guideline under the CA 1998.

3.32 As noted in the OFT guidance, 'the core concept of the [SLC] test is a comparison of the prospects for competition with and without the merger'.[3] A number of factors are pointed to by the OFT and the CC that will be employed in attempting to identify those mergers which may be expected to lead to a SLC.[4]

3.33 First, the proper 'frame of reference' for the competitive analysis will be identified. In this respect, the concept of market definition is crucial. The essence of the concept is that 'a relevant market is something worth monopolising'.[5] More fully:

> 'The relevant market contains all those substitute products and regions which provide a significant competitive constraint on the products and regions of interest. The relevant market can be defined as a collection of products such that a (hypothetical) single supplier of that collection would be able to increase price profitably. Defining the

---

[1]   Case T-342/99 [2002] 5 CMLR 317, [2002] UKCLR 642.

[2]   OFT *Mergers*, para 3.2.

[3]   OFT *Mergers*, para 3.9.

[4]   OFT *Mergers*, para 3.10.

[5]   Bishop, S and Walker, M *Economics of EC Competition Law: Concepts, Application and Measurement* (London, Sweet & Maxwell, 1999), para 3.07.

relevant market in this way ensures that all products which pose a significant competitive constraint on the parties under investigation are taken into consideration. ...

For example, if an investigation were concerned with a merger between two malt whisky producers, a first step might be to assess whether a hypothetical single supplier of malt whisky could profitably increase prices above prevailing levels. If the answer to this question is negative, then the next step is to determine whether control over the closest substitute for malt whisky, say, blended whisky, would allow a single supplier to increase price profitably. If the answer to this question is affirmative, then the relevant market would include both malt and blended whiskys but not other alcoholic drinks.'[1]

The CC, in its recent reports, has focused on the hypothetical monopolist test where it has had the information available to it to do so,[2] and it is already the case that 'in practice, the OFT will tend to regard a relevant market as comprising goods or services which are seen by consumers ... as substitutable'.[3]

3.34 It should be noted that there may be some differences between the way in which this analysis is conducted in a merger reference and under the CA 1998 when examining for possible abuses of the Chapter II Prohibition. In

---

[1] Ibid. See generally Chapter 4 for a full discussion of market definition (at **4.47–4.54**).

[2] For example in *P&O Princess Cruises plc and Royal Caribbean Cruises Ltd* (2002), Cm 5536, the CC dealt with the issue of market definition in the following terms:

'5.3 Defining the relevant economic market is the first step in assessing the impact of the proposed merger. It is against the backdrop of the market, however defined, that shares are estimated and the possibility of market power examined.

5.4 One way to define the market is through the "hypothetical monopolist" test. The hypothetical monopolist test provides a framework within which to determine the set of products that currently provide competitive constraints on the merging firms, and the geographic area in which this occurs.

5.5 We start with the narrowest product or group of products of interest and assess whether a single supplier that controlled all these products could increase its profits by a sustained raising of prices by around 5 to 10 per cent. The ability of such a hypothetical monopolist to do so hinges on the extent to which consumers would turn to other products, and on the ability of suppliers of alternative products to switch production without significant investment or delay in response to the hypothesised price rise. The set of products over which the hypothetical monopolist can exercise its monopoly is expanded until a group of products that can sustain a hypothetical 5 to 10 per cent price rise is found. These are seen as constituting the relevant economic market as their prices are not substantially constrained by those of other products.

5.6 An empirical application of the hypothetical monopolist test is hard to carry out as the data that would be necessary is generally not available. Nevertheless we have found it useful to provide some guidance in estimating the proportion of customers an individual cruise operator would be able to lose after a 5 to 10 per cent price raise and remain as profitable ...'

In more recent reports, see also *Compass Group PLC and Rail Gourmet Holding AG, Restorama AG and Gourmet Nova AG* (Cm 5562, 2002), at paras 4.59–4.64, and, in particular, note: 'We have therefore used the hypothetical monopolist test to the extent that we can' (para 4.64); *Cargill Incorporated and Cerestar SA* (Cm 5521, 2002): 'While we begin with the market as defined in the reference, we consider whether the relevant economic market might be either wider or narrower than the reference market' (para 5.2), and 'A methodology commonly used for assessing the degree of substitutability, and therefore establishing the boundaries of the relevant market, is the SSNIP test' (para 5.4).

[3] *Butterworths Competition Law Service*, VII at [69].

the latter case, the cellophane fallacy[1] raises difficulties which do not arise in merger situations unless the market is already highly concentrated. In the case of merger references, the OFT has indicated that where it 'is able to use quantitative price data as a basis for the hypothetical monopolist test, it will generally use prevailing market price data'.[2]

3.35 In its analysis of the competitive nature of the market in which the merger takes place, the CC again covers the same ground as the OFT. It draws particular attention also to the existence of network effects,[3] and the 'tipping' that may take place in such markets. This is to say that 'as one firm, or technology, gains an advantage in the market, in effect the balance of power in the market "tips" in its direction leaving it as the prevalent firm or technology'. The CC notes that:

> 'in these markets, competition takes place for the market as opposed to within the market and traditional methods of analysis, such as market shares and market concentration might not successfully illustrate the degree of competition in the market.'[4]

3.36 Having considered the competitive framework, the OFT and the CC will consider the characteristics of competition in the market, both pre- and post-merger. Here, it must consider the 'counterfactual' – what would the position be were the merger *not* to take place? This can raise some difficult issues in assessing post-merger rivalry:

> '[While] in most cases, the best guide to the appropriate counterfactual will be prevailing conditions of competition … in certain circumstances the OFT may need to take into account likely and imminent changes in the structure of competition in order to reflect as accurately as possible the nature of rivalry without the merger.'[5]

Problems may arise in particular in bidding markets, where it may be more appropriate to consider those who will be bidding in the next round, rather than the situation at the time of the previous bid. Where firms are likely to enter or exit from the relevant market, this should also be considered in the counterfactual, as must likely changes in the regulatory structure in the case of regulated markets.[6]

---

[1]　See *US v EI Du Pont de Nemours & Co* (1956) 351 US 377. Following this case, which related to an alleged monopolisation of the cellophane market, it was recognised that an undertaking with market power might, and indeed should, be already pricing at a level such that to raise the price would be unprofitable as enough customers at the margin would switch to substitute products. In such cases, if the fallacy is not recognised, a SSNIP test might lead to the conclusion that the market was wider than in fact it was.

[2]　OFT *Mergers*, para 3.20.

[3]　The existence of which is not universally accepted by economists. See, eg Gordon, RL *Antitrust Abuse in the New Economy* (Cheltenham, Edward Elgar, 2002).

[4]　CC *Mergers*, para 3.9.

[5]　OFT *Mergers*, para 3.25.

[6]　This would be the case at the time of writing, for example, in relation to mergers in the media industry where the Communications Bill will make a substantial impact upon the overall industry.

3.37 Factors such as buyer power, the failing firm defence, and the effect of any efficiencies argued to arise out of the merger which may increase the competitive pressure in the market in question will also be considered.

3.38 When analysing horizontal mergers, which raise the greatest concern as, by definition, they reduce the number of competitors in an industry, one of the standard tools used by analysts is that of concentration ratios, and the Herfindahl–Hirschman Index (HHI). Concentration ratios are very simple measures that merely reflect in absolute terms the aggregate market share of a number of the largest suppliers in the market in question – typically three or four firms (C3 or C4). They do not reveal anything about the differences in the size of the firms that make up the group. The HHI is more sensitive to the share of supply held by the larger firms, and is relied on by the EC Commission in its assessment of certain horizontal agreements, and by the US authorities in their assessments of certain mergers. Formally, the HHI is the sum of the squared market shares of the companies on the relevant market, or $\Sigma s1^2 \ldots sn^2$ (where sn is the market share of firm n). Thus, in a market with four firms, each of which have a 25% market share, the HHI would be $25^2 + 25^2 + 25^2 + 25^2 = 2500$. In a total monopoly market, the HHI would be 10,000 (100^2), and in a market of 100 firms, each with only 1% market share, it would be 100. The OFT has indicated that it:

> 'is likely to regard any market with a post-merger HHI in excess of 1,800 as highly concentrated, and any market with a post-merger HHI in excess of 1,000 as concentrated. In a highly concentrated market, a merger with a delta[1] in excess of 50 may give rise to potential competition concerns. In a concentrated market, a merger with a delta in excess of 100 may give rise to potential competition concerns.'[2]

The CC, on the other hand, is likely to place less weight on these measures. In its guidelines, it notes that it 'is not involved with the screening [as to whether to refer a merger] and as a result does not propose to place weight on concentration thresholds of this sort'.[3]

3.39 In relation to co-ordinated anti-competitive effects, the OFT and the CC draw upon the *Airtours* case, in which the Court of First Instance held that for tacit collusion to become more likely, three conditions must be met. These are, first, that the market conditions must be such that the firms have the ability to align their behaviour in the absence of an explicit agreement to do so. Secondly, there must be sufficient incentives for the firms to maintain their conduct. This means that there must be a mechanism whereby firms that deviate from the aligned conduct can be effectively 'punished' by the response of the others. Thirdly, the co-ordination should be sustainable in the face of

---

[1] 'Delta' is the change in the HHI achieved by subtracting the pre-merger HHI from the post-merger HHI.

[2] OFT *Mergers*, para 4.3.

[3] CC *Mergers*, para 3.7.

other market pressures, including the possibility of entry into the market by new firms who do not understand the 'rules'. The CC guidelines develop this point further, and also point to the dangers of concluding that a market is characterised by tacit co-ordination where prices converge, as there may be situations in which 'similar or identical prices can result from intense competition'.[1] In such a case, it may be necessary to consider also profit levels in the industry and perhaps compare these with similar industries to determine whether they are excessive and suggestive of a lack of competition. The history of price movements may also be revealing. In a competitive market, even if prices converge, there are likely to be points at which they are different. This will be the case, for example, where there is a shock to the market outside the control of the firms, such as the exit of a competitor. In a market characterised by tacit co-ordination, prices are more likely to be in perpetual alignment than they are in a competitive, yet oligopolistic, market.

3.40 The conditions under which entry may occur into the market occupied by the merging firms is an important factor in relation to both unilateral and co-ordinated anti-competitive effects. Entry will undermine the ability of the strengthened entity to raise its prices unilaterally, acting as a competitive constraint. Entry is also likely to destabilise co-ordinated anti-competitive conduct. Analysis of entry barriers will be necessary where there are initial concerns raised about post-merger competition. These are defined by the OFT as 'any feature of a market that gives incumbent firms an advantage over potential entrants or control of the assets'.[2] In order to alleviate concerns, it should be the case that entry is feasible, and that it can be of sufficient size to act as a genuine competitive constraint. It must also be clear that entry would occur in a sufficiently short space of time – typically less than one year – and that it will be sustainable.

3.41 The existence of buyer power may be advanced in order to counteract perceived competitive restrictions flowing from the merger. In this case, 'the key question is whether buyers will have a sufficiently strong post-merger bargaining position'.[3] Sheer size of the buyer is not necessarily sufficient to guarantee this. The more important question is whether the buyer has sufficient options to be able to put pressure on the supplier.

3.42 Because the SLC analysis requires a consideration of the counterfactual, it is particularly sensitive to the 'failing firm defence'. This arises in situations where one party is genuinely failing, such that, in the absence of the merger, the market would in any event become more concentrated. In such a case, it

---

[1]   CC *Mergers*, para 3.22.
[2]   OFT *Mergers*, para 4.21.
[3]   OFT *Mergers*, para 4.28.

might be that the merger, by keeping the assets of the failing firm in the market, would be pro-competitive.[1] However, the OFT will be sceptical of the merits of the defence, and has set three conditions for its application which 'will probably only be met in rare cases'.[2] These are where: 'the firm must be in such a parlous situation that without the merger it and its assets would exit the market'; 'there must be no serious prospect of reorganising the business'; and 'there should be no less anti-competitive alternative to the merger'.[3] The CC also points to the likely distribution of the customers of the failing firm following its exit from the market. If these customers would switch in any event to the acquiring firm, then the merger might have little impact on the competitive position. If, however, customers would disperse themselves over a number of competitors, but would stay with the merged entity in the event of the merger, then there would be more likely to be an adverse effect.[4]

3.43 Efficiency gains may also be claimed for mergers. The argument may be made either that because of the efficiencies, there is no SLC, or that there is SLC, but that efficiencies following the merger will be passed on to customers. In order to consider such efficiencies, the OFT requires that they be '(a) demonstrable, (b) merger-specific; and (c) likely to be passed on to consumers'.[5]

3.44 Far less attention is paid to vertical mergers than to horizontal mergers in the OFT guidance. This reflects the fact that vertical mergers give rise to far fewer concerns, and may not, axiomatically, be presumed to reduce competition. However, vertical mergers may give rise to market foreclosure by,

---

[1]   This was the case, for example, in *Air Canada and Canadian Airlines Corporation* (Cm 4838, August 2000), in which the CC held that: 'in assessing the effects of this merger, we have to consider what would have happened in the absence of the merger. The only meaningful scenario against which to judge the effects of the merger is the financial failure of Canadian Airlines and its break-up. ... The possible detriments arising from such a lack of competition ... arise as a result of the failure of Canadian Airlines to sustain competition in the Canadian market and on the Canada-UK routes, and irrespective of the merger situations' (para 1.9).

[2]   OFT *Mergers*, para 4.30. In the US, 'a party wishing to rely on that defence must show four things: first, that the failing firm cannot meet its financial obligations; secondly, that it cannot reorganise itself in bankruptcy; thirdly – an important consideration – that it cannot find another buyer whose purchase would pose lesser anti-competitive risks; and fourthly, that in the absence of the merger, its assets will exit from the market' (Mr Waterson, advocating on behalf of the CBI, the adoption of the test in the UK, *Hansard*, Standing Committee B, col 303 – the Opposition abandoned an attempt to include a specific provision in the Act relating to the failing firm defence, having been assured that the SLC test would require its consideration).

[3]   OFT *Mergers*, paras 4.31–4.33.

[4]   CC *Mergers*, para 3.56.

[5]   OFT *Mergers*, para 4.39. At the Committee stage, the Under-Secretary of State argued that:
'A merger that results in a substantial lessening of competition is almost invariably harmful to customer and consumer interests. It should be possible to allow such a merger to proceed only where the authorities are confident that there are offsetting customer benefits. We do not think that the regime should be structured to take account of benefits that benefit only upstream suppliers and their shareholders, but have no wider benefits for customers' (*Hansard*, Standing Committee B, col 308).

for example, depriving a rival producer of a distribution network if a producer merges with a retail chain. In such cases, the OFT may be concerned where rivals at the horizontal level lack a genuine alternative, either upstream or downstream, to the assets being acquired. In some cases, vertical mergers may also give rise to concerns about co-ordinated conduct. This may be the position, for example, where there is a degree of vertical integration into the retail market where prices are more transparent than in the wholesale market, facilitating co-ordination. In such cases, the analysis will be the same as for horizontal mergers.

3.45 There is also generally less concern regarding conglomerate mergers, which are mergers between firms operating in different markets. As the OFT recognises, 'such mergers rarely lead to a [SLC] as a result solely of their conglomerate effects'.[1] There is, however, the possibility that in some rare cases, a portfolio of products might be built up which is sufficiently large to deter entry, or to act to the detriment of existing competitors, in relation to particular products in the portfolio.

Further questions to be decided by the CC

3.46 If the CC determines that the effect of the merger will be to lead to SLC, it is required further to consider what actions should be taken by it in order to remedy, mitigate, or prevent the SLC (s 35(3)(a)).[2] It may also recommend that others take action. In examining this point, the CC is required:

> 'to have regard to the need to achieve as comprehensive a solution as is reasonable and practicable to the substantial lessening of competition and any adverse effects arising from it.'[3]

The position is considered in the *Explanatory Notes*:

> 'The reference to a "comprehensive solution" will require the CC to consider remedies that address the substantial lessening of competition itself (eg the features arising from the merger that give rise to the creation of market power) because it is generally more effective to tackle the cause of any problems at their source rather than by tackling the symptoms or adverse effects.'[4]

This appears to be suggesting that structural remedies – either blocking an anticipated merger, or requiring divestiture post-merger – are to be generally preferred to conduct remedies where the CC has found that there is SLC flowing from the merger. The application of remedies by the CC is considered in Part 4 of its merger guidelines.

---

[1]   OFT *Mergers*, para 6.1.
[2]   Section 36 is in largely the same terms, in relation to anticipated mergers.
[3]   Section 35(4).
[4]   Paragraph 127.

3.47 The CC is also to have regard to the effect of any action it takes or recommends on any customer benefits arising from the merger. Relevant customer benefits are dealt with in s 30, and arise where there is, or is expected to be,[1] as a result of the merger, 'lower prices, higher quality or greater choice of goods or services' or 'greater innovation in relation to such goods or services'. These benefits may arise either in the market in which the SLC occurs or in other related markets. It may appear counter-intuitive to be looking for these benefits in situations where there has already been found to be SLC, and the *Explanatory Notes* recognise that 'they are not expected to arise very often'.[2] It is sometimes argued, however, that while a merger may reduce competition, it may also create efficiencies from which customers and consumers will benefit.[3] The Irish Delegation expressed some concern about the Commission's suggestion that an efficiency defence be explicitly recognised in EC merger control:

> 'The Green Paper seems to us to be inherently correct in expressing scepticism about efficiencies arising from mergers.
>
> - Empirical studies indicate that, on aggregate, the *ex post* performance of merged companies is, at best, mixed, suggesting that efficiencies may systematically fall below the parties' genuine expectations.
> - From an economic theory perspective, there is a fundamental doubt about efficiencies in mergers where market power increases. If we believe that competition is fundamental to driving cost reductions, then efficiencies are less likely to be attained precisely in the case where a merger creates market power …
> - It is not always obvious that a merger (involving market power) is necessary to achieve many efficiency benefits.
> - If an efficiency defence is allowed, then firms will have a strong incentive to exaggerate the efficiencies and it can be extremely difficult for a competition authority to verify them in advance. For this reason, the burden should likely lie on the parties to show the efficiencies, and a high standard of proof should be required.'

In the *Explanatory Notes*, three examples of mergers that might produce relevant customer benefits are set out. These are:

> '●   a merger producing so-called "network benefits". A merger might give customers of one enterprise improved access to a wider network operated by the other enterprise, with the wider choice of complementary products that this brings. For example, in mobile telecommunications, the more users who join a particular mobile network, the more valuable the network becomes to those users as they can contact more people, in more locations, at lower cost as the network increases. In the transport sector, network benefits can improve service quality through strengthened hubs, better through-ticketing arrangements or better-connected services;

---

[1]   In the case of anticipated benefits these must 'be expected to accrue within a reasonable period of time' (s 30(3)(a)).

[2]   Paragraph 115.

[3]   At the same time, absent competitive pressure, there may be little incentive to pass the benefit of any such efficiencies onto customers.

- mergers leading to large economies of scale where the effect of scale economies on prices is sufficient to outweigh the effect of a substantial lessening of competition. Such circumstances could lead to an overall reduction in prices and be beneficial to both consumers and business, provided that the authorities were satisfied that the economies of scale would be realised in spite of a significant reduction in competition and that prices after the merger would remain lower than they were pre-merger;

- mergers producing more innovation through research and development benefits. Investment in research and development often involves large fixed costs and there may be circumstances where critical mass is needed – in terms of research expertise or capital or both – that can only be secured through a merger.'[1]

3.48   Customers are only regarded as such for the purpose of establishing a relevant customer benefit if they are direct customers of the merged entity, or if they are in a direct chain of customers (s 30(4)).

3.49   Where the CC identifies that a merger has an anti-competitive outcome, it is under a duty, imposed on it by s 41, so far as it is practicable and reasonable to do so, to remedy, mitigate or prevent the adverse effects in relation both to the SLC itself and from any effects of the SLC. In doing so, it is given the discretion to take into account any relevant customer benefits, and has scope:

> 'if it considers that customer benefits are of sufficient importance, to impose a lesser competition remedy or no remedy at all if the only steps that the CC could take to remedy the competition problem are steps that would mean that the customer benefits could not be realised.'[2]

The CC itself has indicated that it would be likely that remedial action would be required in situations in which it determined that a merger would be likely to result in a SLC, unless it did identify the existence of customer benefits. There might also be some other rare cases, such as where any remedial action lay outside the jurisdiction of the UK, where it would be outside the power of the CC to impose a remedy.[3]

3.50   The CC will also consider the cost of any remedy when considering whether to impose it. However, the CC has indicated that in the case of completed mergers, it will 'not consider the costs of divestment to the parties',[4] pointing out that the parties would have had the opportunity to seek a clearance of the merger prior to its consummation. Nor will the CC consider costs outside the competitive structure, such as environmental costs, or the social costs of unemployment, unless it is required to do so by the Secretary of

[1]   Paragraph 117.
[2]   *Explanatory Notes*, para 142.
[3]   CC *Mergers*, para 4.6.
[4]   CC *Mergers*, para 4.8.

State through the imposition of a specified public interest consideration (see **3.58**).

3.51   Remedies should also be proportional to the harm identified as arising out of the merger. This means that where two remedies are being considered, each of which is equally effective, the cheaper should be the one chosen.

3.52   A number of factors are relevant to a consideration of the effectiveness of proposed remedies. In particular, the remedy should be clear to the person to whom it is directed, as well as to other parties who may be called upon to enforce the remedy, or who are affected by it. Secondly, remedies should be crafted so that they are likely to be complied with. A third general consideration relating to remedies is the time-scale within which they will be effective.[1]

3.53   The types of remedies that are available to the CC are set out at para 4.17 of its guidelines as follows:

'The CC will consider any of the following types of remedies:

(a)   remedies that are intended to restore all or part of the *status quo ante* market structure, for example:
   –   prohibition of a proposed merger;
   –   divestment of a completed acquisition;
   –   partial prohibition or divestment;

(b)   remedies that are intended to increase the competition that will be faced by the merged firm (whether from existing competitors or new entrants), for example
   –   requiring access to essential inputs/facilities;
   –   licensing know-how or IPRs;
   –   dismantling exclusive distribution arrangements;
   –   removing no-competition clauses in customer contracts;

(c)   remedies aimed at excluding or limiting the possibility that the merged firm will take advantage of the increased market power resulting from the merger to behave anti-competitively or to exploit its customers or suppliers, for example:
   –   a price cap or other restraint on prices;
   –   a commitment to non-discriminatory behaviour;
   –   an obligation to increase the transparency of prices;
   –   an obligation to refrain from conduct, the main purpose of which is to inhibit entry.'

3.54   The starting point for the CC when considering its approach to the remedy, if one is considered necessary, will be to choose the action that is most likely to restore the competition that has been damaged by the merger. This is to say that, like the OFT, it is more likely to favour structural remedies than behavioural remedies. An additional factor in favour of structural remedies is that they do not require on-going policing. The CC may also

---

[1]   CC *Mergers*, paras 4.14–4.16.

recommend that action be taken by others, for example, by way of legislation, where regulations exist that limit entry, or to amend licence conditions in the case of regulated undertakings.

Merger reports

3.55   The CC is required to publish a report on a merger reference within a period of 24 weeks from the date of the reference concerned (ss 38(1) and 39(1)), although, in exceptional circumstances, this period may be extended by up to a further 8 weeks (s 39(3)). The period may also be extended where a relevant person has failed to comply with the requirements of s 109, which relates to the attendance of witnesses and the production of documents (see **3.100**). This report is to contain its decision, the reasons for its decision, and any information necessary to understand the decision. It has the power to carry out necessary investigations in order to prepare the report (s 38(2)). The Secretary of State has the power to amend s 389 so as to reduce, but not increase, the applicable time-limits. The procedures to be adopted by the CC in relation to merger references are illustrated at **3.111**.

PUBLIC INTEREST CASES

Public intervention notices

3.56   The residual power of the Secretary of State to intervene in the merger process by issuing public intervention notices in accordance with Chapter 2 of the Act has attracted some comment, but it is unlikely that in practice these powers will be substantially used.[1]

3.57   Section 44 gives the Secretary of State the power to intervene in cases where a relevant merger situation raises public interest issues which are specified in s 58. This is to say that:

> 'the Secretary of State should have the power to refer a case that qualifies for investigation if he or she believes that the merger may operate against the public interest. The result will be that the Secretary of State will refer cases to the Competition Commission. The public interest test that the Secretary of State will apply under the new regime will be more limited than that in the [FTA 1973]. The Secretary of State will be limited to taking account of the relevant public interest considerations and any substantial lessening of competition.'[2]

---

[1]   The OFT has a duty to notify the Secretary of State in any case where it is considering making a reference under s 22 or s 33 of any matter which it believes to relate to public interest considerations (s 57(1)). The CC has a duty to bring to the attention of the Secretary of State any representations made about the exercise of his powers under s 57(2).

[2]   *Hansard*, Standing Committee B, col 347.

At the time of Royal Assent, the only such consideration was that of national security, defined to include 'public security', and having the same meaning as that conferred by the EC Merger Regulation, Art 21(3). The term is not defined in that Regulation, and has a wide meaning, drawn in part from other provisions of the EC Treaty.[1] The power exists for the Secretary of State to specify further considerations, and he may issue a notice in respect of such a consideration, but is then under an obligation to finalise it as soon as is practicable (s 41(7)).[2] There are no plans to introduce additional public interest considerations to the one set out in the Act.[3]

3.58   Intervention notices may be issued only where the OFT has not yet made a decision in respect of a merger situation. However, a notice may be issued where the OFT has made a decision to accept undertakings under s 71 as an alternative to making a reference (see **3.74**). Only one notice may be issued in respect of any merger. The details that must be included in intervention notices are set out in s 43. They come into force when they are given, and cease to be in force at the point when the matter is finally determined.[4]

3.59   Where an intervention notice has been given, the OFT is required to give to the Secretary of State a report containing its advice on the considerations relevant to the making of a standard reference under s 22 or s 33 (s 44).[5] The Secretary of State will thus have had advice about the competition issues relating to the merger, and the OFT is obliged also to report back on any representations it has received in relation to the public interest considerations. In essence, the report is to be the summary of the position that the OFT would take in relation to the making of a merger reference, and may also 'include advice and recommendations on any public interest consideration mentioned in the intervention notice concerned' (s 44(6)).

3.60   Following the receipt of the OFT's report, it is for the Secretary of State to refer the matter to the Commission if he is minded to do so. References may be made, either where the Secretary of State believes at the time of the receipt of the OFT report that there is, or there is not, SLC as a result of the merger, as long as he believes that 'the situation operates or may be expected to operate against the public interest'. The Secretary of State is bound in this

---

[1]   See Arts 30, 46, 54 and 297, for example. See Cook, CJ and Kerse, CS *EC Merger Control* (London, Sweet & Maxwell, 2000, 3rd edn), at para 8.4.2.1.

[2]   Public interest considerations are finalised where an order is made and approved by Parliament in accordance with s 124(6).

[3]   *Hansard*, Standing Committee B, col 343.

[4]   The conditions which satisfy this requirement are set out in s 43(4).

[5]   The time-limit within which the report must be prepared is to be determined by the Secretary of State in each case (s 44(2)).

respect by the views of the OFT as regards the competition matters, but not as regards matters relating to the public interest consideration. Section 45(6) therefore provides that *any* anti-competitive outcome identified by the OFT shall be treated as being against the public interest, unless it is outweighed by the relevant public interest consideration. Some qualifications on the power to refer are set out in s 46. These mirror those which limit the OFT's power to make references set out in ss 22 and 33. Where the Secretary of State decides, having received the report of the OFT, that there is no public interest consideration to which he is able to have regard, and therefore does not make a reference, the matter is to be remitted to the OFT for it to deal with as it considers appropriate under the normal merger rules (s 56(1)).

Reports on references made by the Secretary of State

3.61 The requirements of reports made by the CC in response to a reference made by the Secretary of State are at first the same as for those in the case of references made by the OFT. However, the CC must also consider:

> 'whether, taking account only of any substantial lessening of competition and the admissible public interest consideration or considerations concerned, the creation of that situation operates or may be expected to operate against the public interest.'[1]

As with references made by the OFT, the CC also has a duty to determine what action should be taken to remedy the situation, the difference being that in this case, the recommendation will be for action to be taken by the Secretary of State under s 55 (enforcement action taken by the Secretary of State is considered in **3.64**), or by itself or by others. The CC may cancel a reference made under s 45 where it is in relation to an anticipated merger which has been abandoned (s 48(1)). The CC may also cancel a reference if it was made on the basis of a public interest consideration which was not finalised at the time the reference was made, and was not finalised within 24 weeks of the giving of the notice (s 53(1)).[2] It may vary a reference if it considers that it is justified in doing so on the facts, but may not vary it so as to be a reference made under s 22 or s 33. Where the relevant intervention notice has ceased to be in force, the CC will revert to an analysis of the merger as if the reference had been made under s 22 or s 33, as appropriate. In this case, it will have an extra 20 days in which to produce its report from the date set by the Secretary of State (s 56(3)–(5)).

3.62 Any reports made by the CC on the basis of a reference made under s 45 are to be made to the Secretary of State. The deadline for doing so is the

---

[1]   Section 47(2)(b). Subsections (3), (5) and (6) also provide for the CC to reach a view on the relationship between any SLC and the public interest consideration.

[2]   Further technical provisions relating to cases in which a public interest consideration has not been finalised are set out in s 53.

same as in the case of a s 22 or s 33 report, and the rules in relation to the relevant time-limits and extensions thereof are the same.

Decisions of the Secretary of State and enforcement actions

3.63 Where the Secretary of State has received a report from the CC, he 'shall decide whether to make an adverse public interest finding in relation to a relevant merger situation or whether to make no finding in the matter at all' (s 54(2)). No finding shall be made in situations in which the Secretary of State decides that there is no public interest consideration which is relevant to the consideration of the merger situation (s 54(4)). An adverse decision may be made in any case in which the Secretary of State, taking into account the public interest consideration, finds that the merger may be expected to operate against the public interest. The Secretary of State is bound by any decision taken by the CC in relation to the competitive effects of the merger. Any decision shall be made within 30 days of the receipt of the CC's report (s 54(5)).

3.64 Where the Secretary of State makes an adverse finding, he may take such action under Sch 7, para 9 or para 11 as he considers reasonable in order to remedy, mitigate or prevent any of the adverse effects of the merger on the public interest. Where there is also SLC, the Secretary of State may have regard to any relevant customer benefits in determining what action to take (s 55).

OTHER SPECIAL CASES

Special public interest cases

3.65 In addition to the category of public interest cases considered above, there is a special category of public interest cases which allows for the examination of mergers which fail to meet the thresholds to be considered as a 'relevant merger situation'. These are cases involving 'relevant government contractors' which have 'been notified ... of information, documents or other articles relating to defence and of a confidential nature' (s 59(8)).[1] In such a case, a 'special intervention notice' may be issued. In these cases, the OFT is required to report to the Secretary of State, and the Secretary of State then has the power to refer the matter to the CC under s 62. The CC is required to determine whether a 'special merger situation' has been created, and, if so, whether that merger situation may be expected to operate against the public

---

[1] 'Defence' has the same meaning as under Official Secrets Act 1989, s 2.

interest. As with other references, the CC is to identify what action should be taken to mitigate any adverse effects that flow from the merger. Reports are addressed to the Secretary of State, and it is for him to determine what enforcement action needs to be taken.

Newspaper mergers

3.66 No references are to be made under s 22, s 33, s 45 or s 62 in relation to newspaper mergers – technically referred to as the transfer of newspapers or newspaper assets – and s 58(1) of the FTA 1973 continues to apply to these situations (s 69). However, where a transaction falls under s 59(2) of the FTA 1973, which precludes the Secretary of State from making a reference, the provisions of the Act may be applied if the relevant thresholds are fulfilled. In this case, the industry will be treated like any other, notwithstanding its privileged position under the FTA 1973 regime.

3.67 The Communications Bill (see **1.62–1.63**) brings forward provisions for the treatment of newspaper mergers in the future (cols 359–375), and the policy is to adopt a 'lighter touch regulation for the vast majority of newspaper cases that do not raise competition or plurality concerns'.[1] The new regime will 'be fully integrated with the new arrangements [of the Enterprise Act 2002]'.[2] One of the key differences between the new regime and the existing newspaper merger regime is that there will be no pre-notification requirement, subject to the power of the OFT to refer transfers post-completion. The Department of Trade and Industry (DTI) has already indicated that it intends to relax provisions on 'foreign' ownership and cross-media ownership.

3.68 Within the Enterprise Act framework, the test of the acceptance of a newspaper merger that otherwise meets the thresholds of the Act for intervention will be that of an additional public interest requirement. It is envisaged that the new public interest test will relate to: (a) accurate presentation of the news; (b) free expression of opinion; and (c) the maintenance of plurality of views.[3] Cases relating to newspapers may be dealt with either under the general merger provisions of the Enterprise Act 2002, or

---

[1] DTI Memorandum: *Communications Bill – Reform of the Newspaper Merger Regime*, 3 July 2002, para 1.1.

[2] Ibid, para 2.1. However, in some cases, non-competition concerns may still be raised:

    'Those newspaper transfers that potentially raise plurality concerns will require wider regulatory scrutiny in order to protect the additional public interest involved in such transfers. In relation to these transfers, therefore, the Secretary of State will retain the power to refer transfers for wider investigation by the Competition Commission by an extension of the provisions in the Enterprise Bill dealing with "exceptional public interest (EPI)" cases. This will be directed to those cases that involve the public interest in accurate presentation of the news, free expression of opinion and plurality of views in the Press – plurality for short' (policy narrative accompanying the draft Communications Bill, para 9(7)(4)).

[3] Ibid, para 4.9.

under the newspaper public interest considerations. In the latter case, the Chairman of the CC may appoint members of the CC to be 'newspaper panel members'. Completed reports will be delivered to the Secretary of State and to the Office of Communications (OFCOM). It is to be for the Secretary of State to make the final decision in respect of newspaper public interest findings, and on remedies, although the CC may make recommendations, and there will be provision for OFCOM also to make its views known.

Water and sewerage mergers

3.69 Sections 32–35 of the Water Industry Act 1991 (WIA 1991) are replaced by the Act (s 70). Under the new rules, it is for the OFT to make a reference in relation to a merger between two water enterprises where it appears to the OFT that the turnover of the enterprise being taken over exceeds £10m, or that the enterprises belonging to the person doing the taking over do not exceed a turnover of £10m. The role of the Secretary of State is thus supplanted by the role of the OFT. Schedule 6 of the Act replaces s 34 of, and inserts a new Sch 4ZA into, the WIA 1991. The principle in relation to water mergers was that:

> 'once a qualifying merger has been referred, the FTA 1973 "public interest" test is applied in a way that attaches particular weight to the principle that the ability of the Director General of Water Services in carrying out his or her functions under the WIA to make comparisons between water enterprises should not be prejudiced. If the CC makes an adverse finding, the Secretary of State is responsible for determining the final remedies.'[1]

Under the new system, the responsibility for determining the final remedy moves from the Secretary of State to the CC.[2]

European mergers

3.70 Sections 67 and 68 relate to mergers covered by the EC Merger Regulation, and deal with 'intervention to protect legitimate interests'. Where a merger is covered by the Regulation such that a reference to the UK authorities is not possible, but raises issues in relation to Art 21(3) of the EC Merger Regulation, the Secretary of State may give a notice to the OFT if a public interest consideration is relevant. The UK authorities may then make a request to the EC Commission relating to the merger, and have the power to scrutinise it in relation to the interests set out in Art 21. Section 68 provides

---

[1] *Explanatory Notes*, para 199.
[2] These changes apply only to England and Wales, as the WIA 1991 does not apply to Scotland or Northern Ireland.

that the Secretary of State may make Orders relating to the taking of action in the case of such mergers taking place.

ENFORCEMENT AND PROCEDURE

3.71   There are a number of powers available to the OFT, the CC and the Secretary of State in respect of merger control. These may broadly be divided into powers to accept or impose undertakings on enterprise, powers to prevent mergers being consummated, or to impose divestiture requirements where they have been consummated (by way of orders, rather than voluntary undertakings), and powers relating to the investigation of merger situations, under which the OFT or the CC may request or compel the presentation of evidence, or attendance at hearings.

Initial and interim measures, and undertakings in lieu of references

3.72   Where the OFT is considering whether to make a reference under s 22, it may, for the purpose of preventing pre-emptive action,[1] accept undertakings from the relevant parties to take such action(s) as it considers to be appropriate (s 71). The OFT may not accept an undertaking under this section unless it has reasonable grounds to believe that a relevant merger situation has been created. Any undertaking made under this section comes into force when it is given, and may be varied or superseded by another undertaking, or released by the OFT. Some indication of when these powers might be used may be found in past practice:

> 'Undertakings in lieu have typically been used in merger cases in the past where a substantial lessening of competition arises from an overlap that is relatively small in the context of the merger (eg, a few local markets affected by a national merger). In such cases the company may be willing to resolve the problem by divesting itself of part of its business (a structural undertaking); alternatively, in order to remove the concerns that have been raised, it may give a formal commitment about its future conduct.'[2]

3.73   As an alternative to accepting undertakings under s 71, the OFT may make initial enforcement orders. The OFT may require the doing, or restrict the doing, of any thing which would constitute pre-emptive action (s 72(2)(a)), or may impose obligations requiring that activities continued to be carried on,

---

[1]   'Pre-emptive action' is defined as 'action which might prejudice the reference concerned or impede the taking of any action under this Part which may be justified by the Commission's decisions on the reference' (s 71(8)).

[2]   OFT *Mergers*, para 8.4.

or that assets be safeguarded (s 72(2)(b)), and may appoint a person to ensure that this happens (s 72(2)(c)), or anything which may be done by Sch 8, para 19 (see **3.81**). For such an order to be made, the OFT has to believe not only that a relevant merger situation has been created, but also that pre-emptive action is either in progress or in contemplation. It is highly unlikely that orders will ever be imposed on those other than the parties to the merger.

3.74 The OFT may also seek undertakings in lieu of references under s 22 or s 33 (s 73).[1] Section 73 may be invoked where the OFT considers that it is under a duty to make a reference, but taking into account its power not to do so. As indicated in the *Explanatory Notes*:

> 'The purpose of accepting undertakings is to allow the OFT (where it is confident about the problem that needs to be addressed and the appropriate solution) to correct the competition problem the merger presents without recourse to a potentially time-consuming and costly investigation.'

Since the concern raised by mergers is a structural one, the OFT has indicated that it is more likely to accept structural than behavioural undertakings. Once an undertaking has been accepted, the OFT is prevented from making a reference in relation to the merger situation, unless material facts have not been notified to the OFT or made public before the undertaking concerned was accepted (s 73(2)).

3.75 Where an undertaking made under s 73 is not being fulfilled, or where information given to the OFT or made public, which informed the undertaking, was false or misleading, the OFT may make an order compelling performance, or anything permitted by Sch 8 (see **3.81**) (s 75). A further interim power to make orders where it is considering making an order under s 75 is found in s 76. This:

> 'allows the OFT to act quickly to put in place an interim order while it prepares the main remedial order, including carrying out any consultation. The interim order can prevent the parties from taking any action that might prejudice the main order.'[2]

3.76 Standstill provisions are enshrined in ss 77 and 78. In the first case, once a completed merger has been referred to the CC, the parties are

---

[1] The provision has its counterpart in s 75G of the FTA 1973, save that the power there fell to the Secretary of State.

[2] *Explanatory Notes*, para 221. The power can also be used by the CC when it is considering replacing final undertakings with a final order (see **3.79**). As noted in committee:

> 'If a merged entity makes staff redundant, sells off assets, integrates computer systems or takes any other similar action, it could be very difficult for the Commission to effect a divestment of the merger business thereafter.
>
> In the past, the authorities have sought to prevent such further integration by seeking voluntary undertakings from the parties or by imposing an interim order. It is clearer, simpler and more efficient to create a new prohibition that applies to all' (*Hansard*, Standing Committee B, cols 371–372).

prevented[1] from completing any arrangements which have resulted in the merger, or making further arrangements in consequence of that result, or transferring the ownership or control of any enterprises to which the reference relates (s 77(2)). The consent of the CC may be given to such transactions, however. These provisions apply also to a person's conduct outside the UK, but only if he is: (a) a UK national;[2] or (b) a body incorporated under the law of the UK, or any part of the UK; or (c) a person carrying on business in the UK. Section 78 operates in relation to anticipated mergers, and imposes a prohibition on the acquisition or transfer of shares (directly or indirectly) in a company in any enterprise to which the merger reference relates during the relevant period.[3] Section 79(3) provides further clarification in relation to the circumstances in which a person may be deemed to have acquired shares. This provision does not apply to situations in which the person concerned 'acquires an interest in pursuance of an obligation assumed before the publication by the OFT of the reference concerned' (s 79(4)).

3.77   Section 80 gives the CC the new power to accept interim undertakings once a reference has been made to it. These undertakings may be, in addition to any initial undertakings, accepted by the OFT, or may be a re-adoption of OFT undertakings in the appropriate circumstances.[4]

3.78   Mirroring the provisions relating to initial undertakings and orders, the CC may also make orders for the purpose of preventing pre-emptive action. This provision is based on that in FTA 1973, s 74. It does not appear to be limited in the way that the power of the OFT is in relation to initial orders made under s 72 (see **3.73**). Thus, for example, there is no requirement set out to the effect that the CC must believe that either a relevant merger situation has been created, or that steps may be taken by way of pre-emptive action that would jeopardise any subsequent conclusion drawn by the CC.[5]

---

[1]   As long as no undertakings or orders are in force.

[2]   'United Kingdom national' throughout the Act means an individual who is: '(a) a British citizen, a British overseas territory citizen, a British National (Overseas) or a British Overseas citizen; (b) a person who under the British Nationality Act 1981 is a British subject; or (c) a British protected person within the meaning of that Act' (s 129(1)).

[3]   'Relevant period' means the period beginning with the making of the reference concerned and ending when the reference is finally determined (s 78(6)).

[4]   This provision enshrines the practice, but not the law of the FTA 1973, under which interim undertakings, which were not legally enforceable, were sought to deal with anticipated concerns (see *Explanatory Notes*, para 225).

[5]   Under FTA 1973, s 74, the Secretary of State had the power to make interim orders of limited duration following the making of a reference in order to preserve the status quo. These powers were not often used, the practice instead being to seek undertakings which were usually acceded to on the grounds that the power to make an order existed, and the outcome could be worse for the enterprises concerned than might be the case where undertakings were accepted. However, orders were occasionally made, as was the case, for example, in the course of the investigation into *Elders IXL Ltd and Scottish & Newcastle Breweries plc* (1989), Cm 654 – see the Merger Reference (Elders IXL Limited and Scottish & Newcastle

Final powers

3.79 The CC has the power to accept final undertakings from parties in order to remedy concerns raised in its reports (s 82).[1] It also has the power to make orders where any such final undertakings are not fulfilled, or where information which was false or misleading in a material respect was given to it or to the OFT.[2] If an order is made under this section, it may not be varied or revoked unless the OFT advises that such a change is appropriate in the light of changed circumstances. Final orders may also be made by the CC, in accordance with s 41 (s 84). Any order made under this section may contain anything permitted by Sch 8 (see **3.80**). No order shall be made under this section if an undertaking has been accepted and is being complied with under s 82. An undertaking made under s 82 may contain matters *not* set out in Sch 8 (s 89).[3]

Schedule 8 – Provisions that may be contained in merger enforcement orders

3.80 Schedule 8 contains the list of matters that may be imposed in orders for the purpose of remedying any adverse effects of mergers identified by the CC in its report. The list is based on that in FTA 1973, Sch 8, but has been supplemented by six new remedies. Most of the items set out in the Schedule are self-explanatory. The most significant of the new items included on the list is that at para 10, under which an order may require any relevant person to supply goods or services 'to a particular standard or in a particular manner'. An example of the way in which this provision might be applied is given in the *Explanatory Notes* and relates to the fact that it would be possible to tell a bus company to maintain a certain frequency of service.[4] Paragraph 18 has been added to the section relating to the provision of information, so that, *inter alia*, it is possible to compel the publication of information on the Internet.

Enforcement regime in relation to public interest and special public interest cases

3.81 Schedule 7 lays out what is in effect a separate enforcement regime for public interest and special public interest merger references[5] (see **3.57–3.66**).

Breweries plc) Order 1988, SI 1988/1965. See generally, Livingston, D, *Competition Law and Practice* (London, FT Law and Tax, 1995), at 41.17–41.18.
[1]   This power mirrors that of FTA 1973, s 88.
[2]   Note that these powers may be linked back to s 41 (see **3.49**).
[3]   As indeed may any 'enforcement undertaking' – which is to say those made under s 71, s 73, or s 80 in addition to s 82.
[4]   Paragraph 230.
[5]   See also s 85.

As indicated in the *Explanatory Notes*, this regime is a mirror of the main regime, the difference being that the Secretary of State is given the powers which, in other cases, belong to the OFT and the CC. Thus, the Secretary of State may accept pre-emptive undertakings (para 1(2)); make pre-emptive orders (para 2(2)); accept undertakings in lieu of a reference (para 3(2)); or make orders where undertakings are not being adhered to, or where information was given which was false or misleading (para 5). Standstill provisions in relation to these two categories of mergers are contained in paras 7 and 8. Provision for final undertakings and orders is made at paras 9–11. Any orders of the Secretary of State made under this Schedule are to be made by way of statutory instrument and are subject to annulment by way of resolution in Parliament (s 124(5)).

General measures relating to enforcement orders

3.82   Schedule 10[1] makes provision for the general procedural requirements for enforcement undertakings and orders made under this Part of the Act. The provisions relating to the procedures to be followed in making such orders or accepting undertakings are set out in paras 1–5. Paragraphs 6–8 deal with the revocation of orders, or the releasing of parties from undertakings. In all cases, there are publicity and information requirements imposed on the relevant authorities, and consultation periods are required, of 30 days in the case of orders, and 15 days in the case of undertakings. However, para 9 provides that the authority can dispense with *any* of the requirements of this Schedule if there are 'special reasons for doing so'.

3.83   Where the CC or the OFT are considering accepting undertakings, the OFT may be required to consult with the relevant persons to determine if they would be prepared to offer undertakings which the authority would be prepared to accept (s 93(2)).

3.84   The OFT is to maintain a register of undertakings and orders (s 91) and has a general duty, imposed on it by s 92, to keep under review the carrying out of any enforcement undertaking or order.[2] It is required to consider whether these are being complied with, but also whether the undertaking or order remains appropriate in the light of changing circumstances. It must also give advice to the CC or the Secretary of State in relation to enforcement actions taken by them.

---

[1]   See s 90.

[2]   This power mirrors that of FTA 1973, s 88.

Territorial limitations

3.85 An enforcement order may extend to a person's conduct outside the UK, but only if that person is a UK national, or a body incorporated under the law of the UK or of a part of the UK, or a person carrying on business in the UK (s 86(1)).

Intellectual property licences

3.86 Although the CC has indicated that it may require the licensing of intellectual property as part of its portfolio of available remedies, there are limitations to its power to do so, and nothing in an order may have the effect of cancelling or modifying conditions in licences granted under the Patents Act 1977, or in relation to European Patents, or may make available licences under patent or design rights to be available as of right (s 86(2)). This limitation follows that of FTA 1973, s 90(5).[1]

Delegated power of direction

3.87 Section 87 allows any person making an order to give to specified persons or to the holders of specified officers directions relating to actions that must be taken, or to refrain from taking specific actions. The failure to comply with any such direction is actionable before a court, and, in that case, the court may order that the person comply with it. The continued failure to do so would then be actionable as contempt of court. Court orders made under this section may also provide for all the costs of the action to be borne either by the individual, or by the officers of a body corporate or unincorporated responsible for its default.

Enforcement of undertakings, orders and statutory restrictions – third-party rights

3.88 Sections 94 and 95 ensure that those injured by the breach of enforcement undertakings, orders, and statutory restrictions[2] may bring actions before the courts. A duty is owed 'to any person who may be affected by a contravention of the undertaking or (as the case may be) order' (s 94(3)).[3] Any breach which results in loss or damage is actionable. It is a defence, however, for the defendant 'to show that he took all reasonable steps and exercised all due diligence to avoid contravening the undertaking or order' (s 94(5)).[4]

---

[1] See *Butterworths Competition Law Service*, at X[2058]–[2059].

[2] Statutory restrictions are those which automatically prohibit further integration (s 77), and the acquisition of further shares (s 78) (see **3.76**).

[3] In respect of statutory restrictions, see s 95(1).

[4] In respect of statutory restrictions, see s 95(3).

3.89 In addition to private enforcement, the OFT, the CC, and the Secretary of State may also bring civil actions to enforce undertakings, orders, and statutory restrictions, as appropriate.

Merger notices

3.90 Sections 96–102 update the merger notice procedure set out in ss 75A–75H of the FTA 1973. Section 96 requires that any notice of a merger made must be in the prescribed form, as determined by the OFT. Notice of a merger may be given to the OFT only by a person authorised to do so by way of the Regulations to be made on the basis of s 101. Once a merger notice is made, the OFT may request such other information of the person making the notice as it needs to perform its tasks (s 99(2)). Merger notices may be rejected where they are in any material respect false or misleading, or where it is suspected that the merger will not be carried out, or where prescribed information is not given, or where the OFT considers that the merger has a Community dimension and therefore falls to be considered by the EC Commission (s 99(5)). Where the time-limit for the making of a reference has been exceeded and no reference has been made, a notice may not be made in respect of that merger.

3.91 Once a notice has been received by the OFT, there is a 20-day period during which the OFT may decide whether to refer the merger.[1] In cases in which no intervention notice has been issued, the OFT may, by notice, extend the period of consideration by a further 10 days (s 97(2)). Where an intervention notice has been given, a further 20 days' extension may be made by notice (s 97(3)).[2]

3.92 There are some circumstances in which the time-limit can be further extended. These arise where: the person making the merger notice has failed to provide information requested of him (s 97(5)–(6)); the OFT, or the Secretary of State, is considering seeking undertakings (s 97(7)–(8)); the Secretary of State is considering making a reference under s 45 (s 97(9)–(10)) (see **3.60**); or the EC Commission is in the process of deciding whether the case is one falling within its jurisdiction (s 97(11)–(13)). The overall time-limit under the Act is slightly longer than is the case under the EC Merger Regulation – in which only a single body is involved in the procedure – and slightly shorter than was the case under the FTA 1973.

---

[1] This is conditional upon the relevant fee, payable by virtue of s 121, being paid to the OFT. Further technical provisions relating to these time-limits are set out in s 98.

[2] These provisions do not operate cumulatively. The maximum possible extension to the original 20-day period is 20 days (subject to information being properly provided).

3.93 Where a merger notice is given to the OFT, the OFT has an obligation, so far as is practicable, to bring the facts to the attention 'of those whom the OFT considers would be affected if the arrangements were put into effect' (s 99(1)).

3.94 While the function of a merger notice is to protect the merger from being referred to the CC outside the time-limits provided for in s 97, there are circumstances in which this will not operate. These are set out in s 100, and include, *inter alia*, the rejection of the notice by the OFT (see **3.90**), where the merger is consummated within the time period for the consideration of the notice, where any other relevant merger takes place involving any of the parties referred to in the notice, or where the notice is withdrawn. If the parties do not merge within the 6-month time period to which a notice may be limited, the fact that the OFT did not make a reference in that time period does not prevent the OFT making a reference if the merger is subsequently completed (s 100(1)(e)). In this case, the parties would be better advised to make a new notice to the OFT.

3.95 Section 101 provides for the making of regulations for the purposes of ss 96–99. In addition, the Secretary of State may modify ss 97–99 (s 100).

General duties in relation to references

3.96 The OFT (or the Secretary of State, as appropriate) has a general duty to make decisions as to whether to make a reference as soon as possible (s 103).

3.97 Where any decision is being made which the relevant authority 'considers is likely to be adverse to the interests of a relevant party' (s 104(1)), the relevant authority is obliged, so far as is practicable, to consult that party about what is proposed before making that decision. This includes decisions by the OFT or the Secretary of State to make a reference to the CC in respect of a merger.

3.98 Where the OFT undertakes an investigation for the purposes of determining whether to make a reference, it is to take reasonable steps to bring information about that investigation to the attention of those whom it considers might be affected by the creation of the relevant situation.[1] The OFT is obliged to give the CC any information that it has which the CC may reasonably require, and any other assistance which the CC may reasonably

---

[1] This does not apply in the case where a merger notice has been given, and the appropriate procedures complied with, under s 96.

require. Similar responsibilities are placed on the OFT and the CC where the Secretary of State is considering taking any authorised action.

3.99 The OFT has a general duty to publish general advice and guidance about the making of references by it under s 22 or s 33 (s 106). The preliminary version of this advice has been widely relied upon in the preparation of this chapter. Likewise, the CC is under an obligation to publish advice relating to the way in which it will treat references made to it. Further publicity requirements relating to specific decisions in relation to references, undertakings and orders, are provided for in s 107.

Powers of investigation

3.100 Sections 109–117 deal with the power of the CC to require the presentation of evidence and documents[1] needed for the purposes of a merger inquiry. Broadly, these are similar to the equivalent powers as laid out in the FTA 1973, although the CC has enhanced powers to deal directly with those who do not comply with requirements imposed upon them.

3.101 Section 109 confers on the CC the power to compel the attendance of witnesses and the production of documents. A notice may be given to any person requiring him to attend a specified hearing, and to give evidence to the CC or a person nominated by the CC (s 109(1)). A similar power exists in relation to the presentation of documents. The CC may also require the supply of 'estimates, forecasts returns or other information' (s 109(3)). Although this gives the CC a wide power to demand specified information, the practice to date has been for it to be flexible as regards the format in which that information is required to be presented. For example, an enterprise asked for its records has not typically been required to present these outside its standard collation of the material – ie financial years are likely to be accepted as they stand, etc. The CC may take evidence on oath (s 109(5)). No material may be required where the production of such could not be compelled in civil proceedings before a court. This preserves the right against self-incrimination, and a protection in respect of legally privileged material. In the context of a wide-ranging mergers investigation, it is unlikely that these limitations would be often invoked.

3.102 Where the CC finds that a person has, without reasonable cause, failed to comply with an obligation imposed by way of s 109, it may directly impose a penalty on that person, subject to an appeal to the CAT (s 110(1)). Any penalty

---

[1]   The production of a document 'includes a reference to the production of a legible and intelligible copy of information recorded otherwise than in legible form' (s 110(10)).

imposed under this section 'shall be of such an amount as the Commission considers appropriate' (s 111(1)). The amount may be fixed, or may be calculated on a daily rate until such time as compliance is ensured.[1] The imposition of a penalty does not preclude the CC from increasing the period within which it may prepare its report under s 39(4) or s 51(4). An offence is committed if any person intentionally alters, suppresses or destroys any document which he has been required to produce, and, on conviction, he may face a fine not exceeding the statutory maximum, or a term of imprisonment not exceeding two years, or a combination of the two. However, no offence may be deemed to have been committed if the CC has acted under s 110(1) and imposed its own penalty.[2] The maximum penalty that may be imposed in the case of a fixed amount is £30,000, and, in the case of a daily penalty, the maximum amount per day is £15,000 (s 111(7)).[3] The Secretary of State is to specify the allowable amounts, which may not exceed those set out, by way of an order (s 111(4)). Where it imposes a penalty, the CC is required, as soon as is practicable, to give a notice relating to the penalty, setting out the information specified in s 112, which includes the amount of the penalty, and the manner and place in which it is to be paid. The person to whom the notice is addressed may, within 14 days, apply to the CC for it to specify a different rate, or different dates for payment of the penalty. Where a penalty is not paid by the due time, interest shall be added to the outstanding amount, as specified in the Judgments Act 1838. The CC is required to publish a statement of policy regarding the application of s 109 (s 116), which:

> 'will include the considerations that will be relevant to determining the nature and amount of any monetary penalty. These considerations will be for the CC to identify, but it is envisaged that they could include:
>
> - the nature and gravity of the omission;
> - the size and financial resources of the defaulter;
> - the size of the penalty that will encourage the party to co-operate;
> - the scale of costs and other disbenefits that will be incurred by the CC if an inquiry has to be extended to take account of the information provided late.'[4]

3.103 The CC has published (in draft) its *Statement of Policy on Penalties*, which deals in particular with the assessment of situations in which there has been a failure to comply with the requirement to supply information, and the imposition of penalties in relation to this. In relation to the failure to supply information, the CC will consider 'whether there is any reasonable excuse for the contravention', and, in particular, 'the extent to which the contravention or

---

[1]   Although, in the case where there has been an obstruction or delay to a person in the exercise of his powers (s 110(3)), the penalty will be a fixed one.

[2]   Double-jeopardy is also avoided by virtue of s 110(8), which provides that the CC may not proceed under s 110(1) against any person where they have been convicted of an offence in relation to the suppression or destruction of that evidence.

[3]   Broadly, these provisions are modelled on those available under Regulation 17/62.

[4]   *Explanatory Notes*, para 272.

failure arose from circumstances outside the control of the person who has contravened ... for example, the information had been accidentally destroyed'.[1] Five factors are set out as being likely to increase the prospect of a penalty being imposed:

(i)   the failure affected the efficient carrying out of the CC's functions;
(ii)   other persons were adversely affected;
(iii)   deterrence of future non-compliance;
(iv)   the degree of culpability; and
(v)   whether the person failing to comply sought to gain, or did gain, by so doing.[2]

3.104 Appeals against penalties may be made to the CAT. Appeals may be made against the imposition or nature of the penalty, the amount of the penalty, and the date on which the penalty is to be paid (s 114). The CAT may not substitute its own assessment of the penalty unless the substituted figure is lower than the figure that would be required by the CC. A further appeal may be made to the Court of Appeal[3] against the judgment of the CAT (s 114(10)).

3.105 An offence is committed in any case if a person supplies the OFT or the CC or the Secretary of State with information that is false or misleading in a material respect, and he knows that to be the case, or is reckless to that effect (s 117).

Reports

3.106 Where a report is published following a reference, the Secretary of State may 'exclude a matter from the report concerned if he considers that publication of the matter would be inappropriate' (s 118(2)).[4] Either the OFT, or the CC, as appropriate, shall advise the Secretary of State as to the matters which it considers should be excluded.[5]

3.107 Where there is a disagreement amongst the members of the CC dealing with the reference, s 119 provides that the report may include, if the

---

[1]   Paragraph 12.

[2]   The statement applies equally to market investigation references.

[3]   Or in Scotland, the Court of Session.

[4]   In determining what material to exclude, the Secretary of State is to have regard to s 239, which makes reference to 'information whose disclosure the authority thinks is contrary to the public interest', as well as 'commercial information whose disclosure the authority thinks might significantly harm the legitimate business interests of the undertaking to which it relates' or 'information relating to the private affairs of an individual whose disclosure the authority thinks might significantly harm the individual's interests'.

[5]   Both existing decisions and appeals under the CA 1998, and monopolies and merger reference reports under the FTA 1973, exclude matters whose publication is deemed to be a matter of commercial confidentiality, or contrary to the public interest.

member(s) so wish(es), a statement of the disagreement and of the reasons for the disagreement. While this has happened in the past, the value of this practice must be doubted. CC reports do not constitute a body of precedent in the way that court judgments do, as they are exquisitely sensitive to the facts of the particular case.

Appeals

3.108 Any decision of the OFT or the Secretary of State in connection with a merger reference may be appealed to the CAT (s 120).[1] The time-limit for the making of applications under this section is three months from the date of the decision.[2] While it might appear that this is a significant concession to the position of enterprises who might be aggrieved by a reference decision, it is unlikely to be of great application in practice. The standard for appeals is that of judicial review, meaning that the focus will be on the procedures adopted rather than the substance of the decision taken. As noted in the *Explanatory Notes*:

> 'Case law suggests such grounds could include: (i) that an error of law was made; (ii) that there was a material procedural error; such as a material failure of an inquiry panel to comply with the Chairman's procedural rules; (iii) that a material error as to the facts has been made; and (iv) that there was some other material illegality (such as unreasonableness or lack of proportionality). Judicial review evolves over time and the approach in subsection (6) has been taken to ensure the grounds of review continue to mirror any such developments.'[3]

When it reviews any decision, the CAT may quash the whole decision, or only a part of that decision. Further appeals on points of law only may be made to the Court of Appeal or the Court of Session, with the leave of the CAT.

3.111 It should be stressed that this right to appeal is available to third parties, as well as to those subject to the reference. This is a new direct right, and was opposed by, amongst others, the CBI. On the other hand, third parties have always had the right to seek judicial review of merger decisions, and, as the standard is the same, the effect of this is again likely to be very limited in practice. Schedule 3 provides for tribunal rules that may, *inter alia*, permit the CAT to reject proceedings if it appears to it that the persons bringing them do not have sufficient interest in a decision, or where it believes that the appeal is vexatious.

---

[1] This section does not apply to any decision to impose a penalty under s 110, as separate provisions are made in respect of appeals in this context (see **3.104**).

[2] Tribunal rules may modify this limit.

[3] Paragraph 276.

Offences

3.112 Section 125 provides that where an offence has been committed in relation to this part of the Act by a body corporate, which may be attributable to any neglect on the part of a director, manager, secretary or similar officer, that person, as well as the body corporate, commits the offence and may be punished accordingly.

3.113 *Figure 1 – Typical Shape of a Merger Inquiry*

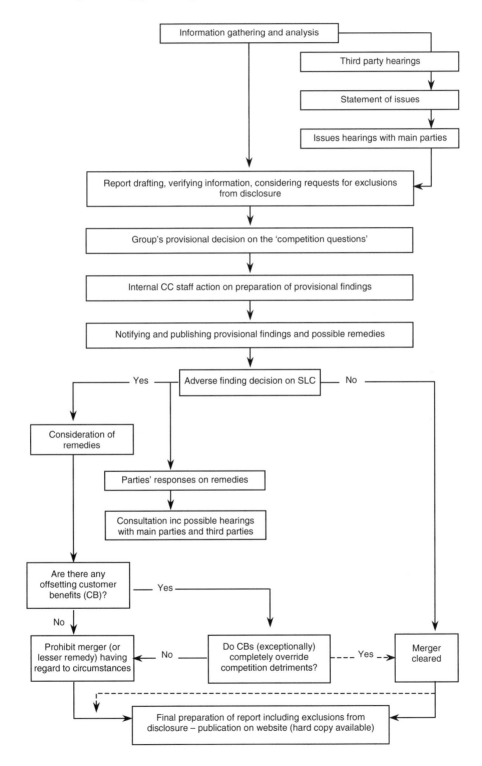

Chapter Four

MARKET INVESTIGATIONS

INTRODUCTION

4.1   In draft Office of Fair Trading (OFT) guidance relating to market investigation references it is noted that:

> 'Competition … is not a static state of affairs but a process by which firms strive in various ways to win customers from rivals. Competition will be effective and markets will work well when firms engaged in the market are subject to competitive constraints from other firms already in the market and/or from firms that could readily enter it, perhaps with new products, and from their customers.'[1]

The process by which this competition functions may be disrupted, not only by unilateral anti-competitive conduct on the part of those holding market power, or anti-competitive agreements, but also by entrenched market conditions. These are difficult to regulate and control under a prohibition-based system, but have been tackled with a degree of success in the UK under the FTA 1973.

4.2   Part 4 of the Act makes provision for the carrying out of 'market investigations'. These replace the monopoly provisions of the FTA 1973, discussed at **1.7–1.13**. The new provisions are 'not fundamentally different from the 1973 Act, many of the provisions of which are drawn and modernised in the [Act]'.[2] In the White Paper, it was recognised that 'the complex monopoly provisions of the Fair Trading Act 1973 provide a very effective means for taking action',[3] but that 'these important provisions are in need of modernisation'.[4] In the *Explanatory Notes*, it was indicated that:

---

[1]   OFT *Market Investigation References: A Consultation Paper* (July 2002) (hereinafter, OFT *Market Investigation References*), para 4.1.

[2]   Mr Alexander, *Hansard*, Standing Committee B, col 442.

[3]   Paragraph 6.1.

[4]   Paragraph 6.4.

'The purpose of these investigations is to inquire into markets where it appears that competition has been prevented, restricted or distorted by the structure of a market (or any aspect of its structure), the conduct of firms (ie persons supplying or acquiring goods or services in the course of business)[1] operating within it, or the conduct of such firms' customers, but there has been no obvious breach of the prohibitions on anti-competitive agreements or arrangements or abuse of a dominant position under CA 1998 or Arts 81 or 82 EC. An example of the sort of circumstances in which these provisions might be used would be a situation where a few large firms supplied almost the whole of the market and, without there being any agreement between them (ie a non-collusive oligopoly), they all tended to follow parallel courses of conduct (eg in relation to pricing), while new competitors faced significant barriers to entry into the market, and there was little or no evidence of vigorous competition between the existing players.'[2]

This is to say that the key feature of market investigation references is that they focus on the functioning of an entire market, rather than on the way in which a single firm behaves.

4.3 From 1994 to October 2002, there had been 20 reports on monopoly references under the FTA 1973, 14 of which were concerned with complex monopolies.[3] It is believed that there will be about the same number of market investigation references – around two each year – as there have been monopolies references under the FTA 1973 (see also **4.28**).

4.4   Part 4 of the Act is in four chapters:

Chapter 1: Market investigation references (ss 131–138);
Chapter 2: Public interest cases (ss 139–153);
Chapter 3: Enforcement (ss 154–167);
Chapter 4: Supplementary (ss 167–184).

Schedules 8, 9 and 12 are also relevant to this Part of the Act.

The relationship of market investigations with the CA 1998 and EC competition law

The Competition Act 1998

4.5 As noted in Chapter 1, the relationship between the CA 1998 and the FTA 1973 was not formalised. However, the policy was that the scale monopoly provisions of the latter would be used only in situations in which there had already been a finding of a breach of the Chapter II Prohibition,

---

[1]   The text here will be updated in the final version of the *Explanatory Notes*, as the reference to 'in the course of business' in the Act was removed at the insistence of the Lords so as to make it clear that the conduct of public bodies buying goods or services could be taken into account.

[2]   Paragraph 282.

[3]   OFT *Market Investigation References*, para 1.1, footnote 1.

coupled to a belief that market structure made further abuse likely. Following the introduction of the Chapter II Prohibition, there was in fact no case in which this scenario arose, and the scale monopoly provisions of the FTA 1973 had, in effect, fallen into disuse. At the Committee stage, the Government explained that:

> 'In general, we would expect the OFT to use the Competition Act in cases in which it suspects that the Act's prohibitions on anti-competitive agreements or abuse of dominance are being infringed, *and market investigation powers in cases in which the Act is not applicable.* Whenever the choice is less straightforward, the decision about which powers to use will be at the OFT's discretion, on examination of all the facts of the case in question.'[1]

The effect of this is that the scale monopoly investigations will, for the most part, disappear, with the market investigation provisions applying to situations in which neither allegations of single-firm abusive conduct falling within the Chapter II Prohibition, nor the application of that law to joint dominance abuse, may be sustained.[2]

4.6 However, there may be some circumstances in which a market investigation reference may be an appropriate response to single-firm conduct. This might be the case, for example, where a firm has market power,[3] but where it does not reach the threshold required to be found to be dominant.[4] An alternative situation might arise where the Chapter II Prohibition is being infringed, but where 'the only effective remedies for the problem are structural ones'.[5]

4.7 In its draft guidance, the OFT indicates that:

---

[1] Col 427, emphasis added.

[2] In the White Paper, it was recognised that the development of the law of joint dominance under Art 82 EC might impact in the UK via the Chapter II Prohibition and s 60 of the CA 1998. Even so, it was suggested that 'regardless of the development of the concept of collective dominance … domestic monopoly provisions currently allow us to tackle a much larger range of market failures than does Community law' (para 6.5).

[3] 'Market power' is a difficult concept to pin down. It is usually defined by economists as the ability to raise prices above the competitive level. The OFT has issued general guidance in relation to the assessment of market power: OFT technical guideline, *Assessment of Market Power*, para 5.2 ([2000] UKCLR 40); while the EC Commission has to date published guidance only in relation to a specific market, *Commission Guidelines on Market Analysis and the Assessment of Significant Market Power under the Community Regulatory Framework for Electronic Communications Networks and Services* (2002) OJ C165/6. In this notice, the Commission notes that the fact that an undertaking is designated as having significant market power for the purposes of *ex ante* regulation does not automatically imply that the undertaking would be dominant for the purposes of the *ex post* application of Art 82 EC.

[4] This possibility is recognised in OFT *Market Investigation References*, para 2.7, but is, in practice, likely to arise only rarely.

[5] OFT *Market Investigation References*, para 2.7(b). The new EC Procedural Regulation makes provision for structural remedies in Art 7 in relation to breaches of Arts 81 and 82 EC. It is not yet clear whether these will then enter the canon of remedies available to the OFT in relation to the Chapter I Prohibition and the Chapter II Prohibition by way of CA 1998, s 60.

'When dealing with a suspected competition problem it is the OFT policy always to consider first whether it may involve an infringement of one or both of the CA 1998 prohibitions and to investigate accordingly. It will only go on to consider a reference to the CC in one of two circumstances:

(a)   When it has reasonable grounds to suspect that there are market features which prevent, restrict or distort competition, but not to establish a breach of the CA 1998 prohibitions.

(b)   When action under CA 1998 has been or is likely to be ineffective at dealing with the adverse effects on competition identified.'[1]

In the White Paper, the Department of Trade and Industry (DTI) recognised that there would be some circumstances in which a reference would not be necessary, even where the markets in question were not working perfectly, as the process of the OFT investigation alone might bear beneficial results: 'in some cases a quick report, which shines a light into a dark corner, will prove sufficient'.[2]

EC competition law

4.8   The application of the new Art 3 of the EC Procedural Regulation[3] in respect of market investigations is somewhat complicated.[4] It seems clear that where such investigations go to conduct which could not be attacked under either Art 81 or Art 82 EC, then they are not precluded under the terms of the new Regulation. The difficulty here is that complex monopoly investigations in the past have tended to deal with wide-ranging issues, which might include any or all of conduct that might be classed as single-firm abuse, collective dominance abuse, and the maintenance of anti-competitive agreements. As to whether it is necessary to show that a market investigation deals *exclusively* with situations which cannot be analysed under the terms of Art 81 or Art 82 EC, the better answer is probably that this is *not* the case. If this is the case, then there is no doubt that the task of the authorities will be difficult.

4.9   It would appear to be possible, within the terms of the 'competition test' on which such investigations are to proceed, to take into account the application of Arts 81 and 82 EC as appropriate, and the Regulation makes it clear that national authorities are free to use their own procedures when applying Arts 81 and 82 EC. Even if such an approach is not taken, as suggested in **1.44**, the subject matter of the more recent complex monopoly

[1]   OFT *Market Investigation References*, para 2.3.

[2]   Paragraph 4.16.

[3]   Council Regulation (EC) 1/2003, but note that this does not enter into force until 1 May 2004. See **1.42–1.49**.

[4]   The OFT has recognised simply that this reform 'may have an impact on the scope of market investigation references, particularly where agreements between undertakings are involved. The OFT will issue further guidance about the effect of modernisation when the position is clearer' (OFT *Market Investigation References*, para 2.8).

investigations could almost certainly not be tackled under either Art 81 or Art 82 EC.

MARKET INVESTIGATION REFERENCES – THE ROLE OF THE OFT

4.10 Section 131(1) provides that the OFT has the power to make a reference to the Competition Commission (CC) where it:

'has reasonable grounds for suspecting that any feature, or combination of features, of a market in the United Kingdom for goods or services prevents, restricts or distorts competition[1] in connection with the supply or acquisition of any goods or services in the United Kingdom or a part of the United Kingdom.'

This is a broad provision, and 'feature' is given a wide interpretation in s 123(2), extending to market structure, and any conduct – which need not be in the market concerned – whether it relates to conduct by suppliers or customers. 'Conduct' also includes 'any failure to act', whether that is intentional or not (s 131(3)). The matters that may fall to be considered in such a reference are considered below, at **4.38–4.41**. Consequential amendments to special sector Acts mean that the regulators also have the power to make references, where specified.[2]

4.11 In July 2002, the OFT published a consultation paper, *Market Investigation References*, which, at the time of writing, remains to be finalised. This sets out the views of the OFT regarding the process by which it may make references to the CC. The guidance, when finalised, will not be binding, 'but will help business and its advisers, and consumers to understand the grounds on which the OFT may decide that a market investigation reference is justified'.[3] The CC has also published its consultation document, *Market Investigation References: Competition Commission Guidelines*, in September 2002.[4]

---

[1]   For the sake of convenience, in the narrative for the remainder of this chapter, this rubric will be reduced to 'adverse effect on competition'.

[2]   These powers are found as follows: Director General of Telecommunications, Telecommunications Act 1984, s 50 (note that this situation will change with the proposed launch of the general communications regulator – OFCOM – dealt with in the Communications Bill); Gas and Electricity Markets Authority, Gas Act 1986, s 36A, and Electricity Act 1989, s 43; Director General of Water Services, Water Industry Act 1991, s 31; Director General of Electricity Supply for Northern Ireland, Electricity (Northern Ireland) Order 1992, SI 1992/231, art 46; Rail Regulator, Railways Act 1993, s 67; Director General of Gas for Northern Ireland, Gas (Northern Ireland) Order 1996, SI 1996/275, art 23; Civil Aviation Authority, Transport Act 2000, s 86. See s 128(7) of the Act.

[3]   Paragraph 1.4.

[4]   Hereinafter, CC *Market Investigation References*.

4.12   The appropriate Minister – who will, in most circumstances, be the Secretary of State for Trade and Industry – also has the power to make a reference on the same terms as the OFT (s 132(3)). This is the case in situations where 'the appropriate Minister is not satisfied with a decision of the OFT not to make a reference under s 131' (s 132(1)). This power can also be invoked where the Minister has brought the matter of concern to the attention of the OFT, and is not satisfied that the OFT will make a reference within a reasonable period of time.[1]

4.13   In neither case can the OFT or the Minister make a reference in situations in which, within the previous 12 months, an undertaking in lieu of a reference has been accepted in accordance with s 156 (ss 131(4) and 132(4)). Undertakings in lieu are discussed further below, at **4.32–4.37**.

4.14   Prior to the making of a reference, the OFT[2] must consult on this (s 169), and shall consult with any person on whom the decision 'is likely to have a substantial impact' (s 169(1)). The OFT is obliged to give its reasons for making the proposed reference (s 169(3)). Whilst these reasons will vary from decision to decision, it is anticipated that the statement will include:

'(a)   a description of the goods or services concerned;
(b)   the identity of the main parties affected by the reference, whether as suppliers or as customers – this may involve the identification of categories of persons rather than individuals;
(c)   a view as to the possible definition of the market (or markets) affected;
(d)   the evidence that has led the OFT to have a reasonable suspicion that competition has been prevented, restricted or distorted, including that possible market features that may be relevant.'[3]

4.15   There is no formal time period set out in the Act within which the consultation process is to take place, but the OFT has suggested that a period of 'about two weeks' is appropriate.[4]

4.16   Section 172 provides that both the OFT (s 172(1)) and the Secretary of State (s 172(3)) have a duty to publish references made by them (or variations to that reference (see below)). This section also obliges the person making the reference to publish the reasons for making it (s 172(5)), although this need not be done at the same time as the publication of the reference (s 172(6)).

---

[1]   See Sufrin, B and Furse, M 'Market Investigations' [2002] Comp Law 244 at 247: 'It is worth noting that the reference in the recent banking services inquiry was made under s 51 [FTA 1973] by the Secretary of State and the Chancellor jointly and such an event could equally occur under the new law if the OFT declined to act'.

[2]   Or Minister, as appropriate.

[3]   OFT *Market Investigation References*, para 3.6.

[4]   Ibid, para 3.8.

4.17   Once a reference has been made, it may be varied by the person making the reference, although there is a duty to consult the CC before doing so (s 135).[1] A variation cannot have the effect of increasing the time period permitted for the determination of the reference (s 135(4)).

4.18   Variations may be made either by the person making the reference, or at the request of the CC itself. In the latter case, the OFT has recognised that:

> 'The content of references gives the CC scope to identify markets affected which differ from those that were considered by the OFT when making the reference, and to identify features giving rise to adverse effects on competition of which the OFT was not aware. Notwithstanding this scope, it may be that the goods and services described in the reference are sufficiently complicated that as the CC proceeds with its investigations it discovers that the description of the goods or services in the reference is inadequate. For example it may find that certain related goods and services are affected by the same market features as those it is investigating or, conversely, that some of the goods or services specified are not affected by these features and need not be investigated further. In those circumstances it may wish to ask the OFT to vary the reference. *It is very likely that the OFT would respond positively to such requests.*'[2]

4.19   Persons who are aggrieved by any decision taken by the OFT or Secretary of State may apply to the Competition Appeals Tribunal (CAT) for a review of that decision (s 179(1)). An application under this section must be brought within three months of the date of the contested decision. The making of an application does not suspend the reference, unless the CAT determines otherwise (s 179(5)). The standard of review is that of an application for judicial review, which is to say that it is that of *Wednesbury* unreasonableness.[3] Appeals from decisions of the CAT in this regard may be made to the Court of Appeal or Court of Session on points of law only (s 179(6)).[4]

---

[1]   There is no duty to consult the CC if the variation is made at its request (s 135(3)).

[2]   OFT *Market Investigation References*, para 3.12, emphasis added.

[3]   *Associated Provincial Picture Houses Ltd v Wednesbury Corpn* [1948] 1 KB 223. It has been noted that the success of judicial review actions is low when they relate to situations in which the views of bodies being examined are conditioned by detailed economic analyses (Borrie, G 'The Regulation of Public and Private Power' [1989] PL 552). It is likely to be easier to review a decision to make a reference than it is a final determination of that reference, but the record generally of reviews in the competition law arena is not one in which there have been a great many successes. However, the CAT has already shown that it is likely to review OFT actions (and presumably those of other bodies over which it jurisdiction extends) vigorously.

[4]   Note that. in *Napp v Director General of Fair Trading* [2002] EWCA Civ 796, [2002] UKCLR 726, the Court of Appeal was concerned to draw a distinction between matters of economic analysis and matters of law, expressing the opinion that in that case the appellant had conflated the two, and in fact had no reasonable case to make out in relation to the law.

Factors influencing the making of a reference

4.20 It was the view of the Confederation of British Industry (CBI) that, notwithstanding this right of appeal, the threshold for the making of references was too low. It feared that, coupled with the provisions for 'super-complaints' (see **6.5–6.14**), the result would be that domestic business would be 'rather beleaguered as a result of the provisions'.[1] Amendments were therefore brought forward which were 'designed to produce a higher threshold for the provisions', or, depending on one's perspective, were 'blatant attempts to restrict the basis on which references will be made'.[2] One Committee member suggested that it was possible that 'a proactive DGFT could become a competition tsar who runs around looking for causes to take up'.[3] An attempt was made to substitute the requirement that there be reasonable grounds for suspecting an adverse effect on competition with a belief that such a situation existed. For the Government, it was argued that there might be situations in which a suspicion existed, and where companies could benefit from a higher hurdle by not co-operating with the OFT to give it the information it needed in order to have a belief. It was further suggested that, in practice, the distinction between 'belief' and 'suspicion' would be a moot one.[4]

4.21 In response to an amendment which would have required that there be a 'significant' or 'substantial' adverse effect on competition, the Government pointed out that the OFT's 'resources will always be finite and it will naturally want to concentrate them on the most serious cases'.[5] The amendment was withdrawn.

4.22 The OFT itself notes, in its draft guidance, that:

> 'when deciding whether to make a reference the OFT will consider whether the suspected adverse effects on competition are likely to have a significant detrimental effect on customers … Where it seems likely that this effect is not significant the OFT will normally take the view that the burden on business, particularly in terms of management time, and the public expenditure costs of an investigation by the CC, are likely to be disproportionate in relation to any benefits that may be obtained from remedying the adverse effects.'[6]

It is not easy to make the assessment hinted at in this paragraph. The costs and benefits of competition investigations are difficult to quantify, although an

---

[1] *Hansard*, Standing Committee B, col 422.

[2] *Hansard*, Standing Committee B, col 430.

[3] *Hansard*, Standing Committee B, col 423.

[4] *Hansard*, Standing Committee B, cols 424–425. For the Government, Mr Alexander described 'belief' as 'a tricky concept to pin down'.

[5] *Hansard*, Standing Committee B, col 426, but note that this issue was raised repeatedly during the passage of the Bill.

[6] OFT *Market Investigation References*, para 2.16.

unpublished OFT research paper suggested that benefits could flow from inquiries that were somewhat specific and 'marginal'.[1]

4.23 The OFT is not *obliged* to make a reference in a situation where it has the power to do so, as s 131(1) provides that it '*may*' make a reference where the relevant criteria are fulfilled. In its draft guidance, the OFT indicates that it:

> 'will make references to the CC when the reference test set out in [s 131] *and each of the following criteria have been met*:
>
> (a) It would not be more appropriate to deal with the competition issues identified by applying CA 1998 or using other powers available to the OFT or, where appropriate, to sectoral regulators.
>
> (b) It would not be more appropriate to address the problem identified by means of undertakings in lieu of a reference.
>
> (c) The scale of the suspected problem, in terms of its detrimental effect on customers, is such that a reference would be an appropriate response to it.
>
> (d) There is a reasonable chance that appropriate remedies will be available.'[2]

4.24 In its draft guidance, the OFT notes that the following factors are relevant in determining whether to make such a reference:

> '(a) The size of the market. Generally speaking the cost of a CC investigation into a very small market would not be justified. However, problems in some relatively small specialised or local markets could have a detrimental impact on customers affected by them.
>
> (b) The proportion of the market affected by the feature giving rise to adverse effects on competition. … such agreements generally have no appreciable effect on competition if the parties' combined share of the relevant market does not exceed 25%.
>
> (c) The persistence of the feature giving rise to adverse effects on competition.'[3]

In practice, the OFT's 'assessment that a reference would be appropriate is likely to be based on a combination of features and will include evidence about both structure and conduct'.[4]

4.25 It is also the case that the OFT:

> 'is not required to reach firm conclusions before making references and it would be inappropriate for it to engage in extensive research. Provided it has reasonable grounds for suspecting that there are market features that adversely affect competition, the reference test has been met and further investigation can be left to the CC.'[5]

4.26 The OFT will also consider the 'likely availability of remedies in the event that the suspected adverse effects on competition were found by the CC

---

[1] Morrison, E, Sewell, A, Matthew, D, Elliott, D and Parr, M *Cost Benefit Assessment of Competition Inquiries and De Minimis Thresholds*, unpublished (OFT, 1996).

[2] OFT *Market Investigation References*, para 2.1, emphasis added.

[3] Ibid, para 2.17.

[4] Ibid, para 4.4.

[5] Ibid, para 4.7.

to exist'. In particular, 'it will not normally make a reference when it believes that no appropriate remedies ... are likely to be available'. This might be the case, for example, where the market in question is a global one, and where any remedy proposed could go only to conduct in the UK, which would have no significant impact on the market in general, or which might even act to the detriment of those in the relevant market in the UK.[1]

4.27 It is unlikely that the OFT will make a market investigation reference in situations where the 'adverse effects on competition arise primarily from laws, regulations, government policies or the actions of regulators'.[2]

4.28 It is worth noting the view of the Government that:

> 'In short, we do not expect that the new regime's reference criteria will lead to there being many more market investigations than there have been monopoly inquiries in recent years. Any increase in the number of references is likely to result from increased OFT resources, not from changes introduced by the Bill.'[3]

4.29 There was strong opposition to the s 132 power (the power of a Minister to make references). It was argued that this section:

> '... bears re-reading because it leaps off the page. The Bill has been promoted as taking political decisions out of competition policy, which everyone agrees is wonderful, yet this clause, unashamedly, allows a Minister to intervene when he is not satisfied. I suspect that Ministers of all political persuasions are not satisfied a great deal of the time. However, the Minister will be able to intervene when the OFT decides not to make a reference ... Curiously and paradoxically, it makes not a blind bit of difference how dissatisfied the Minister is, if the OFT has decided to make a reference with which he does not agree, because it appears to me that he or she can do nothing about that.'[4]

The Government countered that the power was a weaker one than that under the FTA 1973, and opposition attempts to remove this power were defeated in Committee.

4.30 Those familiar with the monopoly provisions of the FTA 1973 will note that there is no reference in the Act to market shares in relation to the making of market investigation references. In the FTA 1973, the threshold was 25% in relation to both scale and complex monopolies. The Opposition

---

[1] Ibid, para 2.19. In the monopoly inquiry *Supermarkets: A Report on the Supply of Groceries from Multiple Stores in the United Kingdom* (October 2000), Cm 4842, the CC noted that it was unusual for it to identify a situation which operated against the public interest, and at the same time to be unable to recommend any remedy for this.

[2] OFT *Market Investigation References*, para 2.20. For an interesting discussion of the interrelationship between regulation and competition policy, see Amato, G and Laudati, C *The Anti-Competitive Impact of Regulation* (Edgar Allen, 2001), particularly Part III.

[3] *Hansard*, Standing Committee B, cols 426–427.

[4] *Hansard*, Standing Committee B, cols 433–434. Elsewhere, we find 'the provision is completely contrary to the thrust of the Bill and it is astonishing that Ministers should want to include it' (Mr Lansley, col 435), and concerns were expressed about Ministers 'playing to the gallery' (Mr Field, col 436).

unsuccessfully sought to introduce a requirement into the Act that there be a 'significant' impact in relation to the questions asked in a market investigation reference before any remedy could be imposed.

4.31 As with the FTA 1973, there is no formal requirement that a full analysis of the relevant market and alleged harm be carried out before the making of the reference, although clearly ss 131 and 132 set a threshold which requires that some proper consideration be given to possible harms. When a reference is made, it is enough that it specifies 'the description of goods or services to which the feature or combination of features relates' (s 131(1)(c)). It will be for the CC to determine if goods or services of that description constitute a relevant market on which an adverse effect on competition might be identified.

Undertakings in lieu of references

4.32 The OFT may accept undertakings in lieu of making a reference (s 154). Thus, s 154(2) provides that:

> 'The OFT may, instead of making such a reference and for the purpose of remedying, mitigating or preventing –
>
> (a) the adverse effect on competition concerned; or
> (b) any detrimental effect on customers so far as it has resulted from, or may be expected to result from, the adverse effect on competition;
>
> accept, from such persons as it considers appropriate, undertakings to take such action as it considers appropriate.'[1]

4.33 In its draft guidance, the OFT notes that these undertakings in lieu of a reference 'are unlikely to be common'.[2] The reasons for this pessimism are twofold. First, the OFT may not have examined the relevant circumstances as thoroughly as would be needed in order for it to be confident that undertakings would achieve the desired result. Secondly, 'trying to negotiate undertakings with several parties in circumstances in which possible adverse effects on competition have not been comprehensively analysed is likely to pose serious practical difficulties'.[3] The dynamics of negotiating undertakings with a number of parties, particularly in situations where there remains ambiguity, are very complex. In a competitive situation, which may be exacerbated where the market is a tight oligopoly, the stance adopted by a company towards the OFT will itself be part of the competitive process. No one company is likely to accept an undertaking unilaterally, unless it can be persuaded that all of its competitors will do likewise, lest it suffer a competitive

---

[1] This provision mirrors the power set out in FTA 1973, s 56A.
[2] OFT *Market Investigation References*, para 2.11.
[3] Ibid.

disadvantage.[1] It is more likely that undertakings will be accepted in the rare situations when the conduct of a single firm is subject to examination.

4.34 The OFT is required, when considering whether to accept undertakings, to have regard to the need to 'achieve as comprehensive a solution as is reasonable and practicable to the adverse effect on competition and any detrimental effects on customers' (s 154(3)). In addition, it may consider whether there are benefits that flow from the conduct in question, which might be disrupted by the undertaking (s 154(4)).

4.35 Section 146(5) provides that no undertaking shall be accepted in situations in which there is, at the present time, no detrimental impact on customers, and the remedy to the potential detrimental impact will not deal with the current adverse effect on competition.

4.36 The procedural requirements in relation to undertakings in lieu are set out in s 155, and are relatively straightforward. In essence, the OFT is required to consult in relation to these by publishing a notice stating that it intends to accept an undertaking.

4.37 As indicated above, it is unlikely that a great many undertakings in lieu of references will be accepted. The OFT draft guidance notes that in 1994, by virtue of the Deregulation and Contracting Out Act 1994, the FTA 1973 was amended in order to allow it to accept undertakings in lieu of making a monopoly reference (s 56A). However, these provisions have never been used, although, on a number of occasions, informal assurances, which are not normally published, have been accepted.

THE DETERMINATION OF REFERENCES – THE ROLE OF THE CC

Questions to be determined

4.38 Section 134 sets out the role of the CC in relation to market investigations. This is to decide whether there is in fact an adverse effect on competition, as suggested in the reference. The broad methodology to be employed by the CC has been set out in its consultation document, *Market Investigation References: Competition Commission Guidelines*, although it must be

---

[1]   This was reported to have been a problem in the monopoly inquiry *Foreign Package Holidays: A Report on the Supply in the UK of Tour Operators' Services and Travel Agents' Services in Relation to Foreign Package Holidays* (1997), Cm 3813.

noted that, in view of the diverse nature of markets, it may not always be possible to follow a standard analysis, and 'the Commission will consider each reference with due regard to the particular circumstances of each case including the information that is available and the time constraints applicable to the case'.[1] Section 134(2) provides that:

'For the purposes of this Part, in relation to a market investigation reference, there is an adverse effect on competition if any feature, or combination of features, of a market in the United Kingdom for relevant goods or services prevents, restricts or distorts competition in connection with the supply or acquisition of any goods or services in the United Kingdom or a part of the United Kingdom'.

The reference to 'features' of a market is deliberately broad, and relates to both structural and behavioural features. Structural features might include 'not only market shares, concentration, buyer power and entry barriers, but also less obvious aspects of market structure such as information asymmetries and Government regulations'.[2] Conduct features 'include the conduct of buyers and sellers, of the firms in the market and of customers'.[3]

4.39   Where the CC finds that there is an adverse effect on competition, or 'any detrimental effect on customers' (s 134(4)(a)), it is required to determine whether action should be taken by it, or by others, to remedy this (s 134(4)). In either case, it should determine what action should be taken, and what harm exactly is to be remedied.

4.40   The reference to a 'detrimental effect on customers'[4] seems at first sight to add little to the key test of s 134(2), although it is expanded on and highlighted in the following two sub-sections. In s 134(5), a 'detrimental effect on customers' is defined as arising where there are:

---

[1]   CC *Market Investigation References*, para 1.4. An illustration of the procedures to be adopted by the CC is set out at the end of this chapter, at **4.122**.

[2]   CC *Market Investigation References*, para 2.9.

[3]   Ibid.

[4]   The terms 'consumers' and 'customers' are defined in s 183(1):

  ' " Consumer" means any person who is–

  (a)   a person to whom goods are or are sought to be supplied (whether by way of sale or otherwise) in the course of a business carried on by the person supplying or seeking to supply them; or

  (b)   a person for whom services are or are sought to be supplied in the course of a business carried on by the person supplying or seeking to supply them;

  and who does not receive or seek to received the goods or services in the course of a business carried on by him;

  "Customer" includes a customer who is not a consumer.'

'(a)   higher prices, lower quality or less choice of goods or services in any market in the United Kingdom (whether or not the market to which the feature of features concerned relate); or

(b)   less innovation in relation to such goods or services.'

And, by virtue of s 134(6), the CC is obliged, when considering whether action should be taken, to take into account in particular the need, as far as possible, to remedy any such detrimental effect.

4.41   The CC is also required to undertake a balancing exercise in that it may take into account benefits which may flow to any customer arising out of the feature(s) of the markets in question (s 134(7)). 'Relevant customer benefits' are defined in the opposite terms to detrimental effects, and the provision is similar in thrust to Art 81(3) EC and CA 1998, s 9, although it should not be seen as an 'exemption' or 'legal exception', as there is no prohibition. In practice, however, 'they will lead to the consideration of much the same issues in much the same way'.[1] Where there are these benefits, the CC (or the OFT, or the Secretary of State, as appropriate) is required to consider whether these accrue as a result of the particular features of the market and would not accrue without that feature being in place, or whether they may be expected to accrue within a reasonable period of time.[2]

The conduct of the investigation and the report

4.42   Section 136 relates to the report that the CC is required to prepare and publish once a reference has been made. These reports are likely to be similar to those published under the monopoly provisions of the FTA 1973,[3] and in relation to mergers. Copies of reports are to be sent to the person making the reference (s 136(4)).

4.43   The time-limit within which a report must be published is two years from the making of the reference (s 137(1)). This should be seen as a long-stop, and the majority of reports published under the monopoly provisions of the FTA 1973 were concluded in a shorter period. The Secretary of State has been given the power to amend this period, but may only do so downwards (s 137(3) and (4)). The two years may be exceeded by up to 20 days in cases in which the Secretary of State makes an 'intervention notice' (see **4.88–4.93**).

---

[1]   Lord Sainsbury, *Hansard* (HL), 18 July 2002, col 1524.

[2]   The CC is obliged, by virtue of s 171(3), to publish guidance relating to the way in which it will assess customer benefits, and the ways in which this assessment will impact on enforcement actions. See **4.105–4.106**.

[3]   Although the CC is giving some thought to reshaping the way in which the reports are presented.

4.44 Although the Act provides that the report is to contain the answers to questions required by s 134 (see **4.38–4.41**), and should be properly reasoned (s 136(2)), it is silent on the methodology by which the CC should reach these conclusions. This is in part because 'markets and thinking about competition continue to evolve',[1] and in part because different markets may require different approaches, and it is not possible to prescribe a single methodological approach which will be applicable to all markets. Generally, however, competitive situations may be analysed by reference to the following three factors: (1) the structure of the market; (2) the position of parties on the market; and (3) the conduct of the parties.

4.45 One of the strengths of market investigations is that they may be applied to situations in which adverse effects on competition flow from the structure of the market, which may have nothing to do with the conduct of the firms in that market.[2] It might, for example, be the case that there are barriers to entry arising from a chain of actions, each of which, by itself, is 'innocent'. This suggests that the CC will necessarily undertake an extensive and rigorous analysis of the market in question, in much the same way as was the case with monopoly investigations. Section 131(2) (see **4.10**) provides that references to a feature of a market are to be concerned with the structure of the market, conduct of suppliers on that market, and conduct of customers on that market. Some of the economic factors which may fall to be considered in making this analysis are set out in OFT *Market Investigation References*, in relation to the way in which the OFT is likely to assess the situation, and these are likely to apply equally to the CC, although the CC will have more time in which to conduct its analysis, and will be more thorough in doing so.

The structure of the market

4.46 Section 134(3) provides that 'relevant goods or services' referred to in s 134(1) and (2) means 'goods or services of a description to be specified in the reference'. While it is to be hoped that the references are carefully considered, it may be the case that the description of the goods and services in the reference is not found to be an appropriate one once a thorough consideration of the market is begun. The key question to be determined in a market reference is that of whether there is a market in which the outcome of the combination of market structure and conduct is competitively harmful. Such a question cannot be resolved without a careful analysis of the economic context in question. In the case of *European Night Services*,[3] for example, the European Court of Justice (ECJ) held that in assessing potential anti-competitive conduct (in this case, an agreement):

---

[1]   OFT *Market Investigation References*, para 1.4.

[2]   *Hansard*, Standing Committee B, col 430.

[3]   *European Night Services v Commission*, Joined Cases T–374/94, etc [1998] ECR II–3141, at paras 136–137.

'account should be taken of the actual conditions in which it functions, in particular the economic context in which the undertakings operate, the products or services covered by the agreement and the actual structure of the market concerned ... It must be stressed that the examination of conditions of competition is based not only on existing competition between undertakings already present on the relevant market but also on potential competition, in order to ascertain whether, in the light of the structure of the market and the economic and legal context within which it functions, there are real concrete possibilities for the undertakings concerned to compete among themselves or for a new competitor to penetrate the relevant market and compete with undertakings already established in it.'

The concept of the 'relevant market' is crucial to the development of this analysis, although 'the Commission does not regard market definition as an end in itself, but rather as a framework within which to analyse the effects of market features'.[1]

Market definition[2]

4.47 The *Explanatory Notes* point out that:

'the distinction between "structure" and "conduct" in a market is commonly made in economic analysis, and is intended to provide the framework for a wide ranging inquiry into how firms compete in a market and the economic context in which they operate.'[3]

The starting point for an analysis of the market structure will be to define the relevant market, a practice in which the CC is already well versed, and in relation to which it employs, where possible, the standard 'small but significant non-transitory increase in price' (SSNIP) test.[4]

4.48 The relevant market needs to be defined in relation to both the product or service, and the geographical area in which that product or service is supplied. The SSNIP test may be employed in both cases. Its use in relation to the product market is set out in both the EC Commission's[5] and the OFT's[6] guidance relating to market definition. In the OFT guidance, the following explanation is given of the SSNIP – or 'hypothetical monopolist' – test:

'2.8   One way to look at this problem is to consider an undertaking that was the only supplier of the products (or group of products) at the centre of the investigation and use the conceptual framework of whether a hypothetical monopolist of these products would maximise its profits by consistently charging higher prices than it would if it faced competition. The assumption is that this hypothetical undertaking would not be

---

[1]   CC *Market Investigation References*, para 2.12.

[2]   See also **3.33–3.35**. The framework set out in CC *Market Investigation References* (at paras 2.12–2.40) is the same as that set out in the relevant merger guidelines, and places heavy, but not exclusive, reliance on the SSNIP test (see below).

[3]   Paragraph 289.

[4]   For a discussion of the economics of market definition, see Bishop, S and Walker, M *The Economics of EC Competition Law: Concepts, Application and Measurement* (Sweet & Maxwell, London, 1999), Chapter 3.

[5]   'Notice on the Definition of the Relevant Market for the Purposes of Community Competition Law' (1997) OJ C372/5.

[6]   *Market Definition* [2000] UKCLR 61, technical guideline.

constrained by the threat of new entry, which would be considered in any overall assessment of an undertaking's market power – see the Competition Act guideline *Assessment of Market Power*. (Defining the market therefore cannot demonstrate on its own that an undertaking possesses market power.)

2.9 If the undertaking would be prevented from setting prices above competitive levels by substitution to certain products, those substitutes can then be added to the potential market and the test applied again. This involves asking whether an undertaking which was the only supplier of this larger group of products would maximise profits by charging prices above competitive levels. By repeating the process, a definition can eventually be reached where, under the assumptions above, a "hypothetical monopolist" could maintain prices above competitive levels. This will usually be the market definition used. If the market were to be expanded further, the same condition should be met: a "hypothetical monopolist" could set higher prices than an undertaking facing competition. The Director General would usually use the narrowest potential market definition. This will not always be the case, however; the relevant market may be wider in the case of a horizontal agreement, for example. [Internal footnotes omitted.]'

This approach was used often in the later CC monopoly reports, as well as in decisions made under the CA 1998. However, it is not always possible to employ the test. In some circumstances, data might be unavailable and, in others, there are theoretical difficulties.[1] In the case of a monopolist who *already prices above the competitive level,* the application of the test – raising prices *further* – will likely yield a false result and point to substitutes that are not substitutes in fact. This is known as the 'cellophane fallacy'.[2] There is no formal solution to this problem, and the best way to deal with it is to look at historical data, if they exist.

4.49 In its case-law, the ECJ emphasised early on the importance of defining the relevant market in the context of the application of Art 82 EC.[3] In

---

[1] In the case of *Aberdeen Journals Ltd v The Director General of Fair Trading supported by Aberdeen Independent Ltd* [2002] CompAR 167, the Competition Commission Appeals Tribunal (CCAT) set aside a decision of the Director, and remitted the case back for further consideration. The CCAT was highly critical of the approach taken to market definition. At paras 147–148, it held that:

'[147] In order to lay the factual foundation for the definition of the relevant market, we would have expected the Decision to contain a brief factual description, at least in outline, of the objective characteristics of the products concerned – for example the content of each of the three newspapers in question, the kinds of advertisements carried (eg display advertisements, recruitment, property, motors, other trade advertisements, classified, notices, etc), the advertising rates offered by the paid-for and free titles respectively, details of their respective circulations, target audiences and geographical distribution areas.

[148] In our view, such a description of the objective characteristics of the products in question is almost always necessary in cases of disputed market definition, because it is on that foundation that the discussion of the relevant product market must rest. In *Continental Can* [1973] CMLR 199] the Court of Justice held that a sufficient description of the markets concerned, and in particular sufficient data on the particular characteristics of the products in question, are essential elements in appraising whether a dominant position exists': [1973] ECR 215 at paras 32–37.

[2] See **3.34**, fn 3.

[3] Although it should be stressed that market definition is also crucial in relation to merger control, and has become increasingly important in the application of Art 81 EC.

Hoffmann-La Roche,[1] the Court stated that 'the concept of the relevant market presupposes that there is a sufficient degree of interchangeability between all products forming part of the same market', and, in *United Brands*,[2] it considered that the problem of whether bananas constituted a market separate from other soft fruit was one of whether bananas were 'reasonably interchangeable by consumers with other kinds of fresh fruit'.[3] While the Court and the Commission have continued to refer to the characteristics of the relevant products, and, in particular, to the ways in which these are viewed by consumers or customers, there has been a move towards the more formal usage of the SSNIP test, too. The Commission Notice[4] firmly placed the SSNIP test at the heart of market definition, and the Commission has been explicit in its application of the test.[5] However, it has also argued that it is not *compelled* to perform the test in each and every case and, in *Virgin/British Airways*,[6] it maintained that the methodology set out in the Notice was merely an illustration of the way in which markets operated.

4.50　In addition to the demand aspects of market definition, it is necessary to consider the possibilities of supply-side substitution (a factor which is recognised in the application of a properly conducted SSNIP test). Supply-side substitution arises where, in the short-to-medium term, an undertaking which does not currently supply a product might be able to do so. In the case of *Continental Can*,[7] for example, the Commission failed to take into account the fact that consumers of tin cans and metal closures might be able to manufacture these themselves if they used them in sufficient quantities, or that suppliers of alternative forms of packaging might be able to switch production. The OFT guideline provides a good explanation of this factor:

> '**3.14**　An example is the supply of paper for use in publishing. Paper is produced in various different grades dependent on the coating used. From a customer's point of view, the different types of paper are not viewed as substitutes, but because they are produced using the same plant and raw materials, it is relatively easy for manufacturers to switch production between different grades. If a "hypothetical monopolist" in one grade of paper tried to set prices above competitive levels, manufacturers currently producing other grades could easily start supplying that grade – the ability to exploit market power is thus constrained by substitution by suppliers.'

4.51　For the OFT, the relevant time within which substitution must occur on the supply side in order for this to be included in the relevant market is a

---

[1]　*Hoffman-La Roche & Co AG v Commission* Case 85/76 [1979] 3 CMLR 211.

[2]　*United Brands Co v Commission* Case 27/76 [1978] 1 CMLR 429.

[3]　Paragraph 12.

[4]　See **4.48**, fn 5.

[5]　As in, for example, *1998 Football World Cup* 2000/12 (2000) OJ L5/55.

[6]　2000/74 (2000) OJ L30/1.

[7]　*Europemballage Corp and Continental Can Co Inc v Commission* Case 6/72 [1973] CMLR 199, [1973] ECR 215.

period of one year. Thus, 'undertakings would not normally be included if they had to make a significant investment in new production capacity or other fixed assets'.[1] The fact that supply-side substitution may take place over a period that is longer than one year does not mean that this is irrelevant, but rather that it is to be considered in relation to market power, rather than market definition.

4.52 In relation to the geographic market, the SSNIP test may also be employed with similar methodology to that of the product market. The question is whether a hypothetical monopolist of the product in the narrowest possible geographic area would be able to raise prices above the competitive level in that area, or whether substitution by customers in that area to suppliers outside of it would make the price rise unprofitable. It has often been the case that markets have been found by the CC to be national, or regional. This may particularly be so where there is an element of regulation of the relevant market. However, it is increasingly the case that markets are found to be EC-wide, or global. In these circumstances, the wider geographical market may serve as a constraint on a 'monopolist' based in the UK.

4.53 There is also a temporal aspect to the question of market definition, although this is not usually as important as product or geography. In some cases, it is obvious that there are specific temporal markets – as is the case, for example, with train travel at peak times for commuters,[2] or telephone calls for business callers. In some cases, there are specific reasons why a temporal definition might be constrained. This was the case, for example, in *ABG Oil*,[3] in which the Commission found that one consequence of the 1973/74 oil crisis was to create a series of temporarily constrained separate markets in favour of each supplier, as customers were unable to switch between them due to the shortages. More generally, temporal markets might be important in relation to switches between one generation of a product and another – for example, in the case of computer software.

4.54 Although decisions and case-law falling under Art 82 EC and the Chapter II Prohibition may be of use in determining the methodology to be applied in relation to market definition, or in setting precedents, these should be treated with some caution. First, it must be recognised that markets change over time, and place. A finding that sparkling mineral waters constituted a relevant market in France in 1990 does not mean that they will constitute a relevant market in the UK in 2003. Further, the answer to the question 'what is

---

[1]   *Market Definition*, para 3.16, technical guideline.

[2]   See CC *Market Investigation References*, para 2.36.

[3]   *ABG Oil companies operating in the Netherlands* 77/327 (1977) OJ L117/1, overturned on appeal *BP v Commission* Case 77/77 [1978] 3 CMLR 174 – the Court left intact the Commission's arguments relating to temporal markets.

the relevant market?' may depend on the context in which the question is being asked. In the case of Art 82 EC and the Chapter II Prohibition, the question relates usually to specific conduct alleged against a specific monopolist at a reasonably narrow point in time. In relation to market investigations, a wider question is being asked, relating to the features of an entire market, and it is possible that this may affect the answers to the questions relating to market definition.

The assessment of competition in the market

4.55 Once the CC has defined the market, it will then consider the state of competition on that market. This is not likely to be a straightforward analysis:

> 'In a typical case, the Commission will be concerned about a combination of features though there may be cases where, in terms of the structure of the market, the situation is largely sufficient to establish that there is no adverse effect on competition. On the other hand, where the Commission believes that structural features might, of themselves give rise to an adverse effect on competition, it would normally go on to consider conduct firms to see if that offsets its concerns. It is unlikely that the Commission would reach an adverse conclusion about the structural features of a market and not also go on to consider the conduct of firms engaged in that market. Any detrimental effects will usually arise from conduct of firms that is conditioned by the structural features of the market.'[1]

INTER-MARKET RIVALRY, AND THE POSITION OF THE PARTIES

4.56 The first step in the competitive assessment is to consider the position of the parties in that market. The market shares of the relevant parties are a strong indication, but are not by themselves determinative of the competitive position, and the strength of any one party. As the *Explanatory Notes* indicate, market shares and concentration:

> 'can provide a rough indication of the competitive strength of firms operating in a market, although they will seldom in themselves provide an unambiguous indication of market power and the state of competition in that market (eg the fact that three firms each have 30 per cent of a market now does not mean that the market is uncompetitive: it may be that their respective shares a year ago were quite different, or that, although their shares remain broadly stable over time, there is a great deal of customer "churn" between them).'

The EC Commission recently introduced into EC competition law the application of the Herfindahl–Hirshman Index (HHI), used as tool by the US authorities in relation to merger control.[2] The HHI is the sum of the squared market shares of the companies on the relevant market. In a market with four firms, each of which has a 25% market share, the HHI would therefore be $25^2 + 25^2 + 25^2 + 25^2 = 2500$. In a total monopoly, the HHI would be 10,000 (100^2). Where the HHI is less than 1000, it is typically characterised as 'low', and an indicator of a market structure which is conducive to competition. An

[1]   CC *Market Investigation References*, para 3.1.

[2]   In the EC, see the *Guidelines on the Applicability of Article 81 EC to Horizontal Cooperation Agreements*.

HHI of over 1800 is regarded as 'high', and suggests that the market may be conducive to anti-competitive outcomes. Changes in market shares over time may reveal the dynamism in the market, a high fluctuation suggesting a healthy competitive environment.

4.57 Other structural factors, apart from market shares and concentration measures, may also be relevant to the assessment. These might include firms' cost structures, capacity, and the structure of ownership in the market. Network effects might also be relevant (see **3.35**), as might the ability of firms to innovate, the objectives and culture of firms, and their views on the development of the market.[1]

NON-PRICE FACTORS IN COMPETITION

4.58 It is not always going to be the case that price competition is the most important determinant of the competitive health of a market. The CC recognises that:

> 'Competition encompasses both price competition and non-price competition, and the latter can in some markets be more significant. Where applicable, the Commission will consider the effect of non-price competition in a market, for example product development, product range and quality, marketing, servicing and research and development (R&D). An emphasis on non-price competition may reflect the characteristics of the product or customer, but may also result from incentives not to compete on price alone or a desire to raise barriers to entry. Equally, if strong non-price competition in the relevant market leads to substantial product differentiation, then this may mean that co-ordinated price behaviour is more difficult or impossible to achieve.'[2]

BARRIERS TO ENTRY, EXPANSION, AND EXIT

4.59 Whether there are barriers to entry is also an important factor, and one that has been expressly dealt with in a number of CC monopoly reports. If barriers to entry are low, then potential competition is going to be an important constraint on incumbents.[3] The distinction between potential competition and supply-side substitution (see **4.50–4.51**) is a matter of time, with potential competition operating over a longer period – typically in excess of a year. This means that, in the short term, a monopolist can set a price above the competitive level, but that this position will not persist in the long term. Where barriers to entry are low, competition authorities are likely to be

---

[1] CC *Market Investigation References*, paras 3.9–3.12.

[2] Ibid, para 3.13.

[3] In the words of the CC: 'the absence of significant barriers to entry will tend to constrain what might otherwise be scope for the exercise of market power by incumbent firms' (CC *Market Investigation References*, para 3.34).

less concerned about the current structure of the market than where barriers are high. Barriers to entry come in many forms, and are generally defined by the OFT in the following terms:

'One definition of an entry barrier is that it is a cost that must be borne by an undertaking entering a market that does not need to be borne by an incumbent undertaking already operating in the market. The existence of entry barriers may reduce the scope for competition, so that incumbents are able to raise prices above competitive levels. Entry barriers do not arise from cost advantages derived solely from the efficiency of the incumbent, and when assessing barriers to entry the Director General will therefore aim to distinguish between such efficiency-based cost advantages and other cost advantages. In practice, however, this may not be easy (internal footnote omitted).'[1]

The following barriers are identified in the *Explanatory Notes*:

'–   laws and regulations (which include intellectual property rights)[2]
–   sunk costs
–   economies of scale
–   information constraints
–   the strategic behaviour of incumbents
–   the likelihood or rate of market growth.'[3]

In addition, the existence of vertical links, such as a strong distribution network, may also make entry harder.[4] Thus, the OFT suggests that:

'A market investigation reference may be the most appropriate way to proceed where vertical agreements are prevalent in a market and have the effect of preventing the entry of new competitors, but there is no evidence of collusion between the firms involved which might have caused this situation to arise.'[5]

COUNTERVAILING BUYER POWER AND MONOPSONY

4.60   In addition to the position of suppliers, it is necessary to consider the position of customers. In some markets, the focus will be on customers, due

---

[1]   OFT technical guideline, *Assessment of Market Power*, para 5.2 ([2000] UKCLR 40).

[2]   And see CC *Market Investigation References*, paras 3.30–3.31.

[3]   Paragraph 290.

[4]   For a discussion of the foreclosure effect of vertical integration, see, in particular, Dobson, PW and Waterson, M *Vertical Restraints and Competition Policy*, OFT Research Paper 12, 1995. In its draft guidance, the OFT notes that 'market investigation references may, in certain circumstances, also be relevant for dealing with possible competition problems arising from vertical agreements' (OFT *Market Investigation References*, para 2.6). However, this suggestion is predicated in part on the fact that, at the time of the preparation of the Bill and the guidance, vertical agreements were excluded from the ambit of the CA 1998 Chapter I Prohibition, save in highly restricted circumstances, by virtue of the Competition Act 1998 (Land and Vertical Agreements Exclusion) Order 2000, SI 2000/310. This approach will need to be re-examined following the completion of the EC modernisation process. The OFT has also said that 'a market investigation reference might be appropriate, however, if a number of firms in a market are vertically integrated, and they engage in some common form of anti-competitive conduct, for example, discrimination against any non-integrated competitors' (OFT, *Market Investigation References*, para 5.10).

[5]   OFT *Market Investigation References*, para 2.6.

to fears about their power in relation to weaker suppliers.[1] In extreme cases, this is referred to as 'monopsony', and is the opposite of monopoly. The strength of customers facing suppliers with market power is an important factor in determining the likely harms flowing from that supplier market power. This is a factor which is discussed in CC *Market Investigation References*, paras 3.35–3.37, and in Part 6 of the OFT technical guideline, *Market Power*, in the following terms:

> '**6.1** The main potential constraint on market power of a seller is the strength of buyers and the structure of the buyers' side of the market. The potential market power of a seller is offset by the buying power of a buyer if, in the absence of that buyer, prices would have been higher. Buyer power allows an undertaking (or a group of undertakings acting together) to exert a substantial influence on the price, quality or the terms of supply of a good purchased. It requires that a buyer should be large in relation to the relevant market, well informed about alternative sources of supply and that the buyer could readily, and at little cost to itself, switch from one supplier to another, or even commence production of the item himself.
>
> **6.2** In general, buyer power is beneficial in two circumstances: when it exerts downward pressure on a supplier's prices and the lower prices are passed on to the consumer; and when there are large efficiency gains that result from the buyer being large in relation to the market. Countervailing buyer power does not always benefit the consumer, however: if, for example, the buyer also has market power as a seller in the downstream market, it may not pass on lower prices to the consumer; it could even use its combined power strategically to the detriment of competition. Conversely, buyer power may have adverse consequences in the upstream market if it is used to foreclose entry or if it threatens the viability of suppliers. A careful analysis of vertical relationships in the market, on a case-by-case basis, is therefore required to assess buyer power.'

There has also been discussion of this issue in many of the CC reports dealing with mergers. Where the concern has been raised that a merger has made the market more concentrated, the existence of countervailing buyer power may be an important factor in addressing this concern.

4.61 It is not only situations which are monopsonistic which may raise concerns. It will be recalled that s 131(3) provides that '"conduct" includes any failure to act'. The OFT has suggested that there may be situations,

---

[1] This was one of the factors underpinning concerns raised in the report *Supermarkets: A Report on the Supply of Groceries from Multiple Stores in the United Kingdom* (Cm 4842, October 2000). Here, the CC received a number of complaints relating to the purchasing practices of the 24 parties identified as falling within the terms of reference. A list of 52 practices was put to the main parties, including such matters as 'requiring or requesting from some of their suppliers various non-cost related payments or discounts, sometimes retrospectively; imposing charged and making changes to contractual arrangements without adequate notice; and unreasonably transferring risks from the main party to the supplier' (para 1.9). When carried out by parties with market power, these practices were found to 'adversely affect the competitiveness of some of their suppliers and distort competition in the supplier market – and in some cases in the retail market – for the supply of groceries' (para 1.10). The CC acknowledged that there were 'advantages that can result from buyer power in relation to those suppliers with market power', but concluded that the practices nevertheless operated against the public interest (para 1.11).

particularly in relation to search costs, where there is a failure to act by individual customers lacking market power, that might be such as to prompt a market investigation reference. This might be the case, for example, where:

> 'there may remain enough uninformed customers with high search costs who purchase from the first firm they encounter for the seller to be able to charge prices without regard to competition.'[1]

4.62 However, in the absence of such a distinctive feature, 'customers' conduct is unlikely on its own to be sufficient to justify a market investigation reference'.[2]

Conduct of the parties on the market

4.63 The second part of the analysis in a market investigation will be that of the conduct of the firms on the market (s 131(2)). As noted above, 'conduct' 'includes any failure to act'. The CC will, in examining a market investigation reference:

> 'have regard to any conduct of the firms in a market (whether sellers or buyers) that could, in the circumstances of the particular market, have an adverse effect on competition (whether in the market in which the firms themselves are engaged or in some other market, for example, the market of the sellers' suppliers or customers).'[3]

4.64 It is the link between structure and conduct which makes the market reference provisions so powerful, and which sets them apart from Arts 81 and 82 EC, and the CA 1998 equivalents. As the *Explanatory Notes* make clear:

> 'The term "conduct" includes any act and omissions, whether intentional or unintentional, of the persons referred to... By the decisions they take, the way in which they make decisions, and how they respond to their rivals and potential entrants, firms operating within a market can prevent, restrict or distort not only competition within that market, but also competition in the markets in which their immediate suppliers (upstream) and customers (downstream) operate, and in complementary markets (ie the conduct of firms in a market for one pair of complementary markets, such as printers and printer cartridges, may prevent, restrict or distort competition in the market for the other product). The conduct of consumers and other customers, as well as that of the businesses that supply them, can also affect the conditions of competition in a market, and it is therefore included in the definition of features of a market... In some cases, it will be open to debate whether a given feature of a market is structural or an aspect of conduct (for example, information asymmetries and barriers to entry arising from the behaviour of incumbents could equally well belong in either category). However in indicating the range of features of a market which the competition authorities may take into account, the separate references to structure and conduct ... do not require either

---

[1]   OFT *Market Investigation References*, para 7.3.
[2]   Ibid, para 7.11.
[3]   CC *Market Investigation References*, para 3.55.

the [OFT or the CC] to identify particular features of markets that are the subject of a reference as falling entirely within the terms of one of [the relevant] subsections.'[1]

Oligopolistic markets

4.65 The analysis of conduct in situations in which the market is characterised by the existence of a number of firms with significant market shares is likely to be more complex than in the case of a single firm with a high market share. In most cases, as has already been discussed, the latter situation should fall to be considered under the CA 1998, or Art 82 EC, and it is the application of the Act to situations of non-collusive dominance which is both its strength, and which makes the application of the Act more difficult. It is noted in the *Explanatory Notes* that 'potential market investigation cases will often raise many complex issues'.[2]

4.66 In its draft guidance, the OFT notes that, because of its preference to rely on the CA 1998 prohibitions where it can do so:

'Market investigation references are therefore likely to focus on competition problems arising from uncoordinated parallel conduct by several firms or industry-wide features of a market in cases where the OFT does not have reasonable grounds to suspect the existence of anti-competitive agreements or dominance. Such problems may have a variety of sources, such as competition dampening common practices whose origins have long been forgotten, customers who are poorly informed relative to suppliers (information asymmetries), and sheer inertia on the part of ostensible customers.'[3]

4.67 The economic problems that arise when analysing what may formally be referred to as oligopolistic interaction between firms are difficult ones. The issue, in essence, may be expressed in the following terms:

'In most industries, firms recognise that their competitive stance – eg pricing and marketing decisions – affects the competitive stance of rival firms and is in turn affected by the competitive stance of these firms. Recognition of this competitive interdependence raises the question of whether firms will seek to reduce the vigour with which they compete with one another.'[4]

---

[1] Paragraphs 291 and 292. It is also recognised, in OFT *Market Investigation References*, that 'it may not always be clear whether a feature of a market that affects competition is structural or an aspect of conduct; for example, a firm's supply contracts or distribution arrangements may add to entry barriers in the market. However, the separate references to structure and conduct in [s 131] do not require the OFT to state whether particular features of a market that is the subject of a reference are to be considered structural features or some aspect of conduct' (para 1.9).

[2] Paragraph 295.

[3] OFT *Market Investigation References*, para 2.4. Information asymmetries were seen as a particular concern in *The Supply of Banking Services by Clearing Banks to Small and Medium Sized Enterprises within the UK* (March 2002), Cm 5319, and 'can restrict competition by adding to customers' switching costs' (*Market Investigation References*, para 5.22).

[4] Bishop, S and Walker, M *The Economics of EC Competition Law: Concepts, Application and Measurement* (London, Sweet & Maxwell, 1999), para 2.59.

In the case of *Airtours*,[1] the Court of First Instance dealt with the question of when the necessary factors might be in place in the case of the application of collective dominance to Art 82 EC and the EC Merger Regulation (see **3.29** and **3.39**). These factors are not binding on market investigations, as what is being established is a different matter, although the approach set out by the CC is very similar.[2] In reaching the conclusion that there is a detrimental effect on competition in the context of a market investigation, it is not necessary to show that there is a collective dominant position within the meaning of Art 82 EC.

4.68 It is a complicating feature of these markets that often:

> 'competition takes forms other than competition in price ... These forms of conduct are often pro-competitive but they may have effects which, especially when combined with other market features, blunt the competitive process, for example by adding to entry barriers.'[3]

4.69 To a limited extent, it is possible to develop a 'check-list' of when a situation of non-collusive oligopoly might be likely to arise. In its draft guidance, the OFT points to the following factors:

- the existence of substantial barriers to entry;
- the homogeneity of the firms' products;
- the similarity (symmetry) of the firms with respect to their market shares, their cost structures, the time horizons of their decisions and strategies;
- the stability of market conditions on both the demand and the cost sides;
- the degree of excess capacity;
- the extent to which prices, outputs and market shares are transparent;
- the structure of the buying side of the market (if the issue is possible co-ordination amongst sellers);
- the extent of any multi-market contacts.

At the same time, it must be noted that 'it is also quite possible for a market displaying many of these factors to be competitive'.[4]

4.70 Specific evidence that might be considered in this regard includes:

> '(a) the pattern of price changes over time, with a view to establishing the degree of parallelism in the face of any changes in demand or cost conditions, and whether the pattern seems more consistent with collusive than competitive behaviour;[1]

[1] *Airtours plc v Commission of the European Communities* Case T-342/99 [2002] 5 CMLR 317, [2002] UKCLR 642.

[2] CC *Market Investigation References*, paras 3.56–3.63. See also **3.39**.

[3] OFT *Market Investigation References*, para 6.5.

[4] Ibid, paras 5.6 and 5.7.

(b) price inertia, such as when sustained exchange rate advantages are not exploited by importers;

(c) any evidence that, notwithstanding evidence of parallelism in, say, published prices, the oligopolists compete in discounts or other concessions off the published price; and

(d) the oligopolists' rates of return compared to returns in comparable markets or to the cost of capital … however, where there is persistent excess capacity excessive prices may not be reflected in high rates of return.'[2]

4.71 The sorts of factors that might be considered to be 'conduct' resulting in detrimental effects could include, for example: the charging of excessive prices as the result of dampened competition;[3] restricting customer choice;[4] providing unfair terms to customers;[5] maintaining exclusionary distribution networks;[6] anti-competitive use of, or reliance on, intellectual property rights;[7]

---

[1] This was a factor analysed by the Commission and the ECJ in the case of *Re Wood Pulp Cartel: Re A Ahlstrom Oy v Commission* Cases C-89, 104, 116, 117 and 125–129/85 [1993] 4 CMLR 407. Here, the Court held that:

> 'In determining the probative value of those different factors, it must be noted that parallel conduct cannot be regarded as furnishing proof of concertation unless concertation constitutes the only plausible explanation for such conduct. It is necessary to bear in mind that, although Article 81 EC prohibits any form of collusion which distorts competition, it does not deprive economic operators of the right to adapt themselves intelligently to the existing and anticipated conduct of their competitors …
>
> Accordingly it is necessary in this case to ascertain whether the parallel conduct alleged by the Commission cannot, taking account of the nature of the products, the size and number of the undertakings and the volume of the market in question, be explained otherwise than by concertation' (paras 71–72, emphasis added).

In the context of market investigation references, this case is not binding on the CC, but it is illustrative of the difficulties that arise in attempting to prove collusive conduct.

[2] OFT *Market Investigation References*, para 6.7.

[3] As was suggested in *New Cars: A Report on the Supply of New Motor Cars within the UK* (April 2000), Cm 4660. Here, the CC held that 'the persistence of the price differences [shows] that the supposed EC single market is not working as such in the car sector and that the UK car market is not fully competitive' (para 2.230). A number of CC and MMC reports have been prompted by concerns regarding excessive prices but have found, after analysing profit levels, rates of return on capital, and other related factors, that prices were not in fact excessive. See, eg *The Supply of Petrol: A Report on the Supply in the United Kingdom of Petrol by Wholesale* (1990), Cm 972; *The Supply of Recorded Music: A Report on the Supply in the UK of Pre-recorded Compact Discs, Vinyl Discs and Tapes Containing Music* (1994), Cm 2599.

[4] Ibid.

[5] See *The Supply of Banking Services by Clearing Banks to Small and Medium Sized Enterprises within the UK* (March 2002), Cm 5319.

[6] See *The Supply of Impulse Ice Cream: A Report on the Supply of Ice Cream Purchased for Immediate Consumption* (January 2000), Cm 4510. The CC found that the arrangements made by BEW, relating to the use of freezers which prevented the use of the freezer to stock for sale other manufacturers' ice cream products, resulted in a reduction of choice (para 2.208). See also *The Supply of Cinema Advertising Services: A Report on the Supply in the United Kingdom of Cinema Advertising Services* (1990), Cm 1080.

[7] Note that this area is one which is particularly sensitive, and that it has recently been revisited by the Court of First Instance in the case of *IMS Health Inc v Commission* Case T-184/01R [2002] 4 CMLR 1. In the context of a scale monopoly inquiry, the MMC considered the issue in *Ford Motor Company Ltd: A Report on the Policy and Practice of the Ford Motor Company Ltd of Not Granting Licences to Manufacture or Sell in the United Kingdom Certain Replacement Body Parts for Ford Vehicles* (1985), Cmnd 9437.

refusals to supply;[1] and anti-competitive use of professional rules.[2] In some reports, the CC has considered a great range of conduct[3] and not of all it may be easily pigeon-holed. This is one reason why the time-limit allowed for the completion of market investigations is so long.

Indicators of the extent of competition

4.72   The CC will not always be able to determine that there is an adverse effect on competition, or a detrimental impact on customers, purely from an examination of the structure of the market and the conduct of firms on the market. As the CC notes: 'it will normally be helpful to the Commission's assessment to consider the effectiveness of competition by examining the outcome of the competitive process in the particular market'.[4]

4.73   Various factors may be examined in order to shed light on competitive outcomes. One is the extent to which prices change over time, and, in particular, how they change in response to changes in costs and demand. The CC may also look at international price comparisons (although this is not always straightforward), the rate of innovation, the product range, and product quality.

4.74   The CC may also have regard to profit levels of the firms in the market place, although this analysis is not without its problems. This issue is dealt with in paras 3.73–3.75 of the CC guideline:

> 'In some cases the level of profitability may be the only way to distinguish whether a pattern of similar prices across a market reflects intense competition or significantly co-ordinated behaviour. The Commission, therefore, will normally seek to identify profit levels, usually in terms of rates of return in the market or markets concerned, as a further indicator of competitive conditions. The Commission will normally seek to identify returns on the depreciated replacement cost of assets, unless there are specific reasons why this is inappropriate.

> Low profits, on the other hand, may conceal ineffective competition if firms with market power are able to operate with higher costs than would be sustainable with keener rivalry in the market. ...

---

[1]   An issue which can arise in a number of circumstances, including the operation of selective distribution systems, *Fine Fragrances: A Report on the Supply in the UK for Retail Sale of Fine Fragrances* (1993), Cm 2380.

[2]   In a number of reports into professional rules, including *Services of Professionally Regulated Osteopaths: A Report on the Supply of the Services of Professionally Regulated Osteopaths in Relation to Restrictions on Advertising* (1989), Cm 583. In its draft guidance, the OFT notes that 'Competition can also be affected by the rules emanating from systems of self-regulation, for example, those applicable to financial services and to a number of occupations and professions. In many cases this can be adequately addressed using CA 1998 or sector-specific legislation. Where it cannot the market affected might be suitable for a reference to the CC' (OFT *Market Investigation References*, para 5.20).

[3]   This was particularly evident in *The Supply of Banking Services by Clearing Banks to Small and Medium Sized Enterprises within the UK* (March 2002), Cm 5319, where the three-volume final report condemned a wide range of practices.

[4]   CC *Market Investigation References*, para 3.70.

In assessing levels of profitability the Commission will have regard to firms' cost of capital, where identifiable, though it would not normally expect to apply this as a rigid benchmark. Comparisons with businesses operating in different but similar markets may on occasions be helpful, but will be of limited usefulness unless the Commission can confirm the validity of the comparison and identify the competitive conditions in the other market.'

The duty to remedy adverse effects

4.75 A fundamental difference between the new market investigations regime and those of the FTA 1973 relates to the way in which any remedies are to be dealt with. Once a report has been published and an adverse effect on competition identified, s 138 of the Act creates an obligation on the CC to:

'take such action under section 159 or 161 as it considers to be reasonable and practicable –

(a) to remedy, mitigate or prevent the adverse effect on competition concerned; and

(b) to remedy, mitigate or prevent any detrimental effects on customers so far as they have resulted from, or may be expected to result from, the adverse effect on competition (s 138(2)).'

4.76 The approach to remedies in market investigation references may be different from the approach in relation to mergers. In the latter case, structural remedies are to be preferred wherever possible, while in the former, these may be inappropriate, and there may be a greater willingness to resort to behavioural remedies.

4.77 Sections 159 and 161 relate to final undertakings and final orders, and are discussed at **4.103** and **4.104**, respectively. Unless there has been a material change in the circumstances, the decisions taken in relation to remedying adverse effects are to be consistent with the arguments advanced in the report. The Commission is, in particular, required to 'have regard to the need to achieve as comprehensive a solution as is reasonable and practicable' (s 138(4)). It may further take into account, although it is not obliged to do so, 'the effect of any action on any relevant customer benefits of the feature or features of the market concerned' (s 138(5)). This, again, permits the Commission to undertake a balancing act, contrasting the detriments of the identified features of the market with any benefits that customers derive from those features.

4.78 Section 138(6), which is also mirrored in ss 147(6) and 154(5), is a little complicated. It provides that *no action* shall be taken in the circumstances set out there. In the *Explanatory Notes*, this is explained in the following way:

'where the CC has found that a detrimental effect on customers may be expected to result from a particular adverse effect on competition, but that no detrimental effect has yet resulted from that adverse effect, then the CC may only take action to remedy, mitigate or prevent the detrimental effect that may be expected to arise if it remedies, mitigates or prevents the adverse effect on competition.'[1]

In understanding this provision, it is necessary to remember that there may be more than one adverse effect on competition identified in a report, and not all of these may lead to a detrimental effect on customers. This section relates to situations in which it may be expected that the adverse effect on competition will lead to a detrimental effect on customers, but has not yet done so. This might be the case, for example, where the adverse effect on competition relates to the future development of the market, such as product innovation. In these cases, the CC (or the OFT, if it is considering accepting an undertaking in lieu of making a reference) may impose a remedy for the customer effect *only* if it simultaneously deals with the competition effect. It may be surmised that the intention behind this clause is to limit the power of the CC (or the OFT, as the case may be) to introduce remedies which are too deeply grounded in speculation as to how the market might develop in the future, rather than by reference to the situation already pertaining in the market. In essence, the *anticipated* customer detriment may be dealt with only by measures which simultaneously deal with the *current* adverse effect on competition.

4.79 The broader impact of the drawing of a distinction between the adverse effect on competition of the feature(s) of the market place, and the detrimental effect on customers, is that 'remedial action may deal with the cause of the problem or with its consequences'.[2]

4.80 The approach to be taken to remedial action is dealt with in Part 4 of the CC guidelines. Generally, it is unlikely that the CC, having identified an adverse effect on competition, would not impose a remedy. Exceptional circumstances where this might be the case, however, could include the situation where the costs of any practicable remedy outweighed the benefit, or where the remedy would need to be implemented outside the UK. It might also be the case that customer benefits arising from the feature or features of the market might mitigate against the imposition of penalties, although 'it would not normally be expected that market features that adversely affect

---

[1]   Paragraph 312.
[2]   CC *Market Investigation References*, para 4.6.

competition could have beneficial rather than detrimental effects on customers'.[1]

4.81 With the exception of the statutory limits, there are no restrictions on the remedies which the CC may seek to impose in market investigation reference cases. Remedies set out in the guidelines include: divestment; remedies designed to reduce barriers to entry; recommendations of changes to regulations; behavioural orders requiring firms, whether buyers or sellers, to cease certain activity; price-caps; and monitoring remedies (ie imposing a reporting requirement to provide the OFT with information on prices or profits, or conduct).

4.82 The CC may also recommend that action be taken by others. Typically, this would relate to situations in which regulations have been identified as giving rise to the harm. It has no power to compel such changes, but 'the government has given a commitment to consider any Commission recommendation and to give a public response within 90 days of publication of the Commission's report'.[2]

4.83 In deciding what remedies to implement, the situation is similar to that in relation to mergers, in that the CC will attempt to impose the remedy which most effectively addresses the problem, at the least possible cost. To this end, the CC will first look for a remedy which 'would be effective in dealing with the adverse effects on competition of the market features'.[3] What remedy will therefore be appropriate will depend on the nature of the adverse effect on competition. Where it is the conduct of firms that gives rise to the detriment, it is more likely that remedies will be behavioural rather than structural. Behavioural remedies, which are more likely to be used in market investigation references than in merger references:

> '… can take many forms but can have a number of shortcomings. They can involve detailed prescription of rules of conduct, for example relating to the terms of trade with customers and suppliers, though there may, in some cases, be a danger of restraining legitimate competitive behaviour and otherwise being overly intrusive. They can require detailed monitoring by the OFT or the sector regulator. Notwithstanding the ability to vary any remedy imposed, behavioural remedies can be difficult to keep in tune with

---

[1]   CC *Market Investigation References*, para 4.27. The CC has noted that 'it is not possible to give detailed guidance on particular benefits that may be relevant customer benefits in market investigations, as this will tend to reflect the characteristics of a particular market' (para 4.32). Examples of benefits that might arise include: economies of scale (where competitive pressure ensures that these are passed onto customers); innovation; regulations that are restrictive but that raise quality or competence; 'vertical integration and vertical agreements [that] can have beneficial effects through the better coordination of activities at different stages of the supply chain and savings in transactions and inventory costs … in a competitive market'; and tie-in sales or product bundling which is convenient to customers (see paras 4.33–4.38).

[2]   CC *Market Investigation References*, para 4.21.

[3]   Ibid, para 4.22.

developing market conditions. For example, cost or demand structures might be changed by technological developments with the consequence that the remedy might introduce its own distortions of competition. Nevertheless, behavioural remedies of one kind or another are a likely outcome of some market investigations.'[1]

PUBLIC INTEREST CASES

4.84   Both the OFT and the CC have a duty to bring to the attention of the Secretary of State any case which, in their opinion, raises public interest issues, as specified in the legislation. This is provided for in s 152. At the time of writing, the only such interest is that of national security (see **4.86**), and thus the OFT notes that it is unlikely that this provision will be invoked. No recent FTA 1973 monopoly inquiry has involved issues relating to public security. Nevertheless, these provisions attracted much attention during the debates on this Part of the Enterprise Bill.

4.85   In situations where the attention of the Secretary of State has been drawn to a public interest consideration, the Secretary of State has the power to intervene in the market investigation reference (s 139). Where a reference has already been made to the CC, the Secretary of State may issue a public interest notice where the reference has not been concluded, or where less than 4 months has elapsed since the date of the reference. Where the OFT is dealing with the matter, by way of considering whether to accept an undertaking in lieu of a reference, or whether to vary an undertaking already accepted, the Secretary of State may issue a notice to the OFT. Only one intervention notice may be given in the course of any market investigation reference.

4.86   A public interest consideration must be one which 'at the time of the giving of the intervention notice concerned, is specified in section 153 or is not so specified but, in the opinion of the Secretary of State, ought to be so specified' (s 139(5)). There is an obligation on the Secretary of State to finalise a public interest consideration which is not specified in s 153 as soon as is practicable if a notice is issued in relation to any consideration not set out in s 153. At the time of Royal Assent, 'national security' was the only public interest consideration specified in s 153. This has the same meaning as in Art 21(3) of the EC Merger Regulation. Unhelpfully, the term is not defined in

---

[1]   CC *Market Investigation References*, para 4.24.

that Regulation, and has a wide meaning, drawn in part from other provisions of the EC Treaty.[1]

4.87 Although s 153(3) gives the Secretary of State the power by Order to modify s 153(2), during the debates, the Government assured a seemingly sceptical opposition that there was no intention at the present time to use this power, and that this measure was designed expressly to 'deal solely with the unforeseeable'.[2] If Orders are made, they may be 'retrospective' in as much as they may relate to situations already under investigation by the OFT or the CC (s 153(4)).

Intervention notices and their effects

4.88 The requirements relating to intervention notices are set out in s 140. Once properly issued, notices come into force at the point when they are given, and cease to have effect at the time when the matter to which they relate is finally determined. The circumstances in which a final determination is considered to have been made are set out in s 140(5), and include the revocation of the notice by the Secretary of State, and the taking of final action in relation to it following the publication of the CC's report.

4.89 Where an intervention notice is in force, the CC is required to conduct its investigation and prepare its report in the same way as it would in relation to a 'competition only' reference (s 141), but it must decide questions in addition to those which must be determined under the 'competition only' reference. Section 147 gives the Secretary of State the power to take such action as may be necessary under ss 159 and 161 (which relate respectively to final undertakings and orders) in order to remedy the effects on competition and the detrimental effects on customers, as appropriate in the light of the eligible public interest consideration. The CC must, therefore, decide 'whether action should be taken by the Secretary of State under section 147' (s 141(3)). The CC is also to determine, on the assumption that the Secretary of State fails to make a relevant decision, or decides that no eligible public interest consideration is relevant, whether it should take action, as if the reference were a 'competition only' reference. In both cases, the CC is to approach the issue in the same way as required under s 138 (see **4.75**).

4.90 The requirements for the publication of the CC report where an intervention notice has been issued depend upon the conclusion reached in

---

[1]   See Arts 30, 46, 54 and 297, for example. For a discussion of the meaning of the term as it may be applied in the context of the EC Merger Regulation, see Cook, CJ and Kerse, CS *EC Merger Control* (London, Sweet & Maxwell, 2000, 3rd edn), at para 8.4.2.1.

[2]   *Hansard*, Standing Committee B, col 482.

relation to that reference. Where it is decided that there is no adverse effect on competition, or that there is an adverse effect or effects, but that no remedy should be imposed, the CC is to publish its own report. In these cases, there is no further role for the Secretary of State to play in the process.

4.91 In situations in which the CC has determined that there is an adverse effect or effects on competition, and that remedies would be appropriate, the report is to be passed on to the Secretary of State in order to enable him to consider the impact on relevant public interest considerations of the remedies suggested to the adverse effect on competition. It is then for the Secretary of State to publish the report no later than the publication of any decision made under s 146(2) (see **4.94**).

4.92 The time-limits in relation to investigations and the making of reports where a public interest intervention notice has been served are broadly the same as for 'competition only' references. The CC has two years from the making of the reference in order to prepare its report (s 144(1)). As under s 137, the Secretary of State may amend this period, but cannot increase it. However, where an intervention notice is subsequently revoked, or where an investigation is terminated because the Secretary of State has relied on a public interest consideration which is not set out in s 153, and which is not added to it within the relevant time period, the CC has an additional 20 days in which to prepare its report (s 151). Section 151, in effect, ensures that any market investigation reference may, at any one time, be considered *only* as a 'competition only' reference, or as a 'public interest' reference.

4.93 Where the Secretary of State makes an intervention notice in relation to a public interest consideration which is not finalised (ie has not been added to the list in s 153 by virtue of an Order approved by Parliament), the CC is not to make its report until after that matter has been finalised (s 145). If the consideration is not finalised within 24 weeks, the CC may give its report as if the intervention notice had not been made. Because the Secretary of State is required to give an intervention notice within four months of the making of the reference, the effect of this provision is not such as to increase the period of two years within which the report must be made.

The decision of the Secretary of State

4.94 Once a report of the CC has been given to the Secretary of State, a 90-day period is allowed for the Secretary of State to publish his decision in relation to the matters raised. If no decision is made within that time, the matter reverts to the CC, and it may then implement the remedies that it has proposed in the report. The Secretary of State is required to determine whether 'any eligible public interest consideration is relevant ... to any action which is mentioned in the report … and which the Commission should take for the purpose of remedying, mitigating or preventing the adverse effect on competition' (s 146(2)).

4.95 Once the Secretary of State has determined that there is a relevant public interest consideration, he may take such action under s 159 or s 161 as is considered to be 'reasonable and practicable' to remedy or mitigate the adverse effect (the criteria here are the same as for the CC in determining a competition only reference – see **4.38**). The Secretary of State is bound by the decision of the CC as to the adverse effect on competition (s 147(4)), and s 147(6) is in the same terms as ss 138(6) and 154(5) (see **4.78**).

4.96 If the matter reverts to the CC due to the failure of the Secretary of State to make a decision, the procedure, in effect, is the same as that in the case of a 'competition only' reference. However, if the CC decides to proceed in a way which is not consistent with its decisions as included in its report, it shall not do so without the consent of the Secretary of State (s 148(7)). This consent shall not be withheld unless the Secretary of State 'believes that the proposed alternative way of proceeding will operate against the public interest' (s 148(8)).

Intervention notices and undertakings in lieu of references

4.97 Where the Secretary of State makes an intervention notice in respect of a case in which the OFT is considering accepting an undertaking in lieu of a reference, and has published a notice to that effect, the impact is to give the Secretary of State the right to veto the proposed undertaking (s 150). The approval of the Secretary of State will be withheld in situations in which 'he believes that it is or may be the case that the proposed undertaking will, if accepted, operate against the public interest' (s 150(2)). An undertaking will operate against the public interest only in situations in which the public interest consideration outweighs the consideration which has led the OFT to propose the acceptance of the undertaking.

PROCEDURES

Undertakings and orders

4.98 Undertakings are voluntarily accepted commitments entered into by the relevant party or parties. Once they are agreed, however, they become legally binding, and are enforceable in the courts. Orders are made by the relevant authorities, and may be both proscriptive (which has been the usual case in the past), and prescriptive in nature. The CC, but not the OFT, is given the power in the Act to make Orders on its own initiative, whereas under the FTA 1973, Orders could be made only in Parliament by way of statutory instrument.

Undertakings in lieu of references

4.99 The ability of the OFT to accept undertakings in lieu of making references has already been considered at **4.32–4.37**. Once such an undertaking has been accepted, neither the OFT nor any relevant Minister will be able to make a reference in relation to that market within a period of 12 months. This restriction does not apply in situations in which the OFT considers that the undertaking has been breached or, in the view of the OFT, needs to be varied or superseded and notice has been given to the relevant parties, or where the person giving the undertaking supplied information relating to it to the OFT which was false or misleading in a material respect (s 156(2)(b)).

Interim undertakings and orders

4.100 An interim undertaking may be sought only in situations in which a report relating to a market investigation reference has been published, but the reference has not yet been finally determined. Interim undertakings may be accepted 'for the purpose of preventing pre-emptive action'.[1] Once accepted, such undertakings may be varied or superseded by another undertaking, or may be released by the relevant authority (s 156). Any undertaking made under this section will automatically cease to have effect at such time as the reference is finally determined. The powers in this respect will be exercised either by the CC, or, in the case where a public interest notice is in force, the Secretary of State.

4.101 Interim orders may be made in similar circumstances, in order to:

'(a) prohibit or restrict the doing of things which the relevant authority considers would constitute pre-emptive action;

(b) impose on any person concerned obligations as to the carrying on of any activities or the safeguarding of any assets;

(c) provide for the carrying on of any activities or the safeguarding of any assets either by the appointment of a person to conduct or supervise the conduct of any activities (on such times and with such powers as may be specified or described in the order) or in any other manner;

(d) do anything which may be done by virtue of paragraph 19 of Schedule 8).'[2]

---

[1] Pre-emptive action is defined in s 157(6) as meaning 'action which might impede the taking of any action under section 138(2) or (as the case may be) 147(2) in relation to the market investigation reference concerned'.

[2] Section 158(2).

This provision is based on FTA 1973, s 89.

4.102 Where any representation is made to the relevant authority relating to the variation or revocation of any interim undertaking or order, the authority is under an obligation to consider that representation as quickly as possible.

Final undertakings and orders

4.103 The CC and the Secretary of State (in the case where a public intervention notice is in place) have the power to accept final undertakings (s 159). The basis for these is that they may be employed in order to remedy the adverse effects identified in the reports, in accordance with ss 138 (see **4.75**) and 147 (see **4.89**). Undertakings may be released by the CC or the Secretary of State, as appropriate, and may be varied or superseded by another undertaking made under the same authority.[1]

4.104 Where an undertaking made under s 159 is not, or is not considered likely to be, fulfilled, the CC or the Secretary of State may make an order containing anything permitted by Sch 8. The provisions in this respect are the same as those for undertakings, save that an order may only be varied or revoked where the OFT advises that this would be appropriate by reason of a change in circumstances. The same is true of the final orders that may be made by the CC or the Secretary of State containing anything permitted by Sch 8, or any closely related remedy.

Enforcement of undertakings and orders

4.105 The OFT has the lead role in the monitoring and enforcement of orders and undertakings. While the CC (or the Secretary of State, as the case may be) is in the best position to determine and craft the appropriate remedies following the making of the report, the OFT is better placed to monitor the application of these remedies in practice, following through from its general remit of keeping markets under inspection. In situations in which the OFT determines that it is appropriate that an undertaking or order be revoked or varied, it will advise the CC or the Secretary of State accordingly (s 162(3)). Where it determines that an order or undertaking is not being complied with, it may take such action as it considers appropriate, including the initiation of court action against the offending company. Thus, s 167(6) provides that compliance shall be enforceable by civil proceedings brought by the OFT for an injunction, or for interdict, or for any other appropriate remedy or relief.

---

[1] This provision is based on that found in FTA 1973, s 88.

4.106 Third parties also have the right, in certain circumstances, to take action in respect of the breach of undertakings and orders. By virtue of s 167(2), 'any person to whom such an undertaking or order relates shall have a duty to comply with it'. This duty is owed to any person who may be affected by a contravention of the undertaking or order, and any breach 'which causes such a person to sustain loss or damage shall be actionable by him' (s 167(4)). It is a defence for the party allegedly in breach of the undertaking or order to 'show that he took all reasonable steps and exercised all due diligence to avoid contravening the undertaking or (as the case may be) order' (s 167(5)).

Investigations

4.107 The Act gives the OFT and the CC the powers that are necessary in order for investigations in respect of market investigation references to be carried out.

4.108 In the case of the OFT, these powers are set out in s 174, and are exactly the same as those of the CC. It is therefore unlikely, in practice, that the OFT will exercise these powers to the full permitted extent. Neither body has the power to launch dawn raids, and to use the full panoply of investigative powers that are available under the CA 1998. An important power is that of s 174(3), under which:

> 'The OFT may give notice to any person requiring him –
>
> (a)   to attend at a time and place specified in the notice; and
> (b)   to give evidence to the OFT or a person nominated by the OFT for the purpose.'

4.109 The OFT may require any person who carries on business to provide estimates, forecasts, returns, or other specified information (s 174(5)). Information may not be compelled if it is subject to legal privilege (s 174(8)). [1]

4.110 These powers may be used only in situations in which the OFT believes that it has the power to make a market investigation reference. This is to say that the threshold for the exercise of formal investigative powers under s 174 is precisely the same as the threshold for the making of a market investigation reference. It is for this reason that the OFT has noted that 'there will be occasions when the OFT will decide not to use its powers and to move to a reference immediately'. [2] In other cases, however, there will be situations in which 'the OFT will decide that it needs to investigate a market further before

---

[1]   A power to take information under oath was withdrawn in the House of Lords.
[2]   OFT *Market Investigation References*, para 3.1.

making a reference, for example in order to be clearer about the appropriateness of a reference'.[1]

4.111 It is an offence if a person fails to comply, without reasonable excuse, with the requirements of s 174 (s 175).

4.112 Information obtained by the OFT in the course of an investigation under the CA 1998 may be used for the purpose of market investigation references, and vice versa.

Offences

4.113 The Act creates a number of specific offences relating to market investigation references. By virtue of s 180, ss 117 and 125, relating to the provision of false and misleading information, and offences committed by bodies corporate, apply to this area (see **3.6** and **3.11**).

Consultation, information and publicity

4.114 Sections 169–173 relate to general duties to consult with relevant parties, to provide and exchange information, and to provide publicity about market investigation references generally, and specific decisions.

4.115 Any relevant authority contemplating making a decision which 'is likely to have a substantial impact on the interests of any person' is required, so far as is practicable, to 'consult that person about what is proposed before making that decision' (s 169). This does not apply in situations in which there is already a specific obligation of consultation imposed in the Act.

4.116 The purpose of s 170, relating to general information duties, is 'to ensure that in relation to market investigations, the OFT, the CC and the Secretary of State are able to obtain such information and assistance as they need from each other'.[2]

4.117 Section 171 obliges the OFT and the CC to publish certain guidance and information relating to the application of this Part of the Act. The relevant guidance, in its draft form, has been heavily quoted from in this chapter.

4.118 Specific publicity requirements in relation to particular decisions or stages of the market investigation procedures are set out in s 172.

---

[1]   Ibid.
[2]   *Explanatory Notes*, para 165.

CONCURRENCY

4.119 As noted above, amendments are made to sector-specific legislation, enabling relevant sectoral regulators to make market investigation references. In addition, there are obligations of both consultation, and consideration of the role of market regulators by the OFT and the CC.

4.120 Where both the OFT and a sector regulator are contemplating making a reference, they are compelled to consult with each other. The OFT has indicated that:

> 'As a matter of practice where a market investigation reference is appropriate for goods or services which are unambiguously part of a regulated industry, and are the subject of concurrent powers, the reference would normally be made by the regulator. In ambiguous cases it would be made by whichever authority is better placed to do so. The factors to be considered in determining which authority deals with the matter include the extent to which sectoral knowledge is relevant and recent experience of dealing with the markets concerned.'[1]

4.121 The regulators have a role which is based in securing the optimum competition in the industries for which they have responsibility, but which also goes wider than this. This issue is dealt with in the *Explanatory Notes*:

> 'In regulated markets, regulators have a statutory set of objectives that go beyond preventing adverse effects on competition. These objectives are also reflected in the terms and conditions of, for example, the licences under which firms operate in such markets. Whilst the regulators have a duty to promote competition, they have other duties that go further than competition. These duties may have higher priority than the duty to promote competition (eg The Postal Services Commission (POSTCOMM) has an overriding duty to ensure a universal postal service). Therefore, when the CC propose remedies that involve changes to licence conditions, networking arrangements, conditions attached to permissions of airports, rail franchise agreements or access agreements or conditions of appointment in the water sector (ie 'relevant action') the CC should have regard to the regulators' duties.'[2]

This obligation is enshrined in s 168, which requires the Commission (or the Secretary of State in the appropriate circumstances) 'in deciding whether such action would be reasonable and practicable, [to] have regard to the relevant statutory functions of the sectoral regulator concerned'.

---

[1] OFT *Market Investigation References*, para 3.15. Under the CA 1998 regime, the relevant technical guideline is 'Concurrent Application to Regulated Industries' [2000] UKCLR 153, and rules governing the allocation of cases are set out in the Competition Act 1998 (Concurrency) Regulations 2000, SI 2000/261.

[2] Paragraph 364.

4.122 *Figure 2 – Typical Shape of a Market Investigation*

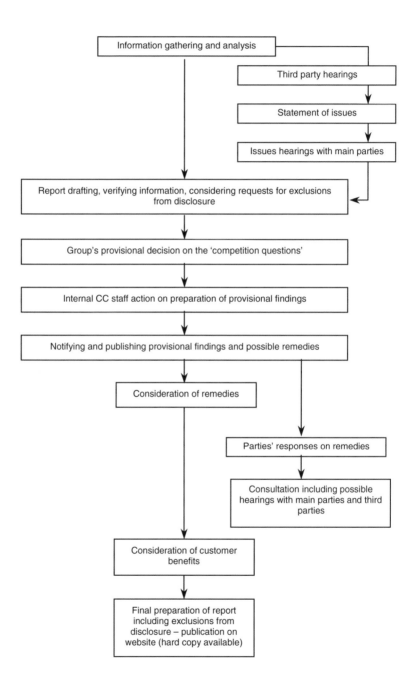

Chapter Five

CARTEL OFFENCES

INTRODUCTION

5.1   The introduction in the Act of a stand-alone criminal offence relating to the pursuit of certain cartel conduct – described by the Opposition as 'great for a headline but not much else'[1] – is a radical departure for competition law in the UK, and it is no surprise that significant opposition to these provisions was expressed during the passage of the Act.[2] It should be noted at the outset that the new offence is *not* related to breaches of the CA 1998, or to other parts of the Act. Likewise, under the EC regime, no criminal sanctions are available in respect of anti-competitive conduct, and it is several hundred years since they were available in the UK.[3] The need to re-introduce such a power into the UK regime was argued for by Margaret Bloom in May 2002:

> 'Are these new powers necessary? Will they be used? The short answer is "Yes". We are uncovering around one cartel a month. We are now uncovering more serious ones. This activity is equivalent to theft. It has no redeeming features. Effective deterrence is very important. However, we will select carefully the cartels for criminal prosecutions, concentrating on the serious ones. We expect that there will be a relatively small number of prosecutions – but they will have a significant deterrent effect. The first prosecutions will reach the courts in a few years.'[4]

---

[1]   Mr Waterson, *Hansard*, 17 June 2002, col 112.

[2]   There have also been a number of articles published on the proposals early on in the process. See, for example, Cutting, M 'Reforming Competition Law' (2001) NLJ 996; and Finfer, A 'That Early-morning Knock may not be the Postman' (2002) *The Times*, 1 October, Supplement, p 9. For a retrospective analysis of the work of the Office of Fair Trading (OFT), see Israel, M 'Cartel Enforcement: How is the OFT Doing?' [2002] Comp Law 237.

[3]   In legislation enacted in the reign of Edward VI, for example 2 Edw 6, c 15, it was provided that a person in breach of certain monopolies laws 'shall forfeit for the first offence Ten pound ... or twenty days imprisonment and shall have only bread and water for his sustenance.' On the second occasion of an offence, a fine of £20 was to be paid or the offender was to be pilloried. On the third occasion, the fine was to be £40, or 'the offender shall sit in the pillory and lose one of his ears, and also shall at all times after that be taken as a man infamous'. It is perhaps to be regretted that this Act was repealed in 1772.

[4]   'Key Challenges in Public Enforcement: A Speech to the British Institute of International and Comparative Law', 17 May 2002, OFT website.

5.2　　In May 2001, a joint Treasury/Department of Trade and Industry (DTI) report into UK productivity and competition argued, *inter alia*, that:

> 'Although the Competition Act 1998 strengthens the deterrent effect against anti-competitive behaviour, the project team is concerned that it may not go far enough. In particular, the penalties for engaging in cartels may not be enough to deter such action.
>
> The project team concludes that American, and other experience suggests that there is a strong case for introducing criminal penalties, including custodial sentences, for those who engage in cartels alongside a new civil sanction of director's disqualification.'[1]

The evidence from America suggests that gaol terms are an effective deterrent. It has been noted that 'corporate officials … belong to a social group that is exquisitely sensitive to status deprivation and censure'.[2] As one American antitrust attorney has put it, the threat of imprisonment in 'real-life federal penitentiaries, with real-life federal convicts'[3] is itself real and plays a significant role in the dynamics of anti-trust investigations.[4] It has been pointed out that, although the Office of Fair Trading (OFT) has stressed the importance of taking action against cartels, it has, at the time of writing, taken only one decision and, in that case, the fine imposed was small when compared to similar enforcement activity in the EC.[5]

5.3　　In the White Paper, it was proposed that criminal penalties should attach to hard-core cartel conduct, with the DTI arguing that:

> '… if fines are to deter firms and their executives effectively, they need to be set at a level which is greater than the expected gains from participating in a cartel.
>
> US evidence shows that cartels often raise prices by around 10%. Increasing prices will have some dampening effect on demand, so a cartelist might increase its profits by a smaller proportion. Conservatively they might do so by around 5%. If the cartel operates for six years (as the average US cartel is thought to do), then the total benefit might be 30% of annual turnover.
>
> The Competition Act 1998 allows fines to be imposed at this level – up to 10% of annual turnover in the relevant market for a maximum of three years. But not all cartels will be caught. In the US, estimates suggest that only a sixth of cartels are detected.

---

[1]　　Quoted in OFT *Proposed Criminalisation of Cartels in the UK* (November 2001), [2002] UKCLR 97, at para 1.3.

[2]　　Geis 'Deterring Corporate Crime' in Ermann, MD and Lundman, RJ (eds) *Corporate and Governmental Deviance: Problems of Organizational Behaviour in Contemporary Society* (Oxford, OUP, 1978), p 278.

[3]　　Unpublished interview, research by the author.

[4]　　Note, however, that it has been argued that the most efficient deterrent is that of very high levels of compensation, or damages, which impose least cost on the public purse: Elzinga, KG and Breit, W *The Antitrust Penalties* (New Haven, Yale UP, 1976). On the other hand, a representative of the US Attorney General has argued that 'I have had numerous lawyers pleading with me to avoid a gaol term for their client and offering to pay any sum imaginable. I have never had anyone offering to spend another week in gaol in return for a lower fine' (quoted in *Hansard*, 2 July 2002, col 157).

[5]　　Israel, M 'Cartel Enforcement: How is the OFT Doing?' [2002] Comp Law 237. The author argues that the OFT target of completing 75% of cases within 12 months of the start of an investigation is ambitious – noting that, in the EC, a time period of 3 years is more standard.

The expected fine for the would-be cartelist is the probability of being caught multiplied by the likely fine (ie a sixth of 30%), around 5% of annual turnover.

Faced with the likely benefits arising from engaging in a cartel, the expected fine is unlikely to act as a meaningful deterrent.'[1]

5.4 Following the DTI proposal, the OFT commissioned a report to investigate the issue. The final report, *Proposed Criminalisation of Cartels in the UK*, was published in November 2001.[2] The authors made a number of recommendations, which are summarised here.

5.5 In relation to the specifics of the offence that should be created, it was suggested that this should:

'... *not* be directly linked to either Article 81 EC or Chapter I of the Competition Act 1998 and should cover more limited ground. This should facilitate distancing the offence from possible defence arguments that the agreement in question might reasonably have been considered to have potentially benefited from an exemption under Article 81(3) EC or sections 4, 6 or 10 of the Competition Act 1998; but it will never be possible completely to preclude such arguments.

(A) We recommend instead that the definition should incorporate the concept of individuals *dishonestly* entering into agreements with each other in order to implement 'hard core' cartel arrangements. We consider that courts would be more likely to convict on the basis of arguments incorporating the concept of dishonesty than would be the case if they had to consider the complex economic arguments that would normally accompany considerations of possible infringements of Article 81 EC or Chapter I of the Competition Act 1998. Furthermore, we consider that the courts are more likely to impose custodial sentences in respect of an offence that is based on the concept of individuals having engaged in dishonest conduct.

The recommended form of definition should also be much easier to frame in terms that are sufficiently clearly defined as to satisfy the requirements of Article 7, ECHR.

We understand that the view of those who are experts in the field of competition law is that the criminal offence should only be applicable to *horizontal* agreements between individuals representing 'competing' undertakings operating at the same level of the supply-chain for the purposes of the agreement in question. It should not apply to vertical agreements, many of which are considered to have pro-competitive or other beneficial effects and consequently are currently excluded from the application of Chapter I of the Competition Act 1998 or alternatively benefit from exemptions under European competition law.'[3]

5.6 In relation to the prosecution process, it was recommended that:

'... the Serious Fraud Office (SFO) should be the lead prosecutor. The SFO has an existing infrastructure and expertise in prosecuting criminal cases of this type whilst the OFT would have to build a prosecution team from scratch and, given the anticipation of a relatively small case-load, we believe that it would not be cost-effective to conduct

---

[1]   Box 7.3.

[2]   [2002] UKCLR 97.

[3]   OFT *Proposed Criminalisation of Cartels in the UK* (November 2001), [2002] UKCLR 97, paras 1.9–1.12.

prosecutions in-house. Additionally, under the circumstances, we consider that the OFT would find it difficult to recruit prosecutors with the requisite skills. Confidence in the efficacy and the fairness in the criminal procedures would be enhanced by giving the conduct of the cases to an independent prosecutor with an established reputation. The SFO's recognised expertise in dealing with serious fraud sits well with the prosecution of hard core cartels.'[1]

5.7   Recommendations were also made relating to the investigation process:

'*(C) We recommend* that criminal investigations should be undertaken by the OFT's existing Investigations Branch under the guidance and direction of an SFO case controller who would be experienced in criminal law. We consider that the specific knowledge of economics and the law relating to cartels possessed by the OFT's investigators will form an integral part of an SFO multi-disciplinary investigative team. The OFT investigators will need to receive training in criminal investigation procedures and familiarise themselves with the appropriate provisions of the Police and Criminal Evidence Act 1984 (PACE). We consider that such training could most appropriately be provided by organisations who currently provide such services to bodies such as HM Customs and Excise and Inland Revenue who already have expertise in the field of criminal investigation.

(E and F) We recommend that appropriate arrangements are made to allow the OFT investigators to utilise the provisions of the Regulation of Investigatory Powers Act 2000 relating to: a) the use of directed surveillance b) the use of covert human intelligence services (CHIS) and c) the acquisition and disclosure of communications data. We further consider that arrangements should be put in place to allow the OFT investigators access to the interception of communications and intrusive surveillance.'[2]

5.8   There was substantial discussion of the interplay between civil and criminal enforcement, with the report's authors concluding that:

'... it should be possible to operate a criminal investigation and prosecution regime applicable to *individuals* participating in cartels in *parallel* with a civil investigation and prosecution regime applicable to *undertakings* engaged in cartel activity; although to do so will not be without certain difficulties.'[3]

It was recommended that documentary evidence obtained in the course of a civil investigation should be able to be relied on in the course of a criminal investigation if the decision was taken to transfer a civil investigation to a criminal one. On the other hand, it was not suggested that it would be possible in all cases to use evidence obtained in a criminal investigation in the course of a civil proceeding if the decision was taken to transfer the case from a criminal one into a civil one. It was noted that the more intrusive powers used in the course of a criminal investigation 'would have been granted specifically for the purposes of investigating suspected criminal offences'.[4] On the other hand, where:

---

[1]   OFT *Proposed Criminalisation of Cartels in the UK* (November 2001), [2002] UKCLR 97, para 1.13.

[2]   Ibid, paras 1.14 and 1.15.

[3]   Ibid, para 1.17.

[4]   Ibid, para 1.18.

'evidence obtained from the use of intrusive surveillance was already in the public domain for the purpose of criminal proceedings, we anticipate that it would be possible to utilise the product of such surveillance in any related civil proceedings without it being considered that the OFT had abused its powers.'[1]

5.9   It was recommended that the criminal sanctions should be applicable exclusively to individuals, and not to undertakings, which would continue to be subject to the civil sanctions provided for in the CA 1998.

5.10   Although it was anticipated that the majority of cartel cases pursued by the OFT would be tackled under the existing civil regime only, it was recommended that:

'those cases which potentially might result in the implementation of criminal proceedings should be pursued to criminal standards of evidence gathering from the outset.'[2]

Further, it was suggested that:

'criminal proceedings against individuals should *precede* civil proceedings against undertakings whenever possible (although we recognise this might not be possible in civil proceedings brought by the EC following its own investigations) in order that any publicity given to the civil proceedings will not prejudice individuals subject to the related criminal proceedings receiving a fair trial.'[3]

5.11   In relation to the prior finding of breaches of the Chapter I Prohibition, scepticism was expressed as to the evidential use of such a finding:

'We do not consider that a prior finding that an *undertaking* had infringed Chapter I would be of much evidential value in subsequent criminal proceedings against the participating *individuals* since the undertaking's participation in the infringement would only have been proved to a *civil* law standard of evidence and it would require to be re-proved to criminal standards.'[4]

5.12   In relation to the penalties that should be available to the enforcers, the report made the following points:

'7.1   We have approached the issue of the appropriate maximum sentence for the new cartels offence against the background that, in section 7 of the White Paper, the Government have said that "hard core cartels are serious conspiracies which defraud business customers and consumers and have wide economic impacts" and "The offence merits a strong sentence".

[1]   OFT *Proposed Criminalisation of Cartels in the UK* (November 2001), [2002] UKCLR 97, para 1.18.
[2]   Ibid, para 1.20.
[3]   Ibid.
[4]   Note, however, the discussion of the burden of proof and the civil law standard by the CCAT in the case of *Napp*, in which it was held that the standard of proof is that of civil cases, but within such civil cases, the more serious the consequence of infringement, the more serious a standard of proof may be required: 'Strong and convincing evidence will be required before infringements of the Chapter I and Chapter II Prohibitions can be found to be proved, even to the "civil standard"' (ibid, para 108). There is an obligation on the DGFT to provide 'strong and compelling evidence ... the undertaking being entitled to the presumption of innocence, and to any reasonable doubt there may be' (ibid, para 109) (*Napp Pharmaceutical Holdings Ltd and Subsidiaries v The Director General of Fair Trading* [2002] CompAR 13).

In considering what should be an appropriate maximum sentence, we have considered the following issues:

- The level of maximum sentences for comparable offences, for example, offences of "insider dealing" and "obtaining property by deception";
- Comparable offences in Canada and Japan carry a maximum sentence of five years and the Republic of Ireland is proposing to increase the maximum for its cartel offence from two to five years;
- The need to have available the powers associated with an arrestable offence as defined in PACE, which requires a maximum sentence of at least five years; and
- The desirability of sending a strong signal to the courts that hard core cartels are very serious offences, which can have important and deleterious economic consequences.

7.2   It will be for the Government to weigh the factors mentioned in paragraph 7.1 and to come to a view on the appropriate level of penalty. We are aware, that in the USA, the maximum sentence available for this type of offence is three years, although related factors can lead to the maximum being increased. In the light of the considerations mentioned above, however, our view is that *(K) this offence merits a maximum penalty of at least five years imprisonment and we so recommend.* We believe that there is a case for imposing a higher maximum penalty of, say, seven years, but we do not make a recommendation on this point. It will, of course, be the case that, in reality, a wide range of penalties are likely to be imposed in individual cases depending on the circumstances, amongst which are:

- The *gravity* and nature of the offence.
- The *duration* of the offence.
- The degree of culpability of the defendant in *implementing* the cartel agreement.
- The degree of culpability of the defendant in *enforcing* the cartel agreement.
- Whether the defendant's conduct was contrary to guidelines laid down in a company *compliance* programme.
- *Mitigating* factors eg any *co-operation* the defendant may have provided in respect of the enquiry; whether or not the defendant was compelled to participate in the cartel under *duress*; whether the offence was a first offence; and any personal circumstances of the defendant which the courts may regard as a factor suggesting leniency.

7.3   We have already pointed out in paragraph 7.1 above that the availability of a sentence of at least five years is required to meet the definition of an arrestable offence as defined in PACE. Certain other powers, such as the intrusive surveillance powers in RIPA [Regulation of Investigatory Powers Act 2000], should be available for cartel offences since they would meet the test in RIPA that their consequences might be either substantial financial gain or serious financial loss to any person and are thus within the definition of "serious arrestable offences".'[1]

5.13   There was also some discussion as to whether it would be appropriate to include a provision allowing for a financial penalty as an alternative to imprisonment. In this respect, the OFT report recommended that:

'the courts should have the power to impose an unlimited fine either in addition to, or instead of, a custodial sentence, on conviction of a cartel offence. We recognise that the objective of criminalising cartels might be diluted if the courts were encouraged to impose fines on

---

[1]   OFT *Proposed Criminalisation of Cartels in the UK* (November 2001), [2002] UKCLR 97, paras 7.1–7.3.

individuals who have participated in cartels rather than to impose custodial sentences on them, particularly if these individuals are, in effect, indemnified by the payment of the fines on their behalf by the undertakings which employ them. Indeed, it is stated in section 7.36 of the White Paper that:

> "The Government is concerned to avoid the possibility of individual fines being paid by employers (who are the main beneficiaries of the cartel) and for this reason does not propose fines as an alternative sanction to a custodial sentence."

7.5   Although the Government's concern is understandable, it would be most unusual to have any offence that was only subject to the imposition of custodial sentences. More importantly, there might be mitigating circumstances of the kind set in paragraph 7.2, which could merit the imposition of a fine, but for which the imposition of a custodial sentence might be considered to be disproportionate. In such circumstances, the absence of a power to fine as an alternative to imprisonment could be counter-productive. It could have the effect that, in certain circumstances, a suspended sentence or conditional discharge rather than an immediate custodial sentence might be imposed whereas the conduct of the defendant might merit the imposition of a substantial financial penalty.'

5.14   The Government, in November 2001, announced its intention to bring into the Enterprise Act 2002 clauses which would make provision for a cartel offence. Under these proposals, the definition of the offence would be one based on parties dishonestly entering into certain horizontal arrangements. The investigations would be carried out by the OFT, acting under the leadership of a case controller from within the SFO. Where a case proceeded to prosecution, the SFO would be the lead prosecutor, although the OFT would be able to issue 'no-action' letters in certain circumstances to protect parties from criminal prosecution. The offence would be triable either way,[1] with the maximum penalty being one of five years' imprisonment, with fines to be available either in addition or in the alternative.

5.15   These proposals were largely adopted in the published Enterprise Bill, which, in Part 6, makes provision for the 'cartel offence'. Although, at 15 sections, this is one of the shortest Parts of the Act, it is likely to be the one that attracts most attention, at least in the popular media.

The offence

5.16   Section 188 provides, therefore, that a person is guilty of a cartel offence if he 'dishonestly agrees with one or more other persons to make or implement, or cause to be made or implemented, arrangements of the following kind relating to at least two undertakings' (s 188(1)). The test for dishonesty in England, Wales and Northern Ireland is the well-established *Ghosh* test.[2] The jury is to determine whether the act done would, according to

---

[1]   Ie in either the magistrates' courts or the Crown Courts.

[2]   Set out in *R v Ghosh* [1982] QB 1053, [1982] 2 All ER 689, CA.

the standards of reasonable people, be considered to be dishonest, and also whether the defendant would have realised that this was the view of reasonable people. If the answer to both questions is in the affirmative, beyond any reasonable doubt, then dishonesty is established. The OFT has indicated the extent of this test in its draft guidance relating to 'no-action letters':

> 'Managers or directors who become aware of the existence of a cartel and then take steps to end it and report its existence to the OFT cannot be said to have behaved dishonestly.
>
> Similarly, an employee who becomes aware of the existence of a cartel and, although not involved in its operation, does nothing to end it is not guilty of a criminal offence.'

5.17 The purpose of basing the offence on the standard of 'dishonest' conduct was to define it tightly, although it was suggested in the debates on the passage of the Act that the definition was anything but tight. However, it was pointed out in Committee that an opposition amendment to replace 'dishonestly' with 'knowingly or recklessly' would have significantly *expanded* the scope of the offence. According to the Under-Secretary of State, the:

> 'sort of evidence that would point to dishonesty is likely to include a failure to seek legal advice, combined with attempts to disguise or hide activity. For example, holding secret meetings and the absence or destruction of records, and other such practices, would be instances of such evidence.'[1]

5.18 It will be noted that it is an offence to 'make' any of the arrangements subsequently referred to. It is not necessary, therefore, for the arrangement to be implemented. However, in relation to arrangements entered into outside the UK, it is necessary that the arrangement be implemented in the UK (see **5.26**). It should be noted further that the inchoate offences of conspiracy and attempt apply under the Criminal Law Act 1977 and the Criminal Attempts Act 1981 automatically to the cartel offence.

5.19 The arrangements referred to in s 188(1) are set out in s 188(2), and are all horizontal arrangements relating to price fixing, the limitation of production or supply, the sharing of markets, and bid-rigging. As noted in the *Explanatory Notes*, these are 'a sub-set of the practices for which undertakings may be pursued under the civil provisions of the CA 1998'. Formally, these are arrangements which:

> '(a) directly or indirectly fix a price for the supply by A in the United Kingdom (otherwise than to B) of a product or service,
>
> (b) limit or prevent supply by A in the United Kingdom of a product or service,
>
> (c) limit or prevent production by A in the United Kingdom of a product,
>
> (d) divide between A and B the supply in the United Kingdom of a product or service to a customer or customers,

---

[1]   *Hansard*, Standing Committee B, col 136.

(e)   divide between A and B customers for the supply in the United Kingdom of a product or service, or

(f)   be bid-rigging arrangements.'

It is further provided in s 188(3) that in the case of s 188(2)(a), (b), and (c), B (as referred to above) must also be engaged in the practice in as much that its price, supply or production must also be fixed, which is to say that the arrangement must be a reciprocal one. There will be no criminal offence in situations in which only one party agrees to limit its conduct. A difficulty that might arise in relation to this test could be that of the situation where A agrees to limit its conduct at one point in time in response to an unwritten commitment from B to limit its conduct in some respect in the future. Such an arrangement could be difficult to prove. It would be a criminal offence for A to fix its price, and B to limit its supply, the effect of which might be the same as if both parties agreed to limit supplies.

5.20   Bid-rigging arrangements are defined in s 188(5) as being those under which, in relation to a request for bids in relation to the supply of a product or service in the UK, or for the production of a product in the UK, either A or B will not make a bid, or both parties will make a bid, but one arrived at in accordance with 'the arrangements'. Arrangements will not be bid-rigging arrangements in situations in which the person requesting the bids is notified of the arrangements. In the *Explanatory Notes*, it is suggested that:

> 'Bid-rigging is the only one of the prohibited activities where for all practical purposes the carrying out of the activity described ... will in itself invariably indicate a dishonest intention and amount to the commission of the offence.'[1]

5.21   Further conditions relating to the horizontal nature of the arrangements are set out in s 189. In each of the instances set out in s 188, it is necessary, as an additional element, that the supply of the product or service by A would be 'at a level in the supply chain at which the product or service would at the same time be supplied by B in the United Kingdom' (s 189(1)).

5.22   It will be noted that the offence is not linked directly to breaches of any existing competition law, and is instead a stand-alone offence. The reasons for this approach, which at first sight seems to add yet another, possibly undesirable, layer to an already complex system, were explained at Committee stage:

> 'there is a fundamental problem with establishing linkage to existing competition law. We have of course considered the approach of a definition based on a direct link to article 81 of the EC Treaty, or on Chapter 1 of the 1998 Act, which comes to the same thing for these purposes. That option was set out in last year's White Paper alongside the dishonesty option. It is superficially attractive, but would present major problems. The

---

[1]   Paragraph 399.

prosecution would need to prove beyond reasonable doubt, in every case, that the agreement would constitute a breach of EC or UK competition law to the satisfaction of a lay jury. I do not think that it is a trivial matter … It would inevitably draw in complex legal and economic argument that is not appropriate for a jury trial.'[1]

THE PENALTY AND PROSECUTION

5.23 As we have seen, the authors of the OFT report suggested that the offence be an arrestable one, carrying a maximum penalty of five years, and that provision should also be made for the imposition of a fine. These recommendations have been followed in the Act, in which s 190 sets out the terms of the penalty. On conviction on indictment, the penalty is 'to imprisonment for a term not exceeding five years, or a fine, or to both' (s 190(1)(a)). On summary conviction, the penalty is 'to imprisonment for a term not exceeding six months or to a fine not exceeding the statutory maximum, or to both' (s 190(1)(b)).

5.24 Proceedings may be brought in England, Wales and Northern Ireland by the Director of the SFO or 'by or with the consent of the OFT' (s 190(2)). The initial expectation is that the SFO will carry out all prosecutions, based in part on its success rates in its prosecutions of fraud.[2] In Scotland, for which no express legislative provision is necessary, the Lord Advocate will be the prosecutor. No private prosecutions may be brought, save with the consent of the OFT, so that there is no prospect of vexatious actions being pursued.

5.25 The OFT has indicated in draft guidance that not all employees who have engaged in cartel conduct will be prosecuted. Thus:

'employees may knowingly have engaged in cartel activity but, provided their involvement is or was peripheral, the exercise of prosecutorial discretion would mean that such individuals would not be prosecuted. Others may have been more closely involved, but their willingness to come forward and co-operate at an early stage of their involvement means that they would be unlikely to face prosecution.'[3]

---

[1]   *Hansard*, Standing Committee B, col 139.

[2]   From 1997 to 2002, the SFO conviction rate was 87% (*Hansard*, Standing Committee B, col 183). See also Lord McIntosh:

'The OFT is included in the Bill as an additional named prosecutor but it is neither expected nor resourced to prosecute initially. It has only been included so that if circumstances justify it in future, the OFT will be able to perform a prosecution role. That might arise if the number of cartel prosecutions created a conflict with other SFO priorities' (*Hansard* (HL), 18 July 2002, col 1542).

[3]   OFT *The Cartel Offence: No-action Letters for Individuals*, consultation document (July 2002), para 1.8.

Territoriality

5.26 Where arrangements are entered into outside the UK, s 190(3) provides that no action may be taken unless the arrangement 'has been implemented in whole or in part in the United Kingdom'. This would mean, for example, that in relation to a bid-rigging arrangement where the tender was invited in any third state and the arrangement was entered into outside the UK by undertakings based in the UK, there would be no jurisdiction under the Act. It is anticipated that the concept of 'implementation' will be given the same meaning as under the CA 1998,[1] which, in turn, flows from the judgment of the European Court of Justice (ECJ) in the case of *Wood Pulp*.[2]

5.27 The relationship of this offence to EC competition law is a complex one. It is clear, for example, that an offence may be committed by a cartel operating in Europe where the arrangements of that cartel are 'implemented' in the UK. *Wood Pulp* implies that the active selling of goods or services whose prices have been affected by the operation of the cartel into the UK would constitute such implementation. However, there would be limitations (discussed in **5.49–5.50**) on the ability to recycle the information and evidence obtained relating to any action taken by the EC Commission or another national competition authority. It has already been made clear that the OFT will not use *both* its civil powers and its new criminal powers in relation to a cartel operating in the UK. A more likely scenario is that cartel arrangements involving undertakings in the UK and elsewhere in the EC might be attacked

---

[1] Section 2(3), for example, limits the application of the Chapter I Prohibition to situations in which the relevant conduct 'is, or is intended to be, *implemented* in the United Kingdom' (emphasis added).

[2] *Re Wood Pulp Cartel: A Ahlstron Oy v Commission* Joined Cases C 89, 104, 114, 116, 117 and 125–129/85 [1988] 4 CMLR 901. Here, the Court, faced with participation in a cartel by undertakings based outside the EC, but with sales being made into the EC, chose not to apply the effects doctrine, although the language it used does not take the 'implementation' principle very far from that doctrine. The Court held that:

> 'It should be observed that an infringement of [Art 81 EC], such as the conclusion of an agreement which has had the effect of restricting competition within the Common Market, consists of conduct made up of two elements, the formation of the agreement … and the implementation thereof. If the applicability of prohibitions laid down under competition law were made to depend on the place where the agreement … was formed, the result would obviously be to give undertakings an easy means of evading those prohibitions. The obvious factor is therefore the place where it is implemented.
>
> The producers in this case implemented their pricing agreement within the Common Market. It is immaterial in that respect whether or not they had recourse to subsidiaries, sub-agents, or branches within the Community in order to make their contacts with purchasers within the Community.
>
> Accordingly the Community's jurisdiction to apply its competition rules to such conduct is covered by the territoriality principle as universally recognised in public international law…' (at paras 16–18).

The UK has resisted the application of the effects doctrine, and, in the debate on the CA 1998, Lord Simon explained that 'by copying out the test in *Wood Pulp* on the face of the Bill, we are also ensuring that in the event that EC jurisprudence develops and creates a pure effects-based doctrine, the application of the UK prohibitions will not follow suit' (*Hansard* (HL) 13 November 1997, col 261).

under Art 81 EC and by the OFT under this Part of the Act. In this case, it is possible that participants in the UK might face penalties that went beyond those imposed on other cartel members. There would appear to be nothing in principle, however, that would prevent the OFT prosecuting all members of the cartel.

5.28   As of September 2002, the OFT has indicated only that it has engaged in extensive discussions with the EC Commission relating to the new offence, and has considered in particular the impact of the offence on leniency policies:

> 'We have worked closely with the European Commission to ensure that the interface between Community and national law is carefully worked out. This has included discussions with the Commission on leniency policies. An undertaking should apply for leniency to both the OFT and the Commission where the cartel involves more member states than the UK. The first undertaking to apply in a cartel should be eligible under the EU civil leniency policy and the UK civil leniency policy for full leniency unless they were the instigator of the cartel, compelled others to take part or played the leading role. Their directors and staff should also be eligible to apply for "no-action" letters in relation to criminal prosecution. These will be issued by the OFT where guilt is admitted, there is a real risk of prosecution and certain other conditions are satisfied. These other conditions are likely to be similar to those which apply for full immunity under the civil leniency policy, ie must not be lead cartel member, must cease involvement in the cartel, must co-operate fully with the investigation and must make a full disclosure. In this way we have ensured the compatible working of the EU and UK regimes. The OFT will discuss with the Commission the handling of individual EC cartel cases where the UK may wish to mount a criminal prosecution. These will be considered case by case.'[1]

'No-action letters'

5.29   Section 190(4) provides that where the OFT issues a written notice to a person 'no proceedings for an offence under s 188 that falls within a description specified in the notice may be brought against that person ... except in the circumstances specified in the notice'. These notices are to be termed 'no-action letters', and are part of the leniency process by which it is hoped to facilitate the investigation of cartel conduct. The process is explained in the *Explanatory Notes*:

> 'It provides the OFT with the power to issue an applicant for leniency with a written notice that he or she will not be prosecuted for the particular matter under investigation provided certain contractual conditions set out in the notice are met. These conditions would be likely to include that the applicant: makes an admission of guilt; must not be the lead cartel member; must cease all involvement in the cartel (except as directed by the OFT to avoid arousing the suspicion of the other parties); must co-operate fully with the investigation; and must make a full disclosure. The notice is intended to encourage informants to come forward by providing them with sufficient comfort that they will not

---

[1]   Bloom, M 'Key Challenges in Public Enforcement: A Speech to the British Institute of International and Comparative Law', 17 May 2002, OFT website.

be prosecuted. In Scotland, the decision to prosecute rests with the Lord Advocate, who will take into account a report from the OFT.'[1]

5.30 Both the OFT and the EC operate leniency programmes, modelled in part on those of the United States, in relation to the application of Art 81 EC and the Chapter I Prohibition.[2] It has proven difficult to prosecute cartels on both sides of the Atlantic. In one American case, it was pointed out that 'the picture of conspiracy as a meeting by twilight of a trio of sinister persons with pointed hats close together belongs to a darker age'[3] and, with increasingly sophisticated organisation amongst cartel members, prosecuting authorities have found it increasingly effective to exploit the inherent weaknesses of cartels and to encourage informants to come forward.[4] Thus, Margaret Bloom commented that:

> 'For cartels, informants are key. Some of these are applications for leniency. By the end of April [2002] we had agreed leniency – with at least one of the parties – in 14 cases (some of which involve resale price maintenance). So far one of these cases has concluded with an infringement decision (*Arriva plc and FirstGroup plc*). In three others we decided the evidence is not sufficient to warrant the commitment of further resources to proceed to an infringement decision. In over half the 14 cases we knew nothing about the cartel (or resale price maintenance) before the leniency application. Even when leniency applicants come in after we have stated an investigation, they can deliver real value. For example, in one case the information provided cut the investigation time by about a half.'[5]

5.31 In July 2002, the OFT released its consultation document entitled *The Cartel Offence: No-action Letters for Individuals*. It is anticipated that no-action letters will be issued primarily to those 'individuals who although not ring leaders or instigators have participated fully in the activities of the cartel, sometimes over an extended period'.[6] In the absence of a no-action letter, such participants may face the risk of prosecution.

---

[1] Paragraph 403. Note that, surprisingly, the OFT *cannot* guarantee immunity from prosecution in Scotland, but it is to be expected that the Lord Advocate will follow the advice of the OFT. The Under-Secretary of State said in Committee that:

> 'The Lord Advocate will prosecute the new offence in Scotland and will not be formally bound by the OFT no-action letter. However ... there are effective working relationships between the OFT, the Serious Fraud Office and the authorities in Scotland. That should avoid inconsistency in practice' (*Hansard*, Standing Committee B, col 174).

[2] In the EC, see the *Commission Notice on Immunity from Fines and Reduction of Fines in Cartel Cases*, 13 February 2002, IP/02/247. In the UK, the policy is set out in Section 9 of the *Director General of Fair Trading's Guidance as to the Appropriate Amount of a Penalty* [2000] UKCLR 431.

[3] *William Goldman Theatres Inc v Loew's Inc* 150 F2d 738, 734n. 15 (3rd Cir 1945).

[4] The story of the uncovering of the vitamins cartel led by the US-based Archer Daniels Midland, and the steps taken by the cartel members to avoid detection, has been grippingly told in Eichenwald, K *The Informant* (New York, Broadway Books, 2000).

[5] 'Key Challenges in Public Enforcement: A Speech to the British Institute of International and Comparative Law', 17 May 2002, OFT website.

[6] Paragraph 1.9.

5.32   In order to be eligible for a no-action letter, the OFT sets as a minimum requirement that the individual must:

(a)   admit participation in the criminal offence;

(b)   provide the OFT with all the information, documents and other evidence available to him or her regarding the existence and activities of the cartel;

(c)   maintain continuous and complete co-operation throughout the investigation until the conclusion of any criminal proceedings arising as a result of the investigation;

(d)   not have acted as the instigator or played the leading role in the cartel nor have compelled others to take part in the cartel;[1] and

(e)   refrain from further participation in the cartel from the time he or she disclosed the cartel except as directed by the investigating authority.[2]

While these are necessary conditions for the issue of a no-action letter, they are not sufficient conditions, and the OFT warns that when it 'already has sufficient information to bring a successful prosecution it will not issue no-action letters'.[3] In this respect, the policy is different from that under the leniency policy in respect of the Chapter I Prohibition, where those co-operating with the investigation once the OFT has launched it may still benefit from a partial reduction in the penalty imposed. Factors such as co-operation during the course of a cartel investigation would presumably be taken into account at the point of sentencing following a conviction, rather than at the point of the decision whether or not to prosecute.

5.33   Those seeking the benefit of a no-action letter may approach the OFT directly, or a lawyer may act on their behalf. In addition, reinforcing the links between the civil and criminal offences of the Chapter I Prohibition and the cartel provisions of the Act, the approach may be made 'on behalf of named employees, directors, ex-employees or ex-directors, by an undertaking seeking leniency in accordance with the *Director General of Fair Trading's Guidance as the Appropriate Amount of a Penalty*.[4] Where the leniency conditions relating to the Chapter I Prohibition or those relating to Art 81 EC, are fulfilled, the OFT will 'normally be prepared to issue no-action letters as well to those individuals who need such letters'.[5]

---

[1]   The OFT has asked specifically what the requirement here should be: 'should the bar on receiving the no-action letters be applied to those who have acted as instigators or played the leading role (a condition rarely met given the collaborative nature of cartels) or should it be only those who have compelled others to take part who are denied the possibility of a no-action letter' (OFT *The Cartel Offence: No-action Letters for Individuals*, consultation document (July 2002), para 2.1(b)).

[2]   OFT *The Cartel Offence: No-action Letters for Individuals*, consultation document (July 2002), para 3.1.

[3]   Ibid, para 3.2.

[4]   Ibid, para 3.3.

[5]   Ibid, para 3.4.

5.34 The OFT will attempt to respond to the request by giving an early indication of the likelihood of the letter being issued.

5.35 Once the OFT has determined that it may be prepared to issue a no-action letter, the prospective recipient will be interviewed, probably over several sessions. At this time, any information provided by the individual:

> 'will not be used against them in criminal proceedings unless they either knowingly or recklessly give false or misleading information, in which case any immunity granted will be withdrawn as if it had never been granted and the OFT may rely on *any* information given by the applicant in a prosecution against them for the cartel offence.'[1]

Following the interview(s), the applicant may discuss with the OFT the prospect of his or her prosecution, and a letter may be issued if the conditions set out in para 3.1 of the guidance are met (see **5.32**), and 'but for the operation of the leniency policy, there is a likelihood of prosecution'.[2]

5.36 No-action letters may be withdrawn in situations in which the recipient breaks the obligations set out in para 3.1, or where there have been material inaccuracies in the information given to the OFT, or where information has been withheld. A draft letter attached to the guidance provides in part that:

> 'If, in the view of the OFT, at any time before the conclusion of any criminal proceedings arising as a result of the investigation into the reported possible offence, the conditions which are set out in this letter have not been complied with in full by the Applicant, the OFT shall give immediate written notice to the Applicant of the nature of the alleged non-compliance and that the OFT is considering revoking the grant of immunity. The Applicant will be given a reasonable opportunity to explain the alleged non-compliance and, if the OFT considers it appropriate, to remedy the breach within a reasonable period of time from the giving of such explanation.'

5.37 Confidentiality of those who come forward is to be protected where possible, and the OFT guidance provides that:

> 'Information from which the identity of individuals who have received no-action letters may be deduced shall not be made public, subject to disclosure obligations in criminal proceedings or when there is an overriding public interest in doing so.'[3]

Extradition

5.38 Section 191 makes express provision for the extradition of those subject to prosecution under this Part of the Act, by way of the application of the Extradition Act 1870, via Sch 1 to the Extradition Act 1989. In respect of those countries with which bilateral extradition treaties were signed prior to 1989, the regime established under the 1870 Act, preserved by the 1989 Act,

---

[1] OFT *The Cartel Offence: No-action Letters for Individuals*, consultation document (July 2002), para 3.5.
[2] Ibid, para 3.6(a).
[3] Ibid, para 3.8.

will be applied. This group includes the US. In respect of countries with which agreements were entered into after 1989, the later Act will apply. The extradition provisions cannot be applied retrospectively. Extradition may be sought where individuals commit an offence under s 188, conspire to commit such an offence, or attempt to commit such an offence. A *quid pro quo* of this approach is that other countries may in turn apply to extradite UK citizens, or those residing in the UK where they have committed offences under that second country's equivalent legislation. In the *Explanatory Notes*, it is explained that:

> 'Dual criminality applies (ie a request for extradition may only ever be made to a country that has criminal penalties for the same activity). Thus the introduction of criminal penalties in the UK will make it possible for other countries that criminalise the same activity to request the extradition of individuals from the UK. Requests made by the UK for the extradition of individuals from other countries will be governed by the law of those countries.'[1]

It will be noted that the US maintains criminal penalties in place in relation to cartel conduct which is in breach of s 1 of the Sherman Act 1890. With respect to the US, the position of Sir Anthony Tennant[2] was discussed at some length in committee. The Under-Secretary of State indicated that, were the provisions in place at the relevant time, he could probably have been extradited to the US. The general position in relation to US law was set out by the Under-Secretary:

> 'Automatic extradition requires both states to prosecute an offender for an identical criminal offence. There are some differences between the United Kingdom offence created under the [Act], and the United States offence brought under the Sherman Act. The US offence is not based on dishonesty, therefore a request would need to be reviewed by the UK courts to establish whether the request fulfils the criteria of it being a case where the offence applies in nature to both jurisdictions. Such a review by the courts provides an extra safeguard against automatic extradition, which is ultimately a matter for the courts to decide.'[3]

PROCEDURE – THE INVESTIGATION OF OFFENCES

5.39 The fact that the same institution – the OFT – will be charged with investigating civil breaches of the CA 1998 and conducting investigations under the market provisions of the Act, as well as enforcing the criminal sanctions in relation to cartel offences, will be a matter of some concern, and it is important that a clear distinction be drawn between the various powers. In particular, the rights accorded to an individual subject to prosecution under this Part of the Act are different from those accorded to an undertaking subject to penalties imposed following breaches of the CA 1998 prohibitions.

---

[1]   Paragraph 405.
[2]   Alleged to have been involved in the cartel arrangements made between Christies and Sothebys.
[3]   *Hansard*, Standing Committee B, cols 188–189.

Evidence gathered in relation to the latter *cannot* be used as the basis for a prosecution of an individual in relation to a cartel offence (although see **5.49**). There are particular problems with human rights jurisprudence, for example, which provides, *inter alia*, that the use of statements obtained using compulsory powers may not be contrary to the European Convention on the Protection of Human Rights and Fundamental Freedoms 1950 (ECHR), Art 6, when they are used in relation to administrative investigations, but may not be relied upon in criminal investigations.[1]

5.40 As early as May 2002, the Director of Competition Enforcement at the OFT was able to say that:

> 'Much preparation has already been done by the OFT and the SFO including planning arrangements for the handling of cases, developing a Memorandum of Understanding covering these arrangements and planning necessary training in criminal investigation proceedings and the appropriate provisions of PACE. This work was started alongside the Hammond/Penrose report that was commissioned and published by the OFT last autumn on *The Proposed Criminalisation of Cartels in the UK*.'[2]

5.41 Broadly, the powers available to the OFT are those available to the SFO under Criminal Justice Act 1987, s 2. The threshold for the launch of an investigation is that 'there are reasonable grounds for suspecting that an offence under section 188 has been committed' (s 192(1)). These powers can be used only in respect of offences under this Part of the Act, and not in relation to the enforcement of the Chapter I and Chapter II Prohibitions of the CA 1998, which are to be enforced by reference to the powers set out in Chapter III of that Act (s 192(2)). In undertaking investigations, the OFT will be required to have regard to the relevant provisions of the Police and Criminal Evidence Act 1984 (PACE 1984), of which s 67(9) provides that:

> 'Persons other than police officers who are charged with the duty of investigating offences or charging offenders shall in the discharge of that duty have regard to any relevant provisions of such a code.'

5.42 The relationship between the OFT and the SFO is to be as described by Margaret Bloom:

> 'The OFT will undertake the initial investigation and will inform the SFO as soon as a case appears likely to lead to criminal prosecution. A decision may be taken at that point to hand the case over to the SFO for prosecution or the OFT may continue the investigation for a period in close co-operation with the SFO (so called "extended vetting") before a decision is taken. Once the SFO has taken over a case, it will appoint a

---

[1] See, for example, *R v Hertfordshire County Council, ex p Green Industries Ltd* [2000] 2 WLR 373. See generally Scanlan, M and Monnick, R 'Investigatory Powers and the Right to a Fair Trial' (2000) 144 SJ 652, and Stallworthy, M 'The Regulation and Investigation of Commercial Activities in the United Kingdom and the Privilege Against Self-Incrimination' [2000] ICCLR 67.

[2] 'Key Challenges in Public Enforcement: A Speech to the British Institute of International and Comparative Law', 17 May 2002, OFT website.

"case controller" to oversee the joint SFO/OFT team which will take it forward. In this way the expertise of the OFT in handling cartel investigations and of the SFO in criminal prosecutions will be used to maximum benefit.'[1]

5.43 The specific powers of investigation set out in ss 193 and 194 are exercisable in situations where it appears to the OFT that there is good reason for using them. Section 193 provides the powers to be used when conducting an investigation, and s 185 the power to enter premises under a warrant.

5.44 Under s 193, the OFT may, by way of written notice, require the person under investigation, or any other person, to answer questions or to provide other information, at a specified time and place. This extends to 'any matter relevant to the investigation' (s 193(1)). The OFT may require that documents[2] be produced, and may take copies of, or extracts from, them and may also require the person producing them to provide explanations relating to them. If documents are not produced, the OFT may require the person to state, to the best of his or her knowledge, where these documents may be found. These powers are similar to those in the CA 1998 relating to the carrying out of investigations for the civil enforcement of the Act. They are not limited to existing employees of companies, and may be applied to persons who are not employees of the undertakings whose conduct is under examination, if those persons are believed to have information relevant to the investigation.

5.45 Section 194 gives the OFT the power to enter premises under a warrant following a successful application to the High Court (or, in Scotland, by the Procurator Fiscal to the Sheriff). Warrants may be granted in circumstances in which the judge is satisfied that there are reasonable grounds for believing that there are, on the premises, documents which the OFT would be entitled to obtain under s 193, and either they have not been supplied under that section, or it is not practicable to serve a s 194 notice, or the service of such a notice might 'seriously prejudice' the investigation (s 185(1)(b)(iii)). The warrant will give the power to a named officer of the OFT, and any other officers of the OFT authorised in writing to enter the premises, using force where necessary, to search for the documents, and to take such steps as are necessary to protect the documents from destruction or interference. Persons who are not employees of the OFT but who are specified in the warrant may accompany the OFT staff. This might include, for example, forensic experts and IT experts, where their skills would assist the investigation. Any person may be required to provide an explanation of the documents, or to state where it may

---

[1]   'Key Challenges in Public Enforcement: A Speech to the British Institute of International and Comparative Law', 17 May 2002, OFT website.

[2]   'Documents' is defined in s 202 to include 'information recorded in any form and, in relation to information recorded otherwise than in a form in which it is visible and legible, references to its production include references to producing it in a form in which it is visible and legible or from which it can readily be produced in a visible and legible form'.

be found. Information held in electronic form, and accessible from the premises, which would include information physically stored elsewhere but accessible, for example, over an intranet, may be required to be produced in a form in which it can be taken away and in which it is legible or from which it can be readily produced in visible and legible form (s 194(2)(d)).

5.46 Section 194(5) also makes an amendment to the Criminal Justice and Police Act 2001, Sch 1, Part 1 to add to it the powers of seizure conferred by s 194(2). This has the effect of incorporating the provisions of the 2001 Act into this part of the Act, and, in particular, those relating to the safeguards surrounding the seizure of material. This includes, in s 52, a requirement to give a written notice in relation to investigations, and, in s 54, a requirement to return any legally privileged material which has been inadvertently seized.

5.47 The OFT may also authorise any competent person who is not an officer of the OFT to exercise on its behalf the powers available under ss 193 and 194. Although the OFT has recruited heavily since the entry into force of the CA 1998, it does not have the staff or the expertise yet to conduct investigations in hostile circumstances with the same efficacy as, say, the SFO or HM Customs & Excise, and it is likely that there may be situations in which the expertise of these organisations is called upon to assist in the carrying out of investigations. It has been suggested that the OFT may sub-contract out some of the investigation process, and, in committee, the prospect was raised that 'it may wish to hive off some of its work to private-practice law firms' – a prospect which, although unlikely, was not expressly refuted by the Under-Secretary of State.[1]

5.48 Sections 196, 197 and 198 provide some safeguards in relation to the exercise of the investigatory powers. The first of these relates to privileged information. In the case of legal professional privilege, a person may not be required to disclose 'any information or produce any document which he would be entitled to refuse to disclose or produce on grounds of legal professional privilege in proceedings in the High Court' (s 196(1)). The second relates to information or documents 'in respect of which he owes an obligation of confidence by virtue of carrying on any banking business' (s 196(2)). However, in this second case, the general protection may be overridden by an express authorisation made by the OFT. This latter provision is based on Criminal Justice Act 1987, s 2. In each case, the OFT board will have to consider whether it is appropriate to respect banking privilege or not.[2]

---

[1] Mr Field, *Hansard*, Standing Committee B, col 207.
[2] The Under-Secretary said in committee that 'No one would deny that the ability to follow money trails is an important power for a cartel investigator. Corrupt payments can be made to seal cartel deals, and individuals involved in bid-rigging and market-sharing can receive sweeteners and pay-offs' (col 209).

5.49 Section 197 relates to the use of statements obtained under compulsion, and limits the uses to which these can be put. The first instance in which such a statement may be relied upon in court flows from the application of s 201(2), which provides that a person who makes a statement which he or she knows to be false, or is reckless as to its truth, is guilty of an offence. The second instance in which such a statement may be relied upon is where, in relation to the prosecution of some other offence – which would include the primary cartel offence – he or she makes a statement which is inconsistent with it.[1] It should be noted that where the compulsory powers available under the CA 1998 are used to gather information, PACE 1984 does not apply (see **5.41**).[2]

5.50 The CA 1998 is amended with the insertion of a new s 30A so that statements obtained in the course of civil proceedings under CA 1998, ss 26, 27 and 28 may not be used against someone in the course of criminal proceedings under this Part of the Act. There are two exceptions to this principle. The first arises where the person makes a statement in giving evidence which is inconsistent with that made in the course of the CA 1998 proceeding. The second occurs where a question relating to that evidence is asked by the person or on his behalf (s 198).

Surveillance

5.51 The OFT is given the power, by virtue of s 199, to carry out covert surveillance in the course of its investigations into a cartel offence. This is effected by way of an amendment made to the Regulation of Investigatory Powers Act 2000 (RIPA 2000). These powers have been summarised by Margaret Bloom:

> 'The Bill grants the OFT access to intrusive surveillance powers through amending the Regulation of Investigatory Powers Act 2000 (RIPA). The Chairman of the OFT may issue an authorisation for the planting of surveillance devices. One of the criteria for which an authorisation may be granted under RIPA is for "the purpose of preventing or detecting serious crime". Surveillance must be necessary and proportionate. All applications for authorisation are subject to the scrutiny and approval of the surveillance commissioners. The OFT intends to outsource the technical deployment of intrusive surveillance to either HM Customs & Excise or the National Crime Squad. Memoranda of Understanding have been drawn up for this. The OFT has applied separately to the Home Office for an Order to grant authorised officers access to directed surveillance (essentially monitoring the movement of people and vehicles) and covert human intelligence sources (essentially the use of informants). The OFT has also applied to the

---

[1]   This approach is consistent with CJA 1987, s 2(8) and (8AA).

[2]   In relation to Scotland, 'in the case of suspects being cautioned ... PACE does not apply. When the OFT is seeking voluntary statements from suspects in Scotland, it will nevertheless give a caution in line with normal practice under Scots common law. Omitting to give a common law caution before questioning a suspect would place the admissibility of the evidence in doubt' (*Hansard*, Standing Committee B, col 203).

Home Office for an order to grant authorised officers access to communication data (primarily postal and telephone records). Both of these applications are under RIPA, The Orders will require affirmative resolution by Parliament.'[1]

These powers are extensive, and may include, for example, the planting of surveillance devices in residential premises, hotel accommodation, and private vehicles. As the *Explanatory Notes* suggest, 'acting on information received from an informant, the OFT could, for example, use these powers to record a meeting of cartelists in a hotel room'.[2] The OFT has already applied to the Home Office for Orders under ss 28 and 29 of RIPA 2000 to grant authorised officers access to directed surveillance (the monitoring of people's movements), and covert human intelligence sources (the use of informants), as well as, under s 22 of RIPA 2000, for an Order to grant authorised officers access to communications data such as postal and telecommunication records. Given the strength of the powers available to the OFT, 'the intrusive surveillance powers will only be used in the most serious cases and when the OFT has specific information about a meeting from an informant'. It must also be the case that the evidence that would be obtained using such methods would not be available by another method.[3]

5.52   Section 200 further grants the OFT power to take action in respect of private property by amending the Police Act 1997, ss 93 and 94. This essentially allows an authorised officer of the OFT to gain access to premises to undertake intrusive surveillance.

OFFENCES

5.53   A number of offences, apart from the general cartel offence set out in s 181, are created by s 201. First, it is an offence for any person to fail to comply with any requirement imposed on him or her by the OFT under ss 193 and 194. The penalty for breach is a term of imprisonment not exceeding six months, or to a fine not exceeding level 5 on the standard scale, or both (s 201(1)). Where statements are made which are false, an offence is committed, and the penalty in this respect is, on conviction on indictment, imprisonment for a term not exceeding two years, or to a fine, or both; and, on summary conviction, imprisonment for a term not exceeding six months, or a fine not exceeding the statutory maximum, or both ('the usual penalty') (s 201(2) and (3)). Where evidence is destroyed or tampered with, in

---

[1]   Bloom, M 'Key Challenges in Public Enforcement: A Speech to the British Institute of International and Comparative Law', 17 May 2002, OFT website.

[2]   Paragraph 420.

[3]   *Hansard*, Committee B, col 213.

circumstances in which the person doing so knows or suspects that an investigation by the OFT or the SFO is being carried out, an offence has been committed, unless the person 'proves that he had no intention of concealing the facts disclosed by the documents from the persons carrying out such an investigation' (s 201(4)). This offence carries the penalty of up to seven years' imprisonment, or a fine, or both, following conviction on indictment, or the usual penalty in relation to a summary conviction. Finally, a person who intentionally obstructs a person exercising his or her powers under a warrant issued under s 194 is guilty of an offence, and may, on conviction by indictment, face a prison term not exceeding two years, or a fine, or both, and, in relation to a summary conviction, to a fine not exceeding the statutory maximum.

Chapter Six

THIRD PARTY ENGAGEMENT – COMPLAINTS AND ACTIONS

INTRODUCTION

6.1   The vibrant role played by third parties in the enforcement of the US antitrust system is a key factor in the efficacy of enforcement of that law.[1] In the EC, the Commission has expressed frustration at the lack of private enforcement, and has attempted to redress the perceived imbalance between the public and private role. In its *Notice on Cooperation between National Courts and the Commission*,[2] the European Commission made clear its view that there are strong advantages to claimants in bringing private actions. In particular, the Commission pointed out that where it is unable to award damages, the courts can order interim measures which are specific to the claimant, and may be able to award costs to the claimant.

6.2   The CA 1998 gave third parties the right of action in respect of breaches of the Chapter I and Chapter II Prohibitions, but these rights have not been often invoked before the national courts, although Lord Simon, at the time of the passage of that Act, claimed that 'the 1998 Act will give businesses and consumers effective rights of redress'.[3]

6.3   In its White Paper, the Department of Trade and Industry (DTI) stressed the need to provide 'real redress for harmed parties'.[4] Here, the

---

[1]   See generally, Jones, CA *Private Enforcement of Antitrust Law in the EU, UK and USA* (Oxford, OUP, 1999). Section 4 of the Clayton Act provides that 'any person who shall be injured in his business or property by reason of anything forbidden in the antitrust laws may sue therefore … and shall recover threefold the damages by him sustained, and the cost of suit, including a reasonable attorney's fee (15 USC, s 15).

[2]   (1993) OJ C39/6.

[3]   *Hansard* (HL), 30 October 1997, col 1146. The position of third-party rights is explained in part at **6.15–6.41**.

[4]   Chapter 8 of the White Paper.

Government dealt with private actions, and actions on behalf of consumers. In the first regard, the Government stated its intention to:

'... expand the role of the Competition Commission Appeal Tribunals enabling them to hear claims for damages in competition cases brought by harmed parties. This would make better use of existing judicial resources. It is also likely to reduce the costs for the parties. The Tribunals currently do not award costs and operate less expensive procedures. Although their rules on costs would need to be revised in light of their new powers it might be possible to retain some flexibility in awarding costs where a private action is also in the public interest.

The Tribunals could hear damages claims both immediately after considering the substantive appeal against a decision of the OFT and in cases where the OFT's decision is accepted and no appeal is subsequently made. This would bring procedural efficiencies as the Tribunals would be able to act more swiftly where they are already familiar with the facts of a case against an undertaking. Clear tests of whether a claimant had just cause and the formula by which the Tribunals would calculate damages would be laid out.'[1]

In relation to actions on behalf of consumers, the position set out in the White Paper recognised the difficulties in this regard, but stressed the benefits:

'Enabling a representative body to take a claim on behalf of a group of consumers is not without its difficulties. In the majority of competition cases, especially those involving long-standing breaches of competition law which affect consumer markets, identifying exactly who has been harmed and in what way is a significant hurdle. The would-be plaintiffs are either not known or a huge additional effort would be required to identify them.

The Government is concerned that consumer groups will have little incentive to bring cases if they are required to identify large numbers of harmed parties. This will be further compounded if the court is then unable to award damages. However, the principle of allowing action in the wider public interest where harm to consumers can be shown is an important one. The Government therefore wishes to consider further how to enable cases to be brought in seemingly intractable areas such as competition.'[2]

6.4 In Part 2 of the Act, various amendments are made to the CA 1998 relating to monetary claims, and to claims brought on behalf of consumers. An amendment is also made to improve the procedures under which third parties may appeal decisions made by the Office of Fair Trading (OFT) to the Competition Appeals Tribunal (CAT). In Part 1 of the Act, provision is made for 'super-complaints' to the OFT, and the position in respect of super-complaints to regulators other than the OFT is dealt with in Part 7 (s 205). All of these provisions are explained in this chapter. Other arrangements relating to third party rights in relation to market investigations and cartel investigations are dealt with as appropriate in the relevant chapters.

---

[1] Paragraphs 8.7 and 8.8.

[2] Paragraphs 8.19 and 8.20.

SUPER-COMPLAINTS

6.5   'Super-complaints' are dealt with in ss 11 and 205 of the Act. The arrival of the super-complaint was described in the committee stages of the debates as being 'like the arrival of gunpowder and cannons to the proprietor of a medieval castle – alarming and impressive at the same time'.[1] Section 11 applies where 'a designated consumer body makes a complaint to the OFT that any feature, or combination of features, of a market in the United Kingdom for goods or services is or appears to be significantly harming the interests of consumers'. Section 205 gives the Secretary of State the power to make orders to apply s 11 to other specified regulators. In August 2002, the OFT published its consultation paper, *Super-complaints: Guidance for Designated Consumer Bodies*, which is designed to help those making super-complaints to the OFT, and which sheds light on the way in which the OFT expects super-complaints to be framed and considered. The aim of this provision, as explained in the *Explanatory Notes*, is to 'encourage groups who represent consumers to make relevant complaints on their collective behalf, and the OFT will be obliged to respond to a super-complaint within a specified time'.[2] These words were echoed by the Under-Secretary of State when she explained that the intention underlying the introduction of the super-complaint was 'to ensure that consumers receive better protection by enabling consumer bodies to complain about any market failure that causes significant harm to consumers'.[3] A further broad statement about the role of the super-complaint clarifies the position:

> 'It is important to remember that the policy's focus is to alert the OFT to market failures that significantly harm the interest of consumers … individual consumers do not necessarily have access to the information, skills, resources and expertise required to put together cogent complaints about the failure of particular markets. That is why we want to enable consumer bodies to do that on their behalf and formalise the process so that consumer interests are protected. That is why the Bill does not envisage that the procedure will be available other than to those who are designated as consumer bodies.'[4]

6.6   Once a super-complaint is made, the OFT is obliged to respond within 90 days, explaining the reasons for its decisions.[5] Super-complaints then are differentiated from normal complaints by virtue of the tight timetable within

---

[1]   Mr Waterson (*Hansard*, Standing Committee B, col 70). The CBI was sceptical about the value of the super-complaint, and concerned about the harms that would flow from ill-directed complaints. This concern was raised by Mr Field in committee: 'The CBI suggests equality of treatment and that the Government should hear all complaints equally. The concept of a super complaint procedure is cause for great concern, because people will assume that complaints have substance if they are put forward by a consumer group on that elevated scale' (*Hansard*, Standing Committee B, col 75).

[2]   Paragraph 48.

[3]   *Hansard*, Standing Committee B, col 71.

[4]   *Hansard*, Standing Committee B, col 112.

[5]   The Under-Secretary of State noted that 'it is also important to stress that the OFT will be required to give a full and reasoned response to super complaints' (*Hansard*, Standing Committee B, col 86).

which the OFT is obliged to reach a decision as to what the response to the complaint should be, and the rigour with which it must explain this response. Super-complaints are not designed to deal with conduct undertaken by specific companies (in which case, complaints may be made under the CA 1998, where the appropriate thresholds are met), but rather with 'features' of a market,[1] and are thus more closely related to market investigation references under Part 4 of the Act than they are to the CA 1998, although they are not part of the formal procedure relating to market investigation references. In fact, super-complaints:

> 'should not be limited to being a preliminary to a particular type of competition investigation; they should be an open-ended vehicle for the OFT to launch investigations under any of its consumer and competition powers.'[2]

As the OFT has indicated, super-complaints 'are distinct from complaints that consumer protection law or competition law has been breached. It is possible, however, that an initiation of a super-complaint could uncover evidence that leads to enforcement action'.[3] It is possible, for example, that super-complaints may be made in respect of conduct which is not illegal at the time when the complaint is made. In such a case, the result might be that a market investigation reference is made where genuine concerns are raised.[4]

6.7　It is for the Secretary of State to designate the 'consumer bodies' empowered to make super-complaints. It is likely that the list will include at least the National Consumers' Council (NCC) and the Consumers' Association (CA), both of which are specifically mentioned in the White Paper.[5] In relation to the regulated sectors, there are in existence consumer representative organisations which would be the appropriate bodies on which to confer the power if orders are made under s 205.[6] No body will be designated unless it applies to be so, and additional government funding will not be given to consumer groups that are so designated in order to assist them in making super-complaints.[7] The NCC, for example, has already indicated that it would seek the designation, and that its resources would enable it to bring such complaints forward. Criteria relating to designation will be published by the

---

[1]　Discussed in Chapter 4 at **4.10** ff.

[2]　Lord Sainsbury, *Hansard* (HL), 16 July 2002, col 1191.

[3]　OFT *Super-complaints: Guidance for Designated Consumer Bodies* (August 2002), para 2.2.

[4]　See, for example, *Hansard*, Standing Committee B, col 76.

[5]　Paragraph 8.21. The National Association of Citizens Advice Bureaux has also indicated that it would apply for designation.

[6]　The DTI will issue final guidance in relation to the criteria for achieving designation status and the application process. The OFT, in its draft guidance, points out that 'if an order is made extending super-complaint powers and duties to specified sectoral regulators any super-complainant will be able to make a complaint directly to a specified regulator rather than the OFT. In that event, the super-complainant should consider which organisation is best placed to deal with the complaint prior to making one' (OFT *Super-complaints: Guidance for Designated Consumer Bodies* (August 2002), para 3.2).

[7]　*Hansard*, Standing Committee B, col 100.

Secretary of State.[1] Once a body has been designated, that status may be removed if the DTI or the OFT is concerned about its operation.

6.8   Just as the OFT is obliged to explain the reasons for its decisions when responding to a super-complaint, there is an expectation that the body making the complaint will do so in a reasoned and well-supported fashion.[2] The guidance to be finalised by the OFT will set out what is expected. Section 11(7) of the Act obliges the OFT to publish this guidance.

6.9   At paras 2.6 and 2.7 of the draft guidance, the OFT sets out what needs to be in a super-complaint. It is doubtful that there will be much, if any, change in relation to this by the time the guidance is finalised:

> '2.6 When making a complaint, the super-complainant should provide a short paper setting out the reasons why they consider that a UK market for goods or services has a feature, or features, that are or appear to be, significantly harming the interests of consumers and should therefore be investigated. This paper should be supported, wherever possible, by documented facts and evidence.

> 2.7 Super-complainants are not expected to provide the level of evidence necessary for the OFT to decide that its investigation criteria are satisfied. However, they should present a reasoned case, supported by evidence. The objective of presenting the case and supporting evidence is to help the OFT to undertake a fuller appraisal of whether there are factors indicating market failure that may warrant launching an MPI[3] market investigation or whether on of the other outcomes … may be appropriate. Complaints that are not supported by a reasoned case, or contain little or no supporting evidence may not be progressed. Complaints that are, or that appear to be, frivolous or vexatious will be rejected.'

6.10   The OFT will adopt a fast-track procedure once a complaint is received that meets these criteria, and within five working days, the complainant will be

---

[1]   These are likely to be based, in the first instance, on the criteria for the designation of bodies in relation to the Stop Now Orders (EC Directive) Regulations 2001, SI 2001/1422 (*Hansard*, Standing Committee B, col 101). The Government will be 'looking for such things as capacity and track record in the appropriate area' (*Hansard*, Standing Committee B, col 103).

[2]   The Under-Secretary of State made this clear in committee:

> 'A concern is floating around that people may make frivolous super complaints and that organisations that are authorised to act in this capacity – that will be a careful process in itself – will come forward with something that is not sensible. I can assure the Committee that organisations will be expected to base their complaint on a reasoned case. If they do not, the OFT will take no action beyond initial consideration' (*Hansard*, Standing Committee B, col 75).

See also col 87:

> 'The consumer body would have to submit considerable resources to produce such a case, so they are unlikely to make frivolous complaints';

and col 88:

> 'I assume, for the sake of argument, that if an utterly frivolous super complaint were submitted, the OFT could rapidly decide that it did not meet the criteria and dismiss it well within the 90-day time limit. Obviously we do not anticipate that such an event will occur because the reputation of organisations designated to bring forward super complaints will itself be on the line in the way in which they deal with those matters. That will be under the public gaze.'

[3]   The Markets and Policy Initiatives Division of the OFT

notified that the complaint has been received, and who the main OFT contact is to be during the examination of the complaint. The OFT team will notify the complainant as soon as possible if the complaint would be better dealt with by an appropriate sector regulator. If further information, or clarification, in relation to the complaint is needed, the super-complainant will be given a set time to respond, which, if not met, may result in the decision being taken formally not to proceed with the complaint.

6.11   A fuller indication of the sorts of evidence which would be 'indicative of the kind and level of information the OFT would normally expect a super-complaint to contain' is set out in Annexes A and B of the draft guidance. These are a detailed set of requirements, although the OFT recognises that not all the information suggested may be available or appropriate in all cases. Some of the 21 items dealt with in Annex A are as follows:

–   details of the market to which the complaint relates;
–   details of the nature of the complaint;
–   how consumers' interests are harmed;
–   whether there is a particularly vulnerable set of consumers;
–   information on market shares;
–   evidence of barriers to entry;
–   information relating to the impact and existence of buyer power;
–   details or information on prices, discounts, discriminatory prices, price dispersions, price trends, comparative price information across suppliers;
–   information relating to profitability;
–   evidence relating to sales techniques;
–   details relating to the consumer switching;
–   indicators of consumer knowledge of the market.

It will be apparent that these criteria, if followed by the super-complainant, will address concerns raised by the OFT relating to the quality of complaints made under the Act.[1]

6.12   Annex B sets out some factors which may indicate that markets are not working effectively. It is not enough, therefore, for a complaint to be a generalised one about 'high prices', or 'lack of competition'. Rather, it should first consider whether any of the key factors indicate that the competitive process in a market is not working well for consumers. These are low productivity, high profitability (reflected in prices that are dispersed substantially, or that do not reflect costs), poor quality and/or variety, or a poor record of innovation. However, 'none of these factors on its own necessarily indicates competition problems. For example, high profitability

---

[1]   See **1.28**.

might simply reflect high levels of efficiency and innovation'.[1] A number of secondary factors relating to market structure that might be considered when analysing whether a particular market has features which act to the detriment of the competitive process are therefore also set out.

6.13 Seven possible outcomes are set out in the draft guidance as flowing from a super-complaint. These are:

– launching MPI market investigation into the issue;
– referring for possible enforcement action by the OFT's competition or consumer regulation divisions;
– making a market investigation reference to the Competition Commission (CC);
– referring the complaint to a sectoral regulator for enforcement action under sectoral powers;
– transferring the complaint to one of the sectoral regulators with concurrent powers as being a more appropriate body to deal with the complaint;
– dismissing the complaint as frivolous or vexatious; and
– dismissing the complaint as unfounded.

6.14 As noted in Chapter 1,[2] the OFT has already accepted two 'super-complaints', even though, at the time of their acceptance, no such official designation existed. Both have been well publicised, and the OFT has indicated in each case its preliminary timetable for action.

THIRD PARTY APPEALS UNDER THE COMPETITION ACT 1998

6.15 As originally written, s 47 of the CA 1998 allowed any person who was not directly the subject of a decision made by the Director General of Fair Trading ('the Director') to 'apply to the Director asking him to withdraw or vary a decision'. It was for the Director to determine whether the applicant had 'a sufficient interest in the relevant decision' (s 47(3)(a)). The Director would deal with the application, and appeals from decisions of the Director could be further appealed to the Competition Commission Appeals Tribunal (CCAT). As noted at the time, 'the "sufficient interest" qualification test for third party appeals may be wider than the equivalent test "direct and individual

1   OFT *Super-complaints: Guidance for Designated Consumer Bodies* (August 2002), para B.5.
2   See **1.29**.

concern" laid down in Art 230 EC and means that consumers and consumer protection organisations may be able to contest the Director's decisions'.[1]

6.16 In the case of *IIB*,[2] criticisms were made of this appeal process. In that case, the Director had taken a decision that the rules of the General Insurance Standards Council (GISC) were non-discriminatory, transparent and based on objective standards and, as such, did not infringe the Chapter I Prohibition.[3] Following applications made under s 47 of the CA 1998 to the Director by the Institute of Independent Insurance Brokers (IIB) and the Association of British Travel Agents (ABTA), the Director refused to withdraw or vary the negative clearance decision.[4] The decision taken in relation to ABTA's application was not published, but, in that relating to the IIB, the Director held that the applicant did have sufficient interest in the matter, but rejected the application on its substance. When the case was appealed to the CCAT, the original decision was set aside. The CCAT also commented, in the following terms, on the procedure under s 47:

> 'Although not entirely relevant to the substance, this case has perhaps highlighted the somewhat cumbersome nature of the procedure under s 47 of the Act, which does not confer on an interested person, who is not a party to an agreement, the right to appeal directly to this Tribunal against an adverse decision of the Director, without going through the s 47 procedure. In this particular case, it is unfortunate that, for whatever reason, nearly six months passed before the IIB, in particular, was able to bring its complaint before this Tribunal. That delay was detrimental to the IIB who, in the meantime had to close its regulatory division, and damaging to GISC because it has delayed for a substantial period the final resolution of its notification to the Director. We hope that this issue can be addressed in future, both from the administrative point of view, and from the perspective of a possible modification to the Act.'[5]

6.17 The CCAT did not probably expect that the legislative response would be so swift – indeed, that it would be introduced before any other decision taken under s 47 had been published. The new s 47, introduced by s 17 of the Act, streamlines the procedure considerably. It allows for an appeal directly to

---

[1]   Livingston, D *The Competition Act 1998: A Practical Guide* (London, Sweet & Maxwell, 2001), para 9.8.1. It should also be noted that s 48 of the CA 1998, is repealed by virtue of Sch 5(3) to the Act. This related to the setting up of the Appeals Tribunal, a matter superseded by the provisions of the Act relating to the CAT (see further, Chapter 2).

[2]   *The Institute of Independent Insurance Brokers v The Director General of Fair Trading supported by the General Insurance Standards Council; Association of British Travel Agents Ltd v The Director General of Fair Trading supported by the General Insurance Standards Council* [2001] CompAR 62.

[3]   *Notification by the General Insurance Standards Council* Decision No CA98/1/2001, [2001] UKCLR 331.

[4]   *Decision of the Director General of Fair Trading pursuant to s 47(4): Application by the Institute of Insurance Brokers under s 47(1)*, 11 May 2001, [2001] UKCLR 838.

[5]   Paragraph 270. It had already been pointed out by Livingston (fn 1 above) that: 'There is, in the case of every application under s 47, some ability for a third party to cause delay and uncertainty while the Director satisfies himself there is no new matter which would cause him to change his decision, even if only by adding an additional condition or obligation, and its is possible that there could be a prolonged period of uncertainty.' (para 9.8.5)

the Competition Appeals Tribunal (CAT), rather than to the Director. The decisions which may be appealed are the same as before, which is to say, those falling within paras (a)–(f) of s 46(3).[1]

6.18   As with the original s 47, there is no definition of 'sufficient interest', and the limits of this are left to be worked out by way of case-law.[2] The likely parties to be able to demonstrate a sufficient interest include relevant trade associations, and close competitors. In general, it is unlikely that a general consumer of a product, or a general customer of the undertaking in respect of whom the decision is made, will have the close connection with the facts that would be required.

6.19   The Government also intends to add a new category to the list of appealable decisions set out in s 46(3) of the CA 1998, allowing appeals against decisions not to grant interim measures under s 35. Although an amendment to the Act was brought forward by the Opposition to achieve this,[3] this was resisted at the time. The Government indicated, however, that secondary legislation would be brought forward, independently of the Act, to effect the change.

CLAIMS FOR DAMAGES

The Competition Act 1998 prior to the amendments

6.20   Damages have been available for injured parties under the terms of the CA 1998 since the entry into force of the two prohibitions. In relation to the application of Arts 81 and 82 EC, it was recognised in the case of *Garden Cottage Foods*[4] that:

> 'A breach of the duty imposed by [Art 82 EC] not to abuse a dominant position in the Common Market or a substantial part of it can thus be categorised in English law as a breach of statutory duty that is imposed not only for the purpose of promoting the general economic prosperity of the Common Market but also for the benefit of private individuals in whom loss or damage is caused by a breach of that duty.'[5]

---

[1]   These are decisions: (a) as to whether the Chapter I Prohibition has been infringed, (b) as to whether the Chapter II Prohibition has been infringed, (c) as to whether to grant an individual exemption, (d) in respect of individual exemptions whether to grant conditions or obligations, or the time-limits applicable, (e) as to extensions to exemptions, (f) as to whether to cancel any exemption.

[2]   In the *Explanatory Notes*, the position is that the 'responsibility for determining whether the party has sufficient interest will lie with the CAT' (para 72).

[3]   See *Hansard* (HL), 18 July 2002, col 1428.

[4]   *Garden Cottage Foods Ltd v Milk Marketing Board* [1983] 2 All ER 770, HL.

[5]   At pp 775–776.

6.21 Notwithstanding the longevity of this right, there is no reported case in which damages have been awarded in the UK in relation to a breach of either Art 81 or Art 82 EC, or the CA 1998 prohibitions. This position stands in stark contrast to that in the US, where private actions, fuelled by the availability of treble damages, and the recovery of an attorney's reasonable fee, are commonplace. Precisely what the factors are that have limited the bringing of private actions is not a matter into which any reliable research has been published. It is generally accepted that the legal culture in the UK is somewhat different from that in the US, and that there is a lesser tendency to litigate generally. It is also undeniable that the great majority of the judiciary in the UK have little, or no, experience of competition, and indeed little knowledge of the general economic principles that are applied in competition cases.[1] In the White Paper, the Government noted that:

> 'at present, private actions are likely to be brought before the High Court or, in the case of Scotland, the Court of Session. The costs can be high, and the judge considering the case is likely to have limited knowledge of competition law. The Government intends to streamline the judicial process so as to make it easier to bring these cases.'[2]

6.22 The only solace that third parties could take from the CA 1998, apart from the general right to damages based on breaches of the two prohibitions, lay in s 58, which provides that a Director's finding relevant to an issue in proceedings is binding on the parties, and that proceedings 'means proceedings which are brought otherwise than by the Director' (s 58(2)).[3] However, this presumption could be overturned if 'the court directs otherwise' (s 58(1)). It is hard to contemplate the circumstances in which a court *would* direct otherwise. One possibility might be where the market conditions had changed since the relevant decision was made, where the claim related to injunctive relief rather than damages for the past harm. Generally, however,

---

[1]   In this regard, it is perhaps instructive to compare the result reached by the court in the case of *Claritas (UK) Ltd v The Post Office and Postal Preference Service Ltd* [2001] UKCLR 2, with that of the OFT in its decision relating to a complaint in respect of the same conduct, *Consignia plc and Postal Preference Service Ltd* Decision CA98/4/2001, [2001] UKCLR 846. Note further that, in the case of *Napp Pharmaceutical Holdings Ltd and Subsidiaries v The Director General of Fair Trading* [2002] EWCA Civ 796, [2002] UKCLR 726, the Court of Appeal recognised the specialist nature of competition law, holding that the CCAT was 'an expert and specialist tribunal, specifically constituted by Parliament to make judgments in an area in which judges have no expertise' (para 34). In such a case, the court would be slow to overturn conclusions reached by the CCAT. In the House of Lords, an attempt was made to introduce into the domestic system a mechanism which would be similar to that of Art 234 EC. This provision, drafted by Sir Jeremy Lever QC, would have allowed courts faced with actions founded on competition law to refer certain points to the CAT for preliminary rulings, which would then be returned to the referring court for application (see, for example, *Hansard* (HL), 15 October 2002, cols 782–788). This attempt was rejected by the Government at Third Reading (see *Hansard*, 30 October 2002, cols 915–919).

[2]   Paragraph 8.6.

[3]   Livingston is somewhat critical, and pessimistic, regarding the state of the 'right' itself in domestic law, and its relationship with the rights available under Community law (see para 10.2.5). It was clear, however, that Parliament intended that there be rights, and s 58 makes no sense if it was not contemplated that there be private actions.

the effect of s 58 is to say that findings of fact made by the Director are binding on the courts where those findings have not been successfully challenged before the CCAT/CAT. As of September 2002, there had been only three sustainable decisions in which the Director had identified that there had been a breach of either the Chapter I Prohibition or the Chapter II Prohibition: *Napp*,[1] *John Bruce*,[2] and *Arriva/FirstGroup*.[3] While it may be presumed that in each of these cases some harm was suffered by either customers or competitors of the undertakings, there have been no reported actions brought against them. Allegations of excessive pricing in *Napp*, albeit not vigorously pursued on appeal, would presumably lead to quantifiable damages. It might be somewhat harder to calculate the damages flowing from the market-sharing arrangements on bus routes in Leeds, or from resale price maintenance of automatic slack adjusters.[4]

Section 58A of the CA 1998

6.23 A new s 58A, which reinforces the provisions of s 58, and makes clearer the relationship between the prohibitions of the CA 1998 and the right to civil damages, is inserted into the CA 1998 (by s 20 of the Act). This now makes express the fact that there may be proceedings before the court in which damages may be claimed. This applies not only to the prohibitions, but also to Arts 81 and 82 EC, where the OFT in the future makes a decision following the implementation of the 'new Regulation 17'.[5] No mention is made here of decisions made by the EC Commission which are, in any event, binding on the courts under the principles of direct effect and the supremacy of EC law.[6] Any court is bound, in such proceedings, by decisions of the OFT or the CAT, to the effect that any of these relevant provisions have been infringed. This section does *not*, for reasons which are unclear, apply to actions other than those related to damages or claims for money. There seems to be no logical reason why it should not equally apply to claims for other forms of relief. However, the existing s 58 applies to *all* claims, and it might be argued that s 58A does little more than clarify the already existing position.

---

[1] *Napp Pharmaceutical Holdings Ltd* Decision No CA98/2/2001, [2001] UKCLR 597, upheld on appeal *Napp Pharmaceutical Holdings Ltd v The Director General of Fair Trading* [2002] CompAR 13.

[2] *Price Fixing Agreements Involving John Bruce (UK) Ltd, Fleet Parts Ltd and Truck and Trailer Components* Decision No CA98/12/2002, [2002] UKCLR 435.

[3] *Market Sharing by Arriva Plc and FirstGroup plc* Decision No CA98/9/2002, [2002] UKCLR 322.

[4] The issue of the calculation of damages is considered at **6.31–6.37**.

[5] Council Regulation (EC) 1/2003; see **1.32**.

[6] This issue was re-opened in the case of *Masterfoods Ltd v HB Ice Cream Ltd; HB Ice Cream Ltd v Masterfoods Ltd* Case C-344/98, [2001] 4 CMLR 14. Here, the ECJ held that 'where a national court is ruling on an agreement or practice the compatibility of which with articles 81(1) and 82 of the Treaty is already the subject of a Commission decision, it cannot take a decision running counter to that of the Commission, even if the latter's decision conflicts with a decision given by a national court of first instance' (at para 60).

Section 47A of the CA 1998

6.24 Section 18 of the Act inserts into the CA 1998 a new s 47A, which greatly facilitates the ability of injured third parties to claim damages in respect of harms following on from breaches of the two prohibitions. It also applies in respect of Arts 81 and 82 EC, and the equivalent provisions in the European Coal and Steel Community (ECSC) Treaty. This provision does not replace, or in any way prejudice, the existing rights of third parties to bring actions in the courts independently of any administrative action.

6.25 The new section applies to 'any claim for damages' or 'any other claim for a sum of money', which 'a person who has suffered loss or damage as a result of the infringement of a relevant prohibition may make in civil proceedings' (CA 1998, s 47A(1)).[1] Claims to which this provision applies may be made in proceedings before the CAT. However, no such claim may be made until such time as there has been a decision as specified in s 47A(6). The relevant decisions are ones of either the OFT or the EC Commission, to the effect that there has been an infringement of the Chapter I or Chapter II Prohibitions, or of Art 81 or Art 82 EC (whether that decision is made by the EC Commission, or, post-modernisation, by the OFT), or of Arts 65(1) and 66(7) of the ECSC Treaty.[2] It was pointed out in committee that the Government had rejected such an approach at the time of the introduction of the CA 1998.[3]

6.25 The key element in s 47A is sub-section (9), in which it is set out that:

> 'In determining a claim to which this section applies the Tribunal is bound by any decision mentioned in subsection (6) which establishes that the prohibition in question has been infringed.'

6.26 The time-limits set out in s 47A(7) and (8) exclude the bringing of claims in the periods during which appeals against those decisions· may be made, or in which appeals against rulings of the CAT (or the CFI, as appropriate) may be further appealed. This ensures that the provision applies

---

[1] The CAT may not therefore hear cases relating to claims for injunctive or other relief.

[2] Although note that the ECSC Treaty expired on 23 July 2002. However, actions brought on the basis of breaches of its provisions may continue for some time.

[3] Mr Djanogly quoted a Library research paper: 'We have considered carefully the option of making the Competition Commission, as opposed to the Courts, the forum to hear private law actions for breach of the prohibition such as claims by third parties for damages or interim relief. We have concluded that there are significant drawbacks to such private actions being heard in the tribunal. In practice the application of the prohibition would often by one of many areas of the commercial dispute to resolve which, in turn, could lead to an unnecessary duplication of fact finding as the tribunal heard competition law points and the courts heard other aspects of the same case. Moreover, if the tribunal were to hear such private law actions, this could prejudice its primary objective of providing a quick and efficient review of DGFT decisions. We have therefore decided that such private actions should be heard in the courts' (*Hansard*, Standing Committee B, col 114).

only to decisions which have either been uncontested, or which have been upheld on appeal. Further, findings of the CAT which alter a Decision of the OFT, and which might, for example find an infringement where the OFT has not found one, may also be relied upon under this section.

6.28 The effect of this is that once the relevant administrative authority has, by way of formal decision, found that there has been an infringement of one of the relevant provisions, and there has either been no appeal, or appeals have been unsuccessful, a claimant may bring an action before the CAT exclusively for damages, without the need to establish any of the matters relating to the substance of the infringement itself. This greatly alters the dynamics of the process, and is certain to encourage claims to be brought forward. One side effect is that it is also likely to encourage more complaints to be brought before the OFT, as an alternative to pursuing cases before the civil courts. Given that, if the OFT pursues the complaint, there are no cost implications to the complainant/claimant in this procedure, and the OFT will bear the burden of investigation, and may, in the appropriate circumstances, issue an interim measures order,[1] there would seem to be little incentive for bearing the costs and risks of initiating a private action.

6.29 It is difficult, at this early stage, to predict how s 47A will relate to s 58A (see **6.23**), and what factors will determine whether an action for damages is brought before the CAT or before any other court.

6.30 This section has a retroactive effect, and therefore allows actions to be initiated on the basis of harm arising prior to the enactment of the Act. Limitations periods will be set in the tribunal rules to be made by the Secretary of State. It is likely that the period will be aligned to Limitation Act 1980, s 2, under which the period in relation to claims before the courts is six years.

The assessment of damages

6.31 The issue of the assessment of damages in competition cases is not a straightforward one, with issues relating to both causation and quantum raising many problems, and it is one in which economic and accountancy evidence is likely to play a significant role. In the White Paper, it is provided that 'clear tests of whether a claimant had just cause and the formula by which the Tribunals would calculate damages would be laid out'.[2]

---

[1] CA 1998, s 35. See the discussion of this in the OFT guideline, *Enforcement*, paras 3.1–3.14.
[2] Paragraph 8.8.

6.32 In the US, there has been substantial case-law relating to the questions of who has standing to bring actions for antitrust injury, and how injuries to these persons are to be calculated.[1]

6.33 In relation to those who have the standing to sue, the US Supreme Court, in *Cargill*,[2] held that 'a showing of antitrust injury is necessary, but not always sufficient, to establish standing … a party may have suffered antitrust injury but may not be a proper plaintiff … for other reasons'.[3] These other reasons 'include the risk of duplication of damages, the indirectness of the harm, the speculativeness of the harm, and the existence of better-situated plaintiffs'.[4] A particular problem relates to that of 'indirect purchasers' of products or services which have been supplied to a first party and then resold. What, for example, is the position to be where a cartel amongst producers of a primary or intermediate product results in the raising of prices to the producers of the final product, which are then passed on to the end customers? Both sides of this equation have been dealt with by the US courts. In *Hanover Shoe*,[5] the court rejected the argument made by the defendant that the plaintiffs had suffered no harm because they had passed on the price increases to their own customers. The court held that to entertain such arguments would be to open up the spectre of increasingly complex litigation, holding that:

> 'we are not impressed with the argument that sound laws of economics require recognizing this defense … Normally the impact of a single change in the relevant conditions cannot be measured after the fact; indeed a businessman may be unable to state whether, had one fact been different … he would have chosen a different price.'[6]

The second part of the equation was dealt with in the case of *Illinois Brick*,[7] where the court held that the flip-side of the ruling in *Hanover Shoe* was that purchasers down the line could not also sue for the injury of higher prices, with the court recognising that 'allowing offensive without defensive use of pass-on would create a serious risk of multiple liability for defendants'.[8]

6.34 In the debates on the passage of the CA 1998, the Government's position was that 'third party rights of action under the domestic regime are to

---

[1]   See generally, Jones, CA *Private Enforcement of Antitrust Law in the EU, UK and USA* (Oxford, OUP, 1999), Chapters 13, 14, 15, 17 and 18. See also American Bar Association, Antitrust Section, *Proving Antitrust Damages: Legal and Economic Issues* (Chicago, ABA, 1996).

[2]   *Cargill, Inc v Monfort, Inc* 479 US 104 (1986).

[3]   At 110, n 5.

[4]   American Bar Association, fn 1 above, p 14.

[5]   *Hanover Shoe, Inc v United Shoe Machinery Corp* 392 US 481 (1968).

[6]   At 492–493, quoted in Jones, fn 1 above, at pp 177–178.

[7]   *Illinois Brick Co v Illinois* 431 US 720 (1977).

[8]   At 730. For references to some of the extensive literature relating to this case, see Jones, fn 1 above, p 179, n 41.

be the same as those under articles 81 and 82 EC'.[1] It is unfortunate, then, that the law relating to the availability of damages is so underdeveloped at the Community level. Indeed, the general principle of EC law in this regard is that questions relating to procedural issues, including civil rights and obligations, are to be resolved by reference to equivalent national principles. In this case, CA 1998, s 60 appears to be of somewhat limited use – the courts are required to be consistent with the principles of EC law, which requires courts in Member States to be consistent with national principles, while ensuring the efficacy of any Community-derived rights. Based on an analysis of existing EC principles, however, Jones argues that:

> 'Community law does not permit adoption of the *Illinois Brick* rule. The rule in *Illinois Brick* would deny compensation to "indirect purchaser" legal and natural persons suffering actual injury from infringement of their directly effective rights. … this would result in an intolerable disparity between the scope of the remedy and the substance of the directly effective rights. Accordingly, it seems that in the Community, indirect purchasers able to prove injury must be allowed to do so without the artificial limitation imposed by *Illinois Brick* in the USA.'[2]

In the *Explanatory Notes*, it is suggested that *Illinois Brick* will not apply in the UK. In relation to claims brought on behalf of consumers (see **6.38–6.42**), the DTI suggests that claims may be sustained where 'a consumer has bought goods for his or her own use, whose price has been inflated by a price-fixing agreement … possibly among the manufacturers' own supplies'.[3] Section 47B of the CA 1998 refers to infringements suffered 'indirectly' (see **6.40**). This is just one of the issues which the CAT or other civil court will have to presumably address at some point.

6.35 In addition to the conceptual problems underpinning the preliminary, but vital, issue of who may be allowed to sue for damages, there are very substantial practical difficulties in proving the assessment of those damages. The issue may be clearly demonstrated with reference to the existing EC and domestic case-law relating to excessive pricing. In the *Napp* decision,[4] the Director argued, applying the OFT guidelines and pre-existing EC case-law, that:

> 'a price is excessive and an abuse if it is above that which would exist in a competitive market, and where it is clear that high profits will not stimulate successful new entry within a reasonable period. Therefore, to show that prices are excessive, it must be demonstrated that (i) prices are higher than would be expected in a competitive market, and (ii) that there is no effective competitor pressure to bring them down to competitive levels, nor is there likely to be.'[5]

---

[1]   *Hansard* (HL), 25 November 1997, col 955.
[2]   At p 195.
[3]   Paragraph 77.
[4]   *Napp Pharmaceutical Holdings Ltd* Decision No CA 98/2/2001, [2001] UKCLR 597.
[5]   Paragraph 203.

Various calculations were made in the decision relating to Napp's prices, costs and profitability, compared to those of its competitors. Comparisons of prices showed that Napp's were, to the relevant sector of the market, between 33% and 67% higher than those of the next nearest competitor.[1] However, no precise figure was given in the decision of what the 'competitive price' would have been, which would have enabled the calculation of the amount of the 'excessive price' to be carried out. The CCAT, on appeal, held that the fact that it was difficult to calculate whether a price is higher than that which would exist in a competitive market does not mean that the exercise should not be undertaken. All the comparisons that could be made in the case were indicative of excessive pricing, and it did not matter that the Director had not been able to specify by how much the prices were excessive.[2] However, in a case for damages, once standing has been established, the first question must be 'how much damage was caused to the claimant?'. In a case brought on the basis of the finding of an abusive excessive price, contrary to the Chapter II Prohibition, it will presumably be necessary for some attempt to be made to calculate the amount by which the price is excessive. It is difficult to see, on a reading of the *Napp* decision, how this could in its present state form the evidentiary basis for the calculation of damages.

6.36   In the US, the courts have been robust in their pragmatism and have not required plaintiffs to follow set models of analysis in relation to the assessment of damages. Thus, in the case of *Lehrman*, the court recognised that:

> '... the law is clear: the courts are to take a charitable view of the difficulties of proving damages in a case when a ... plaintiff must try to prove what would have accrued to him in the absence of the defendant's anti-competitive practice. But this tolerant view is limited by our responsibility not to allow damages to be determined by "guess work" or "speculation"; we must at least insist upon a "just and reasonable estimate of the damage based on relevant data".'[3]

Elsewhere, it has been noted that 'the standards for proving the *fact* that the plaintiff was injured are more stringent than those for proving the *amount* of that injury'.[4] Bearing in mind that damages in the US are to be assessed by juries,[5] it is the position that 'once the plaintiff establishes the fact of damage or injury with reasonable certainty, the jury will be permitted "to make a just

---

[1]   Table 6.

[2]   Paragraphs 392–405.

[3]   *Lehrman v Gulf Oil Corp* 464 F 2d 46 (5th Cir); *cert denied* 409 US 1077 (1972), quoted in Jones, CA *Private Enforcement of Antitrust Law in the EU, UK and USA* (Oxford, OUP, 1999), p 206.

[4]   American Bar Association, Antitrust Section, *Proving Antitrust Damages: Legal and Economic Issues* (Chicago, ABA, 1996), p 31.

[5]   Note also that juries are not told *ex ante* that the award they make will be trebled by the effect of s 4 of the Clayton Act.

and reasonable estimate of the damage based on the relevant data"'.[1] However, the plaintiff does not have carte blanche in this respect and must 'come forward with the best, most accurate measure of damages that is reasonably available'.[2]

6.37 It is beyond the scope of this book to consider the quantitative methods of proof in any detail, and the reader is referred to *Proving Antitrust Damages*,[3] Part Two, which provides an introduction to some of the relevant techniques. It is certain that the leading economic consultancy firms working in this area will make themselves available in the preparation of damages assessments.

CLAIMS ON BEHALF OF CONSUMERS

6.38 In the White Paper, the Government made clear its intention of somehow facilitating the bringing of actions by multiple parties, or 'representative claims' – justifiably described as 'a massive departure for the English legal system'.[4] This proposal was set out at paras 8.17 and 8.18:

> 'The Government wishes to take specific steps to facilitate damages actions on behalf of consumers. Often such cases will involve a large number of harmed parties – each of whom may only have suffered relatively small loss. In such cases, it is much more sensible that claims are brought on behalf of those that suffer by representative consumer bodies.'

Some of the difficulties of devising an effective system of doing this have already been alluded to above (see **6.3**). The proposal met with sharp criticism by the Confederation of British Industry (CBI), which argued that:

> 'In our view, allowing consumer groups the right to bring actions for damages is one of the most ill-conceived and potentially damaging proposals in the entire Bill. Overall, the precedent of class actions in the USA is a very disturbing one and should be avoided here at all costs. The task of consumer organisations should be to bring suspected anti-competitive practices to the attention of the OFT, not to bring proceedings themselves, which would effectively turn such bodies into prosecuting authorities.'[5]

---

[1] American Bar Association, Antitrust Section, *Proving Antitrust Damages: Legal and Economic Issues* (Chicago, ABA, 1996), p 33, quoting *Bigelow v RKO Radio Pictures* 327 US 251.

[2] *Southern Pac. Communications Co v AT&T* 556 F Supp 825, 1090 (DDC 1983).

[3] See fn 1 above.

[4] Mr Waterson (*Hansard*, Standing Committee B, col 123). Such actions have not been permitted in the UK to date, but see LCD *Representative Claims: Proposed New Procedures*, February 2001.

[5] Cited by Mr Waterson (*Hansard*, Standing Committee B, col 124). Dealing with these concerns later on in Committee, the Under-Secretary of State argued that:

> 'The actions in the clause are not exactly the same as US class actions. One of the important differences is that class actions are allowed in the US on behalf of an amorphous and unnamed group of individuals, but consumer claims for damages will be allowed here only on behalf of named, identified consumers – a significant difference – and only with their consent. US class actions are brought in the ordinary courts, but here they will be brought before the CAT only

6.39   One option proposed by the Government was:

> 'to enable selected bodies, such as the Consumers' Association, the National Consumer Council or sectoral consumer bodies, to make a claim for damages on behalf of a wider group or class of consumers in specific circumstances. Following the general legal principle that a plaintiff should have just cause to seek damages and be able to demonstrate the nature and extent of the harm suffered, a representative body would need to be able to identify the numbers of consumers falling into the class and the overall economic harm suffered. This might be possible where the OFT has found that an undertaking is in breach of competition law. In making its decision, the OFT will already have defined a market and determined the economic effect of the company's behaviour. The case would then be brought in the wider public interest.'[1]

6.40   These proposals have taken shape in s 19 of the Act, which inserts a new s 47B into the CA 1998. This allows for the bringing of a claim before the CAT by a 'specified body' where it claims on behalf of at least two specified consumers. There was some pressure from the Opposition, following a suggestion of the CBI, that the number be increased, and a figure of 50 was proposed.[2] It is for the Secretary of State to designate the specified bodies, and they are likely to be the same as those organisations designated in relation to super-complaints (see **6.7**). The consumers may have already initiated those claims – in which case, their approval is required for the claim to be subsumed into the representative action – but this is not a requirement. A 'consumer claim' is one 'to which s 47A [of the CA 1998[3]] applies which an individual has in respect of an infringement affecting (directly or indirectly) goods or services' (s 47B(2)). All consumer claims brought together in a single action must relate to the same infringement. Section 47A(5)–(10), discussed above, applies in relation to s 47B. This, again, means that representative actions may not be brought before the CAT until such time as there has been a sustained adverse decision made by a relevant authority.

6.41   Claims may be brought under this section only in respect of goods or services supplied 'in the course of a business', and received 'otherwise than in

---

following a decision of the OFT or the European Commission that established a breach of competition law' (*Hansard*, Standing Committee B, col 130).

[1]   Paragraph 8.21.

[2]   See *Hansard*, Standing Committee B, cols 120 and 121. In response, the Under-Secretary of State argued that:

> 'Consumer group claims about named individuals are an important part of the strategy to encourage harmed parties to claim redress when damaged by anti-competitive activity. Group claims make it more affordable for the average consumer to gain redress in those cases where a breach of competition laws has already been established. That is another point to bear in mind.
>
> Raising the number required to participate in a group claim merely puts barriers in the way of consumers who are legitimately trying to gain recompense for damage incurred as a result of activities that have already been found to breach the competition law' (*Hansard*, Standing Committee B, cols 121 and 122).

[3]   See **6.24–6.37**.

the course of a business' (s 47B(7)). 'Business' is given a wide meaning in s 47B(8).

6.42 One of the problems with representative claims is to whom the damages should be awarded. In particular, the question arises as to whether it is necessary for damages to be awarded in individual amounts to specified claimants, or whether they may be awarded in aggregate to the representative body, and either held by that body for disbursement to claimants as they come forward, or put to some other approved use. In the White Paper, for example, it was suggested that damages could possibly be awarded in aggregate, and where not disbursed, 'used for other purposes which benefit consumers of the product in question or those in related markets'.[1] The solution adopted in s 47B is to require that damages be awarded 'to the individual concerned' (s 47B(6)). However, 'the Tribunal may, with the consent of the specified body and the individual, order that the sum awarded must be paid to the specified body (acting on behalf of the individual)'. Claims may then be enforced in accordance with Sch 4, paras 2–8. Tribunal rules to be made by the Secretary of State will make provision for the relevant limitation periods.

6.43 Schedule 4, para 6 provides that where an award has been made following a representative action, the individual(s) concerned may enforce the award only with the permission of the relevant court – the expectation being that the award will be enforced by the representative body rather than by the specified individuals.

---

[1] Paragraph 8.22.

Chapter Seven

MISCELLANEOUS PROVISIONS

INTRODUCTION

7.1 This chapter brings together a number of provisions which do not logically belong to any of the other, more specific chapters. Notwithstanding their relegation to a chapter of miscellanies, some of these provisions, particularly those relating to the disqualification of directors, are of the utmost importance.

DIRECTORS' DISQUALIFICATION

7.2 Whilst it is the provisions in the Act relating to criminal enforcement regarding cartels that are likely to attract the greatest media attention, in practice, the threat of directors' disqualification following breaches of competition law will more probably ensure compliance.

7.3 In the White Paper, the Government announced that it would be:

'... in the public interest that directors who have engaged in serious breaches of competition law should be exposed to the possibility of disqualification on that ground alone. It therefore proposes to legislate to enable the OFT to seek a court order disqualifying a director from acting in the management of a limited liability company where breaches of competition law have been found. The OFT would be able to do this irrespective of whether a criminal prosecution has taken place and irrespective of whether the director was aware that agreements were in breach of EC and UK competition law.'[1]

7.4 In accordance with this principle, s 204 of the Act amends the Company Directors Disqualification Act 1986 (CDDA 1986), inserting

---

[1] Paragraph 8.24.

ss 9A–9E.[1] In July 2002, the Office of Fair Trading (OFT) published its consultation paper, *Competition Disqualification Orders*, which is referred to throughout this chapter.

7.5   Section 9A of the CDDA 1986 provides that the appropriate court *must* make a competition disqualification order (CDO) against a person, following an application by the OFT or other appropriate regulator, where the conditions are met. The first condition is that an undertaking[2] of which that person is a director commits a breach of competition law. The relevant competition laws are the Chapter I and Chapter II Prohibitions, and Arts 81 and 82 EC,[3] but not, in this context, Part 6 of the Act relating to cartel offences. The second condition is that the 'court considers that his conduct as a director makes him unfit to be concerned in the management of a company'. In making this determination, the court is to consider the criteria set out later in s 9A(6). These are either that his or her conduct contributed to the breach, that his or her conduct did not contribute to the breach but he or she had reasonable grounds to suspect the breach and took no steps to prevent it, or that he or she did not know of the breach but should have known of it. The court may also consider the involvement of the director in any other breaches of competition law, but cannot have regard to the matters referred to in Sch 1 to the CDDA 1986.

7.6   With regard to the first condition to be met in relation to the individual director, it should be noted that s 9A(7) makes it clear that 'it is immaterial whether the person knew that the conduct of the undertaking constituted the breach'. Where undertakings operate compliance programmes, or where management takes advice in relation to commercial conduct about possible competition law exposure, it is possible that, faced with the threat of disqualification, a director might choose not to seek such advice, or might curtail the ambit of compliance programmes in the hope that, by doing so, he or she could plead ignorance in the event of an eventual breach leading to the threat of disqualification. It is clear from the terms of these provisions that such an approach will not be successful. Directors will face disqualification

---

[1]   Under the existing arrangements, between 1996 and 2001, some 7,607 directors were disqualified (*Hansard*, Standing Committee B, col 218).

[2]   'Undertaking' is to have the same meaning as it does in relation to the application of EC competition law and the CA 1998. 'Company' includes unregistered companies for the purposes of the CDDA 1986 (s 22(2)(b)), and may include companies registered outside Great Britain. Limited liability partnerships are also included within the terms of the CDDA 1986 (Limited Liability Partnership Regulations 2001 (SI 2001/1090), reg 4(2)(a)).

[3]   The OFT has indicated in its guidance that 'it is not the intention of the OFT to apply for CDOs where the infringement to which the determination relates does/did not have an actual or potential effect on the pattern of trade in the United Kingdom' (para 4.5). This is to say that a UK-based company engaged in an abuse of dominant position, or a practice contrary to Art 81 EC *elsewhere* in the EC, with no impact in the UK, will not face the prospect of CDOs being sought against its directors.

where they know, or *should have known*, of the breaches. However, the Under-Secretary of State indicated that 'the vast majority of cases will relate to active involvement in a breach of competition law rather than anything else'.[1]

7.7 When a disqualification order is made, the maximum period of the disqualification is 15 years. By virtue of CDDA 1986, s 13, it is a criminal offence for a person, while disqualified, to be a director of a company, to act as a receiver of a company's property, to take part in any way in the promotion or formation of a company, or to act as an insolvency practitioner. Further, if a person subject to a disqualification order is involved in the management of a company, then he or she is personally liable for all the relevant debts of that company.[2]

7.8 In determining whether to take an action relating to a CDO, the OFT or other regulator has the powers of investigation conferred under CA 1998, ss 26–30. Before using these powers, the relevant authority must issue a notice under CDDA 1986, s 9C (a 'section 9C notice'), giving the director the opportunity to make representations.

7.9 It is for the OFT to apply to the court to seek a CDO (CDDA 1986, s 9A(10)). The OFT has indicated in its guidance that it will consider the following factors in considering whether to apply for a CDO:

'(a) whether there has been a prior determination of a breach of competition law by an undertaking which is a company

(b) whether the undertaking in question has been granted lenient treatment in respect of a financial penalty for that breach of competition law

(c) the seriousness of the case, having regard to any aggravating and mitigating factors. For example, mitigating factors include evidence that before the prior determination of breach a director could not reasonably have known that by carrying out or agreeing to carry out the activity in question the company would breach competition law.'[3]

7.10 The threat of CDOs is clearly being used as part of the incentive for undertakings and their directors to avail themselves of the OFT leniency policy in relation to the application of the Chapter I Prohibition.[4] Thus, the OFT has indicated already that it:

---

[1] *Hansard*, Standing Committee B, col 218.

[2] CDDA 1986, s 15.

[3] OFT *Competition Disqualification Orders* (July 2002), para 4.2.

[4] This applies equally to the EC Commission approach set out in its *Notice on Immunity from Fines and Reduction of Fines in Cartel Cases*.

'will *not* apply for a CDO against *any* current director of an undertaking whose company is the beneficiary of a grant of leniency, in respect of the activities to which the grant of leniency relates.'[1]

7.11   One of the key considerations that will influence the OFT's decision on whether to apply for a CDO is the seriousness of the case, and the guidance goes some way to explaining the approach that will be taken. Six factors are set out as being indicative of 'particularly serious cases'. These are that the director:

'•   planned, devised, approved or encouraged the activity of the undertaking which caused the breach;
•   ordered, encouraged or advocated that his or her undertaking participate in the breach of competition law;
•   ordered or pressured those identified as having a direct or indirect role in the breach to engage in the activity causing the breach;
•   attended meetings (internal or external) in which the activity constituting the breach either occurred or was discussed, or both;
•   directed, ordered or pressured staff of the undertaking to attend meetings (internal or external) for the purpose of participating in or discussing the activity constituting the breach;
•   ordered, encouraged or advocated retaliation against other undertakings who were reluctant to or refused to participate in the activity constituting the breach of competition law.'

Where any two or more of these factors are present, the OFT is very likely to bring an action seeking a CDO. As the OFT explains:

'The key consideration is whether the director had an active role in causing his or her company to carry out or agree to carry out the activity constituting the breach. If the director did not know that by carrying out or agreeing to carry out the activity in question the company would breach competition law, a CDO may still be sought. However, evidence that the director could not reasonably have known that by carrying out or agreeing to carry out [the] activity in question the company would breach competition law will be a mitigating factor when the OFT is considering whether to apply for a CDO.'[2]

7.12   In cases which are 'serious', the view of the OFT is that it is 'likely' to apply for a CDO. Serious cases are those where there is evidence that the director knew, or had reasonable grounds to know, that there was a breach of competition law in the company for which he or she was responsible and did nothing to stop it, or where he or she authorised or approved funds in relation

[1]   OFT *Competition Disqualification Orders* (July 2002), para 4.8. However, the OFT has stated that:
'Where a person ceased to be a director of a company prior to the grant of leniency, the OFT may still consider applying for a CDO against that person. Similarly, where a director has at any time been removed as a director of a company owing to his or her role in the breach of competition law in question, then the OFT may still consider applying for a CDO against that person, irrespective of whether his or her former company has been granted leniency by the OFT or European Commission' (para 4.9).
[2]   Ibid, para 4.12.

to the breach.[1] This might include, for example, authorising expenses incurred during the course of attending a cartel meeting.

7.13 Less serious cases are those in which none of the factors discussed above is present, and 'include situations in which there is no evidence that the director was actually aware of the activity constituting the breach of competition law, but ought to have known'. It might be the case, for example, that 'a director may have deliberately failed to inform himself or herself about the actions of the company'.[2] In these cases, the OFT is not precluded from taking action against a director, although whether it does so will depend on its priorities and commitments at the time. As a general warning, the OFT makes clear that it:

> 'considers that *all* directors of *all* companies may reasonably be expected to *know* that companies must comply with competition law.
>
> The OFT further considers that all directors of a company which in the past has been found to have infringed competition law ought to be actively vigilant against the commission of new competition law breaches by their company.'[3]

7.14 Further aggravating and mitigating factors are set out in paras 4.26–4.28. Aggravating factors include evidence that the director:

– has been involved in competition law breaches previously;
– destroyed or encouraged others to destroy evidence of breaches;
– was unco-operative or obstructive in the course of investigations;
– was engaged in continuing breaches following the initiation of active investigations.

Mitigating factors include evidence to the effect that:

– the director could not, prior to the breach, have reasonably determined that the activity in question would breach competition law. This might be the case, for example, where the conduct was novel, and found to be a breach for the first time, or where an undertaking could not have reasonably known that it was in a dominant position;
– the undertaking committed the breach in response to serious pressure, as might be the case, for example, where an undertaking was coerced into a cartel;
– the director strongly objected to a board resolution determining the breach, or advised that competition law advice should be sought, and, in both cases, voted against the resolution.

---

[1] OFT *Competition Disqualification Orders* (July 2002), para 4.14.
[2] Ibid, para 4.15.
[3] Ibid, paras 4.17 and 4.18.

7.15   In cases in which a director has been convicted of a cartel offence, the CDDA 1986 already provides that that court may make a disqualification order against the individual.[1] In any such case, the OFT is unlikely to use its new powers under CDDA 1986, s 9A. In a case where the OFT has issued a no-action letter in relation to a cartel offence, it will not apply for a CDO against any beneficiary of that letter.

7.16   In large organisations in particular, there will clearly be concerns about the extent to which an individual director may be presumed to have direct knowledge, not of the obligations imposed by the law, but of infringements of it. There have been situations in the past in which companies have sought to avoid liability under the provisions of the FTA 1973 when undertakings or orders have been made, by claiming that subsequent breaches were, in effect, independent actions of rogue employees, and there may well be situations in which an employee would have an incentive to break competition law in order, for example, to achieve targets and earn bonuses. One concern is that directors may be reluctant to become involved in compliance programmes if these are likely to mean that they are considered to have a closer link to breaches of competition law if these are found to have taken place.[2] While this temptation is perhaps understandable, the better approach must be to operate as effective a compliance programme as possible, so as to be able to demonstrate, in the event of any subsequent breach, that it was neither approved of, nor known of, by directors.[3] One of the factors that will be considered by the OFT, for example, is whether any persons committing the breach took steps to conceal it from their colleagues.[4]

7.17   In general, the position of the OFT is that the closer the gap in the company hierarchy is between the director and the person committing the

---

[1]   CDDA 1986, s 2(1) and (2)(b).

[2]   In *Market Sharing by Arriva Plc and First Group plc* Decision No CA98/9/2002, [2002] UKCLR 322, for example, the breach of competition law in question involved managers who failed to comply with the internal compliance programme operated by one of the companies, which required that contacts with competitors be logged.

[3]   In the OFT technical guideline *Enforcement* [1999] UKCLR 217, the position of compliance programmes is dealt with in para 4.35:

'When assessing the amount of any penalty the Director General may take into account, as a mitigating circumstance, the existence of a compliance programme. In order for a compliance programme to reduce a penalty as a mitigating circumstance, the parties will need to show that:
- the programme has been actively implemented;
- it has the visible and continuing support of, and is observed by, senior management;
- there are appropriate compliance policies and procedures in place;
- there is active and ongoing training for employees at all levels who may be involved in activities that are touched by competition law; and
- the programme is evaluated and formal audits are carried out at regular intervals to ensure that it is delivering its objectives.'

[4]   OFT *Competition Disqualification Orders* (July 2002), para 4.22.

breach, the more likely it is that knowledge will be imputed to the director, or that the director ought to have known of the breach.

7.18 In some cases, and particularly where a breach has followed a decision of the board of directors as a whole, the OFT might proceed against all directors. In such a case, the mere fact that a particular director was not present at the operative meeting might not be sufficient to exclude him or her from the action. The question in such a circumstance will be whether the director knew about the action, and took any steps to prevent the board from acting as it did.[1]

7.19 As an alternative to a full court proceeding leading to disqualification, the OFT or relevant regulator may seek a disqualification undertaking from a person whose conduct they believe 'makes him unfit to be concerned in the management of a company' (CDDA 1986, s 9B). The effect of such an undertaking is similar to that of an order. In its guidance, the OFT has indicated that, following the issue of a s 9C notice, it 'will give very serious consideration' to a disqualification undertaking offered. 'Whether or not such an offer will be accepted by the OFT will depend upon the facts of the case, as well as upon the period of disqualification offered.'[2] Any period of disqualification offered in an undertaking must be 'proportionate to the case, taking into account any aggravating or mitigating circumstances'.[3]

7.20 The powers available to the OFT under this part of the CDDA 1986 are, as indicated above, also available to concurrent regulators,[4] and the Secretary of State has been given the power to make regulations for the purpose of co-ordinating the activity of these various bodies in relation to these functions.

COMPETITION ACT 1998 INVESTIGATIONS

7.21 A minor amendment is made to ss 28, 62 and 63 of the CA 1998 which provides that, in the event of entry under a warrant, persons named in it (s 203) may accompany the named or authorised officers executing the warrant. The purpose of this amendment is to allow people who are not

---

[1] OFT *Competition Disqualification Orders* (July 2002), paras 4.23–4.25.

[2] Ibid, para 5.3.

[3] Ibid, para 5.4.

[4] Which, for the purposes of these provisions, are: the Director General of Telecommunications; the Gas and Electricity Markets Authority; the Director General of Water Services; the Rail Regulator; the Civil Aviation Authority.

employees of the OFT, but who have expertise that would be helpful in the course of the investigation, to accompany the OFT staff.

INFORMATION AND ITS EXCHANGE

7.22 Part 9 of the Act relates to the disclosure of information held by the public authorities relating to competition and consumer matters. The general thrust of the Part is explained in the *Explanatory Notes*:

> 'This Part creates a new gateway that sets out general restrictions for the disclosure of specified information held by public authorities. It reflects the Government strategy of widening and harmonising the gateways through which information can be disclosed in the UK and overseas and at the same time introduces appropriate safeguards in respect of permitted disclosure of information.
>
> The Anti-Terrorism, Crime and Security Act 2001 introduced a new gateway (and amended numerous existing gateways) to allow the disclosure of certain information to UK and overseas authorities for the purpose of pursuing criminal investigations or proceedings. The provisions in this Part create a corresponding gateway for disclosure of information relating to consumer and competition matters for the purpose of criminal investigations and proceedings in the UK and overseas. However, they also create a gateway to allow certain information to be disclosed for use in relation to certain civil investigations and proceedings in the UK and overseas. The wider gateway is necessary for the disclosure of information relating to consumer and competition matters as overseas enforcement of such legislation is often under a civil regime.'[1]

7.23 A general restriction on the disclosure of information by any public authority is set out in s 237.[2] Any 'specified information' relating to the affairs of an individual, or any business of an undertaking may not be disclosed unless disclosure is permitted under this Part of the Act. 'Specified information' is defined in s 238 as being that which is obtained by a public authority in connection with the performance of its tasks by virtue, *inter alia*, of Parts 1 (the OFT), 3 (mergers), 4 (market investigations), 6 (cartel offences), and 7 (miscellaneous provisions) of the Act, or where it is obtained under any enactment specified in Sch 14. The restriction does not apply to information which has already been legitimately disclosed. 'Public authority' has the same meaning as under Human Rights Act 1998, s 6.[3]

7.24 In situations where the consent of the person or undertaking to which the information relates is given, the relevant information may be disclosed.

---

[1] Paragraphs 570 and 571.
[2] Part 9 of the Act does not relate, however, to the functions of the CAT.
[3] This includes courts and tribunals, as well as any person exercising functions of a public nature.

7.25 It is an offence to disclose information contrary to this Part of the Act (s 245).

Statutory functions

7.26 There are a number of circumstances in which information may be disclosed. However, in respect of all of these, there is a general obligation on the authority to exclude from disclosure, so far as is practicable, information the disclosure of which would be against the public interest, or information which is commercial information, the disclosure of which would significantly harm the legitimate business interests of the undertaking, or which is private information the disclosure of which would significantly harm the interests of the individual concerned (s 244). The first circumstance where information may be disclosed arises where it is necessary to disclose it for the purpose of fulfilling an obligation relating to the EC (s 235). The second arises in relation to 'facilitating the exercise by the authority of any function it has under or by virtue of this Act or any other enactment' (s 241(1)). Any public authority holding the relevant information may also disclose it to any other authority for the purpose of facilitating their functions under relevant legislation (s 241(3)). This permits, for example, the exchange of information between the OFT and a sector regulator. Relevant enactments are specified in Sch 15. Information exchanged in this way can be used *solely* for the purposes set out in s 241(3).

Criminal proceedings

7.27 Section 242 relates to information disclosed for the purposes of the investigation or the bringing of criminal proceedings. In this regard, there is no restriction relating to statutory functions, and the disclosure may be in respect of the enforcement of any enactment where criminal proceedings may be brought. This would apply, for example, to tax avoidance offences, cartel offences, and fraud offences.

Overseas authorities

7.28 Section 243 is intended to allow information to be given to authorities overseas when they are enforcing, whether by criminal or civil means, competition or consumer legislation ('relevant legislation'). The most important qualification to this provision is that it does not apply to information obtained in relation to merger references and market investigation references.[1] The Secretary of State may also direct that disclosures will not be made in situations in which it appears to him more appropriate to investigate the actions in the UK (s 243(4)).

7.29   A set of factors to be considered in determining whether to disclose the information is set out in s 243(6). These are: whether the matter is sufficiently serious; whether the law of the relevant country provides adequate protection against self-incrimination; and whether mutual assistance arrangements are in place. This list may be modified by the Secretary of State by order.

7.30   Any information disclosed under this section may be used by the relevant overseas authority only for the purposes for which it is disclosed.

REFORM OF EC COMPETITION LAW

7.31   As we have seen in Chapter 1, and throughout the text, domestic competition law interacts extensively with EC competition law. In particular, the CA 1998 is explicitly designed to harmonise the domestic regime with the EC regime to a substantial extent. As a result of the changes being wrought to EC competition law by virtue of the modernisation programme, a number of consequential amendments are going to be necessary to the CA 1998. Section 209 of the Act gives the Secretary of State the power to make necessary amendments to the CA 1998 by regulations, rather than by the fuller legislative process that would ordinarily required. This should ensure that now the new EC Procedural Regulation has been enacted, the UK regime can adapt quickly. In particular, provisions relating to the Chapter I Prohibition, which make reference to the exemption process under Art 81 EC and Regulation 17, will need to be modified.[2] Any such Regulations must be approved by a resolution of each of the Houses of Parliament.

Exclusion of conduct from the Chapter I Prohibition

7.32   Section 209 also allows the Secretary of State to modify any provision of the CA 1998 'which excludes any matter from the Chapter I Prohibition or the Chapter II Prohibition' (s 209(3)). Section 50 of the CA 1998 gave the Secretary of State the power to exclude from the operation of the Chapter I Prohibition vertical agreements and land agreements. The exclusion of vertical

---

[1]   Similarly, it does not apply in relation to information obtained under Parts 4 (monopoly references), 5 (mergers) and 6 (general references) of the FTA 1973.

[2]   See, for example, ss 9 and 10 of the CA 1998.

agreements from the Chapter I Prohibition, save in situations where they were price-fixing agreements,[1] drew a clear wedge between the operation in practice of Art 81 EC and the Chapter I Prohibition, and constituted a 'relevant difference' for the purpose of CA 1998, s 60.

7.33 In the UK, the view was taken that, in the absence of significant market power, vertical agreements were unlikely to be found to be harmful. Lord Simon, therefore, suggested:

> 'There remains a case therefore for special treatment of vertical agreements under the Bill to avoid the burden of unnecessary notification and to ease the so-called "straitjacket" which existing European block exemptions impose.'[2]

This was consistent with the approach advocated by, for example, Dobson and Waterson.[3] In the EC, since the landmark case of *Consten and Grundig*,[4] the approach has been that vertical agreements may be capable of falling within Art 81(1) EC, and, particularly where parallel trade is prevented and absolute territorial protection is conferred, might be incapable of benefiting from an exemption under Art 81(3) EC.

7.34 The more recent EC Block Exemption Regulation on vertical agreements[5] set a threshold of 30% market share, below which agreements would be enabled to benefit from the terms of the Block Exemption Regulation, as long as certain hard-core restrictions were not in place. This brought the approach closer to that of the UK, although there remained the key distinction in the treatment of agreements above this threshold.

7.35 Following the conclusion of the EC modernisation process, and the direct application of EC competition law by national competition authorities parallel with the application of national competition laws, it would be somewhat unfortunate, and indeed impossible, to maintain in place the dual approach to vertical agreements. It has also been recognised that, in some cases, harm does flow in the UK from the operation of vertical agreements, and that the effect of the exclusion is to eliminate the possibility of private actions based on alleged breaches of the Chapter I Prohibition in this respect, although not in relation to vertical agreements that fall to be considered under Art 81 EC.

---

[1]   Competition Act 1998 (Land and Vertical Agreements Exclusion) Order 2000, SI 2000/310. Article 3 of the Order provides that 'The Chapter I Prohibition shall not apply to an agreement to the extent that it is a vertical agreement'.

[2]   *Hansard* (HL), 9 February 1998, col 901.

[3]   See Dobson, PW and Waterson, M *Vertical Restraints in Competition Policy*, OFT Research Paper 12 (1996).

[4]   *Etablissements Consten SARL and Grundig-Verkaufs-GmbH v Commission* Cases 56, 58/64 [1966] 1 CMLR 418.

[5]   Regulation 2790/99 on the application of Art 81(3) of the Treaty to categories of vertical agreements and concerted practices (1999) OJ L336/21.

7.36   The effect of s 209(3) is therefore to allow the Secretary of State to remove this exclusion as soon as it is reasonable to do so, in light of the developments under EC law.

REPEALS AND MODIFICATIONS

The Enterprise Act 2002

7.37   Section 206 of the Act allows the Secretary of State to make modifications to Sch 8, which sets out the remedies available in merger situations and market investigations. This is a straightforward provision which, as explained in the *Explanatory Notes*, is designed to allow the list of remedies that can be used in final orders to 'evolve over time in response to market developments'.[1] As with other similar provisions in the Act, it is to be doubted whether this provision will ever be employed, but is again intended to reduce the need to return to Parliament with further amendments to the competition law legislation.

The Competition Act 1998

Professional rules

7.37   The issue of the relationship between restrictive professional rules, in particular those of bodies governing professions such as law and accountancy, has greatly exercised the OFT since the entry into force of the CA 1998. Schedule 4 to that Act made provision for the exclusion of professional rules from the operation of the Chapter I Prohibition where an appropriate notification to that effect was made to the OFT.[2] In March 2001, the OFT published a *Report on Competition in Professions*.[3] This review raised a number of areas of concern. In an accompanying press release,[4] the OFT's recommendations to ministers were set out. Crucially, these included the removal of the exclusion system established in the CA 1998:

> 'The CA 1998 provides for an exclusion from the Act's prohibition on anti-competitive agreements for agreements which constitute designated professional rules. Specified

---

[1]   Paragraph 432.

[2]   See also the OFT technical guideline *Trade Associations, Professions and Self-Regulating Bodies* [2000] UKCLR 163. In some respects, the Director has a specific remit in relation to professional rules. Thus, for example, under Courts and Legal Services Act 1990, s 29, the Director must be consulted by the Lord Chancellor when changes are proposed to the rules relating, *inter alia*, to the Regulations of the Inns of Court.

[3]   [2001] UKCLR 352.

[4]   'Reform for Competition Needed in Professions' PN 10/01, 7 March 2001, [2001] UKCLR 530.

professions can apply to the Secretary of State for Trade and Industry to have rules designated for exclusion although none has yet done so. The designation would be automatic although it would be subject to revocation on the advice of the Director General. The Director General's view is that this entitlement to exclusion should be removed.'

In April 2002, the OFT published a follow-up report[1] in which, while progress was welcomed, the OFT expressed its continuing concern that 'important freedoms continue to be unnecessarily restricted'.

7.39   Section 207 simply repeals Sch 4 to the CA 1998. The effect of this will be that professional rules now fall to be considered within the mainstream of the application of competition law, primarily within s 2 of the CA 1998, although it is possible, as has been the case in the past in relation to advertising restrictions, that they may fall to be analysed in the course of a market investigation reference. In its progress report, the OFT indicated only that:

'Freedom to compete is a fundamental theme throughout our work. At no point do we prescribe, even tentatively, how professional services should be supplied. We believe that this is generally best determined by unfettered competition between producers for the custom of consumers. Where others restrict the freedom of patterns of supply to evolve and improve, it is right that the onus should be on them to justify the restriction or remove it. The freedom to compete that results will benefit those who use professional services and those who serve them well.'[2]

The Fair Trading Act 1973

7.40   While the FTA 1973 is not completely repealed by the Act, a large part of it is. In addition, the Communications Bill will make further repeals. In addition to those provisions already considered in more detail elsewhere in this book, Part VI of the FTA 1973 is repealed by virtue of s 208. Part VI allowed references other than monopoly references to be made to the Monopolies and Mergers Commission, including, for example, references relating to general commercial practices rather than specific conduct on a specific market (FTA 1973, s 78). This is a power which has very rarely been used.[3] Section 79 allowed references to be made relating to 'restrictive labour practices', and has never been used.

---

[1]   OFT, 'Competition in Professions Progress Statement' [2002] UKCLR 467.
[2]   Ibid, para 5.3.
[3]   See, for example, *Full-Line Forcing and Tie-In Sales* (1981).

APPENDIX

ENTERPRISE ACT 2002

PART 1
THE OFFICE OF FAIR TRADING

Establishment of OFT

1 The Office of Fair Trading

(1) There shall be a body corporate to be known as the Office of Fair Trading (in this Act referred to as 'the OFT').

(2) The functions of the OFT are carried out on behalf of the Crown.

(3) Schedule 1 (which makes further provision about the OFT) has effect.

(4) In managing its affairs the OFT shall have regard, in addition to any relevant general guidance as to the governance of public bodies, to such generally accepted principles of good corporate governance as it is reasonable to regard as applicable to the OFT.

2 The Director General of Fair Trading

(1) The functions of the Director General of Fair Trading (in this Act referred to as 'the Director'), and his property, rights and liabilities, are transferred to the OFT.

(2) The office of the Director is abolished.

(3) Any enactment, instrument or other document passed or made before the commencement of subsection (1) which refers to the Director shall have effect, so far as necessary for the purposes of or in consequence of anything being transferred, as if any reference to the Director were a reference to the OFT.

3 Annual plan

(1) The OFT shall, before each financial year, publish a document (the 'annual plan') containing a statement of its main objectives and priorities for the year.

(2) The OFT shall for the purposes of public consultation publish a document containing proposals for its annual plan at least two months before publishing the annual plan for any year.

(3) The OFT shall lay before Parliament a copy of each document published under subsection (2) and each annual plan.

4 Annual and other reports

(1) The OFT shall, as soon as practicable after the end of each financial year, make to the Secretary of State a report (the 'annual report') on its activities and performance during that year.

(2) The annual report for each year shall include –

(a)   a general survey of developments in respect of matters relating to the OFT's functions;

(b)   an assessment of the extent to which the OFT's main objectives and priorities for the year (as set out in the annual plan) have been met;

(c)   a summary of the significant decisions, investigations or other activities made or carried out by the OFT during the year;

(d)   a summary of the allocation of the OFT's financial resources to its various activities during the year; and

(e)   an assessment of the OFT's performance and practices in relation to its enforcement functions.

(3) The OFT shall lay a copy of each annual report before Parliament and arrange for the report to be published.

(4) The OFT may –

(a)   prepare other reports in respect of matters relating to any of its functions; and

(b)   arrange for any such report to be published.

General functions of OFT

5 Acquisition of information etc

(1) The OFT has the function of obtaining, compiling and keeping under review information about matters relating to the carrying out of its functions.

(2) That function is to be carried out with a view to (among other things) ensuring that the OFT has sufficient information to take informed decisions and to carry out its other functions effectively.

(3) In carrying out that function the OFT may carry out, commission or support (financially or otherwise) research.

6 Provision of information etc to the public

(1) The OFT has the function of –

(a)   making the public aware of the ways in which competition may benefit consumers in, and the economy of, the United Kingdom; and

(b)   giving information or advice in respect of matters relating to any of its functions to the public.

(2) In carrying out those functions the OFT may –

(a)   publish educational materials or carry out other educational activities; or

(b)   support (financially or otherwise) the carrying out by others of such activities or the provision by others of information or advice.

7 Provision of information and advice to Ministers etc

(1) The OFT has the function of –

(a)   making proposals, or

(b)   giving other information or advice,

on matters relating to any of its functions to any Minister of the Crown or other public authority (including proposals, information or advice as to any aspect of the law or a proposed change in the law).

(2) A Minister of the Crown may request the OFT to make proposals or give other information or advice on any matter relating to any of its functions; and the OFT shall, so far as is reasonably practicable and consistent with its other functions, comply with the request.

8 Promoting good consumer practice

(1) The OFT has the function of promoting good practice in the carrying out of activities which may affect the economic interests of consumers in the United Kingdom.

(2) In carrying out that function the OFT may (without prejudice to the generality of subsection (1)) make arrangements for approving consumer codes and may, in accordance with the arrangements, give its approval to or withdraw its approval from any consumer code.

(3) Any such arrangements must specify the criteria to be applied by the OFT in determining whether to give approval to or withdraw approval from a consumer code.

(4) Any such arrangements may in particular –

(a)   specify descriptions of consumer code which may be the subject of an application to the OFT for approval (and any such description may be framed by reference to any feature of a consumer code, including the persons who are, or are to be, subject to the code, the manner in which it is, or is to be, operated and the persons responsible for its operation); and

(b)   provide for the use in accordance with the arrangements of an official symbol intended to signify that a consumer code is approved by the OFT.

(5) The OFT shall publish any arrangements under subsection (2) in such manner it considers appropriate.

(6) In this section 'consumer code' means a code of practice or other document (however described) intended, with a view to safeguarding or promoting the interests of consumers, to regulate by any means the conduct of persons engaged in the supply of goods or services to consumers (or the conduct of their employees or representatives).

Miscellaneous

9 Repeal of certain powers of direction

Section 12 of the Fair Trading Act 1973 (in this Act referred to as 'the 1973 Act') and section 13 of the Competition Act 1980 (powers of Secretary of State to give directions) shall cease to have effect.

10 Part 2 of the 1973 Act

(1) The following provisions of the 1973 Act shall cease to have effect –

- (a) section 3 and Schedule 2 (which establish, and make provision with respect to, the Consumer Protection Advisory Committee);
- (b) sections 13 to 21 (which relate to references made to, and reports of, that Committee); and
- (c) section 22 (power of Secretary of State to make orders in pursuance of a report of that Committee).

(2) But subsection (1)(c) does not affect –

- (a) any order under section 22 of the 1973 Act which is in force immediately before the commencement of this section;
- (b) the continued operation of that section so far as applying to the revocation of any such order.

(3) If the orders saved by subsection (2)(a) have been revoked, the Secretary of State may by order –

- (a) repeal any unrepealed provision of Part 2 of the 1973 Act and subsection (2) above; and
- (b) make such other consequential modifications of any Act or subordinate legislation (whenever passed or made) as he thinks fit.

(4) An order under subsection (3) –

- (a) may make transitional or saving provision in connection with any modification made by the order; and
- (b) shall be made by statutory instrument subject to annulment in pursuance of a resolution of either House of Parliament.

11 Super-complaints to OFT

(1) This section applies where a designated consumer body makes a complaint to the OFT that any feature, or combination of features, of a market in the United Kingdom for goods or services is or appears to be significantly harming the interests of consumers.

(2) The OFT must, within 90 days after the day on which it receives the complaint, publish a response stating how it proposes to deal with the complaint, and in particular –

- (a) whether it has decided to take any action, or to take no action, in response to the complaint, and
- (b) if it has decided to take action, what action it proposes to take.

(3) The response must state the OFT's reasons for its proposals.

(4) The Secretary of State may by order amend subsection (2) by substituting any period for the period for the time being specified there.

(5) 'Designated consumer body' means a body designated by the Secretary of State by order.

(6) The Secretary of State –

    (a)   may designate a body only if it appears to him to represent the interests of consumers of any description, and

    (b)   must publish (and may from time to time vary) other criteria to be applied by him in determining whether to make or revoke a designation.

(7) The OFT –

    (a)   must issue guidance as to the presentation by the complainant of a reasoned case for the complaint, and

    (b)   may issue such other guidance as appears to it to be appropriate for the purposes of this section.

(8) An order under this section –

    (a)   shall be made by statutory instrument, and

    (b)   shall be subject to annulment in pursuance of a resolution of either House of Parliament.

(9) In this section –

    (a)   references to a feature of a market in the United Kingdom for goods or services have the same meaning as if contained in Part 4, and

    (b)   'consumer' means an individual who is a consumer within the meaning of that Part.

PART 2
THE COMPETITION APPEAL TRIBUNAL

The Competition Appeal Tribunal

12 The Competition Appeal Tribunal

(1) There shall be a tribunal, to be called the Competition Appeal Tribunal (in this Part referred to as 'the Tribunal').

(2) The Tribunal shall consist of –

    (a)   a person appointed by the Lord Chancellor to preside over the Tribunal (in this Part referred to as 'the President');

    (b)   members appointed by the Lord Chancellor to form a panel of chairmen; and

    (c)   members appointed by the Secretary of State to form a panel of ordinary members.

(3) The Tribunal shall have a Registrar appointed by the Secretary of State.

(4) The expenses of the Tribunal shall be paid by the Competition Service.

(5) Schedule 2 (which makes further provision about the Tribunal) has effect.

13 The Competition Service

(1) There shall be a body corporate called the Competition Service (in this Part referred to as 'the Service').

(2) The purpose of the Service is to fund, and provide support services to, the Competition Appeal Tribunal.

(3) In subsection (2) 'support services' includes the provision of staff, accommodation and equipment and any other services which facilitate the carrying out by the Tribunal of its functions.

(4) The activities of the Service are not carried out on behalf of the Crown (and its property is not to be regarded as held on behalf of the Crown).

(5) The Secretary of State shall pay to the Service such sums as he considers appropriate to enable it to fund the activities of the Tribunal and to carry out its other activities.

(6) Schedule 3 (which makes further provision about the Service) has effect.

14 Constitution of Tribunal for particular proceedings and its decisions

(1) For the purposes of any proceedings before it the Tribunal shall consist of a chairman and two other members.

(2) The chairman must be the President or a member of the panel of chairmen.

(3) The other members may be chosen from either the panel of chairmen or the panel of ordinary members.

(4) If the members of the Tribunal as constituted in accordance with this section are unable to agree on any decision, the decision is to be taken by majority vote.

(5) This section has effect subject to paragraph 18 of Schedule 4 (consequences of a member of the Tribunal being unable to continue after the proceedings have begun to be heard).

(6) Part 1 of Schedule 4 (which makes further provision about the decisions of the Tribunal and their enforcement) has effect.

15 Tribunal rules

(1) The Secretary of State may, after consulting the President and such other persons as he considers appropriate, make rules (in this Part referred to as 'Tribunal rules') with respect to proceedings before the Tribunal.

(2) Tribunal rules may make provision with respect to matters incidental to or consequential upon appeals provided for by or under any Act to the Court of Appeal or the Court of Session in relation to a decision of the Tribunal.

(3) Tribunal rules may –

    (a)   specify qualifications for appointment as Registrar;

    (b)   confer functions on the President or the Registrar in relation to proceedings before the Tribunal; and

    (c)   contain incidental, supplemental, consequential or transitional provision.

(4) The power to make Tribunal rules is exercisable by statutory instrument subject to annulment in pursuance of a resolution of either House of Parliament.

(5) Part 2 of Schedule 4 (which makes further provision about the rules) has effect, but without prejudice to the generality of subsection (1).

16 Transfers of certain proceedings to and from Tribunal

(1) The Lord Chancellor may by regulations –

    (a)   make provision enabling the court –

        (i)   to transfer to the Tribunal for its determination so much of any proceedings before the court as relates to an infringement issue; and

        (ii)   to give effect to the determination of that issue by the Tribunal; and

    (b)   make such incidental, supplementary, consequential, transitional or saving provision as the Lord Chancellor may consider appropriate.

(2) The power to make regulations under subsection (1) is exercisable by statutory instrument subject to annulment in pursuance of a resolution of either House of Parliament.

(3) Rules of court may prescribe the procedure to be followed in connection with a transfer mentioned in subsection (1).

(4) The court may transfer to the Tribunal, in accordance with rules of court, so much of any proceedings before it as relates to a claim to which section 47A of the 1998 Act applies.

(5) Rules of court may make provision in connection with the transfer from the Tribunal to the High Court or the Court of Session of a claim made in proceedings under section 47A of the 1998 Act.

(6) In this section –

    'the court' means –

        (a)   the High Court or a county court; or

        (b)   the Court of Session or a sheriff court; and

    'infringement issue' means any question relating to whether or not an infringement of –

        (a)   the Chapter I prohibition or the Chapter II prohibition; or

        (b)   Article 81 or 82 of the Treaty,

    has been or is being committed;

but otherwise any terms used in this section and Part 1 of the 1998 Act have the same meaning as they have in that Part.

Proceedings under Part 1 of 1998 Act

17 Third party appeals

For section 47 of the 1998 Act (third party appeals) there is substituted –

'47 Third party appeals

(1) A person who does not fall within section 46(1) or (2) may appeal to the Tribunal with respect to a decision falling within paragraphs (a) to (f) of section 46(3) or such other decision of the OFT under this Part as may be prescribed.

(2) A person may make an appeal under subsection (1) only if the Tribunal considers that he has a sufficient interest in the decision with respect to which the appeal is made, or that he represents persons who have such an interest.

(3) The making of an appeal under this section does not suspend the effect of the decision to which the appeal relates.'

18 Monetary claims

(1) After section 47 of the 1998 Act there is inserted –

'47A Monetary claims before Tribunal

(1) This section applies to –

    (a)   any claim for damages, or
    (b)   any other claim for a sum of money,

which a person who has suffered loss or damage as a result of the infringement of a relevant prohibition may make in civil proceedings brought in any part of the United Kingdom.

(2) In this section "relevant prohibition" means any of the following –

    (a)   the Chapter I prohibition;
    (b)   the Chapter II prohibition;
    (c)   the prohibition in Article 81(1) of the Treaty;
    (d)   the prohibition in Article 82 of the Treaty;
    (e)   the prohibition in Article 65(1) of the Treaty establishing the European Coal and Steel Community;
    (f)   the prohibition in Article 66(7) of that Treaty.

(3) For the purpose of identifying claims which may be made in civil proceedings, any limitation rules that would apply in such proceedings are to be disregarded.

(4) A claim to which this section applies may (subject to the provisions of this Act and Tribunal rules) be made in proceedings brought before the Tribunal.

(5) But no claim may be made in such proceedings –

    (a)   until a decision mentioned in subsection (6) has established that the relevant prohibition in question has been infringed; and

    (b)   otherwise than with the permission of the Tribunal, during any period specified in subsection (7) or (8) which relates to that decision.

(6) The decisions which may be relied on for the purposes of proceedings under this section are –

    (a)   a decision of the OFT that the Chapter I prohibition or the Chapter II prohibition has been infringed;

    (b)   a decision of the OFT that the prohibition in Article 81(1) or Article 82 of the Treaty has been infringed;

    (c)   a decision of the Tribunal (on an appeal from a decision of the OFT) that the Chapter I prohibition, the Chapter II prohibition or the prohibition in Article 81(1) or Article 82 of the Treaty has been infringed;

    (d)   a decision of the European Commission that the prohibition in Article 81(1) or Article 82 of the Treaty has been infringed; or

    (e)   a decision of the European Commission that the prohibition in Article 65(1) of the Treaty establishing the European Coal and Steel Community has been infringed, or a finding made by the European Commission under Article 66(7) of that Treaty.

(7) The periods during which proceedings in respect of a claim made in reliance on a decision mentioned in subsection (6)(a), (b) or (c) may not be brought without permission are –

    (a)   in the case of a decision of the OFT, the period during which an appeal may be made to the Tribunal under section 46, section 47 or the EC Competition Law (Articles 84 and 85) Enforcement Regulations 2001 (SI 2001/2916);

    (b)   in the case of a decision of the OFT which is the subject of an appeal mentioned in paragraph (a), the period following the decision of the Tribunal on the appeal during which a further appeal may be made under section 49 or under those Regulations;

    (c)   in the case of a decision of the Tribunal mentioned in subsection (6)(c), the period during which a further appeal may be made under section 49 or under those Regulations;

    (d)   in the case of any decision which is the subject of a further appeal, the period during which an appeal may be made to the House of Lords from a decision on the further appeal;

and, where any appeal mentioned in paragraph (a), (b), (c) or (d) is made, the period specified in that paragraph includes the period before the appeal is determined.

(8) The periods during which proceedings in respect of a claim made in reliance on a decision or finding of the European Commission may not be brought without permission are –

    (a)   the period during which proceedings against the decision or finding may be instituted in the European Court; and

    (b)   if any such proceedings are instituted, the period before those proceedings are determined.

(9) In determining a claim to which this section applies the Tribunal is bound by any decision mentioned in subsection (6) which establishes that the prohibition in question has been infringed.

(10) The right to make a claim to which this section applies in proceedings before the Tribunal does not affect the right to bring any other proceedings in respect of the claim.'

(2) Section 47A applies to claims arising before the commencement of this section as it applies to claims arising after that time.

19 Claims on behalf of consumers

After section 47A of the 1998 Act (which is inserted by section 18), there is inserted –

'47B Claims brought on behalf of consumers

(1) A specified body may (subject to the provisions of this Act and Tribunal rules) bring proceedings before the Tribunal which comprise consumer claims made or continued on behalf of at least two individuals.

(2) In this section "consumer claim" means a claim to which section 47A applies which an individual has in respect of an infringement affecting (directly or indirectly) goods or services to which subsection (7) applies.

(3) A consumer claim may be included in proceedings under this section if it is –

(a) a claim made in the proceedings on behalf of the individual concerned by the specified body; or

(b) a claim made by the individual concerned under section 47A which is continued in the proceedings on his behalf by the specified body;

and such a claim may only be made or continued in the proceedings with the consent of the individual concerned.

(4) The consumer claims included in proceedings under this section must all relate to the same infringement.

(5) The provisions of section 47A(5) to (10) apply to a consumer claim included in proceedings under this section as they apply to a claim made in proceedings under that section.

(6) Any damages or other sum (not being costs or expenses) awarded in respect of a consumer claim included in proceedings under this section must be awarded to the individual concerned; but the Tribunal may, with the consent of the specified body and the individual, order that the sum awarded must be paid to the specified body (acting on behalf of the individual).

(7) This subsection applies to goods or services which –

(a) the individual received, or sought to receive, otherwise than in the course of a business carried on by him (notwithstanding that he received or sought to receive them with a view to carrying on a business); and

(b)   were, or would have been, supplied to the individual (in the case of goods whether by way of sale or otherwise) in the course of a business carried on by the person who supplied or would have supplied them.

(8) A business includes –

(a)   a professional practice;
(b)   any other undertaking carried on for gain or reward;
(c)   any undertaking in the course of which goods or services are supplied otherwise than free of charge.

(9) "Specified" means specified in an order made by the Secretary of State, in accordance with criteria to be published by the Secretary of State for the purposes of this section.

(10) An application by a body to be specified in an order under this section is to be made in a form approved by the Secretary of State for the purpose.'

Other amendments of 1998 Act

20 Findings of infringements

(1) After section 58 of the 1998 Act there is inserted –

'Findings of infringements

58A Findings of infringements

(1) This section applies to proceedings before the court in which damages or any other sum of money is claimed in respect of an infringement of –

(a)   the Chapter I prohibition;
(b)   the Chapter II prohibition;
(c)   the prohibition in Article 81(1) of the Treaty;
(d)   the prohibition in Article 82 of the Treaty.

(2) In such proceedings, the court is bound by a decision mentioned in subsection (3) once any period specified in subsection (4) which relates to the decision has elapsed.

(3) The decisions are –

(a)   a decision of the OFT that the Chapter I prohibition or the Chapter II prohibition has been infringed;
(b)   a decision of the OFT that the prohibition in Article 81(1) or Article 82 of the Treaty has been infringed;
(c)   a decision of the Tribunal (on an appeal from a decision of the OFT) that the Chapter I prohibition or the Chapter II prohibition has been infringed, or that the prohibition in Article 81(1) or Article 82 of the Treaty has been infringed.

(4) The periods mentioned in subsection (2) are –

(a)   in the case of a decision of the OFT, the period during which an appeal may be made to the Tribunal under section 46 or 47 or the EC Competition Law (Articles 84 and 85) Enforcement Regulations 2001 (SI 2001/2916);

(b)   in the case of a decision of the Tribunal mentioned in subsection (3)(c), the period during which a further appeal may be made under section 49 or under those Regulations;

(c)   in the case of any decision which is the subject of a further appeal, the period during which an appeal may be made to the House of Lords from a decision on the further appeal;

and, where any appeal mentioned in paragraph (a), (b) or (c) is made, the period specified in that paragraph includes the period before the appeal is determined.'

(2) Section 58A does not apply in relation to decisions made before the commencement of this section.

(3) In section 59(1) of that Act (interpretation), in the definition of 'the court', after '58' there is inserted ', 58A'.

21 Amendment of 1998 Act relating to the Tribunal

Schedule 5 (which contains amendments of the 1998 Act relating to, and to the proceedings of, the Tribunal) has effect.

PART 3
MERGERS

CHAPTER 1
DUTY TO MAKE REFERENCES

Duty to make references: completed mergers

22 Duty to make references in relation to completed mergers

(1) The OFT shall, subject to subsections (2) and (3), make a reference to the Commission if the OFT believes that it is or may be the case that –

(a)   a relevant merger situation has been created; and

(b)   the creation of that situation has resulted, or may be expected to result, in a substantial lessening of competition within any market or markets in the United Kingdom for goods or services.

(2) The OFT may decide not to make a reference under this section if it believes that –

(a)   the market concerned is not, or the markets concerned are not, of sufficient importance to justify the making of a reference to the Commission; or

(b)   any relevant customer benefits in relation to the creation of the relevant merger situation concerned outweigh the substantial lessening of competition concerned and any adverse effects of the substantial lessening of competition concerned.

(3) No reference shall be made under this section if –

    (a)   the making of the reference is prevented by section 69(1), 74(1) or 96(3) or paragraph 4 of Schedule 7;

    (b)   the OFT is considering whether to accept undertakings under section 73 instead of making such a reference;

    (c)   the relevant merger situation concerned is being, or has been, dealt with in connection with a reference made under section 33;

    (d)   a notice under section 42(2) is in force in relation to the matter or the matter to which such a notice relates has been finally determined under Chapter 2 otherwise than in circumstances in which a notice is then given to the OFT under section 56(1); or

    (e)   the European Commission is considering a request made, in relation to the matter concerned, by the United Kingdom (whether alone or with others) under article 22(3) of the European Merger Regulations, is proceeding with the matter in pursuance of such a request or has dealt with the matter in pursuance of such a request.

(4) A reference under this section shall, in particular, specify –

    (a)   the enactment under which it is made; and

    (b)   the date on which it is made.

(5) The references in this section to the creation of a relevant merger situation shall be construed in accordance with section 23, the reference in subsection (2) of this section to relevant customer benefits shall be construed in accordance with section 30 and the reference in subsection (3) of this section to a matter to which a notice under section 42(2) relates being finally determined under Chapter 2 shall be construed in accordance with section 43(4) and (5).

(6) In this Part 'market in the United Kingdom' includes –

    (a)   so far as it operates in the United Kingdom or a part of the United Kingdom, any market which operates there and in another country or territory or in a part of another country or territory; and

    (b)   any market which operates only in a part of the United Kingdom;

and references to a market for goods or services include references to a market for goods and services.

(7) In this Part 'the decision-making authority' means –

    (a)   in the case of a reference or possible reference under this section or section 33, the OFT or (as the case may be) the Commission; and

    (b)   in the case of a notice or possible notice under section 42(2) or 59(2) or a reference or possible reference under section 45 or 62, the OFT, the Commission or (as the case may be) the Secretary of State.

23 Relevant merger situations

(1) For the purposes of this Part, a relevant merger situation has been created if –

    (a)   two or more enterprises have ceased to be distinct enterprises at a time or in circumstances falling within section 24; and

(b)   the value of the turnover in the United Kingdom of the enterprise being taken over exceeds £70 million.

(2) For the purposes of this Part, a relevant merger situation has also been created if –

(a)   two or more enterprises have ceased to be distinct enterprises at a time or in circumstances falling within section 24; and

(b)   as a result, one or both of the conditions mentioned in subsections (3) and (4) below prevails or prevails to a greater extent.

(3) The condition mentioned in this subsection is that, in relation to the supply of goods of any description, at least one-quarter of all the goods of that description which are supplied in the United Kingdom, or in a substantial part of the United Kingdom –

(a)   are supplied by one and the same person or are supplied to one and the same person; or

(b)   are supplied by the persons by whom the enterprises concerned are carried on, or are supplied to those persons.

(4) The condition mentioned in this subsection is that, in relation to the supply of services of any description, the supply of services of that description in the United Kingdom, or in a substantial part of the United Kingdom, is to the extent of at least one-quarter –

(a)   supply by one and the same person, or supply for one and the same person; or

(b)   supply by the persons by whom the enterprises concerned are carried on, or supply for those persons.

(5) For the purpose of deciding whether the proportion of one-quarter mentioned in subsection (3) or (4) is fulfilled with respect to goods or (as the case may be) services of any description, the decision-making authority shall apply such criterion (whether value, cost, price, quantity, capacity, number of workers employed or some other criterion, of whatever nature), or such combination of criteria, as the decision-making authority considers appropriate.

(6) References in subsections (3) and (4) to the supply of goods or (as the case may be) services shall, in relation to goods or services of any description which are the subject of different forms of supply, be construed in whichever of the following ways the decision-making authority considers appropriate –

(a)   as references to any of those forms of supply taken separately;

(b)   as references to all those forms of supply taken together; or

(c)   as references to any of those forms of supply taken in groups.

(7) For the purposes of subsection (6) the decision-making authority may treat goods or services as being the subject of different forms of supply whenever –

(a)   the transactions concerned differ as to their nature, their parties, their terms or their surrounding circumstances; and

(b)   the difference is one which, in the opinion of the decision-making authority, ought for the purposes of that subsection to be treated as a material difference.

(8) The criteria for deciding when goods or services can be treated, for the purposes of this section, as goods or services of a separate description shall be such as in any particular case the decision-making authority considers appropriate in the circumstances of that case.

(9) For the purposes of this Chapter, the question whether a relevant merger situation has been created shall be determined as at –

(a) in the case of a reference which is treated as having been made under section 22 by virtue of section 37(2), such time as the Commission may determine; and

(b) in any other case, immediately before the time when the reference has been, or is to be, made.

24 Time-limits and prior notice

(1) For the purposes of section 23 two or more enterprises have ceased to be distinct enterprises at a time or in circumstances falling within this section if –

(a) the two or more enterprises ceased to be distinct enterprises before the day on which the reference relating to them is to be made and did so not more than four months before that day; or

(b) notice of material facts about the arrangements or transactions under or in consequence of which the enterprises have ceased to be distinct enterprises has not been given in accordance with subsection (2).

(2) Notice of material facts is given in accordance with this subsection if –

(a) it is given to the OFT prior to the entering into of the arrangements or transactions concerned or the facts are made public prior to the entering into of those arrangements or transactions; or

(b) it is given to the OFT, or the facts are made public, more than four months before the day on which the reference is to be made.

(3) In this section –

'made public' means so publicised as to be generally known or readily ascertainable; and

'notice' includes notice which is not in writing.

25 Extension of time-limits

(1) The OFT and the persons carrying on the enterprises which have or may have ceased to be distinct enterprises may agree to extend by no more than 20 days the four month period mentioned in section 24(1)(a) or (2)(b).

(2) The OFT may by notice to the persons carrying on the enterprises which have or may have ceased to be distinct enterprises extend the four month period mentioned in section 24(1)(a) or (2)(b) if it considers that any of those persons has failed to provide, within the period stated in a notice under section 31 and in the manner authorised or required, information requested of him in that notice.

(3) An extension under subsection (2) shall be for the period beginning with the end of the period within which the information is to be provided and which is stated in the notice under section 31 and ending with –

> (a)   the provision of the information to the satisfaction of the OFT; or
>
> (b)   if earlier, the cancellation by the OFT of the extension.

(4) The OFT may by notice to the persons carrying on the enterprises which have or may have ceased to be distinct enterprises extend the four month period mentioned in section 24(1)(a) or (2)(b) if it is seeking undertakings from any of those persons under section 73.

(5) An extension under subsection (4) shall be for the period beginning with the receipt of the notice under that subsection and ending with the earliest of the following events –

> (a)   the giving of the undertakings concerned;
>
> (b)   the expiry of the period of 10 days beginning with the first day after the receipt by the OFT of a notice from the person who has been given a notice under subsection (4) and from whom the undertakings are being sought stating that he does not intend to give the undertakings; or
>
> (c)   the cancellation by the OFT of the extension.

(6) The OFT may by notice to the persons carrying on the enterprises which have or may have ceased to be distinct enterprises extend the four month period mentioned in section 24(1)(a) or (2)(b) if the European Commission is considering a request made, in relation to the matter concerned, by the United Kingdom (whether alone or with others) under article 22(3) of the European Merger Regulations (but is not yet proceeding with the matter in pursuance of such a request).

(7) An extension under subsection (6) shall be for the period beginning with the receipt of the notice under that subsection and ending with the receipt of a notice under subsection (8).

(8) The OFT shall, in connection with any notice given by it under subsection (6), by notice inform the persons carrying on the enterprises which have or may have ceased to be distinct enterprises of the completion by the European Commission of its consideration of the request of the United Kingdom.

(9) Subject to subsections (10) and (11), where the four month period mentioned in section 24(1)(a) or (2)(b) is extended or further extended by virtue of this section in relation to a particular case, any reference to that period in section 24 or the preceding provisions of this section shall have effect in relation to that case as if it were a reference to a period equivalent to the aggregate of the period being extended and the period of the extension (whether or not those periods overlap in time).

(10) Subsection (11) applies where –

> (a)   the four month period mentioned in section 24(1)(a) or (2)(b) is further extended;
>
> (b)   the further extension and at least one previous extension is made under one or more of subsections (2), (4) and (6); and
>
> (c)   the same days or fractions of days are included in or comprise the further extension and are included in or comprise at least one such previous extension.

(11) In calculating the period of the further extension, any days or fractions of days of the kind mentioned in subsection (10)(c) shall be disregarded.

(12) No more than one extension is possible under subsection (1).

26 Enterprises ceasing to be distinct enterprises

(1) For the purposes of this Part any two enterprises cease to be distinct enterprises if they are brought under common ownership or common control (whether or not the business to which either of them formerly belonged continues to be carried on under the same or different ownership or control).

(2) Enterprises shall, in particular, be treated as being under common control if they are –

(a) enterprises of interconnected bodies corporate;

(b) enterprises carried on by two or more bodies corporate of which one and the same person or group of persons has control; or

(c) an enterprise carried on by a body corporate and an enterprise carried on by a person or group of persons having control of that body corporate.

(3) A person or group of persons able, directly or indirectly, to control or materially to influence the policy of a body corporate, or the policy of any person in carrying on an enterprise but without having a controlling interest in that body corporate or in that enterprise, may, for the purposes of subsections (1) and (2), be treated as having control of it.

(4) For the purposes of subsection (1), in so far as it relates to bringing two or more enterprises under common control, a person or group of persons may be treated as bringing an enterprise under his or their control if –

(a) being already able to control or materially to influence the policy of the person carrying on the enterprise, that person or group of persons acquires a controlling interest in the enterprise or, in the case of an enterprise carried on by a body corporate, acquires a controlling interest in that body corporate; or

(b) being already able materially to influence the policy of the person carrying on the enterprise, that person or group of persons becomes able to control that policy.

27 Time when enterprises cease to be distinct

(1) Subsection (2) applies in relation to any arrangements or transaction –

(a) not having immediate effect or having immediate effect only in part; but

(b) under or in consequence of which any two enterprises cease to be distinct enterprises.

(2) The time when the parties to any such arrangements or transaction become bound to such extent as will result, on effect being given to their obligations, in the enterprises ceasing to be distinct enterprises shall be taken to be the time at which the two enterprises cease to be distinct enterprises.

(3) In accordance with subsections (1) and (2) (but without prejudice to the generality of those subsections) for the purpose of determining the time at which any two

enterprises cease to be distinct enterprises no account shall be taken of any option or other conditional right until the option is exercised or the condition is satisfied.

(4) Subsections (1) to (3) are subject to subsections (5) to (8) and section 29.

(5) The decision-making authority may, for the purposes of a reference, treat successive events to which this subsection applies as having occurred simultaneously on the date on which the latest of them occurred.

(6) Subsection (5) applies to successive events –

(a)   which occur within a period of two years under or in consequence of the same arrangements or transaction, or successive arrangements or transactions between the same parties or interests; and

(b)   by virtue of each of which, under or in consequence of the arrangements or the transaction or transactions concerned, any enterprises cease as between themselves to be distinct enterprises.

(7) The decision-making authority may, for the purposes of subsections (5) and (6), treat such arrangements or transactions as the decision-making authority considers appropriate as arrangements or transactions between the same interests.

(8) In deciding whether it is appropriate to treat arrangements or transactions as arrangements or transactions between the same interests the decision-making authority shall, in particular, have regard to the persons substantially concerned in the arrangements or transactions concerned.

28 Turnover test

(1) For the purposes of section 23 the value of the turnover in the United Kingdom of the enterprise being taken over shall be determined by taking the total value of the turnover in the United Kingdom of the enterprises which cease to be distinct enterprises and deducting –

(a)   the turnover in the United Kingdom of any enterprise which continues to be carried on under the same ownership and control; or

(b)   if no enterprise continues to be carried on under the same ownership and control, the turnover in the United Kingdom which, of all the turnovers concerned, is the turnover of the highest value.

(2) For the purposes of this Part (other than section 121(4)(c)(ii)) the turnover in the United Kingdom of an enterprise shall be determined in accordance with such provisions as may be specified in an order made by the Secretary of State.

(3) An order under subsection (2) may, in particular, make provision as to –

(a)   the amounts which are, or which are not, to be treated as comprising an enterprise's turnover;

(b)   the date or dates by reference to which an enterprise's turnover is to be determined;

(c)   the connection with the United Kingdom by virtue of which an enterprise's turnover is turnover in the United Kingdom.

(4) An order under subsection (2) may, in particular, make provision enabling the decision-making authority to determine matters of a description specified in the order (including any of the matters mentioned in paragraphs (a) to (c) of subsection (3)).

(5) The OFT shall –

(a) keep under review the sum for the time being mentioned in section 23(1)(b); and

(b) from time to time advise the Secretary of State as to whether the sum is still appropriate.

(6) The Secretary of State may by order amend section 23(1)(b) so as to alter the sum for the time being mentioned there.

29 Obtaining control by stages

(1) Where an enterprise is brought under the control of a person or group of persons in the course of two or more transactions (in this section a 'series of transactions') to which subsection (2) applies, those transactions may, if the decision-making authority considers it appropriate, be treated for the purposes of a reference as having occurred simultaneously on the date on which the latest of them occurred.

(2) This subsection applies to –

(a) any transaction which –

(i) enables that person or group of persons directly or indirectly to control or materially to influence the policy of any person carrying on the enterprise;

(ii) enables that person or group of persons to do so to a greater degree; or

(iii) is a step (whether direct or indirect) towards enabling that person or group of persons to do so; and

(b) any transaction by virtue of which that person or group of persons acquires a controlling interest in the enterprise or, where the enterprise is carried on by a body corporate, in that body corporate.

(3) Where a series of transactions includes a transaction falling within subsection (2)(b), any transaction occurring after the occurrence of that transaction is to be disregarded for the purposes of subsection (1).

(4) Where the period within which a series of transactions occurs exceeds two years, the transactions that may be treated as mentioned in subsection (1) are any of those transactions that occur within a period of two years.

(5) Sections 26(2) to (4) and 127(1), (2) and (4) to (6) shall apply for the purposes of this section to determine –

(a) whether an enterprise is brought under the control of a person or group of persons; and

(b) whether a transaction is one to which subsection (2) applies;

as they apply for the purposes of section 26 to determine whether enterprises are brought under common control.

(6) In determining for the purposes of this section the time at which any transaction occurs, no account shall be taken of any option or other conditional right until the option is exercised or the condition is satisfied.

30 Relevant customer benefits

(1) For the purposes of this Part a benefit is a relevant customer benefit if –

    (a)   it is a benefit to relevant customers in the form of –

        (i)   lower prices, higher quality or greater choice of goods or services in any market in the United Kingdom (whether or not the market or markets in which the substantial lessening of competition concerned has, or may have, occurred or (as the case may be) may occur); or

        (ii)   greater innovation in relation to such goods or services; and

    (b)   the decision-making authority believes –

        (i)   in the case of a reference or possible reference under section 22 or 45(2), as mentioned in subsection (2); and

        (ii)   in the case of a reference or possible reference under section 33 or 45(4), as mentioned in subsection (3).

(2) The belief, in the case of a reference or possible reference under section 22 or section 45(2), is that –

    (a)   the benefit has accrued as a result of the creation of the relevant merger situation concerned or may be expected to accrue within a reasonable period as a result of the creation of that situation; and

    (b)   the benefit was, or is, unlikely to accrue without the creation of that situation or a similar lessening of competition.

(3) The belief, in the case of a reference or possible reference under section 33 or 45(4), is that –

    (a)   the benefit may be expected to accrue within a reasonable period as a result of the creation of the relevant merger situation concerned; and

    (b)   the benefit is unlikely to accrue without the creation of that situation or a similar lessening of competition.

(4) In subsection (1) 'relevant customers' means –

    (a)   customers of any person carrying on an enterprise which, in the creation of the relevant merger situation concerned, has ceased to be, or (as the case may be) will cease to be, a distinct enterprise;

    (b)   customers of such customers; and

    (c)   any other customers in a chain of customers beginning with the customers mentioned in paragraph (a);

and in this subsection 'customers' includes future customers.

31 Information powers in relation to completed mergers

(1) The OFT may by notice to any of the persons carrying on the enterprises which have or may have ceased to be distinct enterprises request him to provide the OFT

with such information as the OFT may require for the purpose of deciding whether to make a reference under section 22.

(2) The notice shall state –

(a) the information required;

(b) the period within which the information is to be provided; and

(c) the possible consequences of not providing the information within the stated period and in the authorised or required manner.

32 Supplementary provision for purposes of sections 25 and 31

(1) The Secretary of State may make regulations for the purposes of sections 25 and 31.

(2) The regulations may, in particular –

(a) provide for the manner in which any information requested by the OFT under section 31 is authorised or required to be provided, and the time at which such information is to be treated as provided (including the time at which it is to be treated as provided to the satisfaction of the OFT for the purposes of section 25(3));

(b) provide for the persons carrying on the enterprises which have or may have ceased to be distinct enterprises to be informed, in circumstances in which section 25(3) applies –

(i) of the fact that the OFT is satisfied as to the provision of the information requested by it or (as the case may be) of the OFT's decision to cancel the extension; and

(ii) of the time at which the OFT is to be treated as so satisfied or (as the case may be) of the time at which the cancellation is to be treated as having effect;

(c) provide for the persons carrying on the enterprises which have or may have ceased to be distinct enterprises to be informed, in circumstances in which section 25(5) applies –

(i) of the OFT's decision to cancel the extension; and

(ii) of the time at which the cancellation is to be treated as having effect;

(d) provide for the time at which any notice under section 25(4), (5)(b), (6) or (8) is to be treated as received;

(e) provide that a person is, or is not, to be treated, in such circumstances as may be specified in the regulations, as acting on behalf of a person carrying on an enterprise which has or may have ceased to be a distinct enterprise.

(3) A notice under section 25(2) –

(a) shall be given within 5 days of the end of the period within which the information is to be provided and which is stated in the notice under section 31; and

(b) shall inform the person to whom it is addressed of –

(i) the OFT's opinion as mentioned in section 25(2); and

(ii) the OFT's intention to extend the period for considering whether to make a reference.

(4) In determining for the purposes of section 25(1) or (5)(b) or subsection (3)(a) above any period which is expressed in the enactment concerned as a period of days or number of days no account shall be taken of –

    (a)   Saturday, Sunday, Good Friday and Christmas Day; and

    (b)   any day which is a bank holiday in England and Wales.

Duty to make references: anticipated mergers

33 Duty to make references in relation to anticipated mergers

(1) The OFT shall, subject to subsections (2) and (3), make a reference to the Commission if the OFT believes that it is or may be the case that –

    (a)   arrangements are in progress or in contemplation which, if carried into effect, will result in the creation of a relevant merger situation; and

    (b)   the creation of that situation may be expected to result in a substantial lessening of competition within any market or markets in the United Kingdom for goods or services.

(2) The OFT may decide not to make a reference under this section if it believes that –

    (a)   the market concerned is not, or the markets concerned are not, of sufficient importance to justify the making of a reference to the Commission;

    (b)   the arrangements concerned are not sufficiently far advanced, or are not sufficiently likely to proceed, to justify the making of a reference to the Commission; or

    (c)   any relevant customer benefits in relation to the creation of the relevant merger situation concerned outweigh the substantial lessening of competition concerned and any adverse effects of the substantial lessening of competition concerned.

(3) No reference shall be made under this section if –

    (a)   the making of the reference is prevented by section 69(1), 74(1) or 96(3) or paragraph 4 of Schedule 7;

    (b)   the OFT is considering whether to accept undertakings under section 73 instead of making such a reference;

    (c)   the arrangements concerned are being, or have been, dealt with in connection with a reference made under section 22;

    (d)   a notice under section 42(2) is in force in relation to the matter or the matter to which such a notice relates has been finally determined under Chapter 2 otherwise than in circumstances in which a notice is then given to the OFT under section 56(1); or

    (e)   the European Commission is considering a request made, in relation to the matter concerned, by the United Kingdom (whether alone or with others) under article 22(3) of the European Merger Regulations, is proceeding with the matter in pursuance of such a request or has dealt with the matter in pursuance of such a request.

(4) A reference under this section shall, in particular, specify –

(a)   the enactment under which it is made; and

(b)   the date on which it is made.

34 Supplementary provision in relation to anticipated mergers

(1) The Secretary of State may by order make such provision as he considers appropriate about the operation of sections 27 and 29 in relation to –

(a)   references under this Part which relate to arrangements which are in progress or in contemplation; or

(b)   notices under section 42(2), 59(2) or 67(2) which relate to such arrangements.

(2) An order under subsection (1) may, in particular –

(a)   provide for sections 27(5) to (8) and 29 to apply with modifications in relation to such references or notices or in relation to particular descriptions of such references or notices;

(b)   enable particular descriptions of events, arrangements or transactions which have already occurred –

(i)   to be taken into account for the purposes of deciding whether to make such references or such references of a particular description or whether to give such notices or such notices of a particular description;

(ii)   to be dealt with under such references or such references of a particular description or under such notices or such notices of a particular description.

Determination of references

35 Questions to be decided in relation to completed mergers

(1) Subject to subsections (6) and (7) and section 127(3), the Commission shall, on a reference under section 22, decide the following questions –

(a)   whether a relevant merger situation has been created; and

(b)   if so, whether the creation of that situation has resulted, or may be expected to result, in a substantial lessening of competition within any market or markets in the United Kingdom for goods or services.

(2) For the purposes of this Part there is an anti-competitive outcome if –

(a)   a relevant merger situation has been created and the creation of that situation has resulted, or may be expected to result, in a substantial lessening of competition within any market or markets in the United Kingdom for goods or services; or

(b)   arrangements are in progress or in contemplation which, if carried into effect, will result in the creation of a relevant merger situation and the creation of that situation may be expected to result in a substantial lessening of competition within any market or markets in the United Kingdom for goods or services.

(3) The Commission shall, if it has decided on a reference under section 22 that there is an anti-competitive outcome (within the meaning given by subsection (2)(a)), decide the following additional questions –

(a) whether action should be taken by it under section 41(2) for the purpose of remedying, mitigating or preventing the substantial lessening of competition concerned or any adverse effect which has resulted from, or may be expected to result from, the substantial lessening of competition;

(b) whether it should recommend the taking of action by others for the purpose of remedying, mitigating or preventing the substantial lessening of competition concerned or any adverse effect which has resulted from, or may be expected to result from, the substantial lessening of competition; and

(c) in either case, if action should be taken, what action should be taken and what is to be remedied, mitigated or prevented.

(4) In deciding the questions mentioned in subsection (3) the Commission shall, in particular, have regard to the need to achieve as comprehensive a solution as is reasonable and practicable to the substantial lessening of competition and any adverse effects resulting from it.

(5) In deciding the questions mentioned in subsection (3) the Commission may, in particular, have regard to the effect of any action on any relevant customer benefits in relation to the creation of the relevant merger situation concerned.

(6) In relation to the question whether a relevant merger situation has been created, a reference under section 22 may be framed so as to require the Commission to exclude from consideration –

(a) subsection (1) of section 23;

(b) subsection (2) of that section; or

(c) one of those subsections if the Commission finds that the other is satisfied.

(7) In relation to the question whether any such result as is mentioned in section 23(2)(b) has arisen, a reference under section 22 may be framed so as to require the Commission to confine its investigation to the supply of goods or services in a part of the United Kingdom specified in the reference.

36 Questions to be decided in relation to anticipated mergers

(1) Subject to subsections (5) and (6) and section 127(3), the Commission shall, on a reference under section 33, decide the following questions –

(a) whether arrangements are in progress or in contemplation which, if carried into effect, will result in the creation of a relevant merger situation; and

(b) if so, whether the creation of that situation may be expected to result in a substantial lessening of competition within any market or markets in the United Kingdom for goods or services.

(2) The Commission shall, if it has decided on a reference under section 33 that there is an anti-competitive outcome (within the meaning given by section 35(2)(b)), decide the following additional questions –

(a)   whether action should be taken by it under section 41(2) for the purpose of remedying, mitigating or preventing the substantial lessening of competition concerned or any adverse effect which may be expected to result from the substantial lessening of competition;

(b)   whether it should recommend the taking of action by others for the purpose of remedying, mitigating or preventing the substantial lessening of competition concerned or any adverse effect which may be expected to result from the substantial lessening of competition; and

(c)   in either case, if action should be taken, what action should be taken and what is to be remedied, mitigated or prevented.

(3) In deciding the questions mentioned in subsection (2) the Commission shall, in particular, have regard to the need to achieve as comprehensive a solution as is reasonable and practicable to the substantial lessening of competition and any adverse effects resulting from it.

(4) In deciding the questions mentioned in subsection (2) the Commission may, in particular, have regard to the effect of any action on any relevant customer benefits in relation to the creation of the relevant merger situation concerned.

(5) In relation to the question whether a relevant merger situation will be created, a reference under section 33 may be framed so as to require the Commission to exclude from consideration –

(a)   subsection (1) of section 23;

(b)   subsection (2) of that section; or

(c)   one of those subsections if the Commission finds that the other is satisfied.

(6) In relation to the question whether any such result as is mentioned in section 23(2)(b) will arise, a reference under section 33 may be framed so as to require the Commission to confine its investigation to the supply of goods or services in a part of the United Kingdom specified in the reference.

37 Cancellation and variation of references under section 22 or 33

(1) The Commission shall cancel a reference under section 33 if it considers that the proposal to make arrangements of the kind mentioned in the reference has been abandoned.

(2) The Commission may, if it considers that doing so is justified by the facts (including events occurring on or after the making of the reference concerned), treat a reference made under section 22 or 33 as if it had been made under section 33 or (as the case may be) 22; and, in such cases, references in this Part to references under those sections shall, so far as may be necessary, be construed accordingly.

(3) Where, by virtue of subsection (2), the Commission treats a reference made under section 22 or 33 as if it had been made under section 33 or (as the case may be) 22,

sections 77 to 81 shall, in particular, apply as if the reference had been made under section 33 or (as the case may be) 22 instead of under section 22 or 33.

(4) Subsection (5) applies in relation to any undertaking accepted under section 80, or any order made under section 81, which is in force immediately before the Commission, by virtue of subsection (2), treats a reference made under section 22 or 33 as if it had been made under section 33 or (as the case may be) 22.

(5) The undertaking or order shall, so far as applicable, continue in force as if –

(a)   in the case of an undertaking or order which relates to a reference made under section 22, accepted or made in relation to a reference made under section 33; and

(b)   in the case of an undertaking or order which relates to a reference made under section 33, accepted or made in relation to a reference made under section 22;

and the undertaking or order concerned may be varied, superseded, released or revoked accordingly.

(6) The OFT may at any time vary a reference under section 22 or 33.

(7) The OFT shall consult the Commission before varying any such reference.

(8) Subsection (7) shall not apply if the Commission has requested the variation concerned.

(9) No variation by the OFT under this section shall be capable of altering the period permitted by section 39 within which the report of the Commission under section 38 is to be prepared and published.

38 Investigations and reports on references under section 22 or 33

(1) The Commission shall prepare and publish a report on a reference under section 22 or 33 within the period permitted by section 39.

(2) The report shall, in particular, contain –

(a)   the decisions of the Commission on the questions which it is required to answer by virtue of section 35 or (as the case may be) 36;

(b)   its reasons for its decisions; and

(c)   such information as the Commission considers appropriate for facilitating a proper understanding of those questions and of its reasons for its decisions.

(3) The Commission shall carry out such investigations as it considers appropriate for the purposes of preparing a report under this section.

(4) The Commission shall, at the same time as a report prepared under this section is published, give it to the OFT.

39 Time-limits for investigations and reports

(1) The Commission shall prepare and publish its report under section 38 within the period of 24 weeks beginning with the date of the reference concerned.

(2) Where article 9(6) of the European Merger Regulations applies in relation to the reference under section 22 or 33, the Commission shall prepare and publish its report under section 38 –

    (a)   within the period of 24 weeks beginning with the date of the reference; or

    (b)   if it is a shorter period, within such period as is necessary to ensure compliance with that article.

(3) The Commission may extend, by no more than 8 weeks, the period within which a report under section 38 is to be prepared and published if it considers that there are special reasons why the report cannot be prepared and published within that period.

(4) The Commission may extend the period within which a report under section 38 is to be prepared and published if it considers that a relevant person has failed (whether with or without a reasonable excuse) to comply with any requirement of a notice under section 109.

(5) In subsection (4) 'relevant person' means –

    (a)   any person carrying on any of the enterprises concerned;

    (b)   any person who (whether alone or as a member of a group) owns or has control of any such person; or

    (c)   any officer, employee or agent of any person mentioned in paragraph (a) or (b).

(6) For the purposes of subsection (5) a person or group of persons able, directly or indirectly, to control or materially to influence the policy of a body of persons corporate or unincorporate, but without having a controlling interest in that body of persons, may be treated as having control of it.

(7) An extension under subsection (3) or (4) shall come into force when published under section 107.

(8) An extension under subsection (4) shall continue in force until –

    (a)   the person concerned provides the information or documents to the satisfaction of the Commission or (as the case may be) appears as a witness in accordance with the requirements of the Commission; or

    (b)   the Commission publishes its decision to cancel the extension.

(9) References in this Part to the date of a reference shall be construed as references to the date specified in the reference as the date on which it is made.

(10) This section is subject to section 40.

40 Section 39: supplementary

(1) No extension is possible under subsection (3) or (4) of section 39 where the period within which the report is to be prepared and published is determined by virtue of subsection (2)(b) of that section.

(2) Where the period within which the report is to be prepared and published is determined by virtue of subsection (2)(a) of section 39, no extension is possible under subsection (3) or (4) of that section which extends that period beyond such period as

is necessary to ensure compliance with article 9(6) of the European Merger Regulations.

(3) A period extended under subsection (3) of section 39 may also be extended under subsection (4) of that section and a period extended under subsection (4) of that section may also be extended under subsection (3) of that section.

(4) No more than one extension is possible under section 39(3).

(5) Where a period within which a report under section 38 is to be prepared and published is extended or further extended under section 39(3) or (4), the period as extended or (as the case may be) further extended shall, subject to subsections (6) and (7), be calculated by taking the period being extended and adding to it the period of the extension (whether or not those periods overlap in time).

(6) Subsection (7) applies where –

    (a)   the period within which the report under section 38 is to be prepared and published is further extended;

    (b)   the further extension and at least one previous extension is made under section 39(4); and

    (c)   the same days or fractions of days are included in or comprise the further extension and are included in or comprise at least one such previous extension.

(7) In calculating the period of the further extension, any days or fractions of days of the kind mentioned in subsection (6)(c) shall be disregarded.

(8) The Secretary of State may by order amend section 39 so as to alter any one or more of the following periods –

    (a)   the period of 24 weeks mentioned in subsection (1) of that section or any period for the time being mentioned in that subsection in substitution for that period;

    (b)   the period of 24 weeks mentioned in subsection (2)(a) of that section or any period for the time being mentioned in that subsection in substitution for that period;

    (c)   the period of 8 weeks mentioned in subsection (3) of that section or any period for the time being mentioned in that subsection in substitution for that period.

(9) No alteration shall be made by virtue of subsection (8) which results in the period for the time being mentioned in subsection (1) or (2)(a) of section 39 exceeding 24 weeks or the period for the time being mentioned in subsection (3) of that section exceeding 8 weeks.

(10) An order under subsection (8) shall not affect any period of time within which the Commission is under a duty to prepare and publish its report under section 38 in relation to a reference under section 22 or 33 if the Commission is already under that duty in relation to that reference when the order is made.

(11) Before making an order under subsection (8) the Secretary of State shall consult the Commission and such other persons as he considers appropriate.

(12) The Secretary of State may make regulations for the purposes of section 39(8).

(13) The regulations may, in particular –

   (a)   provide for the time at which information or documents are to be treated as provided (including the time at which they are to be treated as provided to the satisfaction of the Commission for the purposes of section 39(8));

   (b)   provide for the time at which a person is to be treated as appearing as a witness (including the time at which he is to be treated as appearing as a witness in accordance with the requirements of the Commission for the purposes of section 39(8));

   (c)   provide for the persons carrying on the enterprises which have or may have ceased to be, or may cease to be, distinct enterprises to be informed, in circumstances in which section 39(8) applies, of the fact that –

       (i)   the Commission is satisfied as to the provision of the information or documents required by it; or

       (ii)   the person concerned has appeared as a witness in accordance with the requirements of the Commission;

   (d)   provide for the persons carrying on the enterprises which have or may have ceased to be, or may cease to be, distinct enterprises to be informed, in circumstances in which section 39(8) applies, of the time at which the Commission is to be treated as satisfied as mentioned in paragraph (c)(i) above or the person concerned is to be treated as having appeared as mentioned in paragraph (c)(ii) above.

41 Duty to remedy effects of completed or anticipated mergers

(1) Subsection (2) applies where a report of the Commission has been prepared and published under section 38 within the period permitted by section 39 and contains the decision that there is an anti-competitive outcome.

(2) The Commission shall take such action under section 82 or 84 as it considers to be reasonable and practicable –

   (a)   to remedy, mitigate or prevent the substantial lessening of competition concerned; and

   (b)   to remedy, mitigate or prevent any adverse effects which have resulted from, or may be expected to result from, the substantial lessening of competition.

(3) The decision of the Commission under subsection (2) shall be consistent with its decisions as included in its report by virtue of section 35(3) or (as the case may be) 36(2) unless there has been a material change of circumstances since the preparation of the report or the Commission otherwise has a special reason for deciding differently.

(4) In making a decision under subsection (2), the Commission shall, in particular, have regard to the need to achieve as comprehensive a solution as is reasonable and practicable to the substantial lessening of competition and any adverse effects resulting from it.

(5) In making a decision under subsection (2), the Commission may, in particular, have regard to the effect of any action on any relevant customer benefits in relation to the creation of the relevant merger situation concerned.

CHAPTER 2
PUBLIC INTEREST CASES

Power to make references

42   Intervention by Secretary of State in certain public interest cases

(1) Subsection (2) applies where –

    (a)   the Secretary of State has reasonable grounds for suspecting that it is or may be the case that a relevant merger situation has been created or that arrangements are in progress or in contemplation which, if carried into effect, will result in the creation of a relevant merger situation;

    (b)   no reference under section 22 or 33 has been made in relation to the relevant merger situation concerned;

    (c)   no decision has been made not to make such a reference (other than a decision made by virtue of subsection (2)(b) of section 33 or a decision to accept undertakings under section 73 instead of making such a reference); and

    (d)   no reference is prevented from being made under section 22 or 33 by virtue of –

        (i)   section 22(3)(a) or (e) or (as the case may be) 33(3)(a) or (e); or

        (ii)   Community law or anything done under or in accordance with it.

(2) The Secretary of State may give a notice to the OFT (in this Part 'an intervention notice') if he believes that it is or may be the case that one or more than one public interest consideration is relevant to a consideration of the relevant merger situation concerned.

(3) For the purposes of this Part a public interest consideration is a consideration which, at the time of the giving of the intervention notice concerned, is specified in section 58 or is not so specified but, in the opinion of the Secretary of State, ought to be so specified.

(4) No more than one intervention notice shall be given under subsection (2) in relation to the same relevant merger situation.

(5) For the purposes of deciding whether a relevant merger situation has been created or whether arrangements are in progress or in contemplation which, if carried into effect, will result in the creation of a relevant merger situation, sections 23 to 32 (read together with section 34) shall apply for the purposes of this Chapter as they do for the purposes of Chapter 1 but subject to subsection (6).

(6) In their application by virtue of subsection (5) sections 23 to 32 shall have effect as if –

(a)   for paragraph (a) of section 23(9) there were substituted –

         '(a)   in relation to the giving of an intervention notice, the time when the notice is given;

         (aa)   in relation to the making of a report by the OFT under section 44, the time of the making of the report;

         (ab)   in the case of a reference which is treated as having been made under section 45(2) or (3) by virtue of section 49(1), such time as the Commission may determine; and';

(b)   the references to the OFT in sections 25(1) to (3), (6) and (8) and 31 included references to the Secretary of State;

(c)   the references to the OFT in section 25(4) and (5) were references to the Secretary of State;

(d)   the reference in section 25(4) to section 73 were a reference to paragraph 3 of Schedule 7;

(e)   after section 25(5) there were inserted –

'(5A) The Secretary of State may by notice to the persons carrying on the enterprises which have or may have ceased to be distinct enterprises extend the four month period mentioned in section 24(1)(a) or (2)(b) if, by virtue of section 46(5) or paragraph 3(6) of Schedule 7, he decides to delay a decision as to whether to make a reference under section 45.

(5B) An extension under subsection (5A) shall be for the period of the delay.';

(f)   in section 25(10)(b) after the word '(4)' there were inserted ', (5A)';

(g)   the reference in section 25(12) to one extension were a reference to one extension by the OFT and one extension by the Secretary of State;

(h)   the powers to extend time-limits under section 25 as applied by subsection (5) above, and the power to request information under section 31(1) as so applied, were not exercisable by the OFT or the Secretary of State before the giving of an intervention notice but the existing time-limits in relation to possible references under section 22 or 33 were applicable for the purposes of the giving of that notice;

(i)   the existing time-limits in relation to possible references under section 22 or 33 (except for extensions under section 25(4)) remained applicable on and after the giving of an intervention notice as if any extensions were made under section 25 as applied by subsection (5) above but subject to further alteration by the OFT or the Secretary of State under section 25 as so applied;

(j)   in subsection (1) of section 31 for the words 'section 22' there were substituted 'section 45(2) or (3)' and, in the application of that subsection to the OFT, for the word 'deciding' there were substituted 'enabling the Secretary of State to decide';

(k)   in the case of the giving of intervention notices, the references in sections 23 to 32 to the making of a reference or a reference were, so far as necessary, references to the giving of an intervention notice or an intervention notice; and

(l)   the references to the OFT in section 32(2)(a) to (c) and (3) were construed in accordance with the above modifications.

(7) Where the Secretary of State has given an intervention notice mentioning a public interest consideration which, at that time, is not finalised, he shall, as soon as practicable, take such action as is within his power to ensure that it is finalised.

(8) For the purposes of this Part a public interest consideration is finalised if –

(a)   it is specified in section 58 otherwise than by virtue of an order under subsection (3) of that section; or

(b)   it is specified in that section by virtue of an order under subsection (3) of that section and the order providing for it to be so specified has been laid before, and approved by, Parliament in accordance with subsection (7) of section 124 and within the period mentioned in that subsection.

43 Intervention notices under section 42

(1) An intervention notice shall state –

(a)   the relevant merger situation concerned;

(b)   the public interest consideration or considerations which are, or may be, relevant to a consideration of the relevant merger situation concerned; and

(c)   where any public interest consideration concerned is not finalised, the proposed timetable for finalising it.

(2) Where the Secretary of State believes that it is or may be the case that two or more public interest considerations are relevant to a consideration of the relevant merger situation concerned, he may decide not to mention in the intervention notice such of those considerations as he considers appropriate.

(3) An intervention notice shall come into force when it is given and shall cease to be in force when the matter to which it relates is finally determined under this Chapter.

(4) For the purposes of this Part, a matter to which an intervention notice relates is finally determined under this Chapter if –

(a)   the time within which the OFT is to report to the Secretary of State under section 44 has expired and no such report has been made;

(b)   the Secretary of State decides to accept an undertaking or group of undertakings under paragraph 3 of Schedule 7 instead of making a reference under section 45;

(c)   the Secretary of State otherwise decides not to make a reference under that section;

(d)   the Commission cancels such a reference under section 48(1) or 53(1);

(e)   the time within which the Commission is to prepare a report under section 50 and give it to the Secretary of State has expired and no such report has been prepared and given to the Secretary of State;

(f)   the time within which the Secretary of State is to make and publish a decision under section 54(2) has expired and no such decision has been made and published;

(g)   the Secretary of State decides under section 54(2) to make no finding at all in the matter;

(h)   the Secretary of State otherwise decides under section 54(2) not to make an adverse public interest finding;

(i)   the Secretary of State decides under section 54(2) to make an adverse public interest finding but decides neither to accept an undertaking under paragraph 9 of Schedule 7 nor to make an order under paragraph 11 of that Schedule; or

(j)   the Secretary of State decides under section 54(2) to make an adverse public interest finding and accepts an undertaking under paragraph 9 of Schedule 7 or makes an order under paragraph 11 of that Schedule.

(5) For the purposes of this Part the time when a matter to which an intervention notice relates is finally determined under this Chapter is –

(a)   in a case falling within subsection (4)(a), (e) or (f), the expiry of the time concerned;

(b)   in a case falling within subsection (4)(b), the acceptance of the undertaking or group of undertakings concerned;

(c)   in a case falling within subsection (4)(c), (d), (g) or (h), the making of the decision concerned;

(d)   in a case falling within subsection (4)(i), the making of the decision neither to accept an undertaking under paragraph 9 of Schedule 7 nor to make an order under paragraph 11 of that Schedule; and

(e)   in a case falling within subsection (4)(j), the acceptance of the undertaking concerned or (as the case may be) the making of the order concerned.

44 Investigation and report by OFT

(1) Subsection (2) applies where the Secretary of State has given an intervention notice in relation to a relevant merger situation.

(2) The OFT shall, within such period as the Secretary of State may require, give a report to the Secretary of State in relation to the case.

(3) The report shall contain –

(a)   advice from the OFT on the considerations relevant to the making of a reference under section 22 or 33 which are also relevant to the Secretary of State's decision as to whether to make a reference under section 45; and

(b)   a summary of any representations about the case which have been received by the OFT and which relate to any public interest consideration mentioned in the intervention notice concerned and which is or may be relevant to the Secretary of State's decision as to whether to make a reference under section 45.

(4) The report shall, in particular, include decisions as to whether the OFT believes that it is, or may be, the case that –

(a)   a relevant merger situation has been created or arrangements are in progress or in contemplation which, if carried into effect, will result in the creation of a relevant merger situation;

(b)   the creation of that situation has resulted, or may be expected to result, in a substantial lessening of competition within any market or markets in the United Kingdom for goods or services;

(c)   the market or markets concerned would not be of sufficient importance to justify the making of a reference to the Commission under section 22 or 33;

(d)   in the case of arrangements which are in progress or in contemplation, the arrangements are not sufficiently far advanced, or not sufficiently likely to proceed, to justify the making of such a reference;

(e)   any relevant customer benefits in relation to the creation of the relevant merger situation concerned outweigh the substantial lessening of competition and any adverse effects of the substantial lessening of competition; or

(f)   it would be appropriate to deal with the matter (disregarding any public interest considerations mentioned in the intervention notice concerned) by way of undertakings under paragraph 3 of Schedule 7.

(5) If the OFT believes that it is or may be the case that it would be appropriate to deal with the matter (disregarding any public interest considerations mentioned in the intervention notice concerned) by way of undertakings under paragraph 3 of Schedule 7, the report shall contain descriptions of the undertakings which the OFT believes are, or may be, appropriate.

(6) The report may, in particular, include advice and recommendations on any public interest consideration mentioned in the intervention notice concerned and which is or may be relevant to the Secretary of State's decision as to whether to make a reference under section 45.

(7) The OFT shall carry out such investigations as it considers appropriate for the purposes of producing a report under this section.

45 Power of Secretary of State to refer matter to Commission

(1) Subsections (2) to (5) apply where the Secretary of State –

(a)   has given an intervention notice in relation to a relevant merger situation; and

(b)   has received a report of the OFT under section 44 in relation to the matter.

(2) The Secretary of State may make a reference to the Commission if he believes that it is or may be the case that –

(a)   a relevant merger situation has been created;

(b)   the creation of that situation has resulted, or may be expected to result, in a substantial lessening of competition within any market or markets in the United Kingdom for goods or services;

(c)   one or more than one public interest consideration mentioned in the intervention notice is relevant to a consideration of the relevant merger situation concerned; and

(d)   taking account only of the substantial lessening of competition and the relevant public interest consideration or considerations concerned, the creation of that situation operates or may be expected to operate against the public interest.

(3) The Secretary of State may make a reference to the Commission if he believes that it is or may be the case that –

(a) a relevant merger situation has been created;

(b) the creation of that situation has not resulted, and may be expected not to result, in a substantial lessening of competition within any market or markets in the United Kingdom for goods or services;

(c) one or more than one public interest consideration mentioned in the intervention notice is relevant to a consideration of the relevant merger situation concerned; and

(d) taking account only of the relevant public interest consideration or considerations concerned, the creation of that situation operates or may be expected to operate against the public interest.

(4) The Secretary of State may make a reference to the Commission if he believes that it is or may be the case that –

(a) arrangements are in progress or in contemplation which, if carried into effect, will result in the creation of a relevant merger situation;

(b) the creation of that situation may be expected to result in a substantial lessening of competition within any market or markets in the United Kingdom for goods or services;

(c) one or more than one public interest consideration mentioned in the intervention notice is relevant to a consideration of the relevant merger situation concerned; and

(d) taking account only of the substantial lessening of competition and the relevant public interest consideration or considerations concerned, the creation of the relevant merger situation may be expected to operate against the public interest.

(5) The Secretary of State may make a reference to the Commission if he believes that it is or may be the case that –

(a) arrangements are in progress or in contemplation which, if carried into effect, will result in the creation of a relevant merger situation;

(b) the creation of that situation may be expected not to result in a substantial lessening of competition within any market or markets in the United Kingdom for goods or services;

(c) one or more than one public interest consideration mentioned in the intervention notice is relevant to a consideration of the relevant merger situation concerned; and

(d) taking account only of the relevant public interest consideration or considerations concerned, the creation of the relevant merger situation may be expected to operate against the public interest.

(6) For the purposes of this Chapter any anti-competitive outcome shall be treated as being adverse to the public interest unless it is justified by one or more than one public interest consideration which is relevant.

(7) This section is subject to section 46.

46 References under section 45: supplementary

(1) No reference shall be made under section 45 if –

(a)   the making of the reference is prevented by section 69(1), 74(1) or 96(3) or paragraph 4 of Schedule 7; or

(b)   the European Commission is considering a request made, in relation to the matter concerned, by the United Kingdom (whether alone or with others) under article 22(3) of the European Merger Regulations, is proceeding with the matter in pursuance of such a request or has dealt with the matter in pursuance of such a request.

(2) The Secretary of State, in deciding whether to make a reference under section 45, shall accept the decisions of the OFT included in its report by virtue of subsection (4) of section 44 and any descriptions of undertakings as mentioned in subsection (5) of that section.

(3) Where the decision to make a reference under section 45 is made at any time on or after the end of the period of 24 weeks beginning with the giving of the intervention notice concerned, the Secretary of State shall, in deciding whether to make such a reference, disregard any public interest consideration which is mentioned in the intervention notice but which has not been finalised before the end of that period.

(4) Subject to subsection (5), where the decision to make a reference under section 45(2) or (4) is made at any time before the end of the period of 24 weeks beginning with the giving of the intervention notice concerned, the Secretary of State shall, in deciding whether to make such a reference, disregard any public interest consideration which is mentioned in the intervention notice but which has not been finalised if its effect would be to prevent, or to help to prevent, an anti-competitive outcome from being adverse to the public interest.

(5) The Secretary of State may, if he believes that there is a realistic prospect of the public interest consideration mentioned in subsection (4) being finalised within the period of 24 weeks beginning with the giving of the intervention notice concerned, delay deciding whether to make the reference concerned until the public interest consideration is finalised or, if earlier, the period expires.

(6) A reference under section 45 shall, in particular, specify –

(a)   the subsection of that section under which it is made;

(b)   the date on which it is made; and

(c)   the public interest consideration or considerations mentioned in the intervention notice concerned which the Secretary of State is not under a duty to disregard by virtue of subsection (3) above and which he believes are or may be relevant to a consideration of the relevant merger situation concerned.

Reports on references

47 Questions to be decided on references under section 45

(1) The Commission shall, on a reference under section 45(2) or (3), decide whether a relevant merger situation has been created.

(2) If the Commission decides that such a situation has been created, it shall, on a reference under section 45(2), decide the following additional questions –

    (a)   whether the creation of that situation has resulted, or may be expected to result, in a substantial lessening of competition within any market or markets in the United Kingdom for goods or services; and

    (b)   whether, taking account only of any substantial lessening of competition and the admissible public interest consideration or considerations concerned, the creation of that situation operates or may be expected to operate against the public interest.

(3) If the Commission decides that a relevant merger situation has been created, it shall, on a reference under section 45(3), decide whether, taking account only of the admissible public interest consideration or considerations concerned, the creation of that situation operates or may be expected to operate against the public interest.

(4) The Commission shall, on a reference under section 45(4) or (5), decide whether arrangements are in progress or in contemplation which, if carried into effect, will result in the creation of a relevant merger situation.

(5) If the Commission decides that such arrangements are in progress or in contemplation, it shall, on a reference under section 45(4), decide the following additional questions –

    (a)   whether the creation of that situation may be expected to result in a substantial lessening of competition within any market or markets in the United Kingdom for goods or services; and

    (b)   whether, taking account only of any substantial lessening of competition and the admissible public interest consideration or considerations concerned, the creation of that situation may be expected to operate against the public interest.

(6) If the Commission decides that arrangements are in progress or in contemplation which, if carried into effect, will result in the creation of a relevant merger situation, it shall, on a reference under section 45(5), decide whether, taking account only of the admissible public interest consideration or considerations concerned, the creation of that situation may be expected to operate against the public interest.

(7) The Commission shall, if it has decided on a reference under section 45 that the creation of a relevant merger situation operates or may be expected to operate against the public interest, decide the following additional questions –

    (a)   whether action should be taken by the Secretary of State under section 55 for the purpose of remedying, mitigating or preventing any of the effects adverse to the public interest which have resulted from, or may be expected to result from, the creation of the relevant merger situation;

(b)   whether the Commission should recommend the taking of other action by the Secretary of State or action by persons other than itself and the Secretary of State for the purpose of remedying, mitigating or preventing any of the effects adverse to the public interest which have resulted from, or may be expected to result from, the creation of the relevant merger situation; and

(c)   in either case, if action should be taken, what action should be taken and what is to be remedied, mitigated or prevented.

(8) Where the Commission has decided by virtue of subsection (2)(a) or (5)(a) that there is or will be a substantial lessening of competition within any market or markets in the United Kingdom for goods or services, it shall also decide separately the following questions (on the assumption that it is proceeding as mentioned in section 56(6)) –

(a)   whether action should be taken by it under section 41 for the purpose of remedying, mitigating or preventing the substantial lessening of competition concerned or any adverse effect which has resulted from, or may be expected to result from, the substantial lessening of competition;

(b)   whether the Commission should recommend the taking of action by other persons for the purpose of remedying, mitigating or preventing the substantial lessening of competition concerned or any adverse effect which has resulted from, or may be expected to result from, the substantial lessening of competition; and

(c)   in either case, if action should be taken, what action should be taken and what is to be remedied, mitigated or prevented.

(9) In deciding the questions mentioned in subsections (7) and (8) the Commission shall, in particular, have regard to the need to achieve as comprehensive a solution as is reasonable and practicable to –

(a)   the adverse effects to the public interest; or

(b)   (as the case may be) the substantial lessening of competition and any adverse effects resulting from it.

(10) In deciding the questions mentioned in subsections (7) and (8) in a case where it has decided by virtue of subsection (2)(a) or (5)(a) that there is or will be a substantial lessening of competition, the Commission may, in particular, have regard to the effect of any action on any relevant customer benefits in relation to the creation of the relevant merger situation concerned.

(11) In this section 'admissible public interest consideration' means any public interest consideration which is specified in the reference under section 45 and which the Commission is not under a duty to disregard.

48 Cases where references or certain questions need not be decided

(1) The Commission shall cancel a reference under section 45(4) or (5) if it considers that the proposal to make arrangements of the kind mentioned in that reference has been abandoned.

(2) In relation to the question whether a relevant merger situation has been created or the question whether a relevant merger situation will be created, a reference under section 45 may be framed so as to require the Commission to exclude from consideration –

(a)   subsection (1) of section 23;

(b)   subsection (2) of that section; or

(c)   one of those subsections if the Commission finds that the other is satisfied.

(3) In relation to the question whether any such result as is mentioned in section 23(2)(b) has arisen or the question whether any such result will arise, a reference under section 45 may be framed so as to require the Commission to confine its investigation to the supply of goods or services in a part of the United Kingdom specified in the reference.

49 Variation of references under section 45

(1) The Commission may, if it considers that doing so is justified by the facts (including events occurring on or after the making of the reference concerned), treat –

(a)   a reference made under subsection (2) or (3) of section 45 as if it had been made under subsection (4) or (as the case may be) (5) of that section; or

(b)   a reference made under subsection (4) or (5) of section 45 as if it had been made under subsection (2) or (as the case may be) (3) of that section;

and, in such cases, references in this Part to references under those enactments shall, so far as may be necessary, be construed accordingly.

(2) Where, by virtue of subsection (1), the Commission treats a reference made under subsection (2) or (3) of section 45 as if it had been made under subsection (4) or (as the case may be) (5) of that section, paragraphs 1, 2, 7 and 8 of Schedule 7 shall, in particular, apply as if the reference had been made under subsection (4) or (as the case may be) (5) of that section instead of under subsection (2) or (3) of that section.

(3) Where, by virtue of subsection (1), the Commission treats a reference made under subsection (4) or (5) of section 45 as if it had been made under subsection (2) or (as the case may be) (3) of that section, paragraphs 1, 2, 7 and 8 of Schedule 7 shall, in particular, apply as if the reference had been made under subsection (2) or (as the case may be) (3) of that section instead of under subsection (4) or (5) of that section.

(4) Subsection (5) applies in relation to any undertaking accepted under paragraph 1 of Schedule 7, or any order made under paragraph 2 of that Schedule, which is in force immediately before the Commission, by virtue of subsection (1), treats a reference as mentioned in subsection (1).

(5) The undertaking or order shall, so far as applicable, continue in force as if –

(a)   in the case of an undertaking or order which relates to a reference under subsection (2) or (3) of section 45, accepted or made in relation to a reference made under subsection (4) or (as the case may be) (5) of that section; and

(b)   in the case of an undertaking or order which relates to a reference made
under subsection (4) or (5) of that section, accepted or made in relation
to a reference made under subsection (2) or (as the case may be) (3) of
that section;

and the undertaking or order concerned may be varied, superseded, released or
revoked accordingly.

(6) The Secretary of State may at any time vary a reference under section 45.

(7) The Secretary of State shall consult the Commission before varying any such
reference.

(8) Subsection (7) shall not apply if the Commission has requested the variation
concerned.

(9) No variation by the Secretary of State under this section shall be capable of
altering the public interest consideration or considerations specified in the reference
or the period permitted by section 51 within which the report of the Commission
under section 50 is to be prepared and given to the Secretary of State.

50 Investigations and reports on references under section 45

(1) The Commission shall prepare a report on a reference under section 45 and give it
to the Secretary of State within the period permitted by section 51.

(2) The report shall, in particular, contain –

(a)   the decisions of the Commission on the questions which it is required
to answer by virtue of section 47;

(b)   its reasons for its decisions; and

(c)   such information as the Commission considers appropriate for
facilitating a proper understanding of those questions and of its reasons
for its decisions.

(3) The Commission shall carry out such investigations as it considers appropriate for
the purpose of producing a report under this section.

51 Time-limits for investigations and reports by Commission

(1) The Commission shall prepare its report under section 50 and give it to the
Secretary of State under that section within the period of 24 weeks beginning with the
date of the reference concerned.

(2) Where article 9(6) of the European Merger Regulations applies in relation to the
reference under section 45, the Commission shall prepare its report under section 50
and give it to the Secretary of State –

(a)   within the period of 24 weeks beginning with the date of the reference;
or

(b)   if it is a shorter period, within such period as is necessary to ensure
compliance with that article.

(3) The Commission may extend, by no more than 8 weeks, the period within which
a report under section 50 is to be prepared and given to the Secretary of State if it

considers that there are special reasons why the report cannot be prepared and given to the Secretary of State within that period.

(4) The Commission may extend the period within which a report under section 50 is to be prepared and given to the Secretary of State if it considers that a relevant person has failed (whether with or without a reasonable excuse) to comply with any requirement of a notice under section 109.

(5) In subsection (4) 'relevant person' means –

(a)　　any person carrying on any of the enterprises concerned;

(b)　　any person who (whether alone or as a member of a group) owns or has control of any such person; or

(c)　　any officer, employee or agent of any person mentioned in paragraph (a) or (b).

(6) For the purposes of subsection (5) a person or group of persons able, directly or indirectly, to control or materially to influence the policy of a body of persons corporate or unincorporate, but without having a controlling interest in that body of persons, may be treated as having control of it.

(7) An extension under subsection (3) or (4) shall come into force when published under section 107.

(8) An extension under subsection (4) shall continue in force until –

(a)　　the person concerned provides the information or documents to the satisfaction of the Commission or (as the case may be) appears as a witness in accordance with the requirements of the Commission; or

(b)　　the Commission publishes its decision to cancel the extension.

(9) This section is subject to sections 52 and 53.

52　Section 51: supplementary

(1) No extension is possible under subsection (3) or (4) of section 51 where the period within which the report is to be prepared and given to the Secretary of State is determined by virtue of subsection (2)(b) of that section.

(2) Where the period within which the report is to be prepared and given to the Secretary of State is determined by virtue of subsection (2)(a) of section 51, no extension is possible under subsection (3) or (4) of that section which extends that period beyond such period as is necessary to ensure compliance with article 9(6) of the European Merger Regulations.

(3) A period extended under subsection (3) of section 51 may also be extended under subsection (4) of that section and a period extended under subsection (4) of that section may also be extended under subsection (3) of that section.

(4) No more than one extension is possible under section 51(3).

(5) Where a period within which a report under section 50 is to be prepared and given to the Secretary of State is extended or further extended under section 51(3) or (4), the period as extended or (as the case may be) further extended shall, subject to

subsections (6) and (7), be calculated by taking the period being extended and adding to it the period of the extension (whether or not those periods overlap in time).

(6) Subsection (7) applies where –

    (a)   the period within which the report under section 50 is to be prepared and given to the Secretary of State is further extended;

    (b)   the further extension and at least one previous extension is made under section 51(4); and

    (c)   the same days or fractions of days are included in or comprise the further extension and are included in or comprise at least one such previous extension.

(7) In calculating the period of the further extension, any days or fractions of days of the kind mentioned in subsection (6)(c) shall be disregarded.

(8) The Secretary of State may by order amend section 51 so as to alter any one or more of the following periods –

    (a)   the period of 24 weeks mentioned in subsection (1) of that section or any period for the time being mentioned in that subsection in substitution for that period;

    (b)   the period of 24 weeks mentioned in subsection (2)(a) of that section or any period for the time being mentioned in that subsection in substitution for that period;

    (c)   the period of 8 weeks mentioned in subsection (3) of that section or any period for the time being mentioned in that subsection in substitution for that period.

(9) No alteration shall be made by virtue of subsection (8) which results in the period for the time being mentioned in subsection (1) or (2)(a) of section 51 exceeding 24 weeks or the period for the time being mentioned in subsection (3) of that section exceeding 8 weeks.

(10) An order under subsection (8) shall not affect any period of time within which the Commission is under a duty to prepare and give to the Secretary of State its report under section 50 in relation to a reference under section 45 if the Commission is already under that duty in relation to that reference when the order is made.

(11) Before making an order under subsection (8) the Secretary of State shall consult the Commission and such other persons as he considers appropriate.

(12) The Secretary of State may make regulations for the purposes of section 51(8).

(13) The regulations may, in particular –

    (a)   provide for the time at which information or documents are to be treated as provided (including the time at which they are to be treated as provided to the satisfaction of the Commission for the purposes of section 51(8));

    (b)   provide for the time at which a person is to be treated as appearing as a witness (including the time at which he is to be treated as appearing as a witness in accordance with the requirements of the Commission for the purposes of section 51(8));

(c) provide for the persons carrying on the enterprises which have or may have ceased to be, or may cease to be, distinct enterprises to be informed, in circumstances in which section 51(8) applies, of the fact that –
  (i) the Commission is satisfied as to the provision of the information or documents required by it; or
  (ii) the person concerned has appeared as a witness in accordance with the requirements of the Commission;

(d) provide for the persons carrying on the enterprises which have or may have ceased to be, or may cease to be, distinct enterprises to be informed, in circumstances in which section 51(8) applies, of the time at which the Commission is to be treated as satisfied as mentioned in paragraph (c)(i) above or the person concerned is to be treated as having appeared as mentioned in paragraph (c)(ii) above.

53 Restrictions on action where public interest considerations not finalised

(1) The Commission shall cancel a reference under section 45 if –

(a) the intervention notice concerned mentions a public interest consideration which was not finalised on the giving of that notice or public interest considerations which, at that time, were not finalised;

(b) no other public interest consideration is mentioned in the notice;

(c) at least 24 weeks has elapsed since the giving of the notice; and

(d) the public interest consideration mentioned in the notice has not been finalised within that period of 24 weeks or (as the case may be) none of the public interest considerations mentioned in the notice has been finalised within that period of 24 weeks.

(2) Where a reference to the Commission under section 45 specifies a public interest consideration which has not been finalised before the making of the reference, the Commission shall not give its report to the Secretary of State under section 50 in relation to that reference unless –

(a) the period of 24 weeks beginning with the giving of the intervention notice concerned has expired;

(b) the public interest consideration concerned has been finalised; or

(c) the report must be given to the Secretary of State to ensure compliance with article 9(6) of the European Merger Regulations.

(3) The Commission shall, in reporting on any of the questions mentioned in section 47(2)(b), (3), (5)(b), (6) and (7), disregard any public interest consideration which has not been finalised before the giving of the report.

(4) The Commission shall, in reporting on any of the questions mentioned in section 47(2)(b), (3), (5)(b), (6) and (7), disregard any public interest consideration which was not finalised on the giving of the intervention notice concerned and has not been finalised within the period of 24 weeks beginning with the giving of the notice concerned.

(5) Subsections (1) to (4) are without prejudice to the power of the Commission to carry out investigations in relation to any public interest consideration to which it might be able to have regard in its report.

Decisions of the Secretary of State

54 Decision of Secretary of State in public interest cases

(1) Subsection (2) applies where the Secretary of State has received a report of the Commission under section 50 in relation to a relevant merger situation.

(2) The Secretary of State shall decide whether to make an adverse public interest finding in relation to the relevant merger situation and whether to make no finding at all in the matter.

(3) For the purposes of this Part the Secretary of State makes an adverse public interest finding in relation to a relevant merger situation if, in relation to that situation, he decides –

    (a)   in connection with a reference to the Commission under subsection (2) of section 45, that it is the case as mentioned in paragraphs (a) to (d) of that subsection or subsection (3) of that section;

    (b)   in connection with a reference to the Commission under subsection (3) of that section, that it is the case as mentioned in paragraphs (a) to (d) of that subsection;

    (c)   in connection with a reference to the Commission under subsection (4) of that section, that it is the case as mentioned in paragraphs (a) to (d) of that subsection or subsection (5) of that section; and

    (d)   in connection with a reference to the Commission under subsection (5) of that section, that it is the case as mentioned in paragraphs (a) to (d) of that subsection.

(4) The Secretary of State may make no finding at all in the matter only if he decides that there is no public interest consideration which is relevant to a consideration of the relevant merger situation concerned.

(5) The Secretary of State shall make and publish his decision under subsection (2) within the period of 30 days beginning with the receipt of the report of the Commission under section 50.

(6) In making a decision under subsections (2) to (4), the Secretary of State shall disregard any public interest consideration not specified in the reference under section 45 and any public interest consideration disregarded by the Commission for the purposes of its report.

(7) In deciding whether to make an adverse public interest finding under subsection (2), the Secretary of State shall accept –

    (a)   in connection with a reference to the Commission under section 45(2) or (4), the decision of the report of the Commission under section 50 as to whether there is an anti-competitive outcome; and

    (b)   in connection with a reference to the Commission under section 45(3) or (5) –

(i)   the decision of the report of the Commission under section 50 as to whether a relevant merger situation has been created or (as the case may be) arrangements are in progress or in contemplation which, if carried into effect, will result in the creation of a relevant merger situation; and

(ii)   the decision of the report of the OFT under section 44 as to the absence of a substantial lessening of competition.

(8) In determining for the purposes of subsection (5) the period of 30 days no account shall be taken of –

(a)   Saturday, Sunday, Good Friday and Christmas Day; and

(b)   any day which is a bank holiday in England and Wales.

55 Enforcement action by Secretary of State

(1) Subsection (2) applies where the Secretary of State has decided under subsection (2) of section 54 within the period required by subsection (5) of that section to make an adverse public interest finding in relation to a relevant merger situation and has published his decision within the period so required.

(2) The Secretary of State may take such action under paragraph 9 or 11 of Schedule 7 as he considers to be reasonable and practicable to remedy, mitigate or prevent any of the effects adverse to the public interest which have resulted from, or may be expected to result from, the creation of the relevant merger situation concerned.

(3) In making a decision under subsection (2) the Secretary of State shall, in particular, have regard to the report of the Commission under section 50.

(4) In making a decision under subsection (2) in any case of a substantial lessening of competition, the Secretary of State may, in particular, have regard to the effect of any action on any relevant customer benefits in relation to the creation of the relevant merger situation concerned.

Other

56 Competition cases where intervention on public interest grounds ceases

(1) Where the Secretary of State decides not to make a reference under section 45 on the ground that no public interest consideration to which he is able to have regard is relevant to a consideration of the relevant merger situation concerned, he shall by notice require the OFT to deal with the matter otherwise than under this Chapter.

(2) Where a notice is given to the OFT in the circumstances mentioned in subsection (1), the OFT shall decide whether to make a reference under section 22 or 33; and any time-limits in relation to the Secretary of State's decision whether to make a reference under section 45 (including any remaining powers of extension) shall apply in relation to the decision of the OFT whether to make a reference under section 22 or 33.

(3) Where the Commission cancels under section 53(1) a reference under section 45 and the report of the OFT under section 44 contains the decision that it is or may be the case that there is an anti-competitive outcome in relation to the relevant merger

situation concerned, the Commission shall proceed under this Part as if a reference under section 22 or (as the case may be) 33 had been made to it by the OFT.

(4) In proceeding by virtue of subsection (3) to prepare and publish a report under section 38, the Commission shall proceed as if –

    (a)   the reference under section 22 or 33 had been made at the same time as the reference under section 45;

    (b)   the timetable for preparing and giving its report under section 50 (including any remaining powers of extension and as extended by an additional period of 20 days) were the timetable for preparing and publishing its report under section 38; and

    (c)   in relation to the question whether a relevant merger situation has been created or the question whether arrangements are in progress or in contemplation which, if carried into effect, will result in the creation of a relevant merger situation, the Commission were confined to the questions on the subject to be investigated by it under section 47.

(5) In determining the period of 20 days mentioned in subsection (4) no account shall be taken of –

    (a)   Saturday, Sunday, Good Friday and Christmas Day; and

    (b)   any day which is a bank holiday in England and Wales.

(6) Where the Secretary of State decides under section 54(2) to make no finding at all in the matter in connection with a reference under section 45(2) or (4), the Commission shall proceed under this Part as if a reference under section 22 or (as the case may be) 33 had been made to it instead of a reference under section 45 and as if its report to the Secretary of State under section 50 had been prepared and published by it under section 38 within the period permitted by section 39.

(7) In relation to proceedings by virtue of subsection (6), the reference in section 41(3) to decisions of the Commission as included in its report by virtue of section 35(3) or 36(2) shall be construed as a reference to decisions which were included in the report of the Commission by virtue of section 47(8).

(8) Where the Commission becomes under a duty to proceed as mentioned in subsection (3) or (6), references in this Part to references under sections 22 and 33 shall, so far as may be necessary, be construed accordingly; and, in particular, sections 77 to 81 shall apply as if a reference has been made to the Commission by the OFT under section 22 or (as the case may be) 33.

57 Duties of OFT and Commission to inform Secretary of State

(1) The OFT shall, in considering whether to make a reference under section 22 or 33, bring to the attention of the Secretary of State any case which it believes raises any consideration specified in section 58 unless it believes that the Secretary of State would consider any such consideration immaterial in the context of the particular case.

(2) The OFT and the Commission shall bring to the attention of the Secretary of State any representations about exercising his powers under section 58(3) which have been made to the OFT or (as the case may be) the Commission.

58 Specified considerations

(1) The interests of national security are specified in this section.

(2) In subsection (1) 'national security' includes public security; and in this subsection 'public security' has the same meaning as in article 21(3) of the European Merger Regulations.

(3) The Secretary of State may by order modify this section for the purpose of specifying in this section a new consideration or removing or amending any consideration which is for the time being specified in this section.

(4) An order under this section may, in particular –

  (a) provide for a consideration to be specified in this section for a particular purpose or purposes or for all purposes;

  (b) apply in relation to cases under consideration by the OFT, the Commission or the Secretary of State before the making of the order as well as cases under consideration on or after the making of the order.

CHAPTER 3
OTHER SPECIAL CASES

Special public interest cases

59 Intervention by Secretary of State in special public interest cases

(1) Subsection (2) applies where the Secretary of State has reasonable grounds for suspecting that it is or may be the case that a special merger situation has been created or arrangements are in progress or in contemplation which, if carried into effect, will result in the creation of a special merger situation.

(2) The Secretary of State may give a notice to the OFT (in this Part 'a special intervention notice') if he believes that it is or may be the case that one or more than one consideration specified in section 58 is relevant to a consideration of the special merger situation concerned.

(3) For the purposes of this Part a special merger situation has been created if –

  (a) no relevant merger situation has been created because of section 23(1)(b) and (2)(b); but

  (b) a relevant merger situation would have been created if those enactments were disregarded;

and the conditions mentioned in subsection (4) are satisfied.

(4) The conditions mentioned in this subsection are that, immediately before the enterprises concerned ceased to be distinct –

  (a) at least one of the enterprises concerned was carried on in the United Kingdom or by or under the control of a body corporate incorporated in the United Kingdom; and

(b)   a person carrying on one or more of the enterprises concerned was a relevant government contractor.

(5) For the purposes of deciding whether a relevant merger situation has been created or whether arrangements are in progress or in contemplation which, if carried into effect, will result in the creation of a relevant merger situation, sections 23 to 32 (read together with section 34) shall apply for the purposes of this Chapter as they do for the purposes of Chapter 1 but subject to subsection (6).

(6) In their application by virtue of subsection (5) sections 23 to 32 shall have effect as if –

(a)   for paragraph (a) of section 23(9) there were substituted –

    '(a)   in relation to the giving of a special intervention notice, the time when the notice is given;

    (aa)   in relation to the making of a report by the OFT under section 61, the time of the making of the report;

    (ab)   in the case of a reference which is treated as having been made under section 62(2) by virtue of section 64(2), such time as the Commission may determine; and';

(b)   the references to the OFT in section 24(2)(a) and (b) included references to the Secretary of State;

(c)   the references to the OFT in sections 25(1) to (3), (6) and (8) and 31 included references to the Secretary of State;

(d)   the references to the OFT in section 25(4) and (5) were references to the Secretary of State;

(e)   the reference in section 25(4) to section 73 were a reference to paragraph 3 of Schedule 7;

(f)   the reference in section 25(12) to one extension were a reference to one extension by the OFT and one extension by the Secretary of State;

(g)   the powers to extend time-limits under section 25 as applied by subsection (5) above, and the power to request information under section 31(1) as so applied, were not exercisable by the OFT or the Secretary of State before the giving of a special intervention notice;

(h)   in subsection (1) of section 31 for the words 'section 22' there were substituted 'section 62(2)' and, in the application of that subsection to the OFT, for the word 'deciding' there were substituted 'enabling the Secretary of State to decide';

(i)   in the case of the giving of special intervention notices, the references in sections 23 to 32 to the making of a reference or a reference were, so far as necessary, references to the giving of a special intervention notice or a special intervention notice; and

(j)   the references to the OFT in section 32(2)(a) to (c) and (3) were construed in accordance with the above modifications.

(7) No more than one special intervention notice shall be given under subsection (2) in relation to the same special merger situation.

(8) In this section 'relevant government contractor' means –

(a)   a government contractor –

(i)   who has been notified by or on behalf of the Secretary of State of information, documents or other articles relating to defence and of a confidential nature which the government contractor or an employee of his may hold or receive in connection with being such a contractor; and

(ii)   whose notification has not been revoked by or on behalf of the Secretary of State; or

(b)   a former government contractor who was so notified when he was a government contractor and whose notification has not been revoked by or on behalf of the Secretary of State.

(9) In this section –

'defence' has the same meaning as in section 2 of the Official Secrets Act 1989; and

'government contractor' has the same meaning as in the Act of 1989 and includes any sub-contractor of a government contractor, any sub-contractor of that sub-contractor and any other sub-contractor in a chain of sub-contractors which begins with the sub-contractor of the government contractor.

60 Special intervention notices under section 59

(1) A special intervention notice shall state –

(a)   the special merger situation concerned; and

(b)   the consideration specified in section 58 or considerations so specified which are, or may be, relevant to the special merger situation concerned.

(2) Where the Secretary of State believes that it is or may be the case that two or more considerations specified in section 58 are relevant to a consideration of the special merger situation concerned, he may decide not to mention in the special intervention notice such of those considerations as he considers appropriate.

(3) A special intervention notice shall come into force when it is given and shall cease to be in force when the matter to which it relates is finally determined under this Chapter.

(4) For the purposes of this Part, a matter to which a special intervention notice relates is finally determined under this Chapter if –

(a)   the time within which the OFT is to report to the Secretary of State under section 61 has expired and no such report has been made;

(b)   the Secretary of State decides to accept an undertaking or group of undertakings under paragraph 3 of Schedule 7 instead of making a reference under section 62;

(c)   the Secretary of State otherwise decides not to make a reference under that section;

(d)   the Commission cancels such a reference under section 64(1);

(e)   the time within which the Commission is to prepare a report under section 65 and give it to the Secretary of State has expired and no such report has been prepared and given to the Secretary of State;

(f) the time within which the Secretary of State is to make and publish a decision under section 66(2) has expired and no such decision has been made and published;

(g) the Secretary of State decides under subsection (2) of section 66 otherwise than as mentioned in subsection (5) of that section;

(h) the Secretary of State decides under subsection (2) of section 66 as mentioned in subsection (5) of that section but decides neither to accept an undertaking under paragraph 9 of Schedule 7 nor to make an order under paragraph 11 of that Schedule; or

(i) the Secretary of State decides under subsection (2) of section 66 as mentioned in subsection (5) of that section and accepts an undertaking under paragraph 9 of Schedule 7 or makes an order under paragraph 11 of that Schedule.

(5) For the purposes of this Part the time when a matter to which a special intervention notice relates is finally determined under this Chapter is –

(a) in a case falling within subsection (4)(a), (e) or (f), the expiry of the time concerned;

(b) in a case falling within subsection (4)(b), the acceptance of the undertaking or group of undertakings concerned;

(c) in a case falling within subsection (4)(c), (d) or (g), the making of the decision concerned;

(d) in a case falling within subsection (4)(h), the making of the decision neither to accept an undertaking under paragraph 9 of Schedule 7 nor to make an order under paragraph 11 of that Schedule; and

(e) in a case falling within subsection (4)(i), the acceptance of the undertaking concerned or (as the case may be) the making of the order concerned.

61 Initial investigation and report by OFT

(1) Subsection (2) applies where the Secretary of State has given a special intervention notice in relation to a special merger situation.

(2) The OFT shall, within such period as the Secretary of State may require, give a report to the Secretary of State in relation to the case.

(3) The report shall contain –

(a) advice from the OFT on the considerations relevant to the making of a reference under section 22 or 33 which are also relevant to the Secretary of State's decision as to whether to make a reference under section 62; and

(b) a summary of any representations about the case which have been received by the OFT and which relate to any consideration mentioned in the special intervention notice concerned and which is or may be relevant to the Secretary of State's decision as to whether to make a reference under section 62.

(4) The report shall include a decision as to whether the OFT believes (disregarding section 59(4)(b)) that it is, or may be, the case that a special merger situation has been

created or (as the case may be) arrangements are in progress or in contemplation which, if carried into effect, will result in the creation of a special merger situation.

(5) The report may, in particular, include advice and recommendations on any consideration mentioned in the special intervention notice concerned and which is or may be relevant to the Secretary of State's decision as to whether to make a reference under section 62.

(6) The OFT shall carry out such investigations as it considers appropriate for the purposes of producing a report under this section.

62 Power of Secretary of State to refer the matter

(1) Subsection (2) applies where the Secretary of State –

(a) has given a special intervention notice in relation to a special merger situation; and

(b) has received a report of the OFT under section 61 in relation to the matter.

(2) The Secretary of State may make a reference to the Commission if he believes that it is or may be the case that –

(a) a special merger situation has been created;

(b) one or more than one consideration mentioned in the special intervention notice is relevant to a consideration of the special merger situation concerned; and

(c) taking account only of the relevant consideration or considerations concerned, the creation of that situation operates or may be expected to operate against the public interest.

(3) The Secretary of State may make a reference to the Commission if he believes that it is or may be the case that –

(a) arrangements are in progress or in contemplation which, if carried into effect, will result in the creation of a special merger situation;

(b) one or more than one consideration mentioned in the special intervention notice is relevant to a consideration of the special merger situation concerned; and

(c) taking account only of the relevant consideration or considerations concerned, the creation of that situation may be expected to operate against the public interest.

(4) No reference shall be made under this section if the making of the reference is prevented by section 69(1) or paragraph 4 of Schedule 7.

(5) The Secretary of State, in deciding whether to make a reference under this section, shall accept the decision of the OFT included in its report under section 61 by virtue of subsection (4) of that section.

(6) A reference under this section shall, in particular, specify –

(a) the subsection of this section under which it is made;

(b) the date on which it is made; and

(c)   the consideration or considerations mentioned in the special intervention notice which the Secretary of State believes are, or may be, relevant to a consideration of the special merger situation concerned.

63 Questions to be decided on references under section 62

(1) The Commission shall, on a reference under section 62(2), decide whether a special merger situation has been created.

(2) The Commission shall, on a reference under section 62(3), decide whether arrangements are in progress or in contemplation which, if carried into effect, will result in the creation of a special merger situation.

(3) If the Commission decides that a special merger situation has been created or that arrangements are in progress or in contemplation which, if carried into effect, will result in the creation of a special merger situation, it shall, on a reference under section 62, decide whether, taking account only of the consideration or considerations mentioned in the reference, the creation of that situation operates or may be expected to operate against the public interest.

(4) The Commission shall, if it has decided on a reference under section 62 that the creation of a special merger situation operates or may be expected to operate against the public interest, decide the following additional questions –

(a)   whether action should be taken by the Secretary of State under section 66 for the purpose of remedying, mitigating or preventing any of the effects adverse to the public interest which have resulted from, or may be expected to result from, the creation of the special merger situation concerned;

(b)   whether the Commission should recommend the taking of other action by the Secretary of State or action by persons other than itself and the Secretary of State for the purpose of remedying, mitigating or preventing any of the effects adverse to the public interest which have resulted from, or may be expected to result from, the creation of the special merger situation concerned; and

(c)   in either case, if action should be taken, what action should be taken and what is to be remedied, mitigated or prevented.

64 Cancellation and variation of references under section 62

(1) The Commission shall cancel a reference under section 62(3) if it considers that the proposal to make arrangements of the kind mentioned in that reference has been abandoned.

(2) The Commission may, if it considers that doing so is justified by the facts (including events occurring on or after the making of the reference concerned), treat a reference made under subsection (2) or (3) of section 62 as if it had been made under subsection (3) or (as the case may be) (2) of that section; and, in such cases, references in this Part to references under those enactments shall, so far as may be necessary, be construed accordingly.

(3) Where, by virtue of subsection (2), the Commission treats a reference made under subsection (2) or (3) of section 62 as if it had been made under subsection (3) or (as

the case may be) (2) of that section, paragraphs 1, 2, 7 and 8 of Schedule 7 shall, in particular, apply as if the reference had been made under subsection (3) or (as the case may be) (2) of that section instead of under subsection (2) or (3) of that section.

(4) Subsection (5) applies in relation to any undertaking accepted under paragraph 1 of Schedule 7, or any order made under paragraph 2 of that Schedule, which is in force immediately before the Commission, by virtue of subsection (2), treats a reference made under subsection (2) or (3) of section 62 as if it had been made under subsection (3) or (as the case may be) (2) of that section.

(5) The undertaking or order shall, so far as applicable, continue in force as if –

(a) in the case of an undertaking or order which relates to a reference under subsection (2) of section 62, accepted or made in relation to a reference made under subsection (3) of that section; and

(b) in the case of an undertaking or order which relates to a reference made under subsection (3) of that section, accepted or made in relation to a reference made under subsection (2) of that section;

and the undertaking or order concerned may be varied, superseded, released or revoked accordingly.

(6) The Secretary of State may at any time vary a reference under section 62.

(7) The Secretary of State shall consult the Commission before varying any such reference.

(8) Subsection (7) shall not apply if the Commission has requested the variation concerned.

(9) No variation by the Secretary of State under this section shall be capable of altering the consideration or considerations specified in the reference or the period permitted by virtue of section 65 within which the report of the Commission under that section is to be prepared and given to the Secretary of State.

65 Investigations and reports on references under section 62

(1) The Commission shall prepare a report on a reference under section 62 and give it to the Secretary of State within the period permitted by virtue of this section.

(2) The report shall, in particular, contain –

(a) the decisions of the Commission on the questions which it is required to answer by virtue of section 63;

(b) its reasons for its decisions; and

(c) such information as the Commission considers appropriate for facilitating a proper understanding of those questions and of its reasons for its decisions.

(3) Sections 51 and 52 (but not section 53) shall apply for the purposes of a report under this section as they apply for the purposes of a report under section 50.

(4) The Commission shall carry out such investigations as it considers appropriate for the purpose of producing a report under this section.

66 Decision and enforcement action by Secretary of State

(1) Subsection (2) applies where the Secretary of State has received a report of the Commission under section 65 in relation to a special merger situation.

(2) The Secretary of State shall, in connection with a reference under section 62(2) or (3), decide the questions which the Commission is required to decide by virtue of section 63(1) to (3).

(3) The Secretary of State shall make and publish his decision under subsection (2) within the period of 30 days beginning with the receipt of the report of the Commission under section 65; and subsection (8) of section 54 shall apply for the purposes of this subsection as it applies for the purposes of subsection (5) of that section.

(4) In making his decisions under subsection (2), the Secretary of State shall accept the decisions of the report of the Commission under section 65 as to whether a special merger situation has been created or whether arrangements are in progress or in contemplation which, if carried into effect, will result in the creation of a special merger situation.

(5) Subsection (6) applies where the Secretary of State has decided under subsection (2) that –

    (a)   a special merger situation has been created or arrangements are in progress or in contemplation which, if carried into effect, will result in the creation of a special merger situation;

    (b)   at least one consideration which is mentioned in the special intervention notice concerned is relevant to a consideration of the special merger situation concerned; and

    (c)   taking account only of the relevant consideration or considerations concerned, the creation of that situation operates or may be expected to operate against the public interest;

and has so decided, and published his decision, within the period required by subsection (3).

(6) The Secretary of State may take such action under paragraph 9 or 11 of Schedule 7 as he considers to be reasonable and practicable to remedy, mitigate or prevent any of the effects adverse to the public interest which have resulted from, or may be expected to result from, the creation of the special merger situation concerned.

(7) In making a decision under subsection (6), the Secretary of State shall, in particular, have regard to the report of the Commission under section 65.

European mergers

67 Intervention to protect legitimate interests

(1) Subsection (2) applies where –

    (a)   the Secretary of State has reasonable grounds for suspecting that it is or may be the case that –

        (i)   a relevant merger situation has been created or that arrangements are in progress or in contemplation which, if carried into effect, will result in the creation of a relevant merger situation; and

        (ii)   a concentration with a Community dimension (within the meaning of the European Merger Regulations), or a part of such a concentration, has thereby arisen or will thereby arise;

   (b)   a reference which would otherwise be possible under section 22 or 33 is prevented from being made under that section in relation to the relevant merger situation concerned by virtue of Community law or anything done under or in accordance with it; and

   (c)   the Secretary of State is considering whether to take appropriate measures to protect legitimate interests as permitted by article 21(3) of the European Merger Regulations.

(2) The Secretary of State may give a notice to the OFT (in this section 'a European intervention notice') if he believes that it is or may be the case that one or more than one public interest consideration is relevant to a consideration of the relevant merger situation concerned.

(3) A European intervention notice shall state –

   (a)   the relevant merger situation concerned;

   (b)   the public interest consideration or considerations which are, or may be, relevant to a consideration of the relevant merger situation concerned; and

   (c)   where any public interest consideration concerned is not finalised, the proposed timetable for finalising it.

(4) Where the Secretary of State believes that it is or may be the case that two or more public interest considerations are relevant to a consideration of the relevant merger situation concerned, he may decide not to mention in the intervention notice such of those considerations as he considers appropriate.

(5) No more than one European intervention notice shall be given under subsection (2) in relation to the same relevant merger situation.

(6) Where the Secretary of State has given a European intervention notice mentioning a public interest consideration which, at that time, is not finalised, he shall, as soon as practicable, take such action as is within his power to ensure that it is finalised.

(7) For the purposes of deciding whether a relevant merger situation has been created or whether arrangements are in progress or in contemplation which, if carried into effect, will result in the creation of a relevant merger situation, sections 23 to 32 (read together with section 34) shall apply for the purposes of this section as they do for the purposes of Chapter 1 but subject to subsection (8).

(8) In their application by virtue of subsection (7) sections 23 to 32 shall have effect as if –

   (a)   references in those sections to the decision-making authority were references to the Secretary of State;

(b)   for paragraphs (a) and (b) of section 23(9) there were substituted ', in relation to the giving of a European intervention notice, the time when the notice is given';

(c)   the references to the OFT in section 24(2)(a) and (b) included references to the Secretary of State;

(d)   sections 25, 31 and 32 were omitted; and

(e)   the references in sections 23 to 29 to the making of a reference or a reference were, so far as necessary, references to the giving of a European intervention notice or a European intervention notice.

(9) Section 42(3) shall, in its application to this section and section 68, have effect as if for the words 'intervention notice' there were substituted 'European intervention notice'.

68 Scheme for protecting legitimate interests

(1) The Secretary of State may by order provide for the taking of action, where a European intervention notice has been given, to remedy, mitigate or prevent effects adverse to the public interest which have resulted from, or may be expected to result from, the creation of a European relevant merger situation.

(2) In subsection (1) 'European relevant merger situation' means a relevant merger situation –

(a)   which has been created or will be created if arrangements which are in progress or in contemplation are carried into effect;

(b)   by virtue of which a concentration with a Community dimension (within the meaning of the European Merger Regulations), or a part of such a concentration, has arisen or will arise; and

(c)   in relation to which a reference which would otherwise have been possible under section 22 or 33 was prevented from being made under that section by virtue of Community law or anything done under or in accordance with it.

(3) Provision made under subsection (1) shall include provision ensuring that considerations which are not public interest considerations mentioned in the European intervention notice concerned may not be taken into account in determining whether anything operates, or may be expected to operate, against the public interest.

(4) Provision made under subsection (1) shall include provision –

(a)   applying with modifications sections 23 to 32 for the purposes of deciding for the purposes of this section whether a relevant merger situation has been created or whether arrangements are in progress or in contemplation which, if carried into effect, will result in the creation of a relevant merger situation;

(b)   requiring the OFT to make a report to the Secretary of State before a reference is made;

(c)   enabling the Secretary of State to make a reference to the Commission;

(d)   requiring the Commission to investigate and report to the Secretary of State on such a reference;

(e)   enabling the taking of interim and final enforcement action.

(5) An order under this section may include provision (including provision for the creation of offences and penalties, the payment of fees and the delegation of functions) corresponding to any provision made in, or in connection with, this Part in relation to intervention notices or special intervention notices and the cases to which they relate.

(6) In this section 'European intervention notice' has the same meaning as in section 67.

Other

69 Newspaper mergers

(1) No reference shall, subject to subsection (2), be made under section 22, 33, 45 or 62 in relation to a transfer of a newspaper or of newspaper assets to which section 58(1) of the Fair Trading Act 1973 applies.

(2) Subsection (1) does not apply in a case falling within section 59(2) of the Act of 1973.

(3) In this section 'transfer of a newspaper or of newspaper assets' has the meaning given by section 57(2) of the Act of 1973.

70 Water mergers

(1) For sections 32 to 35 of the Water Industry Act 1991 (special provision for water merger references) there shall be substituted –

'32 Duty to refer merger of water or sewerage undertaking

Subject to section 33 below, it shall be the duty of the OFT to make a merger reference to the Competition Commission if the OFT believes that it is or may be the case –

(a)   that arrangements are in progress which, if carried into effect, will result in a merger of any two or more water enterprises; or

(b)   that such a merger has taken place otherwise than as a result of the carrying into effect of arrangements that have been the subject of a reference by virtue of paragraph (a) above.

33 Exclusion of small mergers from duty to make reference

(1) The OFT shall not make a merger reference under section 32 above in respect of any actual or prospective merger of two or more water enterprises if it appears to the OFT –

(a)   that the value of the turnover of the water enterprise being taken over does not exceed or, as the case may be, would not exceed £10 million; or

(b)   that the only water enterprises already belonging to the person making the take over are enterprises each of which has a turnover the value of which does not exceed or, as the case may be, would not exceed £10 million.

(2) For the purposes of subsection (1)(a) above, the value of the turnover of the water enterprise being taken over shall be determined by taking the total value of the turnover of the water enterprises ceasing to be distinct enterprises and deducting –

    (a)   the turnover of any water enterprise continuing to be carried on under the same ownership and control; or

    (b)   if there is no water enterprise continuing to be carried on under the same ownership and control, the turnover which, of all the turnovers concerned, is the turnover of the highest value.

(3) For the purposes of subsection (1)(b) above –

    (a)   every water enterprise ceasing to be a distinct enterprise and whose turnover is to be deducted by virtue of subsection (2)(a) or (b) above shall be treated as a water enterprise belonging to the person making the take over; and

    (b)   water enterprises shall be treated as separate enterprises so far as they are carried on by different companies holding appointments under Chapter 1 of this Part.

(4) For the purposes of this section the turnover of a water enterprise shall be determined in accordance with such provisions as may be specified in regulations made by the Secretary of State.

(5) Regulations under subsection (4) above may, in particular, make provision as to –

    (a)   the amounts which are, or which are not, to be treated as comprising an enterprise's turnover; and

    (b)   the date or dates by reference to which an enterprise's turnover is to be determined.

(6) Regulations under subsection (4) above may, in particular, make provision enabling the Secretary of State or the OFT to determine matters of a description specified in the regulations (including any of the matters mentioned in paragraphs (a) and (b) of subsection (5) above).

(7) The Secretary of State may by regulations amend subsection (1) above so as –

    (a)   to alter the sum for the time being mentioned in paragraph (a) of that subsection or otherwise to modify the condition set out in that paragraph; or

    (b)   to alter the sum for the time being mentioned in paragraph (b) of that subsection or otherwise to modify the condition set out in that paragraph.

(8) Regulations under subsection (7) above –

    (a)   shall not make any modifications in relation to mergers on or before the coming into force of the regulations; and

    (b)   may, in particular, include supplemental, consequential or transitional provision amending or repealing any provision of this section.

(9) References in this section to enterprises being carried on under the same ownership and control shall be construed in accordance with Part 3 of the 2002 Act.

34 Application of provisions of Enterprise Act 2002

The provisions of Schedule 4ZA to this Act shall have effect with respect to mergers of water enterprises.

35 Construction of merger provisions

(1) In this Chapter (including Schedule 4ZA) –

'enterprise' has the same meaning as in Part 3 of the 2002 Act; and
'water enterprise' means an enterprise carried on by a water undertaker.

(2) References in this Chapter (including Schedule 4ZA), in relation to any two or more enterprises, to the merger of those enterprises are references to those enterprises ceasing, within the meaning of Part 3 of the 2002 Act, to be distinct enterprises; and sections 27 and 29 of that Act and any provision made under section 34 of that Act (time at which enterprises cease to be distinct) shall have effect for the purposes of this Chapter (including Schedule 4ZA) as they have effect for the purposes of that Part.

(3) Nothing in sections 32 to 34 above (including Schedule 4ZA) shall prejudice any power of the OFT or the Secretary of State, in a case in which, or to any extent to which, the OFT is not required to make a reference under section 32 above, to make a reference under Part 3 of the 2002 Act in respect of any actual or prospective merger of two or more water enterprises.

(4) Where two or more enterprises have merged or will merge as part of transactions or arrangements which also involve an actual or prospective merger of two or more water enterprises, Part 3 of the 2002 Act shall apply in relation to the actual or prospective merger of the enterprises concerned excluding the water enterprises; and references in that Part to the creation of a relevant merger situation shall be construed accordingly.

(5) Subject to subsections (3) and (4), Part 3 of the 2002 Act shall not apply in a case in which the OFT is required to make a reference under section 32 above except as applied by virtue of Schedule 4ZA.'

(2) Before Schedule 4A to the Act of 1991 there shall be inserted, as Schedule 4ZA, the Schedule set out in Schedule 6 to this Act.

CHAPTER 4
ENFORCEMENT

Powers exercisable before references under section 22 or 33

71 Initial undertakings: completed mergers

(1) Subsection (2) applies where the OFT is considering whether to make a reference under section 22.

(2) The OFT may, for the purpose of preventing pre-emptive action, accept from such of the parties concerned as it considers appropriate undertakings to take such action as it considers appropriate.

(3) No undertaking shall be accepted under subsection (2) unless the OFT has reasonable grounds for suspecting that it is or may be the case that a relevant merger situation has been created.

(4) An undertaking under this section –

    (a)   shall come into force when accepted;

    (b)   may be varied or superseded by another undertaking; and

    (c)   may be released by the OFT.

(5) An undertaking which –

    (a)   is in force under this section in relation to a possible reference or reference under section 22; and

    (b)   has not been adopted under section 80 or paragraph 1 of Schedule 7;

shall cease to be in force if an order under section 72 or 81 comes into force in relation to that reference or an order under paragraph 2 of that Schedule comes into force in relation to the matter.

(6) An undertaking under this section shall, if it has not previously ceased to be in force and if it has not been adopted under section 80 or paragraph 1 of Schedule 7, cease to be in force –

    (a)   where the OFT has decided to make the reference concerned under section 22, at the end of the period of 7 days beginning with the making of the reference;

    (b)   where the OFT has decided to accept an undertaking under section 73 instead of making that reference, on the acceptance of that undertaking;

    (c)   where an intervention notice is in force, at the end of the period of 7 days beginning with the giving of that notice; and

    (d)   where the OFT has otherwise decided not to make the reference concerned under section 22, on the making of that decision.

(7) The OFT shall, as soon as reasonably practicable, consider any representations received by it in relation to varying or releasing an undertaking under this section.

(8) In this section and section 72 'pre-emptive action' means action which might prejudice the reference concerned or impede the taking of any action under this Part which may be justified by the Commission's decisions on the reference.

72 Initial enforcement orders: completed mergers

(1) Subsection (2) applies where the OFT is considering whether to make a reference under section 22.

(2) The OFT may by order, for the purpose of preventing pre-emptive action –

    (a)   prohibit or restrict the doing of things which the OFT considers would constitute pre-emptive action;

    (b)   impose on any person concerned obligations as to the carrying on of any activities or the safeguarding of any assets;

(c) provide for the carrying on of any activities or the safeguarding of any assets either by the appointment of a person to conduct or supervise the conduct of any activities (on such terms and with such powers as may be specified or described in the order) or in any other manner;

(d) do anything which may be done by virtue of paragraph 19 of Schedule 8.

(3) No order shall be made under subsection (2) unless the OFT has reasonable grounds for suspecting that it is or may be the case that –

(a) a relevant merger situation has been created; and

(b) pre-emptive action is in progress or in contemplation.

(4) An order under this section –

(a) shall come into force at such time as is determined by or under the order; and

(b) may be varied or revoked by another order.

(5) An order which –

(a) is in force under this section in relation to a possible reference or a reference under section 22; and

(b) has not been adopted under section 81 or paragraph 2 of Schedule 7;

shall cease to be in force if an undertaking under section 71 or 80 comes into force in relation to that reference or an undertaking under paragraph 1 of that Schedule comes into force in relation to the matter.

(6) An order under this section shall, if it has not previously ceased to be in force and if it is not adopted under section 81 or paragraph 2 of Schedule 7, cease to be in force –

(a) where the OFT has decided to make the reference concerned under section 22, at the end of the period of 7 days beginning with the making of the reference;

(b) where the OFT has decided to accept an undertaking under section 73 instead of making that reference, on the acceptance of that undertaking;

(c) where an intervention notice is in force, at the end of the period of 7 days beginning with the giving of that notice; and

(d) where the OFT has otherwise decided not to make the reference concerned under section 22, on the making of that decision.

(7) The OFT shall, as soon as reasonably practicable, consider any representations received by it in relation to varying or revoking an order under this section.

73 Undertakings in lieu of references under section 22 or 33

(1) Subsection (2) applies if the OFT considers that it is under a duty to make a reference under section 22 or 33 (disregarding the operation of section 22(3)(b) or (as the case may be) 33(3)(b) but taking account of the power of the OFT under section 22(2) or (as the case may be) 33(2) to decide not to make such a reference).

(2) The OFT may, instead of making such a reference and for the purpose of remedying, mitigating or preventing the substantial lessening of competition

concerned or any adverse effect which has or may have resulted from it or may be expected to result from it, accept from such of the parties concerned as it considers appropriate undertakings to take such action as it considers appropriate.

(3) In proceeding under subsection (2), the OFT shall, in particular, have regard to the need to achieve as comprehensive a solution as is reasonable and practicable to the substantial lessening of competition and any adverse effects resulting from it.

(4) In proceeding under subsection (2), the OFT may, in particular, have regard to the effect of any action on any relevant customer benefits in relation to the creation of the relevant merger situation concerned.

(5) An undertaking under this section –

(a)   shall come into force when accepted;

(b)   may be varied or superseded by another undertaking; and

(c)   may be released by the OFT.

(6) An undertaking under this section which is in force in relation to a relevant merger situation shall cease to be in force if an order comes into force under section 75 or 76 in relation to that undertaking.

(7) The OFT shall, as soon as reasonably practicable, consider any representations received by it in relation to varying or releasing an undertaking under this section.

74 Effect of undertakings under section 73

(1) The relevant authority shall not make a reference under section 22, 33 or 45 in relation to the creation of a relevant merger situation if –

(a)   the OFT has accepted an undertaking or group of undertakings under section 73; and

(b)   the relevant merger situation is the situation by reference to which the undertaking or group of undertakings was accepted.

(2) Subsection (1) does not prevent the making of a reference if material facts about relevant arrangements or transactions, or relevant proposed arrangements or transactions, were not notified (whether in writing or otherwise) to the OFT or made public before any undertaking concerned was accepted.

(3) For the purposes of subsection (2) arrangements or transactions, or proposed arrangements or transactions, are relevant if they are the ones in consequence of which the enterprises concerned ceased or may have ceased, or may cease, to be distinct enterprises.

(4) In subsection (2) 'made public' means so publicised as to be generally known or readily ascertainable.

(5) In this section 'relevant authority' means –

(a)   in relation to a possible reference under section 22 or 33, the OFT; and

(b)   in relation to a possible reference under section 45, the Secretary of State.

75 Order-making power where undertakings under section 73 not fulfilled etc

(1) Subsection (2) applies where the OFT considers that –

    (a)   an undertaking accepted by it under section 73 has not been, is not being or will not be fulfilled; or

    (b)   in relation to an undertaking accepted by it under that section, information which was false or misleading in a material respect was given to the OFT by the person giving the undertaking before the OFT decided to accept the undertaking.

(2) The OFT may, for any of the purposes mentioned in section 73(2), make an order under this section.

(3) Subsections (3) and (4) of section 73 shall apply for the purposes of subsection (2) above as they apply for the purposes of subsection (2) of that section.

(4) An order under this section may contain –

    (a)   anything permitted by Schedule 8; and

    (b)   such supplementary, consequential or incidental provision as the OFT considers appropriate.

(5) An order under this section –

    (a)   shall come into force at such time as is determined by or under the order;

    (b)   may contain provision which is different from the provision contained in the undertaking concerned; and

    (c)   may be varied or revoked by another order.

(6) The OFT shall, as soon as reasonably practicable, consider any representations received by it in relation to varying or revoking an order under this section.

76 Supplementary interim order-making power

(1) Subsection (2) applies where –

    (a)   the OFT has the power to make an order under section 75 in relation to a particular undertaking and intends to make such an order; or

    (b)   the Commission has the power to make an order under section 83 in relation to a particular undertaking and intends to make such an order.

(2) The OFT or (as the case may be) the Commission may, for the purpose of preventing any action which might prejudice the making of that order, make an order under this section.

(3) No order shall be made under subsection (2) unless the OFT or (as the case may be) the Commission has reasonable grounds for suspecting that it is or may be the case that action which might prejudice the making of the order under section 75 or (as the case may be) 83 is in progress or in contemplation.

(4) An order under subsection (2) may –

(a)   prohibit or restrict the doing of things which the OFT or (as the case may be) the Commission considers would prejudice the making of the order under section 75 or (as the case may be) 83;

(b)   impose on any person concerned obligations as to the carrying on of any activities or the safeguarding of any assets;

(c)   provide for the carrying on of any activities or the safeguarding of any assets either by the appointment of a person to conduct or supervise the conduct of any activities (on such terms and with such powers as may be specified or described in the order) or in any other manner;

(d)   do anything which may be done by virtue of paragraph 19 of Schedule 8.

(5) An order under this section –

(a)   shall come into force at such time as is determined by or under the order; and

(b)   may be varied or revoked by another order.

(6) An order under this section shall, if it has not previously ceased to be in force, cease to be in force on –

(a)   the coming into force of an order under section 75 or (as the case may be) 83 in relation to the undertaking concerned; or

(b)   the making of the decision not to proceed with such an order.

(7) The OFT or (as the case may be) the Commission shall, as soon as reasonably practicable, consider any representations received by it in relation to varying or revoking an order under this section.

Interim restrictions and powers

77 Restrictions on certain dealings: completed mergers

(1) Subsections (2) and (3) apply where –

(a)   a reference has been made under section 22 but not finally determined; and

(b)   no undertakings under section 71 or 80 are in force in relation to the relevant merger situation concerned and no orders under section 72 or 81 are in force in relation to that situation.

(2) No relevant person shall, without the consent of the Commission –

(a)   complete any outstanding matters in connection with any arrangements which have resulted in the enterprises concerned ceasing to be distinct enterprises;

(b)   make any further arrangements in consequence of that result (other than arrangements which reverse that result); or

(c)   transfer the ownership or control of any enterprises to which the reference relates.

(3) No relevant person shall, without the consent of the Commission, assist in any of the activities mentioned in paragraphs (a) to (c) of subsection (2).

(4) The prohibitions in subsections (2) and (3) do not apply in relation to anything which the person concerned is required to do by virtue of any enactment.

(5) The consent of the Commission under subsection (2) or (3) –

(a)   may be general or special;

(b)   may be revoked by the Commission; and

(c)   shall be published in such manner as the Commission considers appropriate for the purpose of bringing it to the attention of any person entitled to the benefit of it.

(6) Paragraph (c) of subsection (5) shall not apply if the Commission considers that publication is not necessary for the purpose mentioned in that paragraph.

(7) Subsections (2) and (3) shall apply to a person's conduct outside the United Kingdom if (and only if) he is –

(a)   a United Kingdom national;

(b)   a body incorporated under the law of the United Kingdom or of any part of the United Kingdom; or

(c)   a person carrying on business in the United Kingdom.

(8) In this section 'relevant person' means –

(a)   any person who carries on any enterprise to which the reference relates or who has control of any such enterprise;

(b)   any subsidiary of any person falling within paragraph (a); or

(c)   any person associated with any person falling within paragraph (a) or any subsidiary of any person so associated.

78 Restrictions on certain share dealings: anticipated mergers

(1) Subsection (2) applies where –

(a)   a reference has been made under section 33; and

(b)   no undertakings under section 80 are in force in relation to the relevant merger situation concerned and no orders under section 81 are in force in relation to that situation.

(2) No relevant person shall, without the consent of the Commission, directly or indirectly acquire during the relevant period an interest in shares in a company if any enterprise to which the reference relates is carried on by or under the control of that company.

(3) The consent of the Commission under subsection (2) –

(a)   may be general or special;

(b)   may be revoked by the Commission; and

(c)   shall be published in such manner as the Commission considers appropriate for bringing it to the attention of any person entitled to the benefit of it.

(4) Paragraph (c) of subsection (3) shall not apply if the Commission considers that publication is not necessary for the purpose mentioned in that paragraph.

(5) Subsection (2) shall apply to a person's conduct outside the United Kingdom if (and only if) he is –

(a)   a United Kingdom national;

(b)   a body incorporated under the law of the United Kingdom or of any part of the United Kingdom; or

(c)   a person carrying on business in the United Kingdom.

(6) In this section and section 79 –

'company' includes any body corporate;

'relevant period' means the period beginning with the making of the reference concerned and ending when the reference is finally determined;

'relevant person' means –

(a)   any person who carries on any enterprise to which the reference relates or who has control of any such enterprise;

(b)   any subsidiary of any person falling within paragraph (a); or

(c)   any person associated with any person falling within paragraph (a) or any subsidiary of any person so associated; and

'share' means share in the capital of a company, and includes stock.

79 Sections 77 and 78: further interpretation provisions

(1) For the purposes of this Part a reference under section 22 or 33 is finally determined if –

(a)   the reference is cancelled under section 37(1);

(b)   the time within which the Commission is to prepare and publish a report under section 38 in relation to the reference has expired and no such report has been prepared and published;

(c)   the report of the Commission under section 38 contains the decision that there is not an anti-competitive outcome;

(d)   the report of the Commission under section 38 contains the decision that there is an anti-competitive outcome and the Commission has decided under section 41(2) neither to accept an undertaking under section 82 nor to make an order under section 84; or

(e)   the report of the Commission under section 38 contains the decision that there is an anti-competitive outcome and the Commission has decided under section 41(2) to accept an undertaking under section 82 or to make an order under section 84.

(2) For the purposes of this Part the time when a reference under section 22 or 33 is finally determined is –

(a)   in a case falling within subsection (1)(a), the making of the decision concerned;

(b)   in a case falling within subsection (1)(b), the expiry of the time concerned;

(c)   in a case falling within subsection (1)(c), the publication of the report;

(d)   in a case falling within subsection (1)(d), the making of the decision under section 41(2); and

(e)   in a case falling within subsection (1)(e), the acceptance of the undertaking concerned or (as the case may be) the making of the order concerned.

(3) For the purposes of section 78 and subject to subsection (4) below, the circumstances in which a person acquires an interest in shares include those where –

(a) he enters into a contract to acquire the shares (whether or not for cash);

(b) he is not the registered holder but acquires the right to exercise, or to control the exercise of, any right conferred by the holding of the shares; or

(c) he –

    (i) acquires a right to call for delivery of the shares to himself or to his order or to acquire an interest in the shares; or

    (ii) assumes an obligation to acquire such an interest.

(4) The circumstances in which a person acquires an interest in shares for the purposes of section 78 do not include those where he acquires an interest in pursuance of an obligation assumed before the publication by the OFT of the reference concerned.

(5) The circumstances in which a person acquires a right mentioned in subsection (3) –

(a) include those where he acquires a right, or assumes an obligation, whose exercise or fulfilment would give him that right; but

(b) do not include those where he is appointed as proxy to vote at a specified meeting of a company or of any class of its members or at any adjournment of the meeting or he is appointed by a corporation to act as its representative at any meeting of the company or of any class of its members.

(6) References to rights and obligations in subsections (3) to (5) include conditional rights and conditional obligations.

(7) References in sections 77 and 78 to a person carrying on or having control of any enterprise includes a group of persons carrying on or having control of an enterprise and any member of such a group.

(8) Sections 26(2) to (4) and 127(1), (2) and (4) to (6) shall apply for the purposes of sections 77 and 78 to determine whether any person or group of persons has control of any enterprise and whether persons are associated as they apply for the purposes of section 26 to determine whether enterprises are brought under common control.

(9) Sections 736 and 736A of the Companies Act 1985 shall apply for the purposes of sections 77 and 78 to determine whether a company is a subsidiary of an individual or of a group of persons as they apply to determine whether it is a subsidiary of a company; and references to a subsidiary in subsections (8) and (9) of section 736A as so applied shall be construed accordingly.

80 Interim undertakings

(1) Subsections (2) and (3) apply where a reference under section 22 or 33 has been made but is not finally determined.

(2) The Commission may, for the purpose of preventing pre-emptive action, accept from such of the parties concerned as it considers appropriate undertakings to take such action as it considers appropriate.

(3) The Commission may, for the purpose of preventing pre-emptive action, adopt an undertaking accepted by the OFT under section 71 if the undertaking is still in force when the Commission adopts it.

(4) An undertaking adopted under subsection (3) –

    (a)   shall continue in force, in accordance with its terms, when adopted;

    (b)   may be varied or superseded by an undertaking under this section; and

    (c)   may be released by the Commission.

(5) Any other undertaking under this section –

    (a)   shall come into force when accepted;

    (b)   may be varied or superseded by another undertaking; and

    (c)   may be released by the Commission.

(6) References in this Part to undertakings under this section shall, unless the context otherwise requires, include references to undertakings adopted under this section; and references to the acceptance or giving of undertakings under this section shall be construed accordingly.

(7) An undertaking which is in force under this section in relation to a reference under section 22 or 33 shall cease to be in force if an order under section 81 comes into force in relation to that reference.

(8) An undertaking under this section shall, if it has not previously ceased to be in force, cease to be in force when the reference under section 22 or 33 is finally determined.

(9) The Commission shall, as soon as reasonably practicable, consider any representations received by it in relation to varying or releasing an undertaking under this section.

(10) In this section and section 81 'pre-emptive action' means action which might prejudice the reference concerned or impede the taking of any action under this Part which may be justified by the Commission's decisions on the reference.

81 Interim orders

(1) Subsections (2) and (3) apply where a reference has been made under section 22 or 33 but is not finally determined.

(2) The Commission may by order, for the purpose of preventing pre-emptive action –

    (a)   prohibit or restrict the doing of things which the Commission considers would constitute pre-emptive action;

    (b)   impose on any person concerned obligations as to the carrying on of any activities or the safeguarding of any assets;

    (c)   provide for the carrying on of any activities or the safeguarding of any assets either by the appointment of a person to conduct or supervise the conduct of any activities (on such terms and with such powers as may be specified or described in the order) or in any other manner;

(d)   do anything which may be done by virtue of paragraph 19 of Schedule 8.

(3) The Commission may, for the purpose of preventing pre-emptive action, adopt an order made by the OFT under section 72 if the order is still in force when the Commission adopts it.

(4) An order adopted under subsection (3) –

(a)   shall continue in force, in accordance with its terms, when adopted; and

(b)   may be varied or revoked by an order under this section.

(5) Any other order under this section –

(a)   shall come into force at such time as is determined by or under the order; and

(b)   may be varied or revoked by another order.

(6) References in this Part to orders under this section shall, unless the context otherwise requires, include references to orders adopted under this section; and references to the making of orders under this section shall be construed accordingly.

(7) An order which is in force under this section in relation to a reference under section 22 or 33 shall cease to be in force if an undertaking under section 80 comes into force in relation to that reference.

(8) An order under this section shall, if it has not previously ceased to be in force, cease to be in force when the reference under section 22 or 33 is finally determined.

(9) The Commission shall, as soon as reasonably practicable, consider any representations received by it in relation to varying or revoking an order under this section.

Final powers

82 Final undertakings

(1) The Commission may, in accordance with section 41, accept, from such persons as it considers appropriate, undertakings to take action specified or described in the undertakings.

(2) An undertaking under this section –

(a)   shall come into force when accepted;

(b)   may be varied or superseded by another undertaking; and

(c)   may be released by the Commission.

(3) An undertaking which is in force under this section in relation to a reference under section 22 or 33 shall cease to be in force if an order under section 76(1)(b) or 83 comes into force in relation to the subject-matter of the undertaking.

(4) No undertaking shall be accepted under this section in relation to a reference under section 22 or 33 if an order has been made under –

(a)   section 76(1)(b) or 83 in relation to the subject-matter of the undertaking; or

(b)   section 84 in relation to that reference.

(5) The Commission shall, as soon as reasonably practicable, consider any representations received by it in relation to varying or releasing an undertaking under this section.

83 Order-making power where final undertakings not fulfilled

(1) Subsection (2) applies where the Commission considers that –

(a)   an undertaking accepted by it under section 82 has not been, is not being or will not be fulfilled; or

(b)   in relation to an undertaking accepted by it under that section, information which was false or misleading in a material respect was given to the Commission or the OFT by the person giving the undertaking before the Commission decided to accept the undertaking.

(2) The Commission may, for any of the purposes mentioned in section 41(2), make an order under this section.

(3) Subsections (3) to (5) of section 41 shall apply for the purposes of subsection (2) above as they apply for the purposes of subsection (2) of that section.

(4) An order under this section may contain –

(a)   anything permitted by Schedule 8; and

(b)   such supplementary, consequential or incidental provision as the Commission considers appropriate.

(5) An order under this section –

(a)   shall come into force at such time as is determined by or under the order;

(b)   may contain provision which is different from the provision contained in the undertaking concerned; and

(c)   may be varied or revoked by another order.

(6) No order shall be varied or revoked under this section unless the OFT advises that such a variation or revocation is appropriate by reason of a change of circumstances.

84 Final orders

(1) The Commission may, in accordance with section 41, make an order under this section.

(2) An order under this section may contain –

(a)   anything permitted by Schedule 8; and

(b)   such supplementary, consequential or incidental provision as the Commission considers appropriate.

(3) An order under this section –

(a) shall come into force at such time as is determined by or under the order; and

(b) may be varied or revoked by another order.

(4) No order shall be varied or revoked under this section unless the OFT advises that such a variation or revocation is appropriate by reason of a change of circumstances.

(5) No order shall be made under this section in relation to a reference under section 22 or 33 if an undertaking has been accepted under section 82 in relation to that reference.

Public interest and special public interest cases

85 Enforcement regime for public interest and special public interest cases

(1) Schedule 7 (which provides for the enforcement regime in public interest and special public interest cases) shall have effect.

(2) The OFT may advise the Secretary of State in relation to the taking by him of enforcement action under Schedule 7.

Undertakings and orders: general provisions

86 Enforcement orders: general provisions

(1) An enforcement order may extend to a person's conduct outside the United Kingdom if (and only if) he is –

(a) a United Kingdom national;

(b) a body incorporated under the law of the United Kingdom or of any part of the United Kingdom; or

(c) a person carrying on business in the United Kingdom.

(2) Nothing in an enforcement order shall have effect so as to –

(a) cancel or modify conditions in licences granted –

(i) under a patent granted under the Patents Act 1977 or a European patent (UK) (within the meaning of the Act of 1977); or

(ii) in respect of a design registered under the Registered Designs Act 1949;

by the proprietor of the patent or design; or

(b) require an entry to be made in the register of patents or the register of designs to the effect that licences under such a patent or such a design are to be available as of right.

(3) An enforcement order may prohibit the performance of an agreement already in existence when the order is made.

(4) Schedule 8 (which provides for the contents of certain enforcement orders) shall have effect.

(5) Part 1 of Schedule 9 (which enables certain enforcement orders to modify licence conditions etc in regulated markets) shall have effect.

(6) In this Part 'enforcement order' means an order made under section 72, 75, 76, 81, 83 or 84 or under paragraph 2, 5, 6, 10 or 11 of Schedule 7.

87 Delegated power of directions

(1) An enforcement order may authorise the person making the order to give directions falling within subsection (2) to –

(a)   a person specified in the directions; or

(b)   the holder for the time being of an office so specified in any body of persons corporate or unincorporate.

(2) Directions fall within this subsection if they are directions –

(a)   to take such action as may be specified or described in the directions for the purpose of carrying out, or ensuring compliance with, the enforcement order concerned; or

(b)   to do, or refrain from doing, anything so specified or described which the person might be required by that order to do or refrain from doing.

(3) An enforcement order may authorise the person making the order to vary or revoke any directions so given.

(4) The court may by order require any person who has failed to comply with directions given by virtue of this section to comply with them, or otherwise remedy his failure, within such time as may be specified in the order.

(5) Where the directions related to anything done in the management or administration of a body of persons corporate or unincorporate, the court may by order require the body of persons concerned or any officer of it to comply with the directions, or otherwise remedy the failure to comply with them, within such time as may be specified in the order.

(6) An order under subsection (4) or (5) shall be made on the application of the person authorised by virtue of this section to give the directions concerned.

(7) An order under subsection (4) or (5) may provide for all the costs or expenses of, or incidental to, the application for the order to be met by any person in default or by any officers of a body of persons corporate or unincorporate who are responsible for its default.

(8) In this section 'the court' means –

(a)   in relation to England and Wales or Northern Ireland, the High Court; and

(b)   in relation to Scotland, the Court of Session.

88 Contents of certain enforcement orders

(1) This section applies in relation to any order under section 75, 83 or 84 or under paragraph 5, 10 or 11 of Schedule 7.

(2) The order or any explanatory material accompanying the order shall state –

(a)   the actions that the persons or description of persons to whom the order is addressed must do or (as the case may be) refrain from doing;

(b)   the date on which the order comes into force;

(c)   the possible consequences of not complying with the order; and

(d)   the section of this Part under which a review can be sought in relation to the order.

89 Subject-matter of undertakings

(1) The provision which may be contained in an enforcement undertaking is not limited to the provision which is permitted by Schedule 8.

(2) In this Part 'enforcement undertaking' means an undertaking under section 71, 73, 80 or 82 or under paragraph 1, 3 or 9 of Schedule 7.

90 Procedural requirements for certain undertakings and orders

Schedule 10 (which provides for the procedure for accepting certain enforcement undertakings and making certain enforcement orders and for their termination) shall have effect.

91 Register of undertakings and orders

(1) The OFT shall compile and maintain a register for the purposes of this Part.

(2) The register shall be kept in such form as the OFT considers appropriate.

(3) The OFT shall ensure that the following matters are entered in the register –

(a)   the provisions of any enforcement undertaking accepted under this Part;

(b)   the provisions of any enforcement order made under this Part;

(c)   the details of any variation, release or revocation of such an undertaking or order; and

(d)   the details of any consent given by the Commission under section 77(2) or (3) or 78(2) or by the Secretary of State under paragraph 7(2) or (3) or 8(2) of Schedule 7.

(4) The duty in subsection (3) does not extend to anything of which the OFT is unaware.

(5) The Commission and the Secretary of State shall inform the OFT of any matters which are to be included in the register by virtue of subsection (3) and which relate to enforcement undertakings accepted by them, enforcement orders made by them or consents given by them.

(6) The OFT shall ensure that the contents of the register are available to the public –

(a)   during (as a minimum) such hours as may be specified in an order made by the Secretary of State; and

(b)   subject to such reasonable fees (if any) as the OFT may determine.

(7) If requested by any person to do so and subject to such reasonable fees (if any) as the OFT may determine, the OFT shall supply the person concerned with a copy (certified to be true) of the register or of an extract from it.

Enforcement functions of OFT

92 Duty of OFT to monitor undertakings and orders

(1) The OFT shall keep under review –

    (a)   the carrying out of any enforcement undertaking or any enforcement order; and

    (b)   compliance with the prohibitions in sections 77(2) and (3) and 78(2) and in paragraphs 7(2) and (3) and 8(2) of Schedule 7.

(2) The OFT shall, in particular, from time to time consider –

    (a)   whether an enforcement undertaking or enforcement order has been or is being complied with;

    (b)   whether, by reason of any change of circumstances, an enforcement undertaking is no longer appropriate and –

        (i)   one or more of the parties to it can be released from it; or

        (ii)   it needs to be varied or to be superseded by a new enforcement undertaking; and

    (c)   whether, by reason of any change of circumstances, an enforcement order is no longer appropriate and needs to be varied or revoked.

(3) The OFT shall give the Commission or (as the case may be) the Secretary of State such advice as it considers appropriate in relation to –

    (a)   any possible variation or release by the Commission or (as the case may be) the Secretary of State of an enforcement undertaking accepted by it or (as the case may be) him;

    (b)   any possible new enforcement undertaking to be accepted by the Commission or (as the case may be) the Secretary of State so as to supersede another enforcement undertaking given to the Commission or (as the case may be) the Secretary of State;

    (c)   any possible variation or revocation by the Commission or (as the case may be) the Secretary of State of an enforcement order made by the Commission or (as the case may be) the Secretary of State;

    (d)   any possible enforcement undertaking to be accepted by the Commission or (as the case may be) the Secretary of State instead of an enforcement order or any possible enforcement order to be made by the Commission or (as the case may be) the Secretary of State instead of an enforcement undertaking;

    (e)   the enforcement by virtue of section 94(6) to (8) of any enforcement undertaking or enforcement order; or

    (f)   the enforcement by virtue of section 95(4) and (5) of the prohibitions in sections 77(2) and (3) and 78(2) and in paragraphs 7(2) and (3) and 8(2) of Schedule 7.

(4) The OFT shall take such action as it considers appropriate in relation to –

(a) any possible variation or release by it of an enforcement undertaking accepted by it;

(b) any possible new enforcement undertaking to be accepted by it so as to supersede another enforcement undertaking given to it;

(c) any possible variation or revocation by it of an enforcement order made by it;

(d) any possible enforcement undertaking to be accepted by it instead of an enforcement order or any possible enforcement order to be made by it instead of an enforcement undertaking;

(e) the enforcement by it by virtue of section 94(6) of any enforcement undertaking or enforcement order; or

(f) the enforcement by it by virtue of section 95(4) and (5) of the prohibitions in sections 77(2) and (3) and 78(2) and in paragraphs 7(2) and (3) and 8(2) of Schedule 7.

(5) The OFT shall keep under review the effectiveness of enforcement undertakings accepted under this Part and enforcement orders made under this Part.

(6) The OFT shall, whenever requested to do so by the Secretary of State and otherwise from time to time, prepare a report of its findings under subsection (5).

(7) The OFT shall –

(a) give any report prepared by it under subsection (6) to the Commission;

(b) give a copy of the report to the Secretary of State; and

(c) publish the report.

93 Further role of OFT in relation to undertakings and orders

(1) Subsections (2) and (3) apply where –

(a) the Commission is considering whether to accept undertakings under section 80 or 82; or

(b) the Secretary of State is considering whether to accept undertakings under paragraph 1, 3 or 9 of Schedule 7.

(2) The Commission or (as the case may be) the Secretary of State (in this section 'the relevant authority') may require the OFT to consult with such persons as the relevant authority considers appropriate with a view to discovering whether they will offer undertakings which the relevant authority would be prepared to accept under section 80 or 82 or (as the case may be) paragraph 1, 3 or 9 of Schedule 7.

(3) The relevant authority may require the OFT to report to the relevant authority on the outcome of the OFT's consultations within such period as the relevant authority may require.

(4) A report under subsection (3) shall, in particular, contain advice from the OFT as to whether any undertakings offered should be accepted by the relevant authority under section 80 or 82 or (as the case may be) paragraph 1, 3 or 9 of Schedule 7.

(5) The powers conferred on the relevant authority by subsections (1) to (4) are without prejudice to the power of the relevant authority to consult the persons concerned itself.

(6) If asked by the relevant authority for advice in relation to the taking of enforcement action (whether or not by way of undertaking) in a particular case, the OFT shall give such advice as it considers appropriate.

Other

94 Rights to enforce undertakings and orders

(1) This section applies to any enforcement undertaking or enforcement order.

(2) Any person to whom such an undertaking or order relates shall have a duty to comply with it.

(3) The duty shall be owed to any person who may be affected by a contravention of the undertaking or (as the case may be) order.

(4) Any breach of the duty which causes such a person to sustain loss or damage shall be actionable by him.

(5) In any proceedings brought under subsection (4) against a person to whom an enforcement undertaking or an enforcement order relates it shall be a defence for that person to show that he took all reasonable steps and exercised all due diligence to avoid contravening the undertaking or (as the case may be) order.

(6) Compliance with an enforcement undertaking or an enforcement order shall also be enforceable by civil proceedings brought by the OFT for an injunction or for interdict or for any other appropriate relief or remedy.

(7) Compliance with an undertaking under section 80 or 82, an order made by the Commission under section 76 or an order under section 81, 83 or 84, shall also be enforceable by civil proceedings brought by the Commission for an injunction or for interdict or for any other appropriate relief or remedy.

(8) Compliance with an undertaking under paragraph 1, 3 or 9 of Schedule 7, an order made by the Secretary of State under paragraph 2 of that Schedule or an order under paragraph 5, 6, 10 or 11 of that Schedule, shall also be enforceable by civil proceedings brought by the Secretary of State for an injunction or for interdict or for any other appropriate relief or remedy.

(9) Subsections (6) to (8) shall not prejudice any right that a person may have by virtue of subsection (4) to bring civil proceedings for contravention or apprehended contravention of an enforcement undertaking or an enforcement order.

95 Rights to enforce statutory restrictions

(1) The obligation to comply with section 77(2) or (3) or 78(2) or paragraph 7(2) or (3) or 8(2) of Schedule 7 shall be a duty owed to any person who may be affected by a contravention of the enactment concerned.

(2) Any breach of the duty which causes such a person to sustain loss or damage shall be actionable by him.

(3) In any proceedings brought under subsection (2) against a person who has an obligation to comply with section 77(2) or (3) or 78(2) or paragraph 7(2) or (3) or 8(2)

of Schedule 7 it shall be a defence for that person to show that he took all reasonable steps and exercised all due diligence to avoid contravening the enactment concerned.

(4) Compliance with section 77(2) or (3) or 78(2) shall also be enforceable by civil proceedings brought by the OFT or the Commission for an injunction or for interdict or for any other appropriate relief or remedy.

(5) Compliance with paragraph 7(2) or (3) or 8(2) of Schedule 7 shall also be enforceable by civil proceedings brought by the OFT or the Secretary of State for an injunction or for interdict or for any other appropriate relief or remedy.

(6) Subsections (4) and (5) shall not prejudice any right that a person may have by virtue of subsection (2) to bring civil proceedings for contravention or apprehended contravention of section 77(2) or (3) or 78(2) or paragraph 7(2) or (3) or 8(2) of Schedule 7.

CHAPTER 5
SUPPLEMENTARY

Merger notices

96 Merger notices

(1) A person authorised to do so by regulations under section 101 may give notice to the OFT of proposed arrangements which might result in the creation of a relevant merger situation.

(2) Any such notice (in this Part a 'merger notice') –

    (a)   shall be in the prescribed form; and

    (b)   shall state that the existence of the proposal has been made public.

(3) No reference shall be made under section 22, 33 or 45 in relation to –

    (a)   arrangements of which notice is given under subsection (1) above or arrangements which do not differ from them in any material respect; or

    (b)   the creation of any relevant merger situation which is, or may be, created in consequence of carrying such arrangements into effect;

if the period for considering the merger notice has expired without a reference being made under that section in relation to those arrangements.

(4) Subsection (3) is subject to section 100.

(5) In this section and sections 99(5)(c) and 100(1)(c) 'prescribed' means prescribed by the OFT by notice having effect for the time being and published in the London, Edinburgh and Belfast Gazettes.

(6) In this Part 'notified arrangements' means arrangements of which notice is given under subsection (1) above or arrangements not differing from them in any material respect.

97 Period for considering merger notices

(1) The period for considering a merger notice is, subject as follows, the period of 20 days beginning with the first day after –

    (a)   the notice has been received by the OFT; and

    (b)   any fee payable by virtue of section 121 to the OFT in respect of the notice has been paid.

(2) Where no intervention notice is in force in relation to the matter concerned, the OFT may by notice to the person who gave the merger notice extend by a further 10 days the period for considering the merger notice.

(3) Where an intervention notice is in force in relation to the matter concerned and there has been no extension under subsection (2), the OFT may by notice to the person who gave the merger notice extend by a further 20 days the period for considering the merger notice.

(4) Where an intervention notice is in force in relation to the matter concerned and there has been an extension under subsection (2), the OFT may by notice to the person who gave the merger notice extend the period for considering the merger notice by a further number of days which, including any extension already made under subsection (2), does not exceed 20 days.

(5) The OFT may by notice to the person who gave the merger notice extend the period for considering a merger notice if the OFT considers that the person has failed to provide, within the period stated in a notice under section 99(2) and in the authorised or required manner, information requested of him in that notice.

(6) An extension under subsection (5) shall be for the period until the person concerned provides the information to the satisfaction of the OFT or, if earlier, the cancellation by the OFT of the extension.

(7) The OFT may by notice to the person who gave the merger notice extend the period for considering a merger notice if the OFT is seeking undertakings under section 73 or (as the case may be) the Secretary of State is seeking undertakings under paragraph 3 of Schedule 7.

(8) An extension under subsection (7) shall be for the period beginning with the receipt of the notice under that subsection and ending with the earliest of the following events –

    (a)   the giving of the undertakings concerned;

    (b)   the expiry of the period of 10 days beginning with the first day after the receipt by the OFT of a notice from the person from whom the undertakings are being sought stating that he does not intend to give the undertakings; or

    (c)   the cancellation by the OFT of the extension.

(9) The Secretary of State may by notice to the person who gave the merger notice extend the period for considering a merger notice if, by virtue of paragraph 3(6) of Schedule 7, he decides to delay a decision as to whether to make a reference under section 45.

(10) An extension under subsection (9) shall be for the period of the delay.

(11) The OFT may by notice to the person who gave the merger notice extend the period for considering a merger notice if the European Commission is considering a request made, in relation to the matter concerned, by the United Kingdom (whether alone or with others) under article 22(3) of the European Merger Regulations (but is not yet proceeding with the matter in pursuance of such a request).

(12) An extension under subsection (11) shall be for the period beginning with the receipt of the notice under that subsection and ending with the receipt of a notice under subsection (13).

(13) The OFT shall, in connection with any notice given by it under subsection (11), by notice inform the person who gave the merger notice of the completion by the European Commission of its consideration of the request of the United Kingdom.

98 Section 97: supplementary

(1) A notice under section 97(2), (3), (4), (5), (7), (9) or (11) shall be given, before the end of the period for considering the merger notice, to the person who gave the merger notice.

(2) A notice under section 97(5) –

    (a)   shall also be given within 5 days of the end of the period within which the information is to be provided and which is stated in the notice under section 99(2); and

    (b)   shall also inform the person who gave the merger notice of –

        (i)   the OFT's opinion as mentioned in section 97(5); and

        (ii)   the OFT's intention to extend the period for considering a merger notice.

(3) In determining for the purposes of section 97(1), (2), (3), (4) or (8)(b) or subsection (2)(a) above any period which is expressed in the enactment concerned as a period of days or number of days no account shall be taken of –

    (a)   Saturday, Sunday, Good Friday and Christmas Day; and

    (b)   any day which is a bank holiday in England and Wales.

(4) Any reference in this Part (apart from in section 97(1) and section 99(1)) to the period for considering a merger notice shall, if that period is extended by virtue of any one or more of subsections (2), (3), (4), (5), (7), (9) and (11) of section 97 in relation to a particular case, be construed in relation to that case as a reference to that period as so extended; but only one extension is possible under section 97(2), (3) or (4).

(5) Where the period for considering a merger notice is extended or further extended by virtue of section 97, the period as extended or (as the case may be) further extended shall, subject to subsections (6) and (7), be calculated by taking the period being extended and adding to it the period of the extension (whether or not those periods overlap in time).

(6) Subsection (7) applies where –

    (a)   the period for considering a merger notice is further extended;

    (b)   the further extension and at least one previous extension is made under one or more of subsections (5), (7), (9) and (11) of section 97; and

(c)   the same days or fractions of days are included in or comprise the further extension and are included in or comprise at least one such previous extension.

(7) In calculating the period of the further extension, any days or fractions of days of the kind mentioned in subsection (6)(c) shall be disregarded.

99 Certain functions of OFT and Secretary of State in relation to merger notices

(1) The OFT shall, so far as practicable and when the period for considering any merger notice begins, take such action as the OFT considers appropriate to bring –

(a)   the existence of the proposal;
(b)   the fact that the merger notice has been given; and
(c)   the date on which the period for considering the notice may expire;

to the attention of those whom the OFT considers would be affected if the arrangements were carried into effect.

(2) The OFT may by notice to the person who gave the merger notice request him to provide the OFT with such information as the OFT or (as the case may be) the Secretary of State may require for the purpose of carrying out its or (as the case may be) his functions in relation to the merger notice.

(3) A notice under subsection (2) shall state –

(a)   the information required;
(b)   the period within which the information is to be provided; and
(c)   the possible consequences of not providing the information within the stated period and in the authorised or required manner.

(4) A notice by the OFT under subsection (2) shall be given, before the end of the period for considering the merger notice, to the person who gave the merger notice.

(5) The OFT may, at any time before the end of the period for considering any merger notice, reject the notice if –

(a)   the OFT suspects that any information given in respect of the notified arrangements (whether in the merger notice or otherwise) by the person who gave the notice or any connected person is in any material respect false or misleading;
(b)   the OFT suspects that it is not proposed to carry the notified arrangements into effect;
(c)   any prescribed information is not given in the merger notice or any information requested by notice under subsection (2) is not provided as required; or
(d)   the OFT considers that the notified arrangements are, or if carried into effect would result in, a concentration with a Community dimension within the meaning of the European Merger Regulations.

(6) In this section and section 100 'connected person', in relation to the person who gave a merger notice, means –

(a)   any person who, for the purposes of section 127, is associated with him; or

(b)   any subsidiary of the person who gave the merger notice or of any person so associated with him.

100 Exceptions to protection given by merger notices

(1) Section 96(3) does not prevent any reference being made to the Commission if –

(a)   before the end of the period for considering the merger notice, the OFT rejects the notice under section 99(5);

(b)   before the end of that period, any of the enterprises to which the notified arrangements relate cease to be distinct from each other;

(c)   any information (whether prescribed information or not) that –

(i)   is, or ought to be, known to the person who gave the merger notice or any connected person; and

(ii)   is material to the notified arrangements;

is not disclosed to the OFT by such time before the end of that period as may be specified in regulations under section 101;

(d)   at any time after the merger notice is given but before the enterprises to which the notified arrangements relate cease to be distinct from each other, any of those enterprises ceases to be distinct from any enterprise other than an enterprise to which those arrangements relate;

(e)   the six months beginning with the end of the period for considering the merger notice expires without the enterprises to which the notified arrangements relate ceasing to be distinct from each other;

(f)   the merger notice is withdrawn; or

(g)   any information given in respect of the notified arrangements (whether in the merger notice or otherwise) by the person who gave the notice or any connected person is in any material respect false or misleading.

(2) Subsection (3) applies where –

(a)   two or more transactions which have occurred, or, if any arrangements are carried into effect, will occur, may be treated for the purposes of a reference under section 22, 33 or 45 as having occurred simultaneously on a particular date; and

(b)   section 96(3) does not prevent such a reference in relation to the last of those transactions.

(3) Section 96(3) does not prevent such a reference in relation to any of those transactions which actually occurred less than six months before –

(a)   that date; or

(b)   the actual occurrence of another of those transactions in relation to which such a reference may be made (whether or not by virtue of this subsection).

(4) In determining for the purposes of subsections (2) and (3) the time at which any transaction actually occurred, no account shall be taken of any option or other conditional right until the option is exercised or the condition is satisfied.

(5) In this section references to the enterprises to which the notified arrangements relate are references to those enterprises that would have ceased to be distinct from one another if the arrangements mentioned in the merger notice concerned had been carried into effect at the time when the notice was given.

101 Merger notices: regulations

(1) The Secretary of State may make regulations for the purposes of sections 96 to 100.

(2) The regulations may, in particular –

(a)   provide for section 97(1), (2), (3) or (4) or section 100(1)(e) to apply as if any reference to a period of days or months were a reference to a period specified in the regulations for the purposes of the enactment concerned;

(b)   provide for the manner in which any merger notice is authorised or required to be rejected or withdrawn, and the time at which any merger notice is to be treated as received or rejected;

(c)   provide for the time at which any notice under section 97(7), (8)(b), (11) or (13) is to be treated as received;

(d)   provide for the manner in which any information requested by the OFT or any other material information is authorised or required to be provided or disclosed, and the time at which such information is to be treated as provided or disclosed (including the time at which it is to be treated as provided to the satisfaction of the OFT for the purposes of section 97(6));

(e)   provide for the person who gave the merger notice to be informed, in circumstances in which section 97(6) applies –

  (i)   of the fact that the OFT is satisfied as to the provision of the information requested by the OFT or (as the case may be) of the OFT's decision to cancel the extension; and

  (ii)   of the time at which the OFT is to be treated as so satisfied or (as the case may be) of the time at which the cancellation is to be treated as having effect;

(f)   provide for the person who gave the merger notice to be informed, in circumstances in which section 97(8) applies –

  (i)   of any decision by the OFT to cancel the extension; and

  (ii)   of the time at which such a cancellation is to be treated as having effect;

(g)   provide for the time at which any fee is to be treated as paid;

(h)   provide that a person is, or is not, to be treated, in such circumstances as may be specified in the regulations, as acting on behalf of a person authorised by regulations under this section to give a merger notice or a person who has given such a notice.

102 Power to modify sections 97 to 101

The Secretary of State may, for the purposes of determining the effect of giving a merger notice and the action which may be or is to be taken by any person in connection with such a notice, by order modify sections 97 to 101.

General duties in relation to references

103 Duty of expedition in relation to references

(1) In deciding whether to make a reference under section 22 or 33 the OFT shall have regard, with a view to the prevention or removal of uncertainty, to the need for making a decision as soon as reasonably practicable.

(2) In deciding whether to make a reference under section 45 or 62 the Secretary of State shall have regard, with a view to the prevention or removal of uncertainty, to the need for making a decision as soon as reasonably practicable.

104 Certain duties of relevant authorities to consult

(1) Subsection (2) applies where the relevant authority is proposing to make a relevant decision in a way which the relevant authority considers is likely to be adverse to the interests of a relevant party.

(2) The relevant authority shall, so far as practicable, consult that party about what is proposed before making that decision.

(3) In consulting the party concerned, the relevant authority shall, so far as practicable, give the reasons of the relevant authority for the proposed decision.

(4) In considering what is practicable for the purposes of this section the relevant authority shall, in particular, have regard to –

  (a)   any restrictions imposed by any timetable for making the decision; and
  (b)   any need to keep what is proposed, or the reasons for it, confidential.

(5) The duty under this section shall not apply in relation to the making of any decision so far as particular provision is made elsewhere by virtue of this Part for consultation before the making of that decision.

(6) In this section –

  'the relevant authority' means the OFT, the Commission or the Secretary of State;
  'relevant decision' means –
  (a)   in the case of the OFT, any decision by the OFT –
    (i)   as to whether to make a reference under section 22 or 33 or accept undertakings under section 73 instead of making such a reference; or
    (ii)   to vary under section 37 such a reference;
  (b)   in the case of the Commission, any decision on the questions mentioned in section 35(1) or (3), 36(1) or (2), 47 or 63; and
  (c)   in the case of the Secretary of State, any decision by the Secretary of State –

(i) as to whether to make a reference under section 45 or 62; or

(ii) to vary under section 49 or (as the case may be) 64 such a reference; and

'relevant party' means any person who appears to the relevant authority to control enterprises which are the subject of the reference or possible reference concerned.

Information and publicity requirements

105 General information duties of OFT and Commission

(1) Where the OFT decides to investigate a matter so as to enable it to decide whether to make a reference under section 22 or 33, or so as to make a report under section 44 or 61, it shall, so far as practicable, take such action as it considers appropriate to bring information about the investigation to the attention of those whom it considers might be affected by the creation of the relevant merger situation concerned or (as the case may be) the special merger situation concerned.

(2) Subsection (1) does not apply in relation to arrangements which might result in the creation of a relevant merger situation if a merger notice has been given in relation to those arrangements under section 96.

(3) The OFT shall give the Commission –

(a) such information in its possession as the Commission may reasonably require to enable the Commission to carry out its functions under this Part; and

(b) any other assistance which the Commission may reasonably require for the purpose of assisting it in carrying out its functions under this Part and which it is within the power of the OFT to give.

(4) The OFT shall give the Commission any information in its possession which has not been requested by the Commission but which, in the opinion of the OFT, would be appropriate to give to the Commission for the purpose of assisting it in carrying out its functions under this Part.

(5) The OFT and the Commission shall give the Secretary of State –

(a) such information in their possession as the Secretary of State may by direction reasonably require to enable him to carry out his functions under this Part; and

(b) any other assistance which the Secretary of State may by direction reasonably require for the purpose of assisting him in carrying out his functions under this Part and which it is within the power of the OFT or (as the case may be) the Commission to give.

(6) The OFT shall give the Secretary of State any information in its possession which has not been requested by the Secretary of State but which, in the opinion of the OFT, would be appropriate to give to the Secretary of State for the purpose of assisting him in carrying out his functions under this Part.

(7) The Commission shall have regard to any information given to it under subsection (3) or (4); and the Secretary of State shall have regard to any information given to him under subsection (5) or (6).

(8) Any direction given under subsection (5) –

    (a)   shall be in writing; and

    (b)   may be varied or revoked by a subsequent direction.

106 Advice and information about references under sections 22 and 33

(1) As soon as reasonably practicable after the passing of this Act, the OFT shall prepare and publish general advice and information about the making of references by it under section 22 or 33.

(2) The OFT may at any time publish revised, or new, advice or information.

(3) As soon as reasonably practicable after the passing of this Act, the Commission shall prepare and publish general advice and information about the consideration by it of references under section 22 or 33 and the way in which relevant customer benefits may affect the taking of enforcement action in relation to such references.

(4) The Commission may at any time publish revised, or new, advice or information.

(5) Advice and information published under this section shall be prepared with a view to –

    (a)   explaining relevant provisions of this Part to persons who are likely to be affected by them; and

    (b)   indicating how the OFT or (as the case may be) the Commission expects such provisions to operate.

(6) Advice (or information) published by virtue of subsection (1) or (3) may include advice (or information) about the factors which the OFT or (as the case may be) the Commission may take into account in considering whether, and if so how, to exercise a function conferred by this Part.

(7) Any advice or information published by the OFT or the Commission under this section shall be published in such manner as the OFT or (as the case may be) the Commission considers appropriate.

(8) In preparing any advice or information under this section, the OFT shall consult the Commission and such other persons as it considers appropriate.

(9) In preparing any advice or information under this section, the Commission shall consult the OFT and such other persons as it considers appropriate.

107 Further publicity requirements

(1) The OFT shall publish –

    (a)   any reference made by it under section 22 or 33 or any decision made by it not to make such a reference (other than a decision made by virtue of subsection (2)(b) of section 33);

(b) any variation made by it under section 37 of a reference under section 22 or 33;

(c) such information as it considers appropriate about any decision made by it under section 57(1) to bring a case to the attention of the Secretary of State;

(d) any enforcement undertaking accepted by it under section 71;

(e) any enforcement order made by it under section 72 or 76 or paragraph 2 of Schedule 7;

(f) any variation, release or revocation of such an undertaking or order;

(g) any decision made by it as mentioned in section 76(6)(b); and

(h) any decision made by it to dispense with the requirements of Schedule 10.

(2) The Commission shall publish –

(a) any cancellation by it under section 37(1) of a reference under section 33;

(b) any decision made by it under section 37(2) to treat a reference made under section 22 or 33 as if it had been made under section 32 or (as the case may be) 22;

(c) any extension by it under section 39 of the period within which a report under section 38 is to be prepared and published;

(d) any decision made by it to cancel an extension as mentioned in section 39(8)(b);

(e) any decision made by it under section 41(2) neither to accept an undertaking under section 82 nor to make an order under section 84;

(f) any decision made by it that there has been a material change of circumstances as mentioned in subsection (3) of section 41 or there is another special reason as mentioned in that subsection of that section;

(g) any cancellation by it under section 48(1) or 53(1) of a reference under section 45 or any cancellation by it under section 64(1) of a reference under section 62;

(h) any decision made by it under section 49(1) to treat –

(i) a reference made under subsection (2) or (3) of section 45 as if it had been made under subsection (4) or (as the case may be) (5) of that section; or

(ii) a reference made under subsection (4) or (5) of section 45 as if it had been made under subsection (2) or (as the case may be) (3) of that section;

(i) any extension by it under section 51 of the period within which a report under section 50 is to be prepared and published;

(j) any decision made by it under section 51(8)(b) to cancel such an extension;

(k) any extension by it under section 51 as applied by section 65(3) of the period within which a report under section 65 is to be prepared and published;

(l) any decision made by it under section 51(8)(b) as applied by section 65(3) to cancel such an extension;

(m)   any decision made by it under section 64(2) to treat a reference made under subsection (2) or (3) of section 62 as if it had been made under subsection (3) or (as the case may be) (2) of that section;

(n)   any decision made by it as mentioned in section 76(6)(b);

(o)   any enforcement order made by it under section 76 or 81;

(p)   any enforcement undertaking accepted by it under section 80;

(q)   any variation, release or revocation of such an order or undertaking; and

(r)   any decision made by it to dispense with the requirements of Schedule 10.

(3) The Secretary of State shall publish –

(a)   any intervention notice or special intervention notice given by him;

(b)   any report of the OFT under section 44 or 61 which has been received by him;

(c)   any reference made by him under section 45 or 62 or any decision made by him not to make such a reference;

(d)   any variation made by him under section 49 of a reference under section 45 or under section 64 of a reference under section 62;

(e)   any report of the Commission under section 50 or 65 which has been received by him;

(f)   any decision made by him neither to accept an undertaking under paragraph 9 of Schedule 7 nor to make an order under paragraph 11 of that Schedule;

(g)   any notice given by him under section 56(1);

(h)   any enforcement undertaking accepted by him under paragraph 1 of Schedule 7;

(i)   any variation or release of such an undertaking;

(j)   any decision made by him as mentioned in paragraph 6(6)(b) of Schedule 7; and

(k)   any decision made by him to dispense with the requirements of Schedule 10.

(4) Where any person is under a duty by virtue of subsection (1), (2) or (3) to publish the result of any action taken by that person or any decision made by that person, the person concerned shall, subject to subsections (5) and (6), also publish that person's reasons for the action concerned or (as the case may be) the decision concerned.

(5) Such reasons need not, if it is not reasonably practicable to do so, be published at the same time as the result of the action concerned or (as the case may be) as the decision concerned.

(6) Subsections (4) and (5) shall not apply in relation to any information published under subsection (1)(c).

(7) The Secretary of State shall publish his reasons for –

(a)   any decision made by him under section 54(2) or 66(2); or

(b)   any decision to make an order under section 58(3) or vary or revoke such an order.

(8) Such reasons may be published after –

(a)   in the case of subsection (7)(a), the publication of the decision concerned; and

(b)   in the case of subsection (7)(b), the making of the order or of the variation or revocation;

if it is not reasonably practicable to publish them at the same time as the publication of the decision or (as the case may be) the making of the order or variation or revocation.

(9) The Secretary of State shall publish –

(a)   the report of the OFT under section 44 in relation to a matter no later than publication of his decision as to whether to make a reference under section 45 in relation to that matter; and

(b)   the report of the Commission under section 50 in relation to a matter no later than publication of his decision under section 54(2) in relation to that matter.

(10) The Secretary of State shall publish –

(a)   the report of the OFT under section 61 in relation to a matter no later than publication of his decision as to whether to make a reference under section 62 in relation to that matter; and

(b)   the report of the Commission under section 65 in relation to a matter no later than publication of his decision under section 66(2) in relation to that matter.

(11) Where the Secretary of State has decided under section 55(2) or 66(6) to accept an undertaking under paragraph 9 of Schedule 7 or to make an order under paragraph 11 of that Schedule, he shall (after the acceptance of the undertaking or (as the case may be) the making of the order) lay details of his decision and his reasons for it, and the Commission's report under section 50 or (as the case may be) 65, before each House of Parliament.

108 Defamation

For the purposes of the law relating to defamation, absolute privilege attaches to any advice, guidance, notice or direction given, or decision or report made, by the OFT, the Commission or the Secretary of State in the exercise of any of their functions under this Part.

Investigation powers

109 Attendance of witnesses and production of documents etc

(1) The Commission may, for the purpose of any investigation on a reference made to it under this Part, give notice to any person requiring him –

(a)   to attend at a time and place specified in the notice; and

(b)   to give evidence to the Commission or a person nominated by the Commission for the purpose.

(2) The Commission may, for the purpose of any investigation on a reference made to it under this Part, give notice to any person requiring him –

(a) to produce any documents which –

    (i) are specified or described in the notice, or fall within a category of document which is specified or described in the notice; and

    (ii) are in that person's custody or under his control; and

(b) to produce them at a time and place so specified and to a person so specified.

(3) The Commission may, for the purpose of any investigation on a reference made to it under this Part, give notice to any person who carries on any business requiring him –

(a) to supply to the Commission such estimates, forecasts, returns or other information as may be specified or described in the notice; and

(b) to supply it at a time and place, and in a form and manner, so specified and to a person so specified.

(4) A notice under this section shall include information about the possible consequences of not complying with the notice.

(5) The Commission or any person nominated by it for the purpose may, for the purpose of any investigation on a reference made to it under this Part, take evidence on oath, and for that purpose may administer oaths.

(6) The person to whom any document is produced in accordance with a notice under this section may, for the purpose of any investigation on a reference made to the Commission under this Part, copy the document so produced.

(7) No person shall be required under this section –

(a) to give any evidence or produce any documents which he could not be compelled to give or produce in civil proceedings before the court; or

(b) to supply any information which he could not be compelled to supply in evidence in such proceedings.

(8) No person shall be required, in compliance with a notice under this section, to go more than 10 miles from his place of residence unless his necessary travelling expenses are paid or offered to him.

(9) Any reference in this section to the production of a document includes a reference to the production of a legible and intelligible copy of information recorded otherwise than in legible form.

(10) In this section 'the court' means –

(a) in relation to England and Wales or Northern Ireland, the High Court; and

(b) in relation to Scotland, the Court of Session.

110 Enforcement of powers under section 109: general

(1) Where the Commission considers that a person has, without reasonable excuse, failed to comply with any requirement of a notice under section 109, it may impose a penalty in accordance with section 111.

(2) The Commission may proceed (whether at the same time or at different times) under subsection (1) and section 39(4) or (as the case may be) 51(4) (including that enactment as applied by section 65(3)) in relation to the same failure.

(3) Where the Commission considers that a person has intentionally obstructed or delayed another person in the exercise of his powers under section 109(6), it may impose a penalty in accordance with section 111.

(4) No penalty shall be imposed by virtue of subsection (1) or (3) if more than 4 weeks have passed since the publication of the report of the Commission on the reference concerned; but this subsection shall not apply in relation to any variation or substitution of the penalty which is permitted by virtue of this Part.

(5) A person, subject to subsection (6), commits an offence if he intentionally alters, suppresses or destroys any document which he has been required to produce by a notice under section 109.

(6) A person does not commit an offence under subsection (5) in relation to any act which constitutes a failure to comply with a notice under section 109 if the Commission has proceeded against that person under subsection (1) above in relation to that failure.

(7) A person who commits an offence under subsection (5) shall be liable –

(a)   on summary conviction, to a fine not exceeding the statutory maximum;

(b)   on conviction on indictment, to imprisonment for a term not exceeding two years or to a fine or to both.

(8) The Commission shall not proceed against a person under subsection (1) in relation to an act which constitutes an offence under subsection (5) if that person has been found guilty of that offence.

(9) In deciding whether and, if so, how to proceed under subsection (1) or (3) or section 39(4) or 51(4) (including that enactment as applied by section 65(3)), the Commission shall have regard to the statement of policy which was most recently published under section 116 at the time when the failure concerned or (as the case may be) the obstruction or delay concerned occurred.

(10) The reference in this section to the production of a document includes a reference to the production of a legible and intelligible copy of information recorded otherwise than in legible form; and the reference to suppressing a document includes a reference to destroying the means of reproducing information recorded otherwise than in legible form.

111 Penalties

(1) A penalty imposed under section 110(1) or (3) shall be of such amount as the Commission considers appropriate.

(2) The amount may, in the case of a penalty imposed under section 110(1), be a fixed amount, an amount calculated by reference to a daily rate or a combination of a fixed amount and an amount calculated by reference to a daily rate.

(3) The amount shall, in the case of a penalty imposed under section 110(3), be a fixed amount.

(4) No penalty imposed under section 110(1) shall –

    (a)   in the case of a fixed amount, exceed such amount as the Secretary of State may by order specify;

    (b)   in the case of an amount calculated by reference to a daily rate, exceed such amount per day as the Secretary of State may so specify; and

    (c)   in the case of a fixed amount and an amount calculated by reference to a daily rate, exceed such fixed amount and such amount per day as the Secretary of State may so specify.

(5) In imposing a penalty by reference to a daily rate –

    (a)   no account shall be taken of any days before the service of the notice under section 112 on the person concerned; and

    (b)   unless the Commission determines an earlier date (whether before or after the penalty is imposed), the amount payable shall cease to accumulate at the beginning of –

        (i)   the day on which the requirement of the notice concerned under section 109 is satisfied or (as the case may be) the obstruction or delay is removed; or

        (ii)   if earlier, the day on which the report of the Commission on the reference concerned is published (or, in the case of a report under section 50 or 65, given) or, if no such report is published (or given) within the period permitted for that purpose by this Part, the latest day on which the report may be published (or given) within the permitted period.

(6) No penalty imposed under section 110(3) shall exceed such amount as the Secretary of State may by order specify.

(7) An order under subsection (4) or (6) shall not specify –

    (a)   in the case of a fixed amount, an amount exceeding £30,000;

    (b)   in the case of an amount calculated by reference to a daily rate, an amount per day exceeding £15,000; and

    (c)   in the case of a fixed amount and an amount calculated by reference to a daily rate, a fixed amount exceeding £30,000 and an amount per day exceeding £15,000.

(8) Before making an order under subsection (4) or (6) the Secretary of State shall consult the Commission and such other persons as he considers appropriate.

112 Penalties: main procedural requirements

(1) As soon as practicable after imposing a penalty under section 110(1) or (3), the Commission shall give notice of the penalty.

(2) The notice shall state –

    (a)   that the Commission has imposed a penalty on the person concerned;

(b)   whether the penalty is of a fixed amount, of an amount calculated by reference to a daily rate or of both a fixed amount and an amount calculated by reference to a daily rate;

(c)   the amount or amounts concerned and, in the case of an amount calculated by reference to a daily rate, the day on which the amount first starts to accumulate and the day or days on which it might cease to accumulate;

(d)   the failure or (as the case may be) the obstruction or delay which the Commission considers gave it the power to impose the penalty;

(e)   any other facts which the Commission considers justify the imposition of a penalty and the amount or amounts of the penalty;

(f)   the manner in which, and place at which, the penalty is required to be paid to the Commission;

(g)   the date or dates, no earlier than the end of the relevant period beginning with the date of service of the notice on the person concerned, by which the penalty or (as the case may be) different portions of it are required to be paid;

(h)   that the penalty or (as the case may be) different portions of it may be paid earlier than the date or dates by which it or they are required to be paid; and

(i)   that the person concerned has the right to apply under subsection (3) below or to appeal under section 114 and the main details of those rights.

(3) The person against whom the penalty was imposed may, within 14 days of the date of service on him of a notice under subsection (1), apply to the Commission for it to specify a different date or (as the case may be) different dates by which the penalty or (as the case may be) different portions of it are to be paid.

(4) A notice under this section shall be given by –

(a)   serving a copy of the notice on the person on whom the penalty was imposed; and

(b)   publishing the notice.

(5) In this section 'relevant period' means the period of 28 days mentioned in subsection (3) of section 114 or, if another period is specified by the Secretary of State under that subsection, that period.

113 Payments and interest by instalments

(1) If the whole or any portion of a penalty is not paid by the date by which it is required to be paid, the unpaid balance from time to time shall carry interest at the rate for the time being specified in section 17 of the Judgments Act 1838.

(2) Where an application has been made under section 112(3), the penalty shall not be required to be paid until the application has been determined, withdrawn or otherwise dealt with.

(3) If a portion of a penalty has not been paid by the date required for it, the Commission may, where it considers it appropriate to do so, require so much of the

penalty as has not already been paid (and is capable of being paid immediately) to be paid immediately.

(4) Any sums received by the Commission in or towards the payment of a penalty, or interest on a penalty, shall be paid into the Consolidated Fund.

114 Appeals in relation to penalties

(1) This section applies if a person on whom a penalty is imposed under section 110(1) or (3) is aggrieved by –

 (a) the imposition or nature of the penalty;
 (b) the amount or amounts of the penalty; or
 (c) the date by which the penalty is required to be paid or (as the case may be) the different dates by which portions of the penalty are required to be paid.

(2) The person aggrieved may apply to the Competition Appeal Tribunal.

(3) If a copy of the notice under section 112(1) was served on the person on whom the penalty was imposed, the application to the Competition Appeal Tribunal shall, subject to subsection (4), be made within –

 (a) the period of 28 days starting with the day on which the copy was served on the person concerned; or
 (b) such other period as the Secretary of State may by order specify.

(4) If the application relates to a decision of the Commission on an application by the person on whom the penalty was imposed under section 112(3), the application to the Competition Appeal Tribunal shall be made within –

 (a) the period of 28 days starting with the day on which the person concerned is notified of the decision; or
 (b) such other period as the Secretary of State may by order specify.

(5) On an application under this section, the Competition Appeal Tribunal may –

 (a) quash the penalty;
 (b) substitute a penalty of a different nature or of such lesser amount or amounts as the Competition Appeal Tribunal considers appropriate; or
 (c) in a case falling within subsection (1)(c), substitute for the date or dates imposed by the Commission an alternative date or dates;

if it considers it appropriate to do so.

(6) The Competition Appeal Tribunal shall not substitute a penalty of a different nature under subsection (5)(b) unless it considers that the person on whom the penalty is imposed will, or is likely to, pay less under the substituted penalty than he would have paid under the original penalty.

(7) Where an application has been made under this section –

 (a) the penalty shall not be required to be paid until the application has been determined, withdrawn or otherwise dealt with; and
 (b) the Commission may agree to reduce the amount or amounts of the penalty in settlement of the application.

(8) Where the Competition Appeal Tribunal substitutes a penalty of a different nature or of a lesser amount or amounts it may require the payment of interest on the substituted penalty at such rate or rates, and from such date or dates, as it considers appropriate.

(9) Where the Competition Appeal Tribunal specifies as a date by which the penalty, or a portion of the penalty, is to be paid a date before the determination of the application under this section it may require the payment of interest on the penalty, or portion, from that date at such rate as it considers appropriate.

(10) An appeal lies to the appropriate court –

(a)   on a point of law arising from a decision of the Tribunal in proceedings under this section; or

(b)   from a decision of the Tribunal in such proceedings as to the amount or amounts of a penalty.

(11) An appeal under subsection (10) –

(a)   may be brought by a party to the proceedings before the Tribunal; and

(b)   requires the permission of the Tribunal or the appropriate court.

(12) In this section 'the appropriate court' means the Court of Appeal or, in the case of Tribunal proceedings in Scotland, the Court of Session.

115 Recovery of penalties

Where a penalty imposed under section 110(1) or (3), or any portion of such a penalty, has not been paid by the date on which it is required to be paid and –

(a)   no application relating to the penalty has been made under section 114 during the period within which such an application may be made, or

(b)   any such application which has been made has been determined, withdrawn or otherwise dealt with,

the Commission may recover from the person on whom the penalty was imposed any of the penalty and any interest which has not been paid; and in England and Wales and Northern Ireland such penalty and interest may be recovered as a civil debt due to the Commission.

116 Statement of policy

(1) The Commission shall prepare and publish a statement of policy in relation to the enforcement of notices under section 109.

(2) The statement shall, in particular, include a statement about the considerations relevant to the determination of the nature and amount of any penalty imposed under section 110(1) or (3).

(3) The Commission may revise its statement of policy and, where it does so, it shall publish the revised statement.

(4) The Commission shall consult such persons as it considers appropriate when preparing or revising its statement of policy.

117 False or misleading information

(1) A person commits an offence if –

    (a)   he supplies any information to the OFT, the Commission or the Secretary of State in connection with any of their functions under this Part;

    (b)   the information is false or misleading in a material respect; and

    (c)   he knows that it is false or misleading in a material respect or is reckless as to whether it is false or misleading in a material respect.

(2) A person commits an offence if he –

    (a)   supplies any information to another person which he knows to be false or misleading in a material respect; or

    (b)   recklessly supplies any information to another person which is false or misleading in a material respect;

knowing that the information is to be used for the purpose of supplying information to the OFT, the Commission or the Secretary of State in connection with any of their functions under this Part.

(3) A person who commits an offence under subsection (1) or (2) shall be liable –

    (a)   on summary conviction, to a fine not exceeding the statutory maximum;

    (b)   on conviction on indictment, to imprisonment for a term not exceeding two years or to a fine or to both.

Reports

118 Excisions from reports

(1) Subsection (2) applies where the Secretary of State is under a duty to publish –

    (a)   a report of the OFT under section 44 or 61; or

    (b)   a report of the Commission under section 50 or 65.

(2) The Secretary of State may exclude a matter from the report concerned if he considers that publication of the matter would be inappropriate.

(3) In deciding what is inappropriate for the purposes of subsection (2) the Secretary of State shall have regard to the considerations mentioned in section 244.

(4) The body which has prepared the report shall advise the Secretary of State as to the matters (if any) which it considers should be excluded by him under subsection (2).

(5) References in sections 38(4) and 107(11) to the giving or laying of a report of the Commission shall be construed as references to the giving or laying of the report as published.

119 Minority reports of Commission

(1) Subsection (2) applies where, on a reference to the Commission under this Part, a member of a group constituted in connection with the reference in pursuance of

paragraph 15 of Schedule 7 to the Competition Act 1998, disagrees with any decisions contained in the report of the Commission under this Part as the decisions of the Commission.

(2) The report shall, if the member so wishes, include a statement of his disagreement and of his reasons for disagreeing.

Miscellaneous

120 Review of decisions under Part 3

(1) Any person aggrieved by a decision of the OFT, the Secretary of State or the Commission under this Part in connection with a reference or possible reference in relation to a relevant merger situation or a special merger situation may apply to the Competition Appeal Tribunal for a review of that decision.

(2) For this purpose 'decision' –

   (a)   does not include a decision to impose a penalty under section 110(1) or (3); but
   (b)   includes a failure to take a decision permitted or required by this Part in connection with a reference or possible reference.

(3) Except in so far as a direction to the contrary is given by the Competition Appeal Tribunal, the effect of the decision is not suspended by reason of the making of the application.

(4) In determining such an application the Competition Appeal Tribunal shall apply the same principles as would be applied by a court on an application for judicial review.

(5) The Competition Appeal Tribunal may –

   (a)   dismiss the application or quash the whole or part of the decision to which it relates; and
   (b)   where it quashes the whole or part of that decision, refer the matter back to the original decision maker with a direction to reconsider and make a new decision in accordance with the ruling of the Competition Appeal Tribunal.

(6) An appeal lies on any point of law arising from a decision of the Competition Appeal Tribunal under this section to the appropriate court.

(7) An appeal under subsection (6) requires the permission of the Tribunal or the appropriate court.

(8) In this section –

   'the appropriate court' means the Court of Appeal or, in the case of Tribunal proceedings in Scotland, the Court of Session; and
   'Tribunal rules' has the meaning given by section 15(1).

121 Fees

(1) The Secretary of State may by order require the payment to him or the OFT of such fees as may be prescribed by the order in connection with the exercise by the Secretary of State, the OFT and the Commission of their functions under or by virtue of this Part, Part V of the Fair Trading Act 1973 and sections 32 to 34 of, and Schedule 4ZA to, the Water Industry Act 1991.

(2) An order under this section may, in particular, provide for fees to be payable –

   (a)   in respect of a merger notice;

   (b)   in respect of an application for the consent of the Secretary of State under section 58(1) of the Act of 1973 to the transfer of a newspaper or of newspaper assets; or

   (c)   on the occurrence of any event specified in the order.

(3) The events that may be specified in an order under this section by virtue of subsection (2)(c) include, in particular –

   (a)   the decision by the OFT in relation to a possible reference under section 22 or 33 that it is or may be the case that a relevant merger situation has been created or (as the case may be) that arrangements are in progress or in contemplation which, if carried into effect, will result in the creation of a relevant merger situation;

   (b)   the decision by the Secretary of State in relation to a possible reference under section 45 that it is or may be the case that a relevant merger situation has been created or (as the case may be) that arrangements are in progress or in contemplation which, if carried into effect, will result in the creation of a relevant merger situation;

   (c)   the decision by the Secretary of State in relation to a possible reference under section 62 that –

      (i)   it is or may be the case that a special merger situation has been created or (as the case may be) that arrangements are in progress or in contemplation which, if carried into effect, will result in the creation of a special merger situation; and

      (ii)   one or more than one consideration mentioned in the special intervention notice is relevant to a consideration of the special merger situation concerned; and

   (d)   the decision by the OFT in relation to a possible reference under section 32 of the Act of 1991 that it is or may be the case that arrangements are in progress which, if carried into effect, will result in a merger of any two or more water enterprises or that such a merger has taken place otherwise than as a result of the carrying into effect of arrangements that have been the subject of a reference by virtue of paragraph (a) of that section.

(4) An order under this section may, in particular, contain provision –

   (a)   for ascertaining the persons by whom fees are payable;

   (b)   specifying whether any fee is payable to the Secretary of State or the OFT;

   (c)   for the amount of any fee to be calculated by reference to matters which may include –

(i)   in a case involving functions of the Secretary of State under sections 57 to 61 of the Act of 1973, the number of newspapers concerned, the number of separate editions (determined in accordance with the order) of each newspaper and the average circulation per day of publication (within the meaning of Part V of that Act) of each newspaper; and

(ii)   in any other case, the value of the turnover of the enterprises concerned;

(d)   as to the time when any fee is to be paid; and

(e)   for the repayment by the Secretary of State or the OFT of the whole or part of any fee in specified circumstances.

(5) For the purposes of subsection (4)(c)(ii) the turnover of an enterprise shall be determined in accordance with such provisions as may be specified in an order under this section.

(6) Provision made by virtue of subsection (5) may, in particular, include provision –

(a)   as to the amounts which are, or which are not, to be treated as comprising an enterprise's turnover;

(b)   as to the date or dates by reference to which an enterprise's turnover is to be determined;

(c)   restricting the turnover to be taken into consideration to turnover which has a connection of a particular description with the United Kingdom.

(7) An order under this section may, in particular, in connection with provisions of the kind mentioned in subsection (5) make provision enabling the Secretary of State or the OFT to determine matters of a description specified in the order (including any of the matters mentioned in paragraphs (a) to (c) of subsection (6)).

(8) In determining the amount of any fees to be prescribed by an order under this section, the Secretary of State may take into account all costs incurred by him and by the OFT in respect of the exercise by him, the OFT and the Commission of their respective functions under or by virtue of this Part, Part V of the Act of 1973 and sections 32 to 34 of, and Schedule 4ZA to, the Act of 1991.

(9) Fees paid to the Secretary of State or the OFT under this section shall be paid into the Consolidated Fund.

(10) In this section 'newspaper' has the same meaning as in Part V of the Act of 1973.

122 Primacy of Community law

(1) Advice and information published by virtue of section 106(1) or (3) shall include such advice and information about the effect of Community law, and anything done under or in accordance with it, on the provisions of this Part as the OFT or (as the case may be) the Commission considers appropriate.

(2) Advice and information published by the OFT by virtue of section 106(1) shall, in particular, include advice and information about the circumstances in which the duties

of the OFT under sections 22 and 33 do not apply as a result of the European Merger Regulations or anything done under or in accordance with them.

(3) The duty or power to make a reference under section 22 or 45(2) or (3), and the power to give an intervention notice under section 42, shall apply in a case in which the relevant enterprises ceased to be distinct enterprises at a time or in circumstances not falling within section 24 if the condition mentioned in subsection (4) is satisfied.

(4) The condition mentioned in this subsection is that, because of the European Merger Regulations or anything done under or in accordance with them, the reference, or (as the case may be) the reference under section 22 to which the intervention notice relates, could not have been made earlier than 4 months before the date on which it is to be made.

(5) Where the duty or power to make a reference under section 22 or 45(2) or (3), or the power to give an intervention notice under section 42, applies as mentioned in subsection (3), references in this Part to the creation of a relevant merger situation shall be construed accordingly.

123 Power to alter share of supply test

(1) The Secretary of State may by order amend or replace the conditions which determine for the purposes of this Part whether a relevant merger situation has been created.

(2) The Secretary of State shall not exercise his power under subsection (1) –

(a)   to amend or replace the conditions mentioned in paragraphs (a) and (b) of subsection (1) of section 23;

(b)   to amend or replace the condition mentioned in paragraph (a) of subsection (2) of that section.

(3) In exercising his power under subsection (1) to amend or replace the condition mentioned in paragraph (b) of subsection (2) of section 23 or any condition which for the time being applies instead of it, the Secretary of State shall, in particular, have regard to the desirability of ensuring that any amended or new condition continues to operate by reference to the degree of commercial strength which results from the enterprises concerned having ceased to be distinct.

(4) Before making an order under this section the Secretary of State shall consult the OFT and the Commission.

(5) An order under this section may provide for the delegation of functions to the decision-making authority.

Other

124 Orders and regulations under Part 3

(1) Any power of the Secretary of State to make an order or regulations under this Part shall be exercisable by statutory instrument.

(2) Any power of the Secretary of State to make an order or regulations under this Part –

    (a)   may be exercised so as to make different provision for different cases or different purposes; and

    (b)   includes power to make such incidental, supplementary, consequential, transitory, transitional or saving provision as the Secretary of State considers appropriate.

(3) The power of the Secretary of State under section 34 or 123 (including that power as extended by subsection (2) above) may be exercised by modifying any enactment comprised in or made under this Act, or any other enactment.

(4) The power of the Secretary of State under section 40(8), 52(8) (including that enactment as applied by section 65(3)), 58(3), 68 or 102 as extended by subsection (2) above may be exercised by modifying any enactment comprised in or made under this Act, or any other enactment.

(5) An order made by the Secretary of State under section 28 (including that enactment as applied by section 42(5), 59(5) and 67(7)), 40(8), 52(8) (including that enactment as applied by section 65(3)), 111(4) or (6), 114(3)(b) or (4)(b) or 121 or Schedule 7 shall be subject to annulment in pursuance of a resolution of either House of Parliament.

(6) No order shall be made by the Secretary of State under section 34, 68, 102, 123 or 128(6) unless a draft of it has been laid before, and approved by a resolution of, each House of Parliament.

(7) An order made by the Secretary of State under section 58(3) shall be laid before Parliament after being made and shall cease to have effect unless approved, within the period of 28 days beginning with the day on which it is made, by a resolution of each House of Parliament.

(8) In calculating the period of 28 days mentioned in subsection (7), no account shall be taken of any time during which Parliament is dissolved or prorogued or during which both Houses are adjourned for more than four days.

(9) If an order made by the Secretary of State ceases to have effect by virtue of subsection (7), any modification made by it of an enactment is repealed (and the previous enactment revived) but without prejudice to the validity of anything done in connection with that modification before the order ceased to have effect and without prejudice to the making of a new order.

(10) If, apart from this subsection, an order made by the Secretary of State under section 58(3) would be treated for the purposes of the standing orders of either House of Parliament as a hybrid instrument, it shall proceed in that House as if it were not such an instrument.

125 Offences by bodies corporate

(1) Where an offence under this Part committed by a body corporate is proved to have been committed with the consent or connivance of, or to be attributable to any neglect on the part of –

(a)   a director, manager, secretary or other similar officer of the body corporate, or

(b)   a person purporting to act in such a capacity,

he as well as the body corporate commits the offence and shall be liable to be proceeded against and punished accordingly.

(2) Where the affairs of a body corporate are managed by its members, subsection (1) applies in relation to the acts and defaults of a member in connection with his functions of management as if he were a director of the body corporate.

(3) Where an offence under this Part is committed by a Scottish partnership and is proved to have been committed with the consent or connivance of a partner, or to be attributable to any neglect on the part of a partner, he as well as the partnership commits the offence and shall be liable to be proceeded against and punished accordingly.

(4) In subsection (3) 'partner' includes a person purporting to act as a partner.

126 Service of documents

(1) Any document required or authorised by virtue of this Part to be served on any person may be served –

(a)   by delivering it to him or by leaving it at his proper address or by sending it by post to him at that address;

(b)   if the person is a body corporate other than a limited liability partnership, by serving it in accordance with paragraph (a) on the secretary of the body;

(c)   if the person is a limited liability partnership, by serving it in accordance with paragraph (a) on a member of the partnership; or

(d)   if the person is a partnership, by serving it in accordance with paragraph (a) on a partner or a person having the control or management of the partnership business.

(2) For the purposes of this section and section 7 of the Interpretation Act 1978 (service of documents by post) in its application to this section, the proper address of any person on whom a document is to be served shall be his last known address, except that –

(a)   in the case of service on a body corporate (other than a limited liability partnership) or its secretary, it shall be the address of the registered or principal office of the body;

(b)   in the case of service on a limited liability partnership or a member of the partnership, it shall be the address of the registered or principal office of the partnership;

(c)   in the case of service on a partnership or a partner or a person having the control or management of a partnership business, it shall be the address of the principal office of the partnership.

(3) For the purposes of subsection (2) the principal office of a company constituted under the law of a country or territory outside the United Kingdom or of a

partnership carrying on business outside the United Kingdom is its principal office within the United Kingdom.

(4) Subsection (5) applies if a person to be served under this Part with any document by another has specified to that other an address within the United Kingdom other than his proper address (as determined under subsection (2)) as the one at which he or someone on his behalf will accept documents of the same description as that document.

(5) In relation to that document, that address shall be treated as his proper address for the purposes of this section and section 7 of the Interpretation Act 1978 in its application to this section, instead of that determined under subsection (2).

(6) Any notice in writing or other document required or authorised by virtue of this Part to be served on any person may be served on that person by transmitting the text of the notice or other document to him by means of a telecommunication system (within the meaning of the Telecommunications Act 1984) or by other means but while in electronic form provided the text is received by that person in legible form and is capable of being used for subsequent reference.

(7) This section does not apply to any document if rules of court make provision about its service.

(8) In this section references to serving include references to similar expressions (such as giving or sending).

127 Associated persons

(1) Associated persons, and any bodies corporate which they or any of them control, shall be treated as one person –

   (a)   for the purpose of deciding under section 26 whether any two enterprises have been brought under common ownership or common control; and

   (b)   for the purpose of determining what activities are carried on by way of business by any one person so far as that question arises in connection with paragraph 13(2) of Schedule 8.

(2) Subsection (1) shall not exclude from section 26 any case which would otherwise fall within that section.

(3) A reference under section 22, 33, 45 or 62 (whether or not made by virtue of this section) may be framed so as to exclude from consideration, either altogether or for a specified purpose or to a specified extent, any matter which, apart from this section, would not have been taken into account on that reference.

(4) For the purposes of this section –

   (a)   any individual and that individual's spouse or partner and any relative, or spouse or partner of a relative, of that individual or of that individual's spouse or partner;

   (b)   any person in his capacity as trustee of a settlement and the settlor or grantor and any person associated with the settlor or grantor;

(c)   persons carrying on business in partnership and the spouse or partner and relatives of any of them; or

(d)   two or more persons acting together to secure or exercise control of a body of persons corporate or unincorporate or to secure control of any enterprise or assets,

shall be regarded as associated with one another.

(5) The reference in subsection (1) to bodies corporate which associated persons control shall be construed in accordance with section 26(3) and (4).

(6) In this section 'relative' means a brother, sister, uncle, aunt, nephew, niece, lineal ancestor or descendant (the stepchild of any person, or anyone adopted by a person, whether legally or otherwise, as his child being regarded as a relative or taken into account to trace a relationship in the same way as that person's child); and references to a spouse or partner shall include a former spouse or partner.

128 Supply of services and market for services etc

(1) References in this Part to the supply of services shall be construed in accordance with this section; and references in this Part to a market for services and other related expressions shall be construed accordingly.

(2) The supply of services does not include the provision of services under a contract of service or of apprenticeship whether it is express or implied and (if it is express) whether it is oral or in writing.

(3) The supply of services includes –

(a)   performing for gain or reward any activity other than the supply of goods;

(b)   rendering services to order;

(c)   the provision of services by making them available to potential users.

(4) The supply of services includes making arrangements for the use of computer software or for granting access to data stored in any form which is not readily accessible.

(5) The supply of services includes making arrangements by means of a relevant agreement (within the meaning of section 189(2) of the Broadcasting Act 1990) for sharing the use of telecommunications apparatus.

(6) The supply of services includes permitting or making arrangements to permit the use of land in such circumstances as the Secretary of State may by order specify.

129 Other interpretation provisions

(1) In this Part, unless the context otherwise requires –

'action' includes omission; and references to the taking of action include references to refraining from action;

'agreement' means any agreement or arrangement, in whatever way and whatever form it is made, and whether it is, or is intended to be, legally enforceable or not;

'business' includes a professional practice and includes any other undertaking which is carried on for gain or reward or which is an undertaking in the course of which goods or services are supplied otherwise than free of charge;

'change of circumstances' includes any discovery that information has been supplied which is false or misleading in a material respect;

'Community law' means –

(a)   all the rights, powers, liabilities, obligations and restrictions from time to time created or arising by or under the Community Treaties; and

(b)   all the remedies and procedures from time to time provided for by or under the Community Treaties;

'consumer' means any person who is –

(a)   a person to whom goods are or are sought to be supplied (whether by way of sale or otherwise) in the course of a business carried on by the person supplying or seeking to supply them; or

(b)   a person for whom services are or are sought to be supplied in the course of a business carried on by the person supplying or seeking to supply them;

and who does not receive or seek to receive the goods or services in the course of a business carried on by him;

'customer' includes a customer who is not a consumer;

'enactment' includes an Act of the Scottish Parliament, Northern Ireland legislation and an enactment comprised in subordinate legislation, and includes an enactment whenever passed or made;

'enterprise' means the activities, or part of the activities, of a business;

'the European Merger Regulations' means Council Regulation (EEC) No 4064/89 of 21st December 1989 on the control of concentrations between undertakings as amended by Council Regulation (EC) No 1310/97 of 30th June 1997;

'goods' includes buildings and other structures, and also includes ships, aircraft and hovercraft;

'modify' includes amend or repeal;

'notice' means notice in writing;

'price' includes any charge or fee (however described);

'subordinate legislation' has the same meaning as in the Interpretation Act 1978) and also includes an instrument made under an Act of the Scottish Parliament and an instrument made under Northern Ireland legislation;

'subsidiary' has the meaning given by section 736 of the Companies Act 1985;

'supply', in relation to the supply of goods, includes supply by way of sale, lease, hire or hire-purchase, and, in relation to buildings or other structures, includes the construction of them by a person for another person; and

'United Kingdom national' means an individual who is –

(a)   a British citizen, a British overseas territories citizen, a British National (Overseas) or a British Overseas citizen;

(b)   a person who under the British Nationality Act 1981 is a British subject; or

(c)   a British protected person within the meaning of that Act.

(2) For the purposes of this Part any two bodies corporate are interconnected if –

    (a)   one of them is a body corporate of which the other is a subsidiary; or

    (b)   both of them are subsidiaries of one and the same body corporate;

and in this Part 'interconnected bodies corporate' shall be construed accordingly and 'group of interconnected bodies corporate' means a group consisting of two or more bodies corporate all of whom are interconnected with each other.

(3) References in this Part to a person carrying on business include references to a person carrying on business in partnership with one or more other persons.

(4) Any duty to publish which is imposed on a person by this Part shall, unless the context otherwise requires, be construed as a duty on that person to publish in such manner as he considers appropriate for the purpose of bringing the matter concerned to the attention of those likely to be affected by it.

130 Index of defined expressions

In this Part, the expressions listed in the left-hand column have the meaning given by, or are to be interpreted in accordance with, the provisions listed in the right-hand column.

Expression	Provision of this Act
Action (and the taking of action)	Section 129(1)
Adverse public interest finding	Section 54(3)
Agreement	Section 129(1)
Anti-competitive outcome	Section 35(2)
Business (and carrying on business)	Section 129(1) and (3)
Change of circumstances	Section 129(1)
The Commission	Section 273
Community law	Section 129(1)
Consumer	Section 129(1)
Customer	Section 129(1)
Date of reference	Section 39(9)
The decision-making authority	Section 22(7)
Enactment	Section 129(1)
Enforcement order	Section 86(6)
Enforcement undertaking	Section 89(2)
Enterprise	Section 129(1)
Enterprises ceasing to be distinct	Section 26(1)
European Merger Regulations	Section 129(1)
Final determination of matter to which intervention notice relates	Section 43(4) and (5)
Final determination of matter to which special intervention notice relates	Section 60(4) and (5)
Final determination of reference under section 22 or 33	Section 79(1) and (2)
Goods	Section 129(1)

Expression	Provision of this Act
Interconnected bodies corporate (and a group of interconnected bodies corporate)	Section 129(2)
Intervention notice	Section 42(2)
Market for goods or services	Section 22(6)
Market in the United Kingdom	Section 22(6)
Merger notice	Section 96(2)
Modify	Section 129(1)
Notice	Section 129(1)
Notified arrangements	Section 96(6)
The OFT	Section 273
Orders under section 81	Section 81(6)
Orders under paragraph 2 of Schedule 7	Paragraph 2(7) of Schedule 7
The period for considering a merger notice	Sections 97 and 98
Price	Section 129(1)
Public interest consideration	Sections 42(3) and 67(9)
Public interest consideration being finalised	Section 42(8)
Publish	Section 129(4)
References under section 22, 33, 45 or 62	Sections 37(2), 49(1), 56(8) and 64(2)
Relevant customer benefit	Section 30
Relevant merger situation	Section 23 (as read with other enactments)
Reports of the Commission	Section 118(5)
Special intervention notice	Section 59(2)
Special merger situation	Section 59(3)
Subordinate legislation	Section 129(1)
Subsidiary	Section 129(1)
Supply (in relation to the supply of goods)	Section 129(1)
The supply of services (and a market for services etc)	Section 128
The turnover in the United Kingdom of an enterprise	Section 28(2)
Undertakings under section 80	Section 80(6)
Undertakings under paragraph 1 of Schedule 7	Paragraph 1(7) of Schedule 7
United Kingdom national	Section 129(1)

PART 4
MARKET INVESTIGATIONS

CHAPTER 1
MARKET INVESTIGATION REFERENCES

Making of references

131 Power of OFT to make references

(1) The OFT may, subject to subsection (4), make a reference to the Commission if the OFT has reasonable grounds for suspecting that any feature, or combination of features, of a market in the United Kingdom for goods or services prevents, restricts or distorts competition in connection with the supply or acquisition of any goods or services in the United Kingdom or a part of the United Kingdom.

(2) For the purposes of this Part any reference to a feature of a market in the United Kingdom for goods or services shall be construed as a reference to –

(a)   the structure of the market concerned or any aspect of that structure;

(b)   any conduct (whether or not in the market concerned) of one or more than one person who supplies or acquires goods or services in the market concerned; or

(c)   any conduct relating to the market concerned of customers of any person who supplies or acquires goods or services.

(3) In subsection (2) 'conduct' includes any failure to act (whether or not intentional) and any other unintentional conduct.

(4) No reference shall be made under this section if –

(a)   the making of the reference is prevented by section 156(1); or

(b)   a reference has been made under section 132 in relation to the same matter but has not been finally determined.

(5) References in this Part to a market investigation reference being finally determined shall be construed in accordance with section 183(3) to (6).

(6) In this Part –

'market in the United Kingdom' includes –

(a)   so far as it operates in the United Kingdom or a part of the United Kingdom, any market which operates there and in another country or territory or in a part of another country or territory; and

(b)   any market which operates only in a part of the United Kingdom;

'market investigation reference' means a reference under this section or section 132;

and references to a market for goods or services include references to a market for goods and services.

132 Ministerial power to make references

(1) Subsection (3) applies where, in relation to any goods or services, the appropriate Minister is not satisfied with a decision of the OFT not to make a reference under section 131.

(2) Subsection (3) also applies where, in relation to any goods or services, the appropriate Minister –

 (a) has brought to the attention of the OFT information which the appropriate Minister considers to be relevant to the question of whether the OFT should make a reference under section 131; but

 (b) is not satisfied that the OFT will decide, within such period as the appropriate Minister considers to be reasonable, whether to make such a reference.

(3) The appropriate Minister may, subject to subsection (4), make a reference to the Commission if he has reasonable grounds for suspecting that any feature, or combination of features, of a market in the United Kingdom for goods or services prevents, restricts or distorts competition in connection with the supply or acquisition of any goods or services in the United Kingdom or a part of the United Kingdom.

(4) No reference shall be made under this section if the making of the reference is prevented by section 156(1).

(5) In this Part 'the appropriate Minister' means –

 (a) the Secretary of State; or

 (b) the Secretary of State and one or more than one other Minister of the Crown acting jointly.

133 Contents of references

(1) A market investigation reference shall, in particular, specify –

 (a) the enactment under which it is made;

 (b) the date on which it is made; and

 (c) the description of goods or services to which the feature or combination of features concerned relates.

(2) A market investigation reference may be framed so as to require the Commission to confine its investigation into the effects of features of markets in the United Kingdom for goods or services of a description specified in the reference to the effects of features of such of those markets as exist in connection with –

 (a) a supply, of a description specified in the reference, of the goods or services concerned; or

 (b) an acquisition, of a description specified in the reference, of the goods or services concerned.

(3) A description of the kind mentioned in subsection (2)(a) or (b) may, in particular, be by reference to –

 (a) the place where the goods or services are supplied or acquired; or

 (b) the persons by or to whom they are supplied or by or from whom they are acquired.

Determination of references

134 Questions to be decided on market investigation references

(1) The Commission shall, on a market investigation reference, decide whether any feature, or combination of features, of each relevant market prevents, restricts or distorts competition in connection with the supply or acquisition of any goods or services in the United Kingdom or a part of the United Kingdom.

(2) For the purposes of this Part, in relation to a market investigation reference, there is an adverse effect on competition if any feature, or combination of features, of a relevant market prevents, restricts or distorts competition in connection with the supply or acquisition of any goods or services in the United Kingdom or a part of the United Kingdom.

(3) In subsections (1) and (2) 'relevant market' means –

    (a)   in the case of subsection (2) so far as it applies in connection with a possible reference, a market in the United Kingdom –

        (i)   for goods or services of a description to be specified in the reference; and

        (ii)   which would not be excluded from investigation by virtue of section 133(2); and

    (b)   in any other case, a market in the United Kingdom –

        (i)   for goods or services of a description specified in the reference concerned; and

        (ii)   which is not excluded from investigation by virtue of section 133(2).

(4) The Commission shall, if it has decided on a market investigation reference that there is an adverse effect on competition, decide the following additional questions –

    (a)   whether action should be taken by it under section 138 for the purpose of remedying, mitigating or preventing the adverse effect on competition concerned or any detrimental effect on customers so far as it has resulted from, or may be expected to result from, the adverse effect on competition;

    (b)   whether it should recommend the taking of action by others for the purpose of remedying, mitigating or preventing the adverse effect on competition concerned or any detrimental effect on customers so far as it has resulted from, or may be expected to result from, the adverse effect on competition; and

    (c)   in either case, if action should be taken, what action should be taken and what is to be remedied, mitigated or prevented.

(5) For the purposes of this Part, in relation to a market investigation reference, there is a detrimental effect on customers if there is a detrimental effect on customers or future customers in the form of –

    (a)   higher prices, lower quality or less choice of goods or services in any market in the United Kingdom (whether or not the market to which the feature or features concerned relate); or

    (b)   less innovation in relation to such goods or services.

(6) In deciding the questions mentioned in subsection (4), the Commission shall, in particular, have regard to the need to achieve as comprehensive a solution as is reasonable and practicable to the adverse effect on competition and any detrimental effects on customers so far as resulting from the adverse effect on competition.

(7) In deciding the questions mentioned in subsection (4), the Commission may, in particular, have regard to the effect of any action on any relevant customer benefits of the feature or features of the market concerned.

(8) For the purposes of this Part a benefit is a relevant customer benefit of a feature or features of a market if –

    (a)   it is a benefit to customers or future customers in the form of –

        (i)   lower prices, higher quality or greater choice of goods or services in any market in the United Kingdom (whether or not the market to which the feature or features concerned relate); or

        (ii)   greater innovation in relation to such goods or services; and

    (b)   the Commission, the Secretary of State or (as the case may be) the OFT believes that –

        (i)   the benefit has accrued as a result (whether wholly or partly) of the feature or features concerned or may be expected to accrue within a reasonable period as a result (whether wholly or partly) of that feature or those features; and

        (ii)   the benefit was, or is, unlikely to accrue without the feature or features concerned.

135 Variation of market investigation references

(1) The OFT or (as the case may be) the appropriate Minister may at any time vary a market investigation reference made by it or (as the case may be) him.

(2) The OFT or (as the case may be) the appropriate Minister shall consult the Commission before varying any such reference.

(3) Subsection (2) shall not apply if the Commission has requested the variation concerned.

(4) No variation under this section shall be capable of altering the period permitted by section 137 within which the report of the Commission under section 136 is to be prepared and published or (as the case may be) the period permitted by section 144 within which the report of the Commission under section 142 is to be prepared and published or given.

136 Investigations and reports on market investigation references

(1) The Commission shall prepare and publish a report on a market investigation reference within the period permitted by section 137.

(2) The report shall, in particular, contain –

    (a)   the decisions of the Commission on the questions which it is required to answer by virtue of section 134;

    (b)   its reasons for its decisions; and

(c)   such information as the Commission considers appropriate for facilitating a proper understanding of those questions and of its reasons for its decisions.

(3) The Commission shall carry out such investigations as it considers appropriate for the purposes of preparing a report under this section.

(4) The Commission shall, at the same time as a report under this section is published –

(a)   in the case of a reference under section 131, give it to the OFT; and

(b)   in the case of a reference under section 132, give it to the appropriate Minister and give a copy of it to the OFT.

(5) Where a reference has been made by the OFT under section 131 or by the appropriate Minister under section 132 in circumstances in which a reference could have been made by a relevant sectoral regulator under section 131 as it has effect by virtue of a relevant sectoral enactment, the Commission shall, at the same time as the report under this section is published, give a copy of it to the relevant sectoral regulator concerned.

(6) Where a reference has been made by a relevant sectoral regulator under section 131 as it has effect by virtue of a relevant sectoral enactment, the Commission shall, at the same time as the report under this section is published, give a copy of it to the OFT.

(7) In this Part 'relevant sectoral enactment' means –

(a)   in relation to the Director General of Telecommunications, section 50 of the Telecommunications Act 1984;

(b)   in relation to the Gas and Electricity Markets Authority, section 36A of the Gas Act 1986 or (as the case may be) section 43 of the Electricity Act 1989;

(c)   in relation to the Director General of Water Services, section 31 of the Water Industry Act 1991;

(d)   in relation to the Director General of Electricity Supply for Northern Ireland, article 46 of the Electricity (Northern Ireland) Order 1992 (SI 1992/231 (NI 1));

(e)   in relation to the Rail Regulator, section 67 of the Railways Act 1993;

(f)   in relation to the Director General of Gas for Northern Ireland, article 23 of the Gas (Northern Ireland) Order 1996 (SI 1996/275 (NI 2)); and

(g)   in relation to the Civil Aviation Authority, section 86 of the Transport Act 2000.

(8) In this Part 'relevant sectoral regulator' means the Director General of Telecommunications, the Gas and Electricity Markets Authority, the Director General of Water Services, the Director General of Electricity Supply for Northern Ireland, the Rail Regulator, the Director General of Gas for Northern Ireland or the Civil Aviation Authority.

(9) The Secretary of State may by order modify subsection (7) or (8).

137 Time-limits for market investigations and reports

(1) The Commission shall prepare and publish its report under section 136 within the period of two years beginning with the date of the market investigation reference concerned.

(2) Subsection (1) is subject to section 151(3) and (5).

(3) The Secretary of State may by order amend subsection (1) so as to alter the period of two years mentioned in that subsection or any period for the time being mentioned in that subsection in substitution for that period.

(4) No alteration shall be made by virtue of subsection (3) which results in the period for the time being mentioned in subsection (1) exceeding two years.

(5) An order under subsection (3) shall not affect any period of time within which the Commission is under a duty to prepare and publish its report under section 136 in relation to a market investigation reference if the Commission is already under that duty in relation to that reference when the order is made.

(6) Before making an order under subsection (3) the Secretary of State shall consult the Commission and such other persons as he considers appropriate.

(7) References in this Part to the date of a market investigation reference shall be construed as references to the date specified in the reference as the date on which it is made.

138 Duty to remedy adverse effects

(1) Subsection (2) applies where a report of the Commission has been prepared and published under section 136 within the period permitted by section 137 and contains the decision that there is one or more than one adverse effect on competition.

(2) The Commission shall, in relation to each adverse effect on competition, take such action under section 159 or 161 as it considers to be reasonable and practicable –

    (a)   to remedy, mitigate or prevent the adverse effect on competition concerned; and

    (b)   to remedy, mitigate or prevent any detrimental effects on customers so far as they have resulted from, or may be expected to result from, the adverse effect on competition.

(3) The decisions of the Commission under subsection (2) shall be consistent with its decisions as included in its report by virtue of section 134(4) unless there has been a material change of circumstances since the preparation of the report or the Commission otherwise has a special reason for deciding differently.

(4) In making a decision under subsection (2), the Commission shall, in particular, have regard to the need to achieve as comprehensive a solution as is reasonable and practicable to the adverse effect on competition concerned and any detrimental effects on customers so far as resulting from the adverse effect on competition.

(5) In making a decision under subsection (2), the Commission may, in particular, have regard to the effect of any action on any relevant customer benefits of the feature or features of the market concerned.

(6) The Commission shall take no action under subsection (2) to remedy, mitigate or prevent any detrimental effect on customers so far as it may be expected to result from the adverse effect on competition concerned if –

    (a)   no detrimental effect on customers has resulted from the adverse effect on competition; and

    (b)   the adverse effect on competition is not being remedied, mitigated or prevented.

CHAPTER 2
PUBLIC INTEREST CASES

Intervention notices

139 Public interest intervention by Secretary of State

(1) The Secretary of State may give a notice to the Commission if –

    (a)   a market investigation reference has been made to the Commission;

    (b)   no more than four months has passed since the date of the reference;

    (c)   the reference is not finally determined; and

    (d)   the Secretary of State believes that it is or may be the case that one or more than one public interest consideration is relevant to the case.

(2) The Secretary of State may give a notice to the OFT if –

    (a)   the OFT is considering whether to accept –

        (i)   an undertaking under section 154 instead of making a reference under section 131; or

        (ii)   an undertaking varying or superseding any such undertaking;

    (b)   the OFT has published a notice under section 155(1) or (4); and

    (c)   the Secretary of State believes that it is or may be the case that one or more than one public interest consideration is relevant to the case.

(3) In this Part 'intervention notice' means a notice under subsection (1) or (2).

(4) No more than one intervention notice shall be given under subsection (1) in relation to the same market investigation reference and no more than one intervention notice shall be given under subsection (2) in relation to the same proposed undertaking or in relation to proposed undertakings which do not differ from each other in any material respect.

(5) For the purposes of this Part a public interest consideration is a consideration which, at the time of the giving of the intervention notice concerned, is specified in section 153 or is not so specified but, in the opinion of the Secretary of State, ought to be so specified.

(6) Where the Secretary of State has given an intervention notice mentioning a public interest consideration which, at that time, is not finalised, he shall, as soon as practicable, take such action as is within his power to ensure that it is finalised.

(7) For the purposes of this Part a public interest consideration is finalised if –

(a) it is specified in section 153 otherwise than by virtue of an order under subsection (3) of that section; or

(b) it is specified in that section by virtue of an order under subsection (3) of that section and the order providing for it to be so specified has been laid before, and approved by, Parliament in accordance with subsection (6) of section 181 and within the period mentioned in that subsection.

Intervention notices under section 139(1)

140 Intervention notices under section 139(1)

(1) An intervention notice under section 139(1) shall state –

(a) the market investigation reference concerned;

(b) the date of the market investigation reference concerned;

(c) the public interest consideration or considerations which are, or may be, relevant to the case; and

(d) where any public interest consideration concerned is not finalised, the proposed timetable for finalising it.

(2) Where the Secretary of State believes that it is or may be the case that two or more public interest considerations are relevant to the case, he may decide not to mention in the intervention notice such of those considerations as he considers appropriate.

(3) The Secretary of State may at any time revoke an intervention notice which has been given under section 139(1) and which is in force.

(4) An intervention notice under section 139(1) shall come into force when it is given and shall cease to be in force when the matter to which it relates is finally determined under this Chapter.

(5) For the purposes of subsection (4) a matter to which an intervention notice under section 139(1) relates is finally determined under this Chapter if –

(a) the period permitted by section 144 for the preparation of the report of the Commission under section 142 and for action to be taken in relation to it under section 143(1) or (3) has expired and no such report has been so prepared or no such action has been taken;

(b) the Commission decides under section 145(1) to terminate its investigation;

(c) the report of the Commission has been prepared under section 142 and published under section 143(1) within the period permitted by section 144;

(d) the Secretary of State fails to make and publish a decision under subsection (2) of section 146 within the period required by subsection (3) of that section;

(e) the Secretary of State decides under section 146(2) that no eligible public interest consideration is relevant;

(f) the Secretary of State decides under section 147(2) neither to accept an undertaking under section 159 nor to make an order under section 161;

(g)   the Secretary of State accepts an undertaking under section 159 or makes an order under section 161; or

(h)   the Secretary of State decides to revoke the intervention notice concerned.

(6) For the purposes of subsections (4) and (5) the time when a matter to which an intervention notice under section 139(1) relates is finally determined under this Chapter is –

(a)   in a case falling within subsection (5)(a) or (d), the expiry of the period concerned;

(b)   in a case falling within subsection (5)(b), (e), (f) or (h), the making of the decision concerned;

(c)   in a case falling within subsection (5)(c), the publication of the report concerned; and

(d)   in a case falling within subsection (5)(g), the acceptance of the undertaking concerned or (as the case may be) the making of the order concerned.

(7) In subsection (6)(d) the reference to the acceptance of the undertaking concerned or the making of the order concerned shall, in a case where the enforcement action under section 147(2) involves the acceptance of a group of undertakings, the making of a group of orders or the acceptance and making of a group of undertakings and orders, be treated as a reference to the acceptance or making of the last undertaking or order in the group; but undertakings or orders which vary, supersede or revoke earlier undertakings or orders shall be disregarded for the purposes of subsections (5)(g) and (6)(d).

141 Questions to be decided by Commission

(1) This section applies where an intervention notice under section 139(1) is in force in relation to a market investigation reference.

(2) The Commission shall decide whether any feature, or combination of features, of each relevant market (within the meaning given by section 134(3)) prevents, restricts or distorts competition in connection with the supply or acquisition of any goods or services in the United Kingdom or a part of the United Kingdom.

(3) The Commission shall, if it has decided that there is an adverse effect on competition, decide the following additional questions –

(a)   whether action should be taken by the Secretary of State under section 147 for the purpose of remedying, mitigating or preventing the adverse effect on competition concerned or any detrimental effect on customers so far as it has resulted from, or may be expected to result from, the adverse effect on competition;

(b)   whether the Commission should recommend the taking of other action by the Secretary of State or action by persons other than itself and the Secretary of State for the purpose of remedying, mitigating or preventing the adverse effect on competition concerned or any detrimental effect on customers so far as it has resulted from, or may be expected to result from, the adverse effect on competition; and

(c)   in either case, if action should be taken, what action should be taken and what is to be remedied, mitigated or prevented.

(4) The Commission shall, if it has decided that there is an adverse effect on competition, also decide separately the following questions (on the assumption that it is proceeding as mentioned in section 148(1)) –

(a)   whether action should be taken by it under section 138 for the purpose of remedying, mitigating or preventing the adverse effect on competition concerned or any detrimental effect on customers so far as it has resulted from, or may be expected to result from, the adverse effect on competition;

(b)   whether the Commission should recommend the taking of action by other persons for the purpose of remedying, mitigating or preventing the adverse effect on competition concerned or any detrimental effect on customers so far as it has resulted from, or may be expected to result from, the adverse effect on competition; and

(c)   in either case, if action should be taken, what action should be taken and what is to be remedied, mitigated or prevented.

(5) In deciding the questions mentioned in subsections (3) and (4), the Commission shall, in particular, have regard to the need to achieve as comprehensive a solution as is reasonable and practicable to the adverse effect on competition concerned and any detrimental effects on customers so far as resulting from the adverse effect on competition.

(6) In deciding the questions mentioned in subsections (3) and (4), the Commission may, in particular, have regard to the effect of any action on any relevant customer benefits of the feature or features of the market concerned.

142 Investigations and reports by Commission

(1) Where an intervention notice under section 139(1) is in force in relation to a market investigation reference, the Commission shall prepare a report on the reference and take action in relation to it under section 143(1) or (3) within the period permitted by section 144.

(2) The report shall, in particular, contain –

(a)   the decisions of the Commission on the questions which it is required to answer by virtue of section 141;

(b)   its reasons for its decisions; and

(c)   such information as the Commission considers appropriate for facilitating a proper understanding of those questions and of its reasons for its decisions.

(3) The Commission shall carry out such investigations as it considers appropriate for the purposes of preparing a report under this section.

143 Publication etc of reports of Commission

(1) The Commission shall publish a report under section 142 if it contains –

(a)   the decision of the Commission that there is no adverse effect on competition; or

(b)   the decisions of the Commission that there is one or more than one adverse effect on competition but, on the question mentioned in section 141(4)(a) and in relation to each adverse effect on competition, that no action should be taken by it.

(2) The Commission shall, at the same time as the report is published under subsection (1) –

(a)   in the case of a reference under section 131, give it to the OFT; and

(b)   in the case of a reference under section 132, give it to the appropriate Minister and give a copy of it to the OFT.

(3) Where a report under section 142 contains the decisions of the Commission that there is one or more than one adverse effect on competition and, on the question mentioned in section 141(4)(a) and in relation to at least one such adverse effect, that action should be taken by it, the Commission shall give the report to the Secretary of State.

(4) The Secretary of State shall publish, no later than publication of his decision under section 146(2) in relation to the case, a report of the Commission given to him under subsection (3) and not required to be published by virtue of section 148(2).

(5) The Secretary of State shall, at the same time as a report of the Commission given to him under subsection (3) is published under subsection (4), give a copy of it –

(a)   in the case of a reference under section 131, to the OFT; and

(b)   in the case of a reference under section 132, to any other Minister of the Crown who made the reference and to the OFT.

(6) Where a reference has been made by the OFT under section 131 or by the appropriate Minister under section 132 in circumstances in which a reference could have been made by a relevant sectoral regulator under section 131 as it has effect by virtue of a relevant sectoral enactment, the relevant authority shall, at the same time as the report under section 142 is published under subsection (1) or (4), give a copy of it to the relevant sectoral regulator concerned.

(7) Where a reference has been made by a relevant sectoral regulator under section 131 as it has effect by virtue of a relevant sectoral enactment, the relevant authority shall, at the same time as the report under section 142 is published under subsection (1) or (4), give a copy of it to the OFT.

(8) In subsections (6) and (7) 'the relevant authority' means –

(a)   in the case of a report published under subsection (1), the Commission; and

(b)   in the case of a report published under subsection (4), the Secretary of State.

144 Time-limits for investigations and reports: Part 4

(1) The Commission shall, within the period of two years beginning with the date of the reference, prepare its report under section 142 and publish it under subsection (1)

of section 143 or (as the case may be) give it to the Secretary of State under subsection (3) of that section.

(2) The Secretary of State may by order amend subsection (1) so as to alter the period of two years mentioned in that subsection or any period for the time being mentioned in that subsection in substitution for that period.

(3) No alteration shall be made by virtue of subsection (2) which results in the period for the time being mentioned in subsection (1) exceeding two years.

(4) An order under subsection (2) shall not affect any period of time within which, in relation to a market investigation reference, the Commission is under a duty to prepare its report under section 142 and take action in relation to it under section 143(1) or (3) if the Commission is already under that duty in relation to that reference when the order is made.

(5) Before making an order under subsection (2) the Secretary of State shall consult the Commission and such other persons as he considers appropriate.

145 Restrictions where public interest considerations not finalised: Part 4

(1) The Commission shall terminate its investigation under section 142 if –

    (a)   the intervention notice concerned mentions a public interest consideration which was not finalised on the giving of that notice or public interest considerations which, at that time, were not finalised;

    (b)   no other public interest consideration is mentioned in the notice;

    (c)   at least 24 weeks has elapsed since the giving of the notice; and

    (d)   the public interest consideration mentioned in the notice has not been finalised within that period of 24 weeks or (as the case may be) none of the public interest considerations mentioned in the notice has been finalised within that period of 24 weeks.

(2) Where the intervention notice concerned mentions a public interest consideration which is not finalised on the giving of the notice, the Commission shall not give its report under section 142 to the Secretary of State in accordance with section 143(3) unless the period of 24 weeks beginning with the giving of the intervention notice concerned has expired or the public interest consideration concerned has been finalised.

(3) The Commission shall, in reporting on any of the questions mentioned in section 141(3), disregard any public interest consideration which has not been finalised before the giving of the report.

(4) The Commission shall, in reporting on any of the questions mentioned in section 141(3), disregard any public interest consideration which was not finalised on the giving of the intervention notice concerned and has not been finalised within the period of 24 weeks beginning with the giving of the notice concerned.

(5) Subsections (1) to (4) are without prejudice to the power of the Commission to carry out investigations in relation to any public interest consideration to which it might be able to have regard in its report.

146 Decision of Secretary of State

(1) Subsection (2) applies where the Secretary of State has received a report of the Commission which –

    (a)   has been prepared under section 142;

    (b)   contains the decisions that there is one or more than one adverse effect on competition and, on the question mentioned in section 141(4)(a) and in relation to at least one such adverse effect, that action should be taken by it; and

    (c)   has been given to the Secretary of State as required by section 143(3).

(2) The Secretary of State shall decide whether –

    (a)   any eligible public interest consideration is relevant; or

    (b)   any eligible public interest considerations are relevant;

to any action which is mentioned in the report by virtue of section 141(4)(a) and (c) and which the Commission should take for the purpose of remedying, mitigating or preventing any adverse effect on competition concerned or any detrimental effect on customers so far as it has resulted or may be expected to result from any adverse effect on competition.

(3) The Secretary of State shall make and publish his decision under subsection (2) within the period of 90 days beginning with the receipt of the report of the Commission under section 142.

(4) In this section 'eligible public interest consideration' means a public interest consideration which –

    (a)   was mentioned in the intervention notice concerned; and

    (b)   was not disregarded by the Commission for the purposes of its report under section 142.

147 Remedial action by Secretary of State

(1) Subsection (2) applies where the Secretary of State –

    (a)   has decided under subsection (2) of section 146 within the period required by subsection (3) of that section that an eligible public interest consideration is relevant as mentioned in subsection (2) of that section or eligible public interest considerations are so relevant; and

    (b)   has published his decision within the period required by subsection (3) of that section.

(2) The Secretary of State may, in relation to any adverse effect on competition identified in the report concerned, take such action under section 159 or 161 as he considers to be –

    (a)   reasonable and practicable –

        (i)   to remedy, mitigate or prevent the adverse effect on competition concerned; or

        (ii)   to remedy, mitigate or prevent any detrimental effect on customers so far as it has resulted from, or may be expected to result from, the adverse effect on competition; and

(b)   appropriate in the light of the eligible public interest consideration concerned or (as the case may be) the eligible public interest considerations concerned.

(3) In making a decision under subsection (2), the Secretary of State shall, in particular, have regard to –

(a)   the need to achieve as comprehensive a solution as is reasonable and practicable to the adverse effect on competition concerned and any detrimental effects on customers so far as resulting from the adverse effect on competition; and

(b)   the report of the Commission under section 142.

(4) In having regard by virtue of subsection (3) to the report of the Commission under section 142, the Secretary of State shall not challenge the decision of the Commission contained in the report that there is one or more than one adverse effect on competition.

(5) In making a decision under subsection (2), the Secretary of State may, in particular, have regard to the effect of any action on any relevant customer benefits of the feature or features of the market concerned.

(6) The Secretary of State shall take no action under subsection (2) to remedy, mitigate or prevent any detrimental effect on customers so far as it may be expected to result from the adverse effect on competition concerned if –

(a)   no detrimental effect on customers has resulted from the adverse effect on competition; and

(b)   the adverse effect on competition is not being remedied, mitigated or prevented.

(7) In this section 'eligible public interest consideration' has the same meaning as in section 146.

148 Reversion of the matter to the Commission

(1) If –

(a)   the Secretary of State fails to make and publish his decision under subsection (2) of section 146 within the period required by subsection (3) of that section; or

(b)   the Secretary of State decides that no eligible public interest consideration is relevant as mentioned in subsection (2) of that section;

the Commission shall proceed under section 138 as if the report had been prepared and published under section 136 within the period permitted by section 137.

(2) The Commission shall publish the report which has been prepared by it under section 142 (if still unpublished) as soon as it becomes able to proceed by virtue of subsection (1).

(3) The Commission shall, at the same time as its report is published under subsection (2), give a copy of it –

(a)   in the case of a reference under section 131, to the OFT; and

(b)   in the case of a reference under section 132, to any Minister of the Crown who made the reference (other than the Secretary of State) and to the OFT.

(4) Where a reference has been made by the OFT under section 131 or by the appropriate Minister under section 132 in circumstances in which a reference could have been made by a relevant sectoral regulator under section 131 as it has effect by virtue of a relevant sectoral enactment, the Commission shall, at the same time as its report is published under subsection (2), give a copy of it to the relevant sectoral regulator concerned.

(5) Where a reference has been made by a relevant sectoral regulator under section 131 as it has effect by virtue of a relevant sectoral enactment, the Commission shall, at the same time as its report is published under subsection (2), give a copy of it to the OFT.

(6) In relation to proceedings by virtue of subsection (1), the reference in section 138(3) to decisions of the Commission included in its report by virtue of section 134(4) shall be construed as a reference to decisions which were included in the report of the Commission by virtue of section 141(4).

(7) Where the Commission, in proceeding by virtue of subsection (1), intends to proceed in a way which is not consistent with its decisions as included in its report by virtue of section 141(4), it shall not so proceed without the consent of the Secretary of State.

(8) The Secretary of State shall not withhold his consent under subsection (7) unless he believes that the proposed alternative way of proceeding will operate against the public interest.

(9) For the purposes of subsection (8) a proposed alternative way of proceeding will operate against the public interest only if any eligible public interest consideration or considerations outweigh the considerations which have led the Commission to propose proceeding in that way.

(10) In deciding whether to withhold his consent under subsection (7), the Secretary of State shall accept the Commission's view of what, if the only relevant consideration were how to remedy, mitigate or prevent the adverse effect on competition concerned or any detrimental effect on customers so far as resulting from the adverse effect on competition, would be the most appropriate way to proceed.

(11) In this section 'eligible public interest consideration' has the same meaning as in section 146.

Intervention notices under section 139(2)

149 Intervention notices under section 139(2)

(1) An intervention notice under section 139(2) shall state –

(a)   the proposed undertaking which may be accepted by the OFT;

(b)   the notice under section 155(1) or (4);

(c)   the public interest consideration or considerations which are, or may be, relevant to the case; and

(d)   where any public interest consideration concerned is not finalised, the proposed timetable for finalising it.

(2) Where the Secretary of State believes that it is or may be the case that two or more public interest considerations are relevant to the case, he may decide not to mention in the intervention notice such of those considerations as he considers appropriate.

(3) The Secretary of State may at any time revoke an intervention notice which has been given under section 139(2) and which is in force.

(4) An intervention notice under section 139(2) shall come into force when it is given and shall cease to be in force on the occurrence of any of the events mentioned in subsection (5).

(5) The events are –

(a)   the acceptance by the OFT with the consent of the Secretary of State of an undertaking which is the same as the proposed undertaking mentioned in the intervention notice by virtue of subsection (1)(a) or which does not differ from it in any material respect;

(b)   the decision of the OFT to proceed neither with the proposed undertaking mentioned in the intervention notice by virtue of subsection (1)(a) nor a proposed undertaking which does not differ from it in any material respect; or

(c)   the decision of the Secretary of State to revoke the intervention notice concerned.

150 Power of veto of Secretary of State

(1) Where an intervention notice under section 139(2) is in force, the OFT shall not, without the consent of the Secretary of State, accept the proposed undertaking concerned or a proposed undertaking which does not differ from it in any material respect.

(2) The Secretary of State shall withhold his consent if he believes that it is or may be the case that the proposed undertaking will, if accepted, operate against the public interest.

(3) For the purposes of subsection (2) a proposed undertaking will, if accepted, operate against the public interest only if any public interest consideration which is mentioned in the intervention notice concerned and has been finalised, or any public interest considerations which are so mentioned and have been finalised, outweigh the considerations which have led the OFT to propose accepting the undertaking.

(4) In making his decision under subsection (2) the Secretary of State shall accept the OFT's view of what undertakings, if the only relevant consideration were how to remedy, mitigate or prevent the adverse effect on competition concerned or any detrimental effect on customers so far as resulting from the adverse effect on competition, would be most appropriate.

(5) Where a public interest consideration which is mentioned in the intervention notice concerned is not finalised on the giving of the notice, the Secretary of State shall not make his decision as to whether to give his consent under this section before –

(a)   the end of the period of 24 weeks beginning with the giving of the intervention notice; or

(b)   if earlier, the date on which the public interest consideration concerned has been finalised.

(6) Subject to subsections (2) to (5), the Secretary of State shall not withhold his consent under this section.

Other

151 Further interaction of intervention notices with general procedure

(1) Where an intervention notice under section 139(1) comes into force in relation to a market investigation reference, sections 134(1), (4), (6) and (7), 136(1) to (6), 137(1) to (6) and 138 shall cease to apply in relation to that reference.

(2) Where the Secretary of State revokes an intervention notice which has been given under section 139(1), the Commission shall instead proceed under sections 134 and 136 to 138.

(3) Where the Commission is proceeding by virtue of subsection (2), the period within which the Commission shall prepare and publish its report under section 136 shall be extended by an additional period of 20 days.

(4) Where the Commission terminates its investigation under section 145(1), the Commission shall proceed under sections 134 and 136 to 138.

(5) Where the Commission is proceeding by virtue of subsection (4), the period within which the Commission shall prepare and publish its report under section 136 shall be extended by an additional period of 20 days.

(6) In determining the period of 20 days mentioned in subsection (3) or (5) no account shall be taken of –

(a)   Saturday, Sunday, Good Friday and Christmas Day; and

(b)   any day which is a bank holiday in England and Wales.

152 Certain duties of OFT and Commission

(1) The OFT shall, in considering whether to make a reference under section 131, bring to the attention of the Secretary of State any case which it believes raises any consideration specified in section 153 unless it believes that the Secretary of State would consider any such consideration immaterial in the context of the particular case.

(2) The Commission shall, in investigating any reference made to it under section 131 or 132 within the previous four months, bring to the attention of the Secretary of State any case which it believes raises any consideration specified in section 153 unless

it believes that the Secretary of State would consider any such consideration immaterial in the context of the particular case.

(3) The OFT and the Commission shall bring to the attention of the Secretary of State any representations about exercising his power under section 153(3) which have been made to the OFT or (as the case may be) the Commission.

153 Specified considerations: Part 4

(1) The interests of national security are specified in this section.

(2) In subsection (1) 'national security' includes public security; and in this subsection 'public security' has the same meaning as in article 21(3) of Council Regulation (EEC) No 4064/89 of 21st December 1989 on the control of concentrations between undertakings as amended by Council Regulation (EC) No 1310/97 of 30th June 1997.

(3) The Secretary of State may by order modify this section for the purpose of specifying in this section a new consideration or removing or amending any consideration which is for the time being specified in this section.

(4) An order under this section may apply in relation to cases under consideration by the OFT, by the Secretary of State, by the appropriate Minister (other than the Secretary of State acting alone) or by the Commission before the making of the order as well as cases under consideration on or after the making of the order.

CHAPTER 3
ENFORCEMENT

Undertakings and orders

154 Undertakings in lieu of market investigation references

(1) Subsection (2) applies if the OFT considers that it has the power to make a reference under section 131 and otherwise intends to make such a reference.

(2) The OFT may, instead of making such a reference and for the purpose of remedying, mitigating or preventing –

    (a)   any adverse effect on competition concerned; or

    (b)   any detrimental effect on customers so far as it has resulted from, or may be expected to result from, the adverse effect on competition;

accept, from such persons as it considers appropriate, undertakings to take such action as it considers appropriate.

(3) In proceeding under subsection (2), the OFT shall, in particular, have regard to the need to achieve as comprehensive a solution as is reasonable and practicable to the adverse effect on competition concerned and any detrimental effects on customers so far as resulting from the adverse effect on competition.

(4) In proceeding under subsection (2), the OFT may, in particular, have regard to the effect of any action on any relevant customer benefits of the feature or features of the market concerned.

(5) The OFT shall take no action under subsection (2) to remedy, mitigate or prevent any detrimental effect on customers so far as it may be expected to result from the adverse effect on competition concerned if –

(a) no detrimental effect on customers has resulted from the adverse effect on competition; and

(b) the adverse effect on competition is not being remedied, mitigated or prevented.

(6) An undertaking under this section –

(a) shall come into force when accepted;

(b) may be varied or superseded by another undertaking; and

(c) may be released by the OFT.

(7) The OFT shall, as soon as reasonably practicable, consider any representations received by it in relation to varying or releasing an undertaking under this section.

(8) This section is subject to sections 150 and 155.

155 Undertakings in lieu: procedural requirements

(1) Before accepting an undertaking under section 154 (other than an undertaking under that section which varies an undertaking under that section but not in any material respect), the OFT shall –

(a) publish notice of the proposed undertaking; and

(b) consider any representations made in accordance with the notice and not withdrawn.

(2) A notice under subsection (1) shall state –

(a) that the OFT proposes to accept the undertaking;

(b) the purpose and effect of the undertaking;

(c) the situation that the undertaking is seeking to deal with;

(d) any other facts which the OFT considers justify the acceptance of the undertaking;

(e) a means of gaining access to an accurate version of the proposed undertaking at all reasonable times; and

(f) the period (not less than 15 days starting with the date of publication of the notice) within which representations may be made in relation to the proposed undertaking.

(3) The matters to be included in a notice under subsection (1) by virtue of subsection (2) shall, in particular, include –

(a) the terms of the reference under section 131 which the OFT considers that it has power to make and which it otherwise intends to make; and

(b) the adverse effect on competition, and any detrimental effect on customers so far as resulting from the adverse effect on competition, which the OFT has identified.

(4) The OFT shall not accept the undertaking with modifications unless it –

(a) publishes notice of the proposed modifications; and

(b)   considers any representations made in accordance with the notice and not withdrawn.

(5) A notice under subsection (4) shall state –

(a)   the proposed modifications;

(b)   the reasons for them; and

(c)   the period (not less than 7 days starting with the date of the publication of the notice under subsection (4)) within which representations may be made in relation to the proposed modifications.

(6) If, after publishing notice under subsection (1) or (4), the OFT decides –

(a)   not to accept the undertaking concerned; and

(b)   not to proceed by virtue of subsection (8) or (9);

it shall publish notice of that decision.

(7) As soon as practicable after accepting an undertaking to which this section applies, the OFT shall –

(a)   serve a copy of the undertaking on any person by whom it is given; and

(b)   publish the undertaking.

(8) The requirements of subsection (4) (and those of subsection (1)) shall not apply if the OFT –

(a)   has already published notice under subsection (1) but not subsection (4) in relation to the proposed undertaking; and

(b)   considers that the modifications which are now being proposed are not material in any respect.

(9) The requirements of subsection (4) (and those of subsection (1)) shall not apply if the OFT –

(a)   has already published notice under subsections (1) and (4) in relation to the matter concerned; and

(b)   considers that the further modifications which are now being proposed do not differ in any material respect from the modifications in relation to which notice was last given under subsection (4).

(10) Paragraphs 6 to 8 (but not paragraph 9) of Schedule 10 (procedural requirements before terminating undertakings) shall apply in relation to the proposed release of undertakings under section 154 (other than in connection with accepting an undertaking under that section which varies or supersedes an undertaking under that section) as they apply in relation to the proposed release of undertakings under section 73.

156 Effect of undertakings under section 154

(1) No market investigation reference shall be made by the OFT or the appropriate Minister in relation to any feature, or combination of features, of a market in the United Kingdom for goods or services if –

(a)   the OFT has accepted an undertaking or group of undertakings under section 154 within the previous 12 months; and

(b)   the goods or services to which the undertaking or group of undertakings relates are of the same description as the goods or services to which the feature, or combination of features, relates.

(2) Subsection (1) does not prevent the making of a market investigation reference if –

(a)   the OFT considers that any undertaking concerned has been breached and has given notice of that fact to the person responsible for giving the undertaking; or

(b)   the person responsible for giving any undertaking concerned supplied, in connection with the matter, information to the OFT which was false or misleading in a material respect.

157 Interim undertakings: Part 4

(1) Subsection (2) applies where –

(a)   a market investigation reference has been made;

(b)   a report has been published under section 136 within the period permitted by section 137 or (as the case may be) a report prepared under section 142 and given to the Secretary of State under section 143(3) within the period permitted by section 144 has been published; and

(c)   the market investigation reference concerned is not finally determined.

(2) The relevant authority may, for the purpose of preventing pre-emptive action, accept, from such persons as the relevant authority considers appropriate, undertakings to take such action as the relevant authority considers appropriate.

(3) An undertaking under this section –

(a)   shall come into force when accepted;

(b)   may be varied or superseded by another undertaking; and

(c)   may be released by the relevant authority.

(4) An undertaking under this section shall, if it has not previously ceased to be in force, cease to be in force when the market investigation reference is finally determined.

(5) The relevant authority shall, as soon as reasonably practicable, consider any representations received by the relevant authority in relation to varying or releasing an undertaking under this section.

(6) In this section and section 158 –

'pre-emptive action' means action which might impede the taking of any action under section 138(2) or (as the case may be) 147(2) in relation to the market investigation reference concerned; and

'the relevant authority' means –

(a)   where an intervention notice is in force in relation to the market investigation reference, the Secretary of State;

(b)   in any other case, the Commission.

158 Interim orders: Part 4

(1) Subsection (2) applies where –

    (a)   a market investigation reference has been made;

    (b)   a report has been published under section 136 within the period permitted by section 137 or (as the case may be) a report prepared under section 142 and given to the Secretary of State under section 143(3) within the period permitted by section 144 has been published; and

    (c)   the market investigation reference concerned is not finally determined.

(2) The relevant authority may by order, for the purpose of preventing pre-emptive action –

    (a)   prohibit or restrict the doing of things which the relevant authority considers would constitute pre-emptive action;

    (b)   impose on any person concerned obligations as to the carrying on of any activities or the safeguarding of any assets;

    (c)   provide for the carrying on of any activities or the safeguarding of any assets either by the appointment of a person to conduct or supervise the conduct of any activities (on such terms and with such powers as may be specified or described in the order) or in any other manner;

    (d)   do anything which may be done by virtue of paragraph 19 of Schedule 8.

(3) An order under this section –

    (a)   shall come into force at such time as is determined by or under the order; and

    (b)   may be varied or revoked by another order.

(4) An order under this section shall, if it has not previously ceased to be in force, cease to be in force when the market investigation reference is finally determined.

(5) The relevant authority shall, as soon as reasonably practicable, consider any representations received by the relevant authority in relation to varying or revoking an order under this section.

159 Final undertakings: Part 4

(1) The Commission may, in accordance with section 138, accept, from such persons as it considers appropriate, undertakings to take action specified or described in the undertakings.

(2) The Secretary of State may, in accordance with section 147, accept, from such persons as he considers appropriate, undertakings to take action specified or described in the undertakings.

(3) An undertaking under this section shall come into force when accepted.

(4) An undertaking under subsection (1) or (2) may be varied or superseded by another undertaking under that subsection.

(5) An undertaking under subsection (1) may be released by the Commission and an undertaking under subsection (2) may be released by the Secretary of State.

(6) The Commission or (as the case may be) the Secretary of State shall, as soon as reasonably practicable, consider any representations received by it or (as the case may be) him in relation to varying or releasing an undertaking under this section.

160 Order-making power where final undertakings not fulfilled: Part 4

(1) Subsection (2) applies where the relevant authority considers that –

    (a)   an undertaking accepted by the relevant authority under section 159 has not been, is not being or will not be fulfilled; or

    (b)   in relation to an undertaking accepted by the relevant authority under that section, information which was false or misleading in a material respect was given to the relevant authority or the OFT by the person giving the undertaking before the relevant authority decided to accept the undertaking.

(2) The relevant authority may, for any of the purposes mentioned in section 138(2) or (as the case may be) 147(2), make an order under this section.

(3) Subsections (3) to (6) of section 138 or (as the case may be) 147 shall apply for the purposes of subsection (2) above as they apply for the purposes of that section.

(4) An order under this section may contain –

    (a)   anything permitted by Schedule 8; and

    (b)   such supplementary, consequential or incidental provision as the relevant authority considers appropriate.

(5) An order under this section –

    (a)   shall come into force at such time as is determined by or under the order;

    (b)   may contain provision which is different from the provision contained in the undertaking concerned; and

    (c)   may be varied or revoked by another order.

(6) No order shall be varied or revoked under this section unless the OFT advises that such a variation or revocation is appropriate by reason of a change of circumstances.

(7) In this section 'the relevant authority' means –

    (a)   in the case of an undertaking accepted under section 159 by the Commission, the Commission; and

    (b)   in the case of an undertaking accepted under that section by the Secretary of State, the Secretary of State.

161 Final orders: Part 4

(1) The Commission may, in accordance with section 138, make an order under this section.

(2) The Secretary of State may, in accordance with section 147, make an order under this section.

(3) An order under this section may contain –

    (a)   anything permitted by Schedule 8; and

    (b)   such supplementary, consequential or incidental provision as the person making it considers appropriate.

(4) An order under this section –

    (a)   shall come into force at such time as is determined by or under the order; and

    (b)   may be varied or revoked by another order.

(5) No order shall be varied or revoked under this section unless the OFT advises that such a variation or revocation is appropriate by reason of a change of circumstances.

Enforcement functions of OFT

162 Duty of OFT to monitor undertakings and orders: Part 4

(1) The OFT shall keep under review the carrying out of any enforcement undertaking or any enforcement order.

(2) The OFT shall, in particular, from time to time consider –

    (a)   whether an enforcement undertaking or enforcement order has been or is being complied with;

    (b)   whether, by reason of any change of circumstances, an enforcement undertaking is no longer appropriate and –

        (i)   one or more of the parties to it can be released from it; or

        (ii)   it needs to be varied or to be superseded by a new enforcement undertaking; and

    (c)   whether, by reason of any change of circumstances, an enforcement order is no longer appropriate and needs to be varied or revoked.

(3) The OFT shall give the Commission or (as the case may be) the Secretary of State such advice as it considers appropriate in relation to –

    (a)   any possible variation or release by the Commission or (as the case may be) the Secretary of State of an enforcement undertaking accepted by it or (as the case may be) him;

    (b)   any possible new enforcement undertaking to be accepted by the Commission or (as the case may be) the Secretary of State so as to supersede another enforcement undertaking given to the Commission or (as the case may be) the Secretary of State;

    (c)   any possible variation or revocation by the Commission or (as the case may be) the Secretary of State of an enforcement order made by the Commission or (as the case may be) the Secretary of State;

    (d)   any possible enforcement undertaking to be accepted by the Commission or (as the case may be) the Secretary of State instead of an enforcement order or any possible enforcement order to be made by the Commission or (as the case may be) the Secretary of State instead of an enforcement undertaking; or

(e) the enforcement by virtue of section 167(6) to (8) of any enforcement undertaking or enforcement order.

(4) The OFT shall take such action as it considers appropriate in relation to –

(a) any possible variation or release by it of an undertaking accepted by it under section 154;

(b) any possible new undertaking to be accepted by it under section 154 so as to supersede another undertaking given to it under that section; or

(c) the enforcement by it by virtue of section 167(6) of any enforcement undertaking or enforcement order.

(5) The OFT shall keep under review the effectiveness of enforcement undertakings accepted under this Part and enforcement orders made under this Part.

(6) The OFT shall, whenever requested to do so by the Secretary of State and otherwise from time to time, prepare a report of its findings under subsection (5).

(7) The OFT shall –

(a) give any report prepared by it under subsection (6) to the Commission;

(b) give a copy of the report to the Secretary of State; and

(c) publish the report.

(8) In this Part –

'enforcement order' means an order made under section 158, 160 or 161; and

'enforcement undertaking' means an undertaking accepted under section 154, 157 or 159.

163 Further role of OFT in relation to undertakings and orders: Part 4

(1) Subsections (2) and (3) apply where the Commission or the Secretary of State (in this section 'the relevant authority') is considering whether to accept undertakings under section 157 or 159.

(2) The relevant authority may require the OFT to consult with such persons as the relevant authority considers appropriate with a view to discovering whether they will offer undertakings which the relevant authority would be prepared to accept under section 157 or (as the case may be) 159.

(3) The relevant authority may require the OFT to report to the relevant authority on the outcome of the OFT's consultations within such period as the relevant authority may require.

(4) A report under subsection (3) shall, in particular, contain advice from the OFT as to whether any undertakings offered should be accepted by the relevant authority under section 157 or (as the case may be) 159.

(5) The powers conferred on the relevant authority by subsections (1) to (4) are without prejudice to the power of the relevant authority to consult the persons concerned itself.

(6) If asked by the relevant authority for advice in relation to the taking of enforcement action (whether or not by way of undertakings) in a particular case, the OFT shall give such advice as it considers appropriate.

Supplementary

164 Enforcement undertakings and orders under this Part: general provisions

(1) The provision which may be contained in an enforcement undertaking is not limited to the provision which is permitted by Schedule 8.

(2) The following enactments in Part 3 shall apply in relation to enforcement orders under this Part as they apply in relation to enforcement orders under that Part –

    (a)   section 86(1) to (5) (enforcement orders: general provisions); and

    (b)   section 87 (power of directions conferred by enforcement order).

(3) An enforcement order under section 160 or 161 or any explanatory material accompanying the order shall state –

    (a)   the actions that the persons or description of persons to whom the order is addressed must do or (as the case may be) refrain from doing;

    (b)   the date on which the order comes into force;

    (c)   the possible consequences of not complying with the order; and

    (d)   the section of this Part under which a review can be sought in relation to the order.

165 Procedural requirements for certain undertakings and orders: Part 4

Schedule 10 (procedural requirements for certain undertakings and orders), other than paragraph 9 of that Schedule, shall apply in relation to undertakings under section 159 and orders under section 160 or 161 as it applies in relation to undertakings under section 82 and orders under section 83 or 84.

166 Register of undertakings and orders: Part 4

(1) The OFT shall compile and maintain a register for the purposes of this Part.

(2) The register shall be kept in such form as the OFT considers appropriate.

(3) The OFT shall ensure that the following matters are entered in the register –

    (a)   the provisions of any enforcement undertaking accepted by virtue of this Part (whether by the OFT, the Commission, the Secretary of State or a relevant sectoral regulator);

    (b)   the provisions of any enforcement order made by virtue of this Part (whether by the Commission, the Secretary of State or a relevant sectoral regulator); and

    (c)   the details of any variation, release or revocation of such an undertaking or order.

(4) The duty in subsection (3) does not extend to anything of which the OFT is unaware.

(5) The Commission, the Secretary of State and any relevant sectoral regulator shall inform the OFT of any matters which are to be included in the register by virtue of subsection (3) and which relate to enforcement undertakings accepted by them or enforcement orders made by them.

(6) The OFT shall ensure that the contents of the register are available to the public –

(a)   during (as a minimum) such hours as may be specified in an order made by the Secretary of State; and

(b)   subject to such reasonable fees (if any) as the OFT may determine.

(7) If requested by any person to do so and subject to such reasonable fees (if any) as the OFT may determine, the OFT shall supply the person concerned with a copy (certified to be true) of the register or of an extract from it.

167 Rights to enforce undertakings and orders under this Part

(1) This section applies to any enforcement undertaking or enforcement order.

(2) Any person to whom such an undertaking or order relates shall have a duty to comply with it.

(3) The duty shall be owed to any person who may be affected by a contravention of the undertaking or (as the case may be) order.

(4) Any breach of the duty which causes such a person to sustain loss or damage shall be actionable by him.

(5) In any proceedings brought under subsection (4) against a person to whom an enforcement undertaking or enforcement order relates it shall be a defence for that person to show that he took all reasonable steps and exercised all due diligence to avoid contravening the undertaking or (as the case may be) order.

(6) Compliance with an enforcement undertaking or an enforcement order shall also be enforceable by civil proceedings brought by the OFT for an injunction or for interdict or for any other appropriate relief or remedy.

(7) Compliance with an undertaking accepted under section 157 or 159, or an order under section 158, 160 or 161, shall also be enforceable by civil proceedings brought by the relevant authority for an injunction or for interdict or for any other appropriate relief or remedy.

(8) In subsection (7) 'the relevant authority' means –

(a)   in the case of an undertaking accepted by the Commission or an order made by the Commission, the Commission; and

(b)   in the case of an undertaking accepted by the Secretary of State or an order made by the Secretary of State, the Secretary of State.

(9) Subsections (6) to (8) shall not prejudice any right that a person may have by virtue of subsection (4) to bring civil proceedings for contravention or apprehended contravention of an enforcement undertaking or an enforcement order.

CHAPTER 4
SUPPLEMENTARY

Regulated markets

168 Regulated markets

(1) Subsection (2) applies where the Commission or the Secretary of State is considering for the purposes of this Part whether relevant action would be reasonable and practicable for the purpose of remedying, mitigating or preventing an adverse effect on competition or any detrimental effect on customers so far as resulting from such an effect.

(2) The Commission or (as the case may be) the Secretary of State shall, in deciding whether such action would be reasonable and practicable, have regard to the relevant statutory functions of the sectoral regulator concerned.

(3) In this section 'relevant action' means –

    (a)   modifying the conditions of a licence granted under section 7 of the Telecommunications Act 1984;

    (b)   modifying conditions in force under Part 4 of the Airports Act 1986 other than any conditions imposed or modified in pursuance of section 40(3) or (4) of that Act;

    (c)   modifying the conditions of a licence granted under section 7 or 7A of the Gas Act 1986;

    (d)   modifying the conditions of a licence granted under section 6 of the Electricity Act 1989;

    (e)   modifying networking arrangements (within the meaning given by section 39(1) of the Broadcasting Act 1990);

    (f)   modifying the conditions of a company's appointment under Chapter 1 of Part 2 of the Water Industry Act 1991;

    (g)   modifying the conditions of a licence granted under article 10 of the Electricity (Northern Ireland) Order 1992 (SI 1992/231 (NI 1));

    (h)   modifying the conditions of a licence granted under section 8 of the Railways Act 1993;

    (i)   modifying an access agreement (within the meaning given by section 83(1) of the Act of 1993) or a franchise agreement (within the meaning given by section 23(3) of that Act);

    (j)   modifying conditions in force under Part 4 of the Airports (Northern Ireland) Order 1994 (SI 1994/426 (NI 1)) other than any conditions imposed or modified in pursuance of article 40(3) or (4) of that Order;

    (k)   modifying the conditions of a licence granted under article 8 of the Gas (Northern Ireland) Order 1996 (SI 1996/275 (NI 2));

    (l)   modifying the conditions of a licence granted under section 11 of the Postal Services Act 2000; or

    (m)   modifying the conditions of a licence granted under section 5 of the Transport Act 2000.

(4) In this section 'relevant statutory functions' means –

(a) in relation to any licence granted under section 7 of the Telecommunications Act 1984, the duties and obligations of the Director General of Telecommunications imposed on him by or in pursuance of any enactment or other provision mentioned in section 7(5)(a) of that Act;

(b) in relation to conditions in force under Part 4 of the Airports Act 1986 other than any conditions imposed or modified in pursuance of section 40(3) or (4) of that Act, the duties of the Civil Aviation Authority under section 39(2) and (3) of that Act;

(c) in relation to any licence granted under section 7 or 7A of the Gas Act 1986, the objectives and duties of the Gas and Electricity Markets Authority under section 4AA and 4AB(2) of that Act;

(d) in relation to any licence granted under section 6 of the Electricity Act 1989, the objectives and duties of the Gas and Electricity Markets Authority under section 3A and 3B(2) of that Act;

(e) in relation to any networking arrangements (within the meaning given by section 39(1) of the Broadcasting Act 1990), the duties of the Independent Television Commission under section 2(2) of that Act;

(f) in relation to a company's appointment under Chapter 1 of Part 2 of the Water Industry Act 1991, the duties of the Director General of Water Services under section 2 of that Act;

(g) in relation to any licence granted under article 10 of the Electricity (Northern Ireland) Order 1992 (SI 1992/231 (NI 1)), the duty of the Director General of Electricity Supply for Northern Ireland under article 6 of that Order;

(h) in relation to any licence granted under section 8 of the Railways Act 1993 where none of the conditions of the licence relate to consumer protection, the duties of the Rail Regulator under section 4 of that Act;

(i) in relation to any licence granted under section 8 of the Act of 1993 where one or more than one condition of the licence relates to consumer protection, the duties of the Rail Regulator under section 4 of that Act and the duties of the Strategic Rail Authority under section 207 of the Transport Act 2000;

(j) in relation to any access agreement (within the meaning given by section 83(1) of the Act of 1993), the duties of the Rail Regulator under section 4 of the Act of 1993;

(k) in relation to any franchise agreement (within the meaning given by section 23(3) of the Act of 1993), the duties of the Strategic Rail Authority under section 207 of the Act of 2000;

(l) in relation to conditions in force under Part 4 of the Airports (Northern Ireland) Order 1994 (SI 1994/426 (NI 1)) other than any conditions imposed or modified in pursuance of article 40(3) or (4) of that Order, the duties of the Civil Aviation Authority under article 30(2) and (3) of that Order;

(m) in relation to any licence granted under article 8 of the Gas (Northern Ireland) Order 1996 (SI 1996/275 (NI 2)), the duties of the Director General of Gas for Northern Ireland under article 5 of that Order;

(n)   in relation to any licence granted under section 11 of the Postal Services Act 2000, the duties of the Postal Services Commission under sections 3 and 5 of that Act; and

(o)   in relation to any licence granted under section 5 of the Transport Act 2000, the duties of the Civil Aviation Authority under section 87 of that Act.

(5) In this section 'sectoral regulator' means –

(a)   the Civil Aviation Authority;

(b)   the Director General of Electricity Supply for Northern Ireland;

(c)   the Director General of Gas for Northern Ireland;

(d)   the Director General of Telecommunications;

(e)   the Director General of Water Services;

(f)   the Gas and Electricity Markets Authority;

(g)   the Independent Television Commission;

(h)   the Postal Services Commission;

(i)   the Rail Regulator; or

(j)   the Strategic Rail Authority.

(6) Subsection (7) applies where the Commission or the Secretary of State is considering for the purposes of this Part whether modifying the conditions of a licence granted under section 7 or 7A of the Gas Act 1986 or section 6 of the Electricity Act 1989 would be reasonable and practicable for the purpose of remedying, mitigating or preventing an adverse effect on competition or any detrimental effect on customers so far as resulting from such an effect.

(7) The Commission or (as the case may be) the Secretary of State may, in deciding whether modifying the conditions of such a licence would be reasonable and practicable, have regard to those matters to which the Gas and Electricity Markets Authority may have regard by virtue of section 4AA(4) of the Act of 1986 or (as the case may be) section 3A(4) of the Act of 1989.

(8) The Secretary of State may by order modify subsection (3), (4), (5), (6) or (7).

(9) Part 2 of Schedule 9 (which makes provision for functions under this Part to be exercisable by various sectoral regulators) shall have effect.

Consultation, information and publicity

169 Certain duties of relevant authorities to consult: Part 4

(1) Subsection (2) applies where the relevant authority is proposing to make a relevant decision in a way which the relevant authority considers is likely to have a substantial impact on the interests of any person.

(2) The relevant authority shall, so far as practicable, consult that person about what is proposed before making that decision.

(3) In consulting the person concerned, the relevant authority shall, so far as practicable, give the reasons of the relevant authority for the proposed decision.

(4) In considering what is practicable for the purposes of this section the relevant authority shall, in particular, have regard to –

　(a)　any restrictions imposed by any timetable for making the decision; and

　(b)　any need to keep what is proposed, or the reasons for it, confidential.

(5) The duty under this section shall not apply in relation to the making of any decision so far as particular provision is made elsewhere by virtue of this Part for consultation before the making of that decision.

(6) In this section –

　'the relevant authority' means the OFT, the appropriate Minister or the Commission; and

　'relevant decision' means –

　　(a)　in the case of the OFT, any decision by the OFT –

　　　(i)　as to whether to make a reference under section 131 or accept undertakings under section 154 instead of making such a reference; or

　　　(ii)　to vary under section 135 such a reference;

　　(b)　in the case of the appropriate Minister, any decision by the appropriate Minister –

　　　(i)　as to whether to make a reference under section 132; or

　　　(ii)　to vary under section 135 such a reference; and

　　(c)　in the case of the Commission, any decision on the questions mentioned in section 134 or 141.

170　General information duties

(1) The OFT shall give the Commission –

　(a)　such information in its possession as the Commission may reasonably require to enable the Commission to carry out its functions under this Part; and

　(b)　any other assistance which the Commission may reasonably require for the purpose of assisting it in carrying out its functions under this Part and which it is within the power of the OFT to give.

(2) The OFT shall give the Commission any information in its possession which has not been requested by the Commission but which, in the opinion of the OFT, would be appropriate to give to the Commission for the purpose of assisting it in carrying out its functions under this Part.

(3) The OFT and the Commission shall give the Secretary of State or the appropriate Minister so far as he is not the Secretary of State acting alone –

　(a)　such information in their possession as the Secretary of State or (as the case may be) the appropriate Minister concerned may by direction reasonably require to enable him to carry out his functions under this Part; and

　(b)　any other assistance which the Secretary of State or (as the case may be) the appropriate Minister concerned may by direction reasonably require for the purpose of assisting him in carrying out his functions under this

Part and which it is within the power of the OFT or (as the case may be) the Commission to give.

(4) The OFT shall give the Secretary of State or the appropriate Minister so far as he is not the Secretary of State acting alone any information in its possession which has not been requested by the Secretary of State or (as the case may be) the appropriate Minister concerned but which, in the opinion of the OFT, would be appropriate to give to the Secretary of State or (as the case may be) the appropriate Minister concerned for the purpose of assisting him in carrying out his functions under this Part.

(5) The Commission shall have regard to any information given to it under subsection (1) or (2); and the Secretary of State or (as the case may be) the appropriate Minister concerned shall have regard to any information given to him under subsection (3) or (4).

(6) Any direction given under subsection (3) –

(a)   shall be in writing; and

(b)   may be varied or revoked by a subsequent direction.

171 Advice and information: Part 4

(1) As soon as reasonably practicable after the passing of this Act, the OFT shall prepare and publish general advice and information about the making of references by it under section 131.

(2) The OFT may at any time publish revised, or new, advice or information.

(3) As soon as reasonably practicable after the passing of this Act, the Commission shall prepare and publish general advice and information about the consideration by it of market investigation references and the way in which relevant customer benefits may affect the taking of enforcement action in relation to such references.

(4) The Commission may at any time publish revised, or new, advice or information.

(5) Advice and information published under this section shall be prepared with a view to –

(a)   explaining relevant provisions of this Part to persons who are likely to be affected by them; and

(b)   indicating how the OFT or (as the case may be) the Commission expects such provisions to operate.

(6) Advice and information published by virtue of subsection (1) or (3) shall include such advice and information about the effect of Community law, and anything done under or in accordance with it, on the provisions of this Part as the OFT or (as the case may be) the Commission considers appropriate.

(7) Advice (or information) published by virtue of subsection (1) or (3) may include advice (or information) about the factors which the OFT or (as the case may be) the Commission may take into account in considering whether, and if so how, to exercise a function conferred by this Part.

(8) Any advice or information published by the OFT or the Commission under this section shall be published in such manner as the OFT or (as the case may be) the Commission considers appropriate.

(9) In preparing any advice or information under this section, the OFT shall consult the Commission and such other persons as it considers appropriate.

(10) In preparing any advice or information under this section, the Commission shall consult the OFT and such other persons as it considers appropriate.

(11) In this section 'Community law' means –

    (a)   all the rights, powers, liabilities, obligations and restrictions from time to time created or arising by or under the Community Treaties; and

    (b)   all the remedies and procedures from time to time provided for by or under the Community Treaties.

172 Further publicity requirements: Part 4

(1) The OFT shall publish –

    (a)   any reference made by it under section 131;

    (b)   any variation made by it under section 135 of a reference under section 131;

    (c)   any decision of a kind mentioned in section 149(5)(b); and

    (d)   such information as it considers appropriate about any decision made by it under section 152(1) to bring a case to the attention of the Secretary of State.

(2) The Commission shall publish –

    (a)   any decision made by it under section 138(2) neither to accept an undertaking under section 159 nor to make an order under section 161;

    (b)   any decision made by it that there has been a material change of circumstances as mentioned in section 138(3) or there is another special reason as mentioned in that section;

    (c)   any termination under section 145(1) of an investigation by it;

    (d)   such information as it considers appropriate about any decision made by it under section 152(2) to bring a case to the attention of the Secretary of State;

    (e)   any enforcement undertaking accepted by it under section 157;

    (f)   any enforcement order made by it under section 158; and

    (g)   any variation, release or revocation of such an undertaking or order.

(3) The Secretary of State shall publish –

    (a)   any reference made by him under section 132;

    (b)   any variation made by him under section 135 of a reference under section 132;

    (c)   any intervention notice given by him;

    (d)   any decision made by him to revoke such a notice;

    (e)   any decision made by him under section 147(2) neither to accept an undertaking under section 159 nor to make an order under section 161;

    (f)   any enforcement undertaking accepted by him under section 157;

(g)   any variation or release of such an undertaking; and

(h)   any direction given by him under section 170(3) in connection with the exercise by him of his functions under section 132(3).

(4) The appropriate Minister (other than the Secretary of State acting alone) shall publish –

(a)   any reference made by him under section 132;

(b)   any variation made by him under section 135 of a reference under section 132; and

(c)   any direction given by him under section 170(3) in connection with the exercise by him of his functions under section 132(3).

(5) Where any person is under an obligation by virtue of subsection (1), (2), (3) or (4) to publish the result of any action taken by that person or any decision made by that person, the person concerned shall, subject to subsections (6) and (7), also publish that person's reasons for the action concerned or (as the case may be) the decision concerned.

(6) Such reasons need not, if it is not reasonably practicable to do so, be published at the same time as the result of the action concerned or (as the case may be) as the decision concerned.

(7) Subsections (5) and (6) shall not apply in relation to any case falling within subsection (1)(d) or (2)(d).

(8) The Secretary of State shall publish his reasons for –

(a)   any decision made by him under section 146(2); or

(b)   any decision to make an order under section 153(3) or vary or revoke such an order.

(9) Such reasons may be published after –

(a)   in the case of subsection (8)(a), the publication of the decision concerned; and

(b)   in the case of subsection (8)(b), the making of the order or of the variation or revocation;

if it is not reasonably practicable to publish them at the same time as the publication of the decision or (as the case may be) the making of the order or variation or revocation.

(10) Where the Secretary of State has decided under section 147(2) to accept an undertaking under section 159 or to make an order under section 161, he shall (after the acceptance of the undertaking or (as the case may be) the making of the order) lay details of his decision and his reasons for it, and the Commission's report under section 142, before each House of Parliament.

173 Defamation: Part 4

For the purposes of the law relating to defamation, absolute privilege attaches to any advice, guidance, notice or direction given, or decision or report made, by the OFT, by the Secretary of State, by the appropriate Minister (other than the Secretary of State acting alone) or by the Commission in the exercise of any of their functions under this Part.

Investigation powers

174 Investigation powers of OFT

(1) The OFT may exercise any of the powers in subsections (3) to (5) for the purpose of assisting it in deciding whether to make a reference under section 131 or to accept undertakings under section 154 instead of making such a reference.

(2) The OFT shall not exercise any of the powers in subsections (3) to (5) for the purpose of assisting it as mentioned in subsection (1) unless it already believes that it has power to make such a reference.

(3) The OFT may give notice to any person requiring him –

    (a)   to attend at a time and place specified in the notice; and

    (b)   to give evidence to the OFT or a person nominated by the OFT for the purpose.

(4) The OFT may give notice to any person requiring him –

    (a)   to produce any documents which –

        (i)   are specified or described in the notice, or fall within a category of document which is specified or described in the notice; and

        (ii)   are in that person's custody or under his control; and

    (b)   to produce them at a time and place so specified and to a person so specified.

(5) The OFT may give notice to any person who carries on any business requiring him –

    (a)   to supply to the OFT such estimates, forecasts, returns or other information as may be specified or described in the notice; and

    (b)   to supply it at a time and place, and in a form and manner, so specified and to a person so specified.

(6) A notice under this section shall include information about the possible consequences of not complying with the notice.

(7) The person to whom any document is produced in accordance with a notice under this section may, for the purpose mentioned in subsection (1), copy the document so produced.

(8) No person shall be required under this section –

    (a)   to give any evidence or produce any documents which he could not be compelled to give or produce in civil proceedings before the court; or

    (b)   to supply any information which he could not be compelled to supply in evidence in such proceedings.

(9) No person shall be required, in compliance with a notice under this section, to go more than 10 miles from his place of residence unless his necessary travelling expenses are paid or offered to him.

(10) Any reference in this section to the production of a document includes a reference to the production of a legible and intelligible copy of information recorded otherwise than in legible form.

(11) In this section 'the court' means –

    (a)   in relation to England and Wales or Northern Ireland, the High Court; and

    (b)   in relation to Scotland, the Court of Session.

175 Enforcement of powers under section 174: offences

(1) A person commits an offence if he, intentionally and without reasonable excuse, fails to comply with any requirement of a notice under section 174.

(2) A person commits an offence if he intentionally and without reasonable excuse alters, suppresses or destroys any document which he has been required to produce by a notice under section 174.

(3) A person who commits an offence under subsection (1) or (2) shall be liable –

    (a)   on summary conviction, to a fine not exceeding the statutory maximum;

    (b)   on conviction on indictment, to imprisonment for a term not exceeding two years or to a fine or to both.

(4) A person commits an offence if he intentionally obstructs or delays –

    (a)   the OFT in the exercise of its powers under section 174; or

    (b)   any person in the exercise of his powers under subsection (7) of that section.

(5) A person who commits an offence under subsection (4) shall be liable –

    (a)   on summary conviction, to a fine not exceeding the statutory maximum;

    (b)   on conviction on indictment, to a fine.

176 Investigation powers of the Commission

(1) The following sections in Part 3 shall apply, with the modifications mentioned in subsections (2) and (3) below, for the purposes of references under this Part as they apply for the purposes of references under that Part –

    (a)   section 109 (attendance of witnesses and production of documents etc);

    (b)   section 110 (enforcement of powers under section 109: general);

    (c)   section 111 (penalties);

    (d)   section 112 (penalties: main procedural requirements);

    (e)   section 113 (payments and interest by instalments);

    (f)   section 114 (appeals in relation to penalties);

    (g)   section 115 (recovery of penalties); and

    (h)   section 116 (statement of policy).

(2) Section 110 shall, in its application by virtue of subsection (1) above, have effect as if –

    (a)   subsection (2) were omitted; and

(b)   in subsection (9) the words from 'or section' to 'section 65(3))' were omitted.

(3) Section 111(5)(b)(ii) shall, in its application by virtue of subsection (1) above, have effect as if –

(a)   for the words 'section 50 or 65, given' there were substituted 'section 142, published or given under section 143(1) or (3)'; and

(b)   for the words '(or given)', in both places where they appear, there were substituted '(or published or given)'.

Reports

177 Excisions from reports: Part 4

(1) Subsection (2) applies where the Secretary of State is under a duty to publish a report of the Commission under section 142.

(2) The Secretary of State may exclude a matter from the report if he considers that publication of the matter would be inappropriate.

(3) In deciding what is inappropriate for the purposes of subsection (2) the Secretary of State shall have regard to the considerations mentioned in section 244.

(4) The Commission shall advise the Secretary of State as to the matters (if any) which it considers should be excluded by him under subsection (2).

(5) References in sections 136(4) to (6), 143(2) and (5) to (7), 148(3) to (5) and 172(10) to the giving or laying of a report of the Commission shall be construed as references to the giving or laying of the report as published.

178 Minority reports of Commission: Part 4

(1) Subsection (2) applies where, on a market investigation reference, a member of a group constituted in connection with the reference in pursuance of paragraph 15 of Schedule 7 to the Competition Act 1998, disagrees with any decisions contained in the report of the Commission under this Part as the decisions of the Commission.

(2) The report shall, if the member so wishes, include a statement of his disagreement and of his reasons for disagreeing.

Other

179 Review of decisions under Part 4

(1) Any person aggrieved by a decision of the OFT, the appropriate Minister, the Secretary of State or the Commission in connection with a reference or possible reference under this Part may apply to the Competition Appeal Tribunal for a review of that decision.

(2) For this purpose 'decision' –

(a)   does not include a decision to impose a penalty under section 110(1) or (3) as applied by section 176; but

(b)   includes a failure to take a decision permitted or required by this Part in connection with a reference or possible reference.

(3) Except in so far as a direction to the contrary is given by the Competition Appeal Tribunal, the effect of the decision is not suspended by reason of the making of the application.

(4) In determining such an application the Competition Appeal Tribunal shall apply the same principles as would be applied by a court on an application for judicial review.

(5) The Competition Appeal Tribunal may –

(a)   dismiss the application or quash the whole or part of the decision to which it relates; and

(b)   where it quashes the whole or part of that decision, refer the matter back to the original decision maker with a direction to reconsider and make a new decision in accordance with the ruling of the Competition Appeal Tribunal.

(6) An appeal lies on any point of law arising from a decision of the Competition Appeal Tribunal under this section to the appropriate court.

(7) An appeal under subsection (6) requires the permission of the Tribunal or the appropriate court.

(8) In this section –

'the appropriate court' means the Court of Appeal or, in the case of Tribunal proceedings in Scotland, the Court of Session; and
'Tribunal rules' has the meaning given by section 15(1).

180 Offences

(1) Sections 117 (false or misleading information) and 125 (offences by bodies corporate) shall apply, with the modifications mentioned in subsection (2) below, for the purposes of this Part as they apply for the purposes of Part 3.

(2) Section 117 shall, in its application by virtue of subsection (1) above, have effect as if references to the Secretary of State included references to the appropriate Minister so far as he is not the Secretary of State acting alone.

181 Orders under Part 4

(1) Any power of the Secretary of State to make an order under this Part shall be exercisable by statutory instrument.

(2) Any power of the Secretary of State to make an order under this Part –

(a)   may be exercised so as to make different provision for different cases or different purposes;

(b)   includes power to make such incidental, supplementary, consequential, transitory, transitional or saving provision as the Secretary of State considers appropriate.

(3) The power of the Secretary of State under section 136(9), 137(3), 144(2), 153(3) or 168(8) as extended by subsection (2) above may be exercised by modifying any enactment comprised in or made under this Act, or any other enactment.

(4) An order made by the Secretary of State under section 137(3), 144(2), 158, 160 or 161, or under section 111(4) or (6) or 114(3)(b) or (4)(b) as applied by section 176, shall be subject to annulment in pursuance of a resolution of either House of Parliament.

(5) No order shall be made by the Secretary of State under section 136(9) or 168(8), or section 128(6) as applied by section 183(2), unless a draft of it has been laid before, and approved by a resolution of, each House of Parliament.

(6) An order made by the Secretary of State under section 153(3) shall be laid before Parliament after being made and shall cease to have effect unless approved, within the period of 28 days beginning with the day on which it is made, by a resolution of each House of Parliament.

(7) In calculating the period of 28 days mentioned in subsection (6), no account shall be taken of any time during which Parliament is dissolved or prorogued or during which both Houses are adjourned for more than four days.

(8) If an order made by the Secretary of State ceases to have effect by virtue of subsection (6), any modification made by it of an enactment is repealed (and the previous enactment revived) but without prejudice to the validity of anything done in connection with that modification before the order ceased to have effect and without prejudice to the making of a new order.

(9) If, apart from this subsection, an order made by the Secretary of State under section 153(3) would be treated for the purposes of the standing orders of either House of Parliament as a hybrid instrument, it shall proceed in that House as if it were not such an instrument.

(10) References in this section to an order made under this Part include references to an order made under section 111(4) or (6) or 114(3)(b) or (4)(b) as applied by section 176 and an order made under section 128(6) as applied by section 183(2).

182 Service of documents: Part 4

Section 126 shall apply for the purposes of this Part as it applies for the purposes of Part 3.

183 Interpretation: Part 4

(1) In this Part, unless the context otherwise requires –

    'action' includes omission; and references to the taking of action include references to refraining from action;

    'business' includes a professional practice and includes any other undertaking which is carried on for gain or reward or which is an undertaking in the course of which goods or services are supplied otherwise than free of charge;

    'change of circumstances' includes any discovery that information has been supplied which is false or misleading in a material respect;

'consumer' means any person who is –

    (a)   a person to whom goods are or are sought to be supplied (whether by way of sale or otherwise) in the course of a business carried on by the person supplying or seeking to supply them; or

    (b)   a person for whom services are or are sought to be supplied in the course of a business carried on by the person supplying or seeking to supply them;

and who does not receive or seek to receive the goods or services in the course of a business carried on by him;

'customer' includes a customer who is not a consumer;

'enactment' includes an Act of the Scottish Parliament, Northern Ireland legislation and an enactment comprised in subordinate legislation, and includes an enactment whenever passed or made;

'goods' includes buildings and other structures, and also includes ships, aircraft and hovercraft;

'Minister of the Crown' means the holder of an office in Her Majesty's Government in the United Kingdom and includes the Treasury;

'modify' includes amend or repeal;

'notice' means notice in writing;

'subordinate legislation' has the same meaning as in the Interpretation Act 1978 and also includes an instrument made under an Act of the Scottish Parliament and an instrument made under Northern Ireland legislation; and

'supply', in relation to the supply of goods, includes supply by way of sale, lease, hire or hire-purchase, and, in relation to buildings or other structures, includes the construction of them by a person for another person.

(2) Sections 127(1)(b) and (4) to (6) and 128 shall apply for the purposes of this Part as they apply for the purposes of Part 3.

(3) For the purposes of this Part a market investigation reference is finally determined if –

    (a)   where no intervention notice under section 139(1) has been given in relation to it –

        (i)   the period permitted by section 137 for preparing and publishing a report under section 136 has expired and no such report has been prepared and published;

        (ii)   such a report has been prepared and published within the period permitted by section 137 and contains the decision that there is no adverse effect on competition;

        (iii)   the Commission has decided under section 138(2) neither to accept undertakings under section 159 nor to make an order under section 161; or

        (iv)   the Commission has accepted an undertaking under section 159 or made an order under section 161;

    (b)   where an intervention notice under section 139(1) has been given in relation to it –

        (i)   the period permitted by section 144 for the preparation of the report of the Commission under section 142 and for action to be taken in relation to it under section 143(1) or (3) has expired while the intervention notice is still in force and no such report has been so prepared or no such action has been taken;

(ii) the Commission has terminated under section 145(1) its investigation and the reference is finally determined under paragraph (a) above (disregarding the fact that the notice was given);

(iii) the report of the Commission has been prepared under section 142 and published under section 143(1) within the period permitted by section 144;

(iv) the intervention notice was revoked and the reference is finally determined under paragraph (a) above (disregarding the fact that the notice was given);

(v) the Secretary of State has failed to make and publish a decision under subsection (2) of section 146 within the period permitted by subsection (3) of that section and the reference is finally determined under paragraph (a) above (disregarding the fact that the notice was given);

(vi) the Secretary of State has decided under section 146(2) that no eligible public interest consideration is relevant and the reference is finally determined under paragraph (a) above (disregarding the fact that the notice was given);

(vii) the Secretary of State has decided under 146(2) that a public interest consideration is relevant but has decided under section 147(2) neither to accept an undertaking under section 159 nor to make an order under section 161; or

(viii) the Secretary of State has decided under section 146(2) that a public interest consideration is relevant and has accepted an undertaking under section 159 or made an order under section 161.

(4) For the purposes of this Part the time when a market investigation reference is finally determined is –

(a) in a case falling within subsection (3)(a)(i) or (b)(i), the expiry of the time concerned;

(b) in a case falling within subsection (3)(a)(ii) or (b)(iii), the publication of the report;

(c) in a case falling within subsection (3)(a)(iv) or (b)(viii), the acceptance of the undertaking concerned or (as the case may be) the making of the order concerned; and

(d) in any other case, the making of the decision or last decision concerned or the taking of the action concerned.

(5) The references in subsection (4) to subsections (3)(a)(i), (ii) and (iv) include those enactments as applied by subsection (3)(b)(ii), (iv), (v) or (vi).

(6) In subsection (4)(c) the reference to the acceptance of the undertaking concerned or the making of the order concerned shall, in a case where the enforcement action concerned involves the acceptance of a group of undertakings, the making of a group of orders or the acceptance and making of a group of undertakings and orders, be

treated as a reference to the acceptance or making of the last undertaking or order in the group; but undertakings or orders which vary, supersede or revoke earlier undertakings or orders shall be disregarded for the purposes of subsections (3)(a)(iv) and (b)(viii) and (4)(c).

(7) Any duty to publish which is imposed on a person by this Part shall, unless the context otherwise requires, be construed as a duty on that person to publish in such manner as that person considers appropriate for the purpose of bringing the matter concerned to the attention of those likely to be affected by it.

184 Index of defined expressions: Part 4

In this Part, the expressions listed in the left-hand column have the meaning given by, or are to be interpreted in accordance with, the provisions listed in the right-hand column.

Expression	Provision of this Act
Action (and the taking of action)	Section 183(1)
Adverse effect on competition	Section 134(2)
Appropriate Minister	Section 132(5)
Business	Section 183(1)
Change of circumstances	Section 183(1)
The Commission	Section 273
Consumer	Section 183(1)
Customer	Section 183(1)
Date of market investigation reference	Section 137(7)
Detrimental effect on customers	Section 134(5)
Enactment	Section 183(1)
Enforcement order	Section 162(8)
Enforcement undertaking	Section 162(8)
Feature of a market	Section 131(2)
Final determination of market investigation reference	Section 183(3) to (6)
Goods	Section 183(1)
Intervention notice	Section 139(3)
Market for goods or services	Section 131(6)
Market in the United Kingdom	Section 131(6)
Market investigation reference	Section 131(6)
Minister of the Crown	Section 183(1)
Modify	Section 183(1)
Notice	Section 183(1)
The OFT	Section 273
Public interest consideration	Section 139(5)
Public interest consideration being finalised	Section 139(7)
Publish	Section 183(7)
Relevant customer benefit	Section 134(8)

Relevant sectoral enactment	Section 136(7)
Relevant sectoral regulator	Section 136(8)
Reports of the Commission	Section 177(5)
Subordinate legislation	Section 183(1)
Supply (in relation to the supply of goods)	Section 183(1)
The supply of services (and a market for services etc)	Section 183(2)

PART 5
THE COMPETITION COMMISSION

185 The Commission

Schedule 11 (which amends provisions relating to the constitution and powers of the Commission under Schedule 7 to the 1998 Act) has effect.

186 Annual report of Commission

After paragraph 12 of Schedule 7 to the 1998 Act (the Competition Commission) there is inserted –

'12A Annual reports

(1) The Commission shall make to the Secretary of State a report for each financial year on its activities during the year.

(2) The annual report must be made before the end of August next following the financial year to which it relates.

(3) The Secretary of State shall lay a copy of the annual report before Parliament and arrange for the report to be published.'

187 Commission rules of procedure

(1) In section 45(7) of the 1998 Act (the Competition Commission) for the words 'Schedule 7 makes' there shall be substituted 'Schedules 7 and 7A make'.

(2) In paragraph 19 of Schedule 7 to that Act, after sub-paragraph (4), there shall be inserted –

'(5) This paragraph does not apply to groups for which rules must be made under paragraph 19A.'

(3) After paragraph 19 of that Schedule to that Act there shall be inserted –

'19A

(1) The Chairman must make rules of procedure in relation to merger reference groups, market reference groups and special reference groups.

(2) Schedule 7A makes further provision about rules made under this paragraph but is not to be taken as restricting the Chairman's powers under this paragraph.

(3) The Chairman must publish rules made under this paragraph in such manner as he considers appropriate for the purpose of bringing them to the attention of those likely to be affected by them.

(4) The Chairman must consult the members of the Commission and such other persons as he considers appropriate before making rules under this paragraph.

(5) Rules under this paragraph may –

    (a)   make different provision for different cases or different purposes;

    (b)   be varied or revoked by subsequent rules made under this paragraph.

(6) Subject to rules made under this paragraph, each merger reference group, market reference group and special reference group may determine its own procedure.

(7) In determining how to proceed in accordance with rules made under this paragraph and in determining its procedure under sub-paragraph (6), a group must have regard to any guidance issued by the Chairman.

(8) Before issuing any guidance for the purposes of this paragraph the Chairman shall consult the members of the Commission and such other persons as he considers appropriate.

(9) In this paragraph and in Schedule 7A –

     "market reference group" means any group constituted in connection with a reference under section 131 or 132 of the Enterprise Act 2002 (including that section as it has effect by virtue of another enactment);

     "merger reference group" means any group constituted in connection with a reference under section 59 of the Fair Trading Act 1973, section 32 of the Water Industry Act 1991 or section 22, 33, 45 or 62 of the Enterprise Act 2002; and

     "special reference group" means any group constituted in connection with a reference or (in the case of the Financial Services and Markets Act 2000) an investigation under –

         (a) section 11 of the Competition Act 1980;
         (b) section 13 of the Telecommunications Act 1984;
         (c) section 43 of the Airports Act 1986;
         (d) section 24 or 41E of the Gas Act 1986;
         (e) section 12 or 56C of the Electricity Act 1989;
         (f) Schedule 4 to the Broadcasting Act 1990;
         (g) section 12 or 14 of the Water Industry Act 1991;
         (h) article 15 of the Electricity (Northern Ireland) Order 1992 (SI 1992/231 (NI 1));
         (i) section 13 of, or Schedule 4A to, the Railways Act 1993;
         (j) article 34 of the Airports (Northern Ireland) Order 1994 (SI 1994/426 (NI 1));

(k) article 15 of the Gas (Northern Ireland) Order 1996 (SI 1996/275 (NI 2));

(l) section 15 of the Postal Services Act 2000;

(m) section 162 or 306 of the Financial Services and Markets Act 2000; or

(n) section 12 of the Transport Act 2000.'

(4) After Schedule 7 to that Act there shall be inserted, as Schedule 7A, the Schedule set out in Schedule 12 to this Act.

PART 6
CARTEL OFFENCE

Cartel offence

188 Cartel offence

(1) An individual is guilty of an offence if he dishonestly agrees with one or more other persons to make or implement, or to cause to be made or implemented, arrangements of the following kind relating to at least two undertakings (A and B).

(2) The arrangements must be ones which, if operating as the parties to the agreement intend, would –

(a) directly or indirectly fix a price for the supply by A in the United Kingdom (otherwise than to B) of a product or service,

(b) limit or prevent supply by A in the United Kingdom of a product or service,

(c) limit or prevent production by A in the United Kingdom of a product,

(d) divide between A and B the supply in the United Kingdom of a product or service to a customer or customers,

(e) divide between A and B customers for the supply in the United Kingdom of a product or service, or

(f) be bid-rigging arrangements.

(3) Unless subsection (2)(d), (e) or (f) applies, the arrangements must also be ones which, if operating as the parties to the agreement intend, would –

(a) directly or indirectly fix a price for the supply by B in the United Kingdom (otherwise than to A) of a product or service,

(b) limit or prevent supply by B in the United Kingdom of a product or service, or

(c) limit or prevent production by B in the United Kingdom of a product.

(4) In subsections (2)(a) to (d) and (3), references to supply or production are to supply or production in the appropriate circumstances (for which see section 189).

(5) 'Bid-rigging arrangements' are arrangements under which, in response to a request for bids for the supply of a product or service in the United Kingdom, or for the production of a product in the United Kingdom –

(a) A but not B may make a bid, or

(b)   A and B may each make a bid but, in one case or both, only a bid arrived at in accordance with the arrangements.

(6) But arrangements are not bid-rigging arrangements if, under them, the person requesting bids would be informed of them at or before the time when a bid is made.

(7) 'Undertaking' has the same meaning as in Part 1 of the 1998 Act.

189 Cartel offence: supplementary

(1) For section 188(2)(a), the appropriate circumstances are that A's supply of the product or service would be at a level in the supply chain at which the product or service would at the same time be supplied by B in the United Kingdom.

(2) For section 188(2)(b), the appropriate circumstances are that A's supply of the product or service would be at a level in the supply chain –

(a)   at which the product or service would at the same time be supplied by B in the United Kingdom, or

(b)   at which supply by B in the United Kingdom of the product or service would be limited or prevented by the arrangements.

(3) For section 188(2)(c), the appropriate circumstances are that A's production of the product would be at a level in the production chain –

(a)   at which the product would at the same time be produced by B in the United Kingdom, or

(b)   at which production by B in the United Kingdom of the product would be limited or prevented by the arrangements.

(4) For section 188(2)(d), the appropriate circumstances are that A's supply of the product or service would be at the same level in the supply chain as B's.

(5) For section 188(3)(a), the appropriate circumstances are that B's supply of the product or service would be at a level in the supply chain at which the product or service would at the same time be supplied by A in the United Kingdom.

(6) For section 188(3)(b), the appropriate circumstances are that B's supply of the product or service would be at a level in the supply chain –

(a)   at which the product or service would at the same time be supplied by A in the United Kingdom, or

(b)   at which supply by A in the United Kingdom of the product or service would be limited or prevented by the arrangements.

(7) For section 188(3)(c), the appropriate circumstances are that B's production of the product would be at a level in the production chain –

(a)   at which the product would at the same time be produced by A in the United Kingdom, or

(b)   at which production by A in the United Kingdom of the product would be limited or prevented by the arrangements.

190 Cartel offence: penalty and prosecution

(1) A person guilty of an offence under section 188 is liable –

(a)   on conviction on indictment, to imprisonment for a term not exceeding five years or to a fine, or to both;

(b)   on summary conviction, to imprisonment for a term not exceeding six months or to a fine not exceeding the statutory maximum, or to both.

(2) In England and Wales and Northern Ireland, proceedings for an offence under section 188 may be instituted only –

(a)   by the Director of the Serious Fraud Office, or

(b)   by or with the consent of the OFT.

(3) No proceedings may be brought for an offence under section 188 in respect of an agreement outside the United Kingdom, unless it has been implemented in whole or in part in the United Kingdom.

(4) Where, for the purpose of the investigation or prosecution of offences under section 188, the OFT gives a person written notice under this subsection, no proceedings for an offence under section 188 that falls within a description specified in the notice may be brought against that person in England and Wales or Northern Ireland except in circumstances specified in the notice.

191 Extradition

The offences to which an Order in Council under section 2 of the Extradition Act 1870 (arrangements with foreign states) can apply include –

(a)   an offence under section 188,

(b)   conspiracy to commit such an offence, and

(c)   attempt to commit such an offence.

Criminal investigations by OFT

192 Investigation of offences under section 188

(1) The OFT may conduct an investigation if there are reasonable grounds for suspecting that an offence under section 188 has been committed.

(2) The powers of the OFT under sections 193 and 194 are exercisable, but only for the purposes of an investigation under subsection (1), in any case where it appears to the OFT that there is good reason to exercise them for the purpose of investigating the affairs, or any aspect of the affairs, of any person ('the person under investigation').

193 Powers when conducting an investigation

(1) The OFT may by notice in writing require the person under investigation, or any other person who it has reason to believe has relevant information, to answer questions, or otherwise provide information, with respect to any matter relevant to the investigation at a specified place and either at a specified time or forthwith.

(2) The OFT may by notice in writing require the person under investigation, or any other person, to produce, at a specified place and either at a specified time or

forthwith, specified documents, or documents of a specified description, which appear to the OFT to relate to any matter relevant to the investigation.

(3) If any such documents are produced, the OFT may –

    (a)   take copies or extracts from them;

    (b)   require the person producing them to provide an explanation of any of them.

(4) If any such documents are not produced, the OFT may require the person who was required to produce them to state, to the best of his knowledge and belief, where they are.

(5) A notice under subsection (1) or (2) must indicate –

    (a)   the subject matter and purpose of the investigation; and

    (b)   the nature of the offences created by section 201.

194 Power to enter premises under a warrant

(1) On an application made by the OFT to the High Court, or, in Scotland, by the procurator fiscal to the sheriff, in accordance with rules of court, a judge or the sheriff may issue a warrant if he is satisfied that there are reasonable grounds for believing –

    (a)   that there are on any premises documents which the OFT has power under section 193 to require to be produced for the purposes of an investigation; and

    (b)   that –

        (i)   a person has failed to comply with a requirement under that section to produce the documents;

        (ii)   it is not practicable to serve a notice under that section in relation to them; or

        (iii)   the service of such a notice in relation to them might seriously prejudice the investigation.

(2) A warrant under this section shall authorise a named officer of the OFT, and any other officers of the OFT whom the OFT has authorised in writing to accompany the named officer –

    (a)   to enter the premises, using such force as is reasonably necessary for the purpose;

    (b)   to search the premises and –

        (i)   take possession of any documents appearing to be of the relevant kind, or

        (ii)   take, in relation to any documents appearing to be of the relevant kind, any other steps which may appear to be necessary for preserving them or preventing interference with them;

    (c)   to require any person to provide an explanation of any document appearing to be of the relevant kind or to state, to the best of his knowledge and belief, where it may be found;

    (d)   to require any information which is stored in any electronic form and is accessible from the premises and which the named officer considers relates to any matter relevant to the investigation, to be produced in a form –

(i)   in which it can be taken away, and

(ii)   in which it is visible and legible or from which it can readily be produced in a visible and legible form.

(3) Documents are of the relevant kind if they are of a kind in respect of which the application under subsection (1) was granted.

(4) A warrant under this section may authorise persons specified in the warrant to accompany the named officer who is executing it.

(5) In Part 1 of Schedule 1 to the Criminal Justice and Police Act 2001 (powers of seizure to which section 50 of that Act applies), after paragraph 73 there is inserted –

'73A Enterprise Act 2002

The power of seizure conferred by section 194(2) of the Enterprise Act 2002 (seizure of documents for the purposes of an investigation under section 192(1) of that Act).'

195 Exercise of powers by authorised person

(1) The OFT may authorise any competent person who is not an officer of the OFT to exercise on its behalf all or any of the powers conferred by section 193 or 194.

(2) No such authority may be granted except for the purpose of investigating the affairs, or any aspect of the affairs, of a person specified in the authority.

(3) No person is bound to comply with any requirement imposed by a person exercising powers by virtue of any authority granted under this section unless he has, if required to do so, produced evidence of his authority.

196 Privileged information etc

(1) A person may not under section 193 or 194 be required to disclose any information or produce any document which he would be entitled to refuse to disclose or produce on grounds of legal professional privilege in proceedings in the High Court, except that a lawyer may be required to provide the name and address of his client.

(2) A person may not under section 193 or 194 be required to disclose any information or produce any document in respect of which he owes an obligation of confidence by virtue of carrying on any banking business unless –

(a)   the person to whom the obligation of confidence is owed consents to the disclosure or production; or

(b)   the OFT has authorised the making of the requirement.

(3) In the application of this section to Scotland, the reference in subsection (1) –

(a)   to proceedings in the High Court is to be read as a reference to legal proceedings generally; and

(b)   to an entitlement on grounds of legal professional privilege is to be read as a reference to an entitlement by virtue of any rule of law whereby –

(i)   communications between a professional legal adviser and his client, or

(ii)   communications made in connection with or in contemplation of legal proceedings and for the purposes of those proceedings,

are in such proceedings protected from disclosure on the ground of confidentiality.

197 Restriction on use of statements in court

(1) A statement by a person in response to a requirement imposed by virtue of section 193 or 194 may only be used in evidence against him –

(a)   on a prosecution for an offence under section 201(2); or

(b)   on a prosecution for some other offence where in giving evidence he makes a statement inconsistent with it.

(2) However, the statement may not be used against that person by virtue of paragraph (b) of subsection (1) unless evidence relating to it is adduced, or a question relating to it is asked, by or on behalf of that person in the proceedings arising out of the prosecution.

198 Use of statements obtained under Competition Act 1998

In the 1998 Act, after section 30 there is inserted –

'30A Use of statements in prosecution

A statement made by a person in response to a requirement imposed by virtue of any of sections 26 to 28 may not be used in evidence against him on a prosecution for an offence under section 188 of the Enterprise Act 2002 unless, in the proceedings –

(a)   in giving evidence, he makes a statement inconsistent with it, and

(b)   evidence relating to it is adduced, or a question relating to it is asked, by him or on his behalf.'

199 Surveillance powers

(1) The Regulation of Investigatory Powers Act 2000 is amended as follows.

(2) In section 32 (authorisation of intrusive surveillance) –

(a)   after subsection (3) there is inserted –

'(3A) In the case of an authorisation granted by the chairman of the OFT, the authorisation is necessary on grounds falling within subsection (3) only if it is necessary for the purpose of preventing or detecting an offence under section 188 of the Enterprise Act 2002 (cartel offence).';

(b)   in subsection (6) after paragraph (m) there is inserted '; and

(n)   the chairman of the OFT.'

(3) In section 33 (rules for grant of authorisations) after subsection (4) there is inserted –

'(4A) The chairman of the OFT shall not grant an authorisation for the carrying out of intrusive surveillance except on an application made by an officer of the OFT.'

(4) In subsection (5)(a) of that section, after 'officer' there is inserted 'or the chairman or an officer of the OFT'.

(5) In section 34 (grant of authorisation in the senior officer's absence) –

    (a)   in subsection (1)(a), after 'or by' there is inserted 'an officer of the OFT or';

    (b)   in subsection (2)(a), after 'may be,' there is inserted 'as chairman of the OFT or';

    (c)   in subsection (4), after paragraph (l) there is inserted –

    '(m)   a person is entitled to act for the chairman of the OFT if he is an officer of the OFT designated by it for the purposes of this paragraph as a person entitled so to act in an urgent case.'

(6) In section 35 (notification of authorisations for intrusive surveillance) –

    (a)   in subsections (1) and (10), for 'or customs' there is substituted ', customs or OFT';

    (b)   in subsection (10), after paragraph (b) there is inserted –

    '(ba)   the chairman of the OFT; or';

    (c)   in paragraph (c) of that subsection, at the end there is inserted 'or for a person falling within paragraph (ba).'

(7) In section 36 (approval required for authorisations to take effect) –

    (a)   in subsection (1), after paragraph (d) there is inserted '; or

    (e)   an officer of the OFT.';

    (b)   in subsection (6), after paragraph (g) there is inserted '; and

    (h)   where the authorisation was granted by the chairman of the OFT or a person entitled to act for him by virtue of section 34(4)(m), that chairman.'

(8) In section 37 (quashing of police and customs authorisations etc) in subsection (1), after paragraph (d) there is inserted '; or

    (e)   an officer of the OFT.'

(9) In section 40 (information to be provided to Surveillance Commissioners) after paragraph (d) there is inserted ', and

    (e)   every officer of the OFT,'.

(10) In section 46 (restrictions on authorisations extending to Scotland), in subsection (3), after paragraph (d) there is inserted –

    '(da)   the OFT;'.

(11) In section 48 (interpretation of Part 2), in subsection (1), after the entry relating to 'directed' and 'intrusive' there is inserted –

    '"OFT" means the Office of Fair Trading;'.

200 Authorisation of action in respect of property

(1) Part 3 of the Police Act 1997 (authorisation of action in respect of property) is amended as follows.

(2) In section 93 (authorisation to interfere with property etc) –

 (a)   in subsection (1B), after 'customs officer' there is inserted 'or an officer of the Office of Fair Trading';

 (b)   after subsection (2A) there is inserted –

 '(2AA) Where the authorising officer is the chairman of the Office of Fair Trading, the only purpose falling within subsection (2)(a) is the purpose of preventing or detecting an offence under section 188 of the Enterprise Act 2002.';

 (c)   in subsection (3), after paragraph (d) there is inserted ', or

 (e)   if the authorising officer is within subsection (5)(i), by an officer of the Office of Fair Trading.';

 (d)   in subsection (5), after paragraph (h) there is inserted '; or

 (i)   the chairman of the Office of Fair Trading.'

(3) In section 94 (authorisation given in absence of authorising officer) in subsection (2), after paragraph (f) there is inserted –

 '(g)   where the authorising officer is within paragraph (i) of that subsection, by an officer of the Office of Fair Trading designated by it for the purposes of this section.'

201 Offences

(1) Any person who without reasonable excuse fails to comply with a requirement imposed on him under section 193 or 194 is guilty of an offence and liable on summary conviction to imprisonment for a term not exceeding six months or to a fine not exceeding level 5 on the standard scale or to both.

(2) A person who, in purported compliance with a requirement under section 193 or 194 –

 (a)   makes a statement which he knows to be false or misleading in a material particular; or

 (b)   recklessly makes a statement which is false or misleading in a material particular,

is guilty of an offence.

(3) A person guilty of an offence under subsection (2) is liable –

 (a)   on conviction on indictment, to imprisonment for a term not exceeding two years or to a fine or to both; and

 (b)   on summary conviction, to imprisonment for a term not exceeding six months or to a fine not exceeding the statutory maximum, or to both.

(4) Where any person –

(a)   knows or suspects that an investigation by the Serious Fraud Office or the OFT into an offence under section 188 is being or is likely to be carried out; and

(b)   falsifies, conceals, destroys or otherwise disposes of, or causes or permits the falsification, concealment, destruction or disposal of documents which he knows or suspects are or would be relevant to such an investigation,

he is guilty of an offence unless he proves that he had no intention of concealing the facts disclosed by the documents from the persons carrying out such an investigation.

(5) A person guilty of an offence under subsection (4) is liable –

(a)   on conviction on indictment, to imprisonment for a term not exceeding 5 years or to a fine or to both; and

(b)   on summary conviction, to imprisonment for a term not exceeding six months or to a fine not exceeding the statutory maximum, or to both.

(6) A person who intentionally obstructs a person in the exercise of his powers under a warrant issued under section 194 is guilty of an offence and liable –

(a)   on conviction on indictment, to imprisonment for a term not exceeding 2 years or to a fine or to both; and

(b)   on summary conviction, to a fine not exceeding the statutory maximum.

202 Interpretation of sections 192 to 201

In sections 192 to 201 –

'documents' includes information recorded in any form and, in relation to information recorded otherwise than in a form in which it is visible and legible, references to its production include references to producing it in a form in which it is visible and legible or from which it can readily be produced in a visible and legible form;

'person under investigation' has the meaning given in section 192(2).

PART 7
COMPETITION PROVISIONS

Powers of entry under 1998 Act

203 Powers of entry

(1) The 1998 Act is amended as follows.

(2) In section 28 (power to enter premises under a warrant), after subsection (3) there is inserted –

'(3A) A warrant under this section may authorise persons specified in the warrant to accompany the named officer who is executing it.'

(3) In section 62 (power to enter premises: Commission investigations), after subsection (5) there is inserted –

'(5A) A warrant under this section may authorise persons specified in the warrant to accompany the named officer who is executing it.'

(4) In section 63 (power to enter premises: Director's special investigations), after subsection (5) there is inserted –

'(5A) A warrant under this section may authorise persons specified in the warrant to accompany the named authorised officer who is executing it.'

Directors disqualification

204 Disqualification

(1) The Company Directors Disqualification Act 1986 is amended as follows.

(2) The following sections are inserted after section 9 (matters for determining unfitness in certain cases) –

'Disqualification for competition infringements

9A Competition disqualification order

(1) The court must make a disqualification order against a person if the following two conditions are satisfied in relation to him.

(2) The first condition is that an undertaking which is a company of which he is a director commits a breach of competition law.

(3) The second condition is that the court considers that his conduct as a director makes him unfit to be concerned in the management of a company.

(4) An undertaking commits a breach of competition law if it engages in conduct which infringes any of the following –

　(a)　the Chapter 1 prohibition (within the meaning of the Competition Act 1998) (prohibition on agreements, etc preventing, restricting or distorting competition);
　(b)　the Chapter 2 prohibition (within the meaning of that Act) (prohibition on abuse of a dominant position);
　(c)　Article 81 of the Treaty establishing the European Community (prohibition on agreements, etc preventing, restricting or distorting competition);
　(d)　Article 82 of that Treaty (prohibition on abuse of a dominant position).

(5) For the purpose of deciding under subsection (3) whether a person is unfit to be concerned in the management of a company the court –

　(a)　must have regard to whether subsection (6) applies to him;
　(b)　may have regard to his conduct as a director of a company in connection with any other breach of competition law;
　(c)　must not have regard to the matters mentioned in Schedule 1.

(6) This subsection applies to a person if as a director of the company –

　(a)　his conduct contributed to the breach of competition law mentioned in subsection (2);

(b)   his conduct did not contribute to the breach but he had reasonable grounds to suspect that the conduct of the undertaking constituted the breach and he took no steps to prevent it;

(c)   he did not know but ought to have known that the conduct of the undertaking constituted the breach.

(7) For the purposes of subsection (6)(a) it is immaterial whether the person knew that the conduct of the undertaking constituted the breach.

(8) For the purposes of subsection (4)(a) or (c) references to the conduct of an undertaking are references to its conduct taken with the conduct of one or more other undertakings.

(9) The maximum period of disqualification under this section is 15 years.

(10) An application under this section for a disqualification order may be made by the OFT or by a specified regulator.

(11) Section 60 of the Competition Act 1998 (consistent treatment of questions arising under United Kingdom and Community law) applies in relation to any question arising by virtue of subsection (4)(a) or (b) above as it applies in relation to any question arising under Part 1 of that Act.

9B Competition undertakings

(1) This section applies if –

(a)   the OFT or a specified regulator thinks that in relation to any person an undertaking which is a company of which he is a director has committed or is committing a breach of competition law,

(b)   the OFT or the specified regulator thinks that the conduct of the person as a director makes him unfit to be concerned in the management of a company, and

(c)   the person offers to give the OFT or the specified regulator (as the case may be) a disqualification undertaking.

(2) The OFT or the specified regulator (as the case may be) may accept a disqualification undertaking from the person instead of applying for or proceeding with an application for a disqualification order.

(3) A disqualification undertaking is an undertaking by a person that for the period specified in the undertaking he will not –

(a)   be a director of a company;

(b)   act as receiver of a company's property;

(c)   in any way, whether directly or indirectly, be concerned or take part in the promotion, formation or management of a company;

(d)   act as an insolvency practitioner.

(4) But a disqualification undertaking may provide that a prohibition falling within subsection (3)(a) to (c) does not apply if the person obtains the leave of the court.

(5) The maximum period which may be specified in a disqualification undertaking is 15 years.

(6) If a disqualification undertaking is accepted from a person who is already subject to a disqualification undertaking under this Act or to a disqualification order the periods specified in those undertakings or the undertaking and the order (as the case may be) run concurrently.

(7) Subsections (4) to (8) of section 9A apply for the purposes of this section as they apply for the purposes of that section but in the application of subsection (5) of that section the reference to the court must be construed as a reference to the OFT or a specified regulator (as the case may be).

9C Competition investigations

(1) If the OFT or a specified regulator has reasonable grounds for suspecting that a breach of competition law has occurred it or he (as the case may be) may carry out an investigation for the purpose of deciding whether to make an application under section 9A for a disqualification order.

(2) For the purposes of such an investigation sections 26 to 30 of the Competition Act 1998 apply to the OFT and the specified regulators as they apply to the OFT for the purposes of an investigation under section 25 of that Act.

(3) Subsection (4) applies if as a result of an investigation under this section the OFT or a specified regulator proposes to apply under section 9A for a disqualification order.

(4) Before making the application the OFT or regulator (as the case may be) must –

    (a)   give notice to the person likely to be affected by the application, and

    (b)   give that person an opportunity to make representations.

9D Co-ordination

(1) The Secretary of State may make regulations for the purpose of co-ordinating the performance of functions under sections 9A to 9C (relevant functions) which are exercisable concurrently by two or more persons.

(2) Section 54(5) to (7) of the Competition Act 1998 applies to regulations made under this section as it applies to regulations made under that section and for that purpose in that section –

    (a)   references to Part 1 functions must be read as references to relevant functions;

    (b)   references to a regulator must be read as references to a specified regulator;

    (c)   a competent person also includes any of the specified regulators.

(3) The power to make regulations under this section must be exercised by statutory instrument subject to annulment in pursuance of a resolution of either House of Parliament.

(4) Such a statutory instrument may –

    (a)   contain such incidental, supplemental, consequential and transitional provision as the Secretary of State thinks appropriate;

(b)   make different provision for different cases.

9E Interpretation

(1) This section applies for the purposes of sections 9A to 9D.

(2) Each of the following is a specified regulator for the purposes of a breach of competition law in relation to a matter in respect of which he or it has a function –

(a)   the Director General of Telecommunications;
(b)   the Gas and Electricity Markets Authority;
(c)   the Director General of Water Services;
(d)   the Rail Regulator;
(e)   the Civil Aviation Authority.

(3) The court is the High Court or (in Scotland) the Court of Session.

(4) Conduct includes omission.

(5) Director includes shadow director.'

(3) In section 1(1) (general provision about disqualification orders) for 'section 6' substitute 'sections 6 and 9A'.

(4) In section 8A (variation etc of disqualification undertaking) after subsection (2) there is inserted the following subsection –

'(2A) Subsection (2) does not apply to an application in the case of an undertaking given under section 9B, and in such a case on the hearing of the application whichever of the OFT or a specified regulator (within the meaning of section 9E) accepted the undertaking –

(a)   must appear and call the attention of the court to any matters which appear to it or him (as the case may be) to be relevant;
(b)   may give evidence or call witnesses.'

(5) In section 8A for subsection (3) there is substituted –

'(3) In this section "the court" –

(a)   in the case of an undertaking given under section 9B means the High Court or (in Scotland) the Court of Session;
(b)   in any other case has the same meaning as in section 7(2) or 8 (as the case may be).'

(6) In section 16(3) for 'the Secretary of State or the official receiver or the liquidator' substitute 'a person falling within subsection (4)'.

(7) In section 16 after subsection (3) there is inserted the following subsection –

'(4) The following fall within this subsection –

(a)   the Secretary of State;
(b)   the official receiver;
(c)   the OFT;
(d)   the liquidator;
(e)   a specified regulator (within the meaning of section 9E).'

(8) In section 17 (applications for leave under an order or undertaking) after subsection (3) there is inserted the following subsection –

'(3A) Where a person is subject to a disqualification undertaking accepted at any time under section 9B any application for leave for the purposes of section 9B(4) must be made to the High Court or (in Scotland) the Court of Session.'

(9) In section 17(4) for 'or 1A(1)(a)' substitute '1A(1)(a) or 9B(4)'.

(10) In section 17 after subsection (5) there are inserted the following subsections –

'(6) Subsection (5) does not apply to an application for leave for the purposes of section 1(1)(a) if the application for the disqualification order was made under section 9A.

(7) In such a case and in the case of an application for leave for the purposes of section 9B(4) on the hearing of the application whichever of the OFT or a specified regulator (within the meaning of section 9E) applied for the order or accepted the undertaking (as the case may be) –

(a)   must appear and draw the attention of the court to any matters which appear to it or him (as the case may be) to be relevant;

(b)   may give evidence or call witnesses.'

(11) In section 18 (register of disqualification orders and undertakings) for subsection (2A) substitute –

'(2A) The Secretary of State must include in the register such particulars as he considers appropriate of –

(a)   disqualification undertakings accepted by him under section 7 or 8;

(b)   disqualification undertakings accepted by the OFT or a specified regulator under section 9B;

(c)   cases in which leave has been granted as mentioned in subsection (1)(d).'

Miscellaneous

205 Super-complaints to regulators other than OFT

(1) The Secretary of State may by order provide that section 11 is to apply to complaints made to a specified regulator in relation to a market of a specified description as it applies to complaints made to the OFT, with such modifications as may be specified.

(2) An order under this section –

(a)   shall be made by statutory instrument, and

(b)   shall be subject to annulment in pursuance of a resolution of either House of Parliament.

(3) In this section –

'regulator' has the meaning given in section 54(1) of the 1998 Act; and 'specified' means specified in the order.

206 Power to modify Schedule 8

(1) The Secretary of State may by order made by statutory instrument modify Schedule 8.

(2) An order under this section may make –

(a)   different provision for different cases or different purposes;

(b)   such incidental, supplementary, consequential, transitory, transitional or saving provision as the Secretary of State considers appropriate.

(3) An order under this section may, in particular, modify that Schedule in its application by virtue of Part 3 of this Act, in its application by virtue of Part 4 of this Act, in its application by virtue of any other enactment (whether by virtue of Part 4 of this Act as applied by that enactment or otherwise) or in its application by virtue of every enactment that applies it.

(4) An order under this section as extended by subsection (2) may modify any enactment comprised in or made under this Act, or any other enactment.

(5) No order shall be made under this section unless a draft of it has been laid before, and approved by a resolution of, each House of Parliament.

(6) No modification of Schedule 8 in its application by virtue of Part 3 of this Act shall be made by an order under this section if the modification relates to a relevant merger situation or (as the case may be) a special merger situation which has been created before the coming into force of the order.

(7) No modification shall be made by an order under this section of Schedule 8 in its application in relation to references made under section 22, 33, 45 or 62 before the coming into force of the order.

(8) No modification shall be made by an order under this section of Schedule 8 in its application in relation to references made under section 131 or 132 before the coming into force of the order (including references made under section 131 as applied by another enactment).

(9) Before making an order under this section, the Secretary of State shall consult the OFT and the Commission.

(10) Expressions used in this section which are also used in Part 3 of this Act have the same meaning in this section as in that Part.

207 Repeal of Schedule 4 to the 1998 Act

Section 3(1)(d) of and Schedule 4 to the 1998 Act (which provide for the exclusion from the Chapter 1 prohibition in cases involving designated professional rules) shall cease to have effect.

208 Repeal of Part 6 of Fair Trading Act 1973

Sections 78 to 80 of the 1973 Act (references to Commission other than monopoly and merger references) shall cease to have effect.

209 Reform of Community competition law

(1) The Secretary of State may by regulations make such modifications of the 1998 Act as he considers appropriate for the purpose of eliminating or reducing any differences between –

    (a)   the domestic provisions of the 1998 Act, and

    (b)   European Community competition law,

which result (or would otherwise result) from a relevant Community instrument made after the passing of this Act.

(2) In subsection (1) –

    'the domestic provisions of the 1998 Act' means the provisions of the 1998 Act so far as they do not implement or give effect to a relevant Community instrument;

    'European Community competition law' includes any Act or subordinate legislation so far as it implements or gives effect to a relevant Community instrument;

    'relevant Community instrument' means a regulation or directive under Article 83 of the Treaty establishing the European Community.

(3) The Secretary of State may by regulations repeal or otherwise modify any provision of an Act (other than the 1998 Act) which excludes any matter from the Chapter I prohibition or the Chapter II prohibition (within the meaning of Part 1 of the 1998 Act).

(4) The power under subsection (3) may not be exercised –

    (a)   before the power under subsection (1) has been exercised; or

    (b)   so as to extend the scope of any exclusion that is not being removed by the regulations.

(5) Regulations under this section may –

    (a)   confer power to make subordinate legislation;

    (b)   make such consequential, supplementary, incidental, transitory, transitional or saving provision as the Secretary of State considers appropriate (including provision modifying any Act or subordinate legislation); and

    (c)   make different provision for different cases or circumstances.

(6) The power to make regulations under this section is exercisable by statutory instrument.

(7) No regulations may be made under this section unless a draft of them has been laid before and approved by a resolution of each House of Parliament.

(8) Paragraph 1(1)(c) of Schedule 2 to the European Communities Act 1972 (restriction on powers to legislate) shall not apply to regulations which implement or give effect to a relevant Community instrument made after the passing of this Act.

* * * *

PART 9
INFORMATION

Restrictions on disclosure

237 General restriction

(1) This section applies to specified information which relates to –

    (a)   the affairs of an individual;

    (b)   any business of an undertaking.

(2) Such information must not be disclosed –

    (a)   during the lifetime of the individual, or

    (b)   while the undertaking continues in existence,

unless the disclosure is permitted under this Part.

(3) But subsection (2) does not prevent the disclosure of any information if the information has on an earlier occasion been disclosed to the public in circumstances which do not contravene –

    (a)   that subsection;

    (b)   any other enactment or rule of law prohibiting or restricting the disclosure of the information.

(4) Nothing in this Part authorises a disclosure of information which contravenes the Data Protection Act 1998.

(5) Nothing in this Part affects the Competition Appeal Tribunal.

(6) This Part (except section 244) does not affect any power or duty to disclose information which exists apart from this Part.

238 Information

(1) Information is specified information if it comes to a public authority in connection with the exercise of any function it has under or by virtue of –

    (a)   Part 1, 3, 4, 6, 7 or 8;

    (b)   an enactment specified in Schedule 14;

    (c)   such subordinate legislation as the Secretary of State may by order specify for the purposes of this subsection.

(2) It is immaterial whether information comes to a public authority before or after the passing of this Act.

(3) Public authority (except in the expression 'overseas public authority') must be construed in accordance with section 6 of the Human Rights Act 1998.

(4) In subsection (1) the reference to an enactment includes a reference to an enactment contained in –

    (a)   an Act of the Scottish Parliament;

    (b)   Northern Ireland legislation;

    (c)   subordinate legislation.

(5) The Secretary of State may by order amend Schedule 14.

(6) The power to make an order under subsection (5) includes power to add, vary or remove a reference to any provision of –

    (a)   an Act of the Scottish Parliament;

    (b)   Northern Ireland legislation.

(7) An order under this section must be made by statutory instrument subject to annulment in pursuance of a resolution of either House of Parliament.

(8) This section applies for the purposes of this Part.

Permitted disclosure

239 Consent

(1) This Part does not prohibit the disclosure by a public authority of information held by it to any other person if it obtains each required consent.

(2) If the information was obtained by the authority from a person who had the information lawfully and the authority knows the identity of that person the consent of that person is required.

(3) If the information relates to the affairs of an individual the consent of the individual is required.

(4) If the information relates to the business of an undertaking the consent of the person for the time being carrying on the business is required.

(5) For the purposes of subsection (4) consent may be given –

    (a)   in the case of a company by a director, secretary or other officer of the company;

    (b)   in the case of a partnership by a partner;

    (c)   in the case of an unincorporated body or association by a person concerned in the management or control of the body or association.

240 Community obligations

This Part does not prohibit the disclosure of information held by a public authority to another person if the disclosure is required for the purpose of a Community obligation.

241 Statutory functions

(1) A public authority which holds information to which section 237 applies may disclose that information for the purpose of facilitating the exercise by the authority of any function it has under or by virtue of this Act or any other enactment.

(2) If information is disclosed under subsection (1) so that it is not made available to the public it must not be further disclosed by a person to whom it is so disclosed other than with the agreement of the public authority for the purpose mentioned in that subsection.

(3) A public authority which holds information to which section 237 applies may disclose that information to any other person for the purpose of facilitating the exercise by that person of any function he has under or by virtue of –

(a)   this Act;

(b)   an enactment specified in Schedule 15;

(c)   such subordinate legislation as the Secretary of State may by order specify for the purposes of this subsection.

(4) Information disclosed under subsection (3) must not be used by the person to whom it is disclosed for any purpose other than a purpose relating to a function mentioned in that subsection.

(5) In subsection (1) the reference to an enactment includes a reference to an enactment contained in –

(a)   an Act of the Scottish Parliament;

(b)   Northern Ireland legislation;

(c)   subordinate legislation.

(6) The Secretary of State may by order amend Schedule 15.

(7) The power to make an order under subsection (6) includes power to add, vary or remove a reference to any provision of –

(a)   an Act of the Scottish Parliament;

(b)   Northern Ireland legislation.

(8) An order under this section must be made by statutory instrument subject to annulment in pursuance of a resolution of either House of Parliament.

242 Criminal proceedings

(1) A public authority which holds information to which section 237 applies may disclose that information to any person –

(a)   in connection with the investigation of any criminal offence in any part of the United Kingdom;

(b)   for the purposes of any criminal proceedings there;

(c)   for the purpose of any decision whether to start or bring to an end such an investigation or proceedings.

(2) Information disclosed under this section must not be used by the person to whom it is disclosed for any purpose other than that for which it is disclosed.

(3) A public authority must not make a disclosure under this section unless it is satisfied that the making of the disclosure is proportionate to what is sought to be achieved by it.

243 Overseas disclosures

(1) A public authority which holds information to which section 237 applies (the discloser) may disclose that information to an overseas public authority for the purpose mentioned in subsection (2).

(2) The purpose is facilitating the exercise by the overseas public authority of any function which it has relating to –

    (a)   carrying out investigations in connection with the enforcement of any relevant legislation by means of civil proceedings;

    (b)   bringing civil proceedings for the enforcement of such legislation or the conduct of such proceedings;

    (c)   the investigation of crime;

    (d)   bringing criminal proceedings or the conduct of such proceedings;

    (e)   deciding whether to start or bring to an end such investigations or proceedings.

(3) But subsection (1) does not apply to any of the following –

    (a)   information which is held by a person who is designated by virtue of section 213(4) as a designated enforcer for the purposes of Part 8;

    (b)   information which comes to a public authority in connection with an investigation under Part 4, 5 or 6 of the 1973 Act or under section 11 of the Competition Act 1980;

    (c)   competition information within the meaning of section 351 of the Financial Services and Markets Act 2000;

    (d)   information which comes to a public authority in connection with an investigation under Part 3 or 4 or section 174 of this Act.

(4) The Secretary of State may direct that a disclosure permitted by this section must not be made if he thinks that in connection with any matter in respect of which the disclosure could be made it is more appropriate –

    (a)   if any investigation is to be carried out, that it is carried out by an authority in the United Kingdom or in another specified country or territory;

    (b)   if any proceedings are to be brought, that they are brought in a court in the United Kingdom or in another specified country or territory.

(5) The Secretary of State must take such steps as he thinks are appropriate to bring a direction under subsection (4) to the attention of persons likely to be affected by it.

(6) In deciding whether to disclose information under this section a public authority must have regard in particular to the following considerations –

    (a)   whether the matter in respect of which the disclosure is sought is sufficiently serious to justify making the disclosure;

    (b)   whether the law of the country or territory to whose authority the disclosure would be made provides appropriate protection against self-incrimination in criminal proceedings;

    (c)   whether the law of that country or territory provides appropriate protection in relation to the storage and disclosure of personal data;

    (d)   whether there are arrangements in place for the provision of mutual assistance as between the United Kingdom and that country or territory in relation to the disclosure of information of the kind to which section 237 applies.

(7) Protection is appropriate if it provides protection in relation to the matter in question which corresponds to that so provided in any part of the United Kingdom.

(8) The Secretary of State may by order –

  (a)   modify the list of considerations in subsection (6);
  (b)   add to those considerations;
  (c)   remove any of those considerations.

(9) An order under subsection (8) must be made by statutory instrument subject to annulment in pursuance of a resolution of either House of Parliament.

(10) Information disclosed under this section –

  (a)   may be disclosed subject to the condition that it must not be further disclosed without the agreement of the discloser, and
  (b)   must not otherwise be used by the overseas public authority to which it is disclosed for any purpose other than that for which it is first disclosed.

(11) An overseas public authority is a person or body in any country or territory outside the United Kingdom which appears to the discloser to exercise functions of a public nature in relation to any of the matters mentioned in paragraphs (a) to (e) of subsection (2).

(12) Relevant legislation is –

  (a)   this Act, any enactment specified in Schedule 14 and such subordinate legislation as is specified by order for the purposes of section 238(1);
  (b)   any enactment or subordinate legislation specified in an order under section 211(2);
  (c)   any enactment or subordinate legislation specified in an order under section 212(3);
  (d)   legislation in any country or territory outside the United Kingdom which appears to the discloser to make provision corresponding to this Act or to any such enactment or subordinate legislation.

244 Specified information: considerations relevant to disclosure

(1) A public authority must have regard to the following considerations before disclosing any specified information (within the meaning of section 238(1)).

(2) The first consideration is the need to exclude from disclosure (so far as practicable) any information whose disclosure the authority thinks is contrary to the public interest.

(3) The second consideration is the need to exclude from disclosure (so far as practicable) –

  (a)   commercial information whose disclosure the authority thinks might significantly harm the legitimate business interests of the undertaking to which it relates, or
  (b)   information relating to the private affairs of an individual whose disclosure the authority thinks might significantly harm the individual's interests.

(4) The third consideration is the extent to which the disclosure of the information mentioned in subsection (3)(a) or (b) is necessary for the purpose for which the authority is permitted to make the disclosure.

Offences

245 Offences

(1) A person commits an offence if he discloses information to which section 237 applies in contravention of section 237(2).

(2) A person commits an offence if he discloses information in contravention of a direction given under section 243(4).

(3) A person commits an offence if he uses information disclosed to him under this Part for a purpose which is not permitted under this Part.

(4) A person who commits an offence under this section is liable –

> (a) on summary conviction to imprisonment for a term not exceeding three months or to a fine not exceeding the statutory maximum or to both;
>
> (b) on conviction on indictment to imprisonment for a term not exceeding two years or to a fine or to both.

General

246 Subordinate legislation

In this Part 'subordinate legislation' has the same meaning as in section 21(1) of the Interpretation Act 1978 and includes an instrument made under –

> (a) an Act of the Scottish Parliament;
> (b) Northern Ireland legislation.

247 Repeals

The following enactments (which make provision as to the disclosure of certain information) shall cease to have effect –

> (a) section 28(5) and (5A) of the Trade Descriptions Act 1968;
> (b) sections 30(3) and 133 of the 1973 Act;
> (c) paragraph 12 of the Schedule to the Prices Act 1974;
> (d) section 174 of the Consumer Credit Act 1974;
> (e) section 10 of the Estate Agents Act 1979;
> (f) section 19(1) to (3), (4)(c), (d) and (f) and (5) and (6) of the Competition Act 1980;
> (g) section 38 of the Consumer Protection Act 1987;
> (h) paragraph 7 of the Schedule to the Property Misdescriptions Act 1991;
> (i) paragraph 5 of Schedule 2 to the Timeshare Act 1992;
> (j) sections 55 and 56 of and Schedule 11 to the Competition Act 1998;
> (k) section 351(1) to (3) and (7) of and Schedule 19 to the Financial Services and Markets Act 2000.

* * * *

PART 11
SUPPLEMENTARY

273 Interpretation

In this Act –

'the 1973 Act' means the Fair Trading Act 1973;
'the 1998 Act' means the Competition Act 1998;
'the Commission' means the Competition Commission;
'the Director' means the Director General of Fair Trading; and
'the OFT' means the Office of Fair Trading.

274 Provision of financial assistance for consumer purposes

The Secretary of State may give financial assistance to any person for the purpose of assisting –

(a) activities which the Secretary of State considers are of benefit to consumers; or
(b) the provision of –
  (i) advice or information about consumer matters;
  (ii) educational materials relating to consumer matters; or
  (iii) advice or information to the Secretary of State in connection with the formulation of policy in respect of consumer matters.

275 Financial provision

There shall be paid out of money provided by Parliament –

(a) any expenditure incurred by the OFT, the Secretary of State, any other Minister of the Crown or a government department by virtue of this Act; and
(b) any increase attributable to this Act in the sums payable out of money so provided by virtue of any other Act.

276 Transitional or transitory provision and savings

(1) Schedule 24 (which makes transitional and transitory provisions and savings) has effect.

(2) The Secretary of State may by order made by statutory instrument make such transitional or transitory provisions and savings as he considers appropriate in connection with the coming into force of any provision of this Act.

(3) An order under subsection (2) may modify any Act or subordinate legislation.

(4) Schedule 24 does not restrict the power under subsection (2) to make other transitional or transitory provisions and savings.

277 Power to make consequential amendments etc

(1) The Secretary of State may by order make such supplementary, incidental or consequential provision as he thinks appropriate –

    (a)   for the general purposes, or any particular purpose, of this Act; or

    (b)   in consequence of any provision made by or under this Act or for giving full effect to it.

(2) An order under this section may –

    (a)   modify any Act or subordinate legislation (including this Act);

    (b)   make incidental, supplementary, consequential, transitional, transitory or saving provision.

(3) The power to make an order under this section is exercisable by statutory instrument subject to annulment in pursuance of a resolution of either House of Parliament.

(4) The power conferred by this section is not restricted by any other provision of this Act.

278 Minor and consequential amendments and repeals

(1) Schedule 25 (which contains minor and consequential amendments) has effect.

(2) Schedule 26 (which contains repeals and revocations) has effect.

279 Commencement

The preceding provisions of this Act shall come into force on such day as the Secretary of State may by order made by statutory instrument appoint; and different days may be appointed for different purposes.

280 Extent

(1) Sections 256 to 265, 267, 269 and 272 extend only to England and Wales.

(2) Sections 204, 248 to 255 and 270 extend only to England and Wales and Scotland (but subsection (3) of section 415A as inserted by section 270 extends only to England and Wales).

(3) Any other modifications by this Act of an enactment have the same extent as the enactment being modified.

(4) Otherwise, this Act extends to England and Wales, Scotland and Northern Ireland.

281 Short title

This Act may be cited as the Enterprise Act 2002.

SCHEDULES

SCHEDULE 1
THE OFFICE OF FAIR TRADING

Section 1

Membership

1

(1) The OFT shall consist of a chairman and no fewer than four other members, appointed by the Secretary of State.

(2) The Secretary of State shall consult the chairman before appointing any other member.

Terms of appointment, remuneration, pensions etc

2

(1) Subject to this Schedule, the chairman and other members shall hold and vacate office in accordance with the terms of their respective appointments.

(2) The terms of appointment of the chairman and other members shall be determined by the Secretary of State.

3

(1) An appointment of a person to hold office as chairman or other member shall be for a term not exceeding five years.

(2) A person holding office as chairman or other member –

    (a)   may resign that office by giving notice in writing to the Secretary of State; and

    (b)   may be removed from office by the Secretary of State on the ground of incapacity or misbehaviour.

(3) A previous appointment as chairman or other member does not affect a person's eligibility for appointment to either office.

4

(1) The OFT shall pay to the chairman and other members such remuneration, and such travelling and other allowances, as may be determined by the Secretary of State.

(2) The OFT shall, if required to do so by the Secretary of State –

    (a)   pay such pension, allowances or gratuities as may be determined by the Secretary of State to or in respect of a person who holds or has held office as chairman or other member; or

(b)   make such payments as may be so determined towards provision for the payment of a pension, allowances or gratuities to or in respect of such a person.

(3) If, where any person ceases to hold office as chairman or other member, the Secretary of State determines that there are special circumstances which make it right that he should receive compensation, the OFT shall pay to him such amount by way of compensation as the Secretary of State may determine.

Staff

5

(1) The Secretary of State shall, after consulting the chairman, appoint a person (who may, subject to sub-paragraph (2), also be a member of the OFT) to act as chief executive of the OFT on such terms and conditions as the Secretary of State may think appropriate.

(2) A person appointed as chief executive after the end of the transitional period may not at the same time be chairman.

(3) In sub-paragraph (2) 'the transitional period' means the period of two years beginning with the day on which this paragraph comes into force.

6

The OFT may, with the approval of the Minister for the Civil Service as to numbers and terms and conditions of service, appoint such other staff as it may determine.

Membership of committees or sub-committees of OFT

7

The members of a committee or sub-committee of the OFT may include persons who are not members of the OFT (and a sub-committee may include persons who are not members of the committee which established it).

Proceedings etc

8

(1) The OFT may regulate its own procedure (including quorum).

(2) The OFT shall consult the Secretary of State before making or revising its rules and procedures for dealing with conflicts of interest.

(3) The OFT shall from time to time publish a summary of its rules and procedures for dealing with conflicts of interest.

9

The validity of anything done by the OFT is not affected by a vacancy among its members or by a defect in the appointment of a member.

10

(1) The application of the seal of the OFT shall be authenticated by the signature of –

(a)   any member; or

(b)   some other person who has been authorised for that purpose by the OFT, whether generally or specially.

(2) Sub-paragraph (1) does not apply in relation to any document which is, or is to be, signed in accordance with the law of Scotland.

11

A document purporting to be duly executed under the seal of the OFT, or signed on its behalf, shall be received in evidence and, unless the contrary is proved, be taken to be so executed or signed.

Performance of functions

12

(1) Anything authorised or required to be done by the OFT (including exercising the power under this paragraph) may be done by –

(a)   any member or employee of the OFT who is authorised for that purpose by the OFT, whether generally or specially;

(b)   any committee of the OFT which has been so authorised.

(2) Sub-paragraph (1)(b) does not apply to a committee whose members include any person who is not a member or employee of the OFT.

Supplementary powers

13

The OFT has power to do anything which is calculated to facilitate, or is conducive or incidental to, the performance of its functions.

Parliamentary Commissioner Act 1967

14

In Schedule 2 to the Parliamentary Commissioner Act 1967 (departments and authorities subject to investigation), there is inserted at the appropriate place –

'Office of Fair Trading.'

House of Commons Disqualification Act 1975

15

In Part 2 of Schedule 1 to the House of Commons Disqualification Act 1975 (bodies of which all members are disqualified), there is inserted at the appropriate place –

'The Office of Fair Trading.'

Northern Ireland Assembly Disqualification Act 1975

16

In Part 2 of Schedule 1 to the Northern Ireland Assembly Disqualification Act 1975 (bodies of which all members are disqualified), there is inserted at the appropriate place –

'The Office of Fair Trading.'

SCHEDULE 2
THE COMPETITION APPEAL TRIBUNAL

Section 12

Appointment, etc of President and chairmen

1

(1) A person is not eligible for appointment as President unless –

    (a)   he has a 10 year general qualification;

    (b)   he is an advocate or solicitor in Scotland of at least 10 years' standing; or

    (c)   he is a member of the Bar of Northern Ireland or solicitor of the Supreme Court of Northern Ireland of at least 10 years' standing;

and he appears to the Lord Chancellor to have appropriate experience and knowledge of competition law and practice.

(2) A person is not eligible for appointment as a chairman unless –

    (a)   he has a 7 year general qualification;

    (b)   he is an advocate or solicitor in Scotland of at least 7 years' standing; or

    (c)   he is a member of the Bar of Northern Ireland or solicitor of the Supreme Court of Northern Ireland of at least 7 years' standing;

and he appears to the Lord Chancellor to have appropriate experience and knowledge (either of competition law and practice or any other relevant law and practice).

(3) Before appointing an advocate or solicitor in Scotland under this paragraph, the Lord Chancellor must consult the Lord President of the Court of Session.

(4) In this paragraph 'general qualification' has the same meaning as in section 71 of the Courts and Legal Services Act 1990.

2

(1) The members appointed as President or as chairmen shall hold and vacate office in accordance with their terms of appointment, subject to the following provisions.

(2) A person may not be a chairman for more than 8 years (but this does not prevent a temporary re-appointment for the purpose of continuing to act as a member of the Tribunal as constituted for the purposes of any proceedings instituted before the end of his term of office).

(3) The President and the chairmen may resign their offices by notice in writing to the Lord Chancellor.

(4) The Lord Chancellor may remove a person from office as President or chairman on the ground of incapacity or misbehaviour.

3

If the President is absent or otherwise unable to act the Lord Chancellor may appoint as acting President any person qualified for appointment as a chairman.

Appointment, etc of ordinary members

4

(1) Ordinary members shall hold and vacate office in accordance with their terms of appointment, subject to the following provisions.

(2) A person may not be an ordinary member for more than 8 years (but this does not prevent a temporary re-appointment for the purpose of continuing to act as a member of the Tribunal as constituted for the purposes of any proceedings instituted before the end of his term of office).

(3) An ordinary member may resign his office by notice in writing to the Secretary of State.

(4) The Secretary of State may remove a person from office as an ordinary member on the ground of incapacity or misbehaviour.

Remuneration etc for members

5

(1) The Competition Service shall pay to the President, the chairmen and the ordinary members such remuneration (whether by way of salaries or fees), and such allowances, as the Secretary of State may determine.

(2) The Competition Service shall, if required to do so by the Secretary of State –

    (a)   pay such pension, allowances or gratuities as may be determined by the Secretary of State to or in respect of a person who holds or has held office as President, a chairman or an ordinary member; or

(b)   make such payments as may be so determined towards provision for the payment of a pension, allowance or gratuities to or in respect of such a person.

Compensation for loss of office

6

If, where any person ceases to hold office as President, a chairman or ordinary member, the Secretary of State determines that there are special circumstances which make it right that he should receive compensation, the Competition Service shall pay to him such amount by way of compensation as the Secretary of State may determine.

Staff, accommodation and property

7

Any staff, office accommodation or equipment required for the Tribunal shall be provided by the Competition Service.

Miscellaneous

8

The President must arrange such training for members of the Tribunal as he considers appropriate.

9

In this Schedule 'chairman' and 'ordinary member' mean respectively a member of the panel of chairmen, or a member of the panel of ordinary members, appointed under section 12.

10

In Part 2 of Schedule 1 to the House of Commons Disqualification Act 1975 (bodies of which all members are disqualified), there is inserted at the appropriate place –

'The Competition Appeal Tribunal.'

11

In Part 2 of Schedule 1 to the Northern Ireland Assembly Disqualification Act 1975 (bodies of which all members are disqualified), there is inserted at the appropriate place –

'The Competition Appeal Tribunal.'

SCHEDULE 3
THE COMPETITION SERVICE

Section 13

PART 1
CONSTITUTION ETC

Membership of the Service

1

(1) The Service shall consist of –

    (a)   the President of the Competition Appeal Tribunal;

    (b)   the Registrar of the Competition Appeal Tribunal; and

    (c)   one or more appointed members.

(2) An appointed member shall be appointed by the Secretary of State after consulting the President.

Chairman of Service

2

(1) Subject to sub-paragraph (2), the members shall choose one of their number to be chairman of the Service.

(2) The Secretary of State shall designate one of the members to be the first chairman of the Service for such period as the Secretary of State may determine.

Appointed members

3

An appointed member shall hold and vacate office in accordance with the terms of his appointment (and is eligible for re-appointment).

Allowances, etc for members

4

(1) The Service shall pay –

    (a)   such travelling and other allowances to its members, and

    (b)   such remuneration to any appointed member,

as may be determined by the Secretary of State.

(2) The Service shall, if required to do so by the Secretary of State –

(a)　pay such pension, allowances or gratuities as may be determined by the Secretary of State to or in respect of a person who holds or has held office as an appointed member; or

(b)　make such payments as may be so determined towards provision for the payment of a pension, allowances or gratuities to or in respect of such a person.

5

If, where any person ceases to hold office as an appointed member, the Secretary of State determines that there are special circumstances which make it right that he should receive compensation, the Service shall pay to him such amount by way of compensation as the Secretary of State may determine.

Staff

6

(1) The Service may, with the approval of the Secretary of State as to numbers and terms and conditions of service, appoint such staff as it may determine.

(2) The persons to whom section 1 of the Superannuation Act 1972 (persons to or in respect of whom benefits may be provided by schemes under that section) applies shall include the staff of the Service.

(3) The Service shall pay to the Minister for the Civil Service, at such times as he may direct, such sums as he may determine in respect of any increase attributable to sub-paragraph (2) in the sums payable out of money provided by Parliament under the Superannuation Act 1972.

Procedure

7

(1) The Service may regulate its own procedure (including quorum).

(2) The validity of anything done by the Service is not affected by a vacancy among its members or by a defect in the appointment of a member.

8

(1) The application of the seal of the Service shall be authenticated by the signature of –

(a)　any member; or

(b)　some other person who has been authorised for that purpose by the Service, whether generally or specially.

(2) Sub-paragraph (1) does not apply in relation to any document which is, or is to be, signed in accordance with the law of Scotland.

9

A document purporting to be duly executed under the seal of the Service, or signed on its behalf, shall be received in evidence and, unless the contrary is proved, be taken to be so executed or signed.

The Service's powers

10

The Service has power to do anything which is calculated to facilitate, or is conducive or incidental to, the performance of its functions.

Accounts

11

(1) The Service shall keep proper accounts and proper records in relation to its accounts.

(2) In performing that duty the Service shall, in addition to accounts and records relating to its own activities (including the services provided to the Tribunal), keep separate accounts and separate records in relation to the activities of the Tribunal.

12

(1) The Service shall –

    (a)   prepare a statement of accounts in respect of each of its financial years; and

    (b)   prepare a statement of accounts for the Tribunal for each of its financial years.

(2) The Service must send copies of the accounts required by sub-paragraph (1) to the Secretary of State and to the Comptroller and Auditor General before the end of August following the financial year to which they relate.

(3) Those accounts must comply with any directions given by the Secretary of State with the approval of the Treasury as to –

    (a)   the information to be contained in them;

    (b)   the manner in which that information is to be presented; and

    (c)   the methods and principles according to which they are to be prepared.

(4) The Comptroller and Auditor General shall –

    (a)   examine, certify and report on each statement of accounts received by him; and

    (b)   lay copies of each statement before Parliament.

(5) In this paragraph 'financial year' means the period of 12 months ending with 31st March.

PART 2
TRANSFERS OF PROPERTY ETC BETWEEN THE COMMISSION AND THE SERVICE

13

(1) The Secretary of State may make one or more schemes for the transfer to the Service of defined property, rights and liabilities of the Commission (including rights and liabilities relating to contracts of employment).

(2) A scheme may define the property, rights and liabilities to be transferred by specifying or describing them or by referring to all (or all except anything specified or described) of the property, rights and liabilities comprised in a specified part of the undertaking of the transferor.

(3) The property, rights and liabilities which may be transferred include any that would otherwise be incapable of being transferred or assigned.

(4) A scheme may include supplementary, incidental, transitional and consequential provision.

14

(1) On the day appointed by a scheme under paragraph 13, the property, rights and liabilities which are the subject of the scheme shall, by virtue of this sub-paragraph, be transferred in accordance with the provisions of the scheme.

(2) If, after that day, the Commission and the Service so agree in writing, the scheme shall for all purposes be deemed to have come into force on that day with such modification as may be agreed.

(3) An agreement under sub-paragraph (2) may, in connection with giving effect to modifications to the scheme, include supplemental, incidental, transitional and consequential provision.

15

The transfer by paragraph 14(1) of the rights and liabilities relating to an individual's contract of employment does not break the continuity of his employment and, accordingly –

    (a)   he is not to be regarded for the purposes of Part 11 of the Employment Rights Act 1996 as having been dismissed by virtue of the transfer; and

    (b)   his period of employment with the transferor counts as a period of employment with the transferee for the purposes of that Act.

16

(1) Anything done by or in relation to the transferor for the purposes of or in connection with anything transferred by paragraph 14(1) which is in effect

immediately before it is transferred shall be treated as if done by or in relation to the transferee.

(2) There may be continued by or in relation to the transferee anything (including legal proceedings) relating to anything so transferred which is in the process of being done by or in relation to the transferor immediately before it is transferred.

(3) A reference to the transferor in any document relating to anything so transferred shall be taken (so far as necessary for the purposes of or in consequence of the transfer) as a reference to the transferee.

(4) A transfer under paragraph 14(1) does not affect the validity of anything done by or in relation to the transferor before the transfer takes effect.

PART 3
MISCELLANEOUS

17

In Part 2 of Schedule 1 to the House of Commons Disqualification Act 1975 (bodies of which all members are disqualified), there is inserted at the appropriate place –

'The Competition Service.'

18

In Part 2 of Schedule 1 to the Northern Ireland Assembly Disqualification Act 1975 (bodies of which all members are disqualified), there is inserted at the appropriate place –

'The Competition Service.'

SCHEDULE 4
TRIBUNAL: PROCEDURE

Sections 14 and 15

PART 1
GENERAL

Decisions of the Tribunal

1

(1) A decision of the Tribunal in any proceedings before it must –

    (a)   state the reasons for the decision and whether it was unanimous or taken by a majority;

    (b)   be recorded in a document signed and dated by the chairman of the Tribunal dealing with the proceedings.

(2) In preparing that document the Tribunal shall have regard to the need for excluding, so far as practicable –

    (a)   information the disclosure of which would in its opinion be contrary to the public interest;

    (b)   commercial information the disclosure of which would or might, in its opinion, significantly harm the legitimate business interests of the undertaking to which it relates;

    (c)   information relating to the private affairs of an individual the disclosure of which would, or might, in its opinion, significantly harm his interests.

(3) But the Tribunal shall also have regard to the extent to which any disclosure mentioned in sub-paragraph (2) is necessary for the purpose of explaining the reasons for the decision.

(4) The President shall make such arrangements for the publication of the decisions of the Tribunal as he considers appropriate.

Enforcement of decisions in Great Britain

2

If a decision of the Tribunal is registered in England and Wales in accordance with rules of court or any practice direction –

    (a)   payment of damages which are awarded by the decision;

    (b)   costs or expenses awarded by the decision; and

    (c)   any direction given as a result of the decision,

may be enforced by the High Court as if the damages, costs or expenses were an amount due in pursuance of a judgment or order of the High Court, or as if the direction were an order of the High Court.

3

If a decision of the Tribunal awards damages, costs or expenses, or results in any direction being given, the decision may be recorded for execution in the Books of Council and Session and shall be enforceable accordingly.

4

Subject to rules of court or any practice direction, a decision of the Tribunal may be registered or recorded for execution –

    (a)   for the purpose of enforcing a direction given as a result of the decision, by the Registrar of the Tribunal or a person who was a party to the proceedings;

    (b)   for the purpose of enforcing a decision to award damages, costs or expenses (other than a decision to which paragraph (c) applies), by the person to whom the sum concerned was awarded; and

(c)   for the purpose of enforcing a decision to award damages which is the subject of an order under section 47B(6) of the 1998 Act, by the specified body concerned.

Enforcement of decisions in Northern Ireland

5

(1) A decision of the Tribunal may be enforced in Northern Ireland with the leave of the High Court in Northern Ireland –

    (a)   in the case of a direction given as a result of the decision, by the Registrar of the Tribunal or a person who was a party to the proceedings;

    (b)   for the purpose of enforcing a decision to award damages, costs or expenses (other than a decision to which paragraph (c) applies), by the person to whom the sum concerned was awarded; and

    (c)   for the purpose of enforcing a decision to award damages which is the subject of an order under section 47B(6) of the 1998 Act, by the specified body concerned.

(2) For the purpose of enforcing in Northern Ireland a decision to award damages, costs or expenses –

    (a)   payment may be enforced as if the damages, costs or expenses were an amount due in pursuance of a judgment or order of the High Court in Northern Ireland; and

    (b)   a sum equal to the amount of damages, costs or expenses shall be deemed to be payable under a money judgment within the meaning of Article 2(2) of the Judgments Enforcement (Northern Ireland) Order 1981 (SI 1981/226 (NI 6)) (and the provisions of that Order apply accordingly).

(3) For the purpose of enforcing in Northern Ireland a direction given as a result of a decision of the Tribunal, the direction may be enforced as if it were an order of the High Court in Northern Ireland.

Miscellaneous

6

A decision of the Tribunal in proceedings under section 47B of the 1998 Act which –

    (a)   awards damages to an individual in respect of a claim made or continued on his behalf (but is not the subject of an order under section 47B(6)); or

    (b)   awards costs or expenses to an individual in respect of proceedings in respect of a claim made under section 47A of that Act prior to its being continued on his behalf in the proceedings under section 47B,

may only be enforced by the individual concerned with the permission of the High Court or Court of Session.

7

An award of costs or expenses against a specified body in proceedings under section 47B of the 1998 Act may not be enforced against any individual on whose behalf a claim was made or continued in those proceedings.

8

In this Part of this Schedule any reference to damages includes a reference to any sum of money (other than costs or expenses) which may be awarded in respect of a claim made under section 47A of the 1998 Act or included in proceedings under section 47B of that Act.

PART 2
TRIBUNAL RULES

General

9

In this Schedule 'the Tribunal', in relation to any proceedings before it, means the Tribunal as constituted (in accordance with section 14) for the purposes of those proceedings.

10

Tribunal rules may make different provision for different kinds of proceedings.

Institution of proceedings

11

(1) Tribunal rules may make provision as to the period within which and the manner in which proceedings are to be brought.

(2) That provision may, in particular –

    (a)   provide for time limits for making claims to which section 47A of the 1998 Act applies in proceedings under section 47A or 47B;

    (b)   provide for the Tribunal to extend the period in which any particular proceedings may be brought; and

    (c)   provide for the form, contents, amendment and acknowledgement of the documents by which proceedings are to be instituted.

12

Tribunal rules may provide for the Tribunal to reject any proceedings (other than proceedings under section 47A or 47B of the 1998 Act) if it considers that –

    (a)   the person instituting them does not have a sufficient interest in the decision with respect to which the proceedings are brought; or

(b)   the document by which he institutes them discloses no valid grounds for bringing them.

13

Tribunal rules may provide for the Tribunal –

(a)   to reject the whole of any proceedings under section 47B of the 1998 Act if it considers that the person bringing the proceedings is not entitled to do so or that the proceedings do not satisfy the requirements of section 47B(1);

(b)   to reject any claim which is included in proceedings under section 47B if it considers that –

    (i)   the claim is not a consumer claim (within the meaning of section 47B(2)) which may be included in such proceedings; or

    (ii)   the individual concerned has not consented to its being made or continued on his behalf in such proceedings; or

(c)   to reject any claim made under section 47A of the 1998 Act or included in proceedings under section 47B of that Act if it considers that there are no reasonable grounds for making it.

14

Tribunal rules may provide for the Tribunal to reject any proceedings if it is satisfied that the person instituting the proceedings has habitually and persistently and without any reasonable ground –

(a)   instituted vexatious proceedings (whether against the same person or against different persons); or

(b)   made vexatious applications in any proceedings.

15

Tribunal rules must ensure that no proceedings are rejected without giving the parties the opportunity to be heard.

Pre-hearing reviews and preliminary matters

16

(1) Tribunal rules may make provision for the carrying out by the Tribunal of a preliminary consideration of proceedings (a 'pre-hearing review').

(2) That provision may include –

(a)   provision enabling such powers to be exercised on a pre-hearing review as may be specified in the rules;

(b)   provision for security and supplemental provision relating to security.

(3) For the purposes of sub-paragraph (2)(b) –

(a)   'provision for security' means provision authorising the Tribunal, in specified circumstances, to order a party to the proceedings, if he wishes to continue to participate in them, to pay a deposit not exceeding such sum as may be specified or calculated in a specified manner; and

    (b)   'supplemental provision', in relation to security, means provision as to –

        (i)   the manner in which the amount of a deposit is to be determined;

        (ii)   the consequences of non-payment of a deposit;

        (iii)   the circumstances in which the deposit, or any part of it, may be refunded to the person who paid it or paid to another party to the proceedings.

Conduct of the hearing

17

(1) Tribunal rules may make provision –

    (a)   as to the manner in which proceedings are to be conducted, including provision for any hearing to be held in private if the Tribunal considers it appropriate because it is considering information of a kind mentioned in paragraph 1(2);

    (b)   as to the persons entitled to appear on behalf of the parties;

    (c)   for requiring persons to attend to give evidence and produce documents, and for authorising the administration of oaths to witnesses;

    (d)   as to the evidence which may be required or admitted and the extent to which it should be oral or written;

    (e)   allowing the Tribunal to fix time limits with respect to any aspect of proceedings and to extend any time limit (before or after its expiry);

    (f)   enabling the Tribunal, on the application of any party or on its own initiative, to order –

        (i)   the disclosure between, or the production by, the parties of documents or classes of documents; or

        (ii)   such recovery or inspection of documents as might be ordered by a sheriff;

    (g)   for the appointment of experts for the purposes of proceedings;

    (h)   for the award of costs or expenses, including allowances payable to persons in connection with attendance before the Tribunal;

    (i)   for taxing or otherwise settling any costs or expenses awarded by the Tribunal or for the enforcement of any order awarding costs or expenses.

(2) Rules under sub-paragraph (1)(h) may provide, in relation to a claim made under section 47A of the 1998 Act which is continued on behalf of an individual in proceedings under section 47B of that Act, for costs or expenses to be awarded to or against that individual in respect of proceedings on that claim which took place before it was included in the proceedings under section 47B of that Act.

(3) Otherwise Tribunal rules may not provide for costs or expenses to be awarded to or against an individual on whose behalf a claim is made or continued in proceedings under section 47B of the 1998 Act.

(4) Tribunal rules may make provision enabling the Tribunal to refer any matter arising in any proceedings (other than proceedings under section 47A or 47B of the 1998 Act) back to the authority that made the decision to which the proceedings relate, if it appears that the matter has not been adequately investigated.

(5) A person who without reasonable excuse fails to comply with –

   (a)   any requirement imposed by virtue of sub-paragraph (1)(c); or
   (b)   any requirement with respect to the disclosure, production, recovery or inspection of documents which is imposed by virtue of sub-paragraph (1)(f),

is guilty of an offence and liable on summary conviction to a fine not exceeding level 3 on the standard scale.

Quorum

18

(1) Tribunal rules may make provision as to the consequences of a member of the Tribunal being unable to continue after part of any proceedings have been heard.

(2) The rules may allow the Tribunal to consist of the remaining members for the rest of the proceedings.

(3) The rules may enable the President, if it is the chairman of the Tribunal who is unable to continue –

   (a)   to appoint either of the remaining members to chair the Tribunal; and
   (b)   if that person is not a member of the panel of chairmen, to appoint himself or some other suitably qualified person to attend the proceedings and advise the remaining members on any questions of law arising.

(4) For the purpose of sub-paragraph (3) a person is 'suitably qualified' if he is, or is qualified for appointment as, a member of the panel of chairmen.

Interest

19

(1) Tribunal rules may make provision allowing the Tribunal to order that interest is payable on any sum awarded by the Tribunal or on any fees ordered to be paid under paragraph 20.

(2) That provision may include provision –

   (a)   as to the circumstances in which such an order may be made;
   (b)   as to the manner in which, and the periods in respect of which, interest is to be calculated and paid.

Fees

20

(1) Tribunal rules may provide –

    (a)   for fees to be chargeable in respect of specified costs of proceedings; and

    (b)   for the amount of such costs to be determined by the Tribunal.

(2) Any sums received in respect of such fees shall be paid into the Consolidated Fund.

Withdrawal of proceedings

21

(1) Tribunal rules may make provision –

    (a)   preventing a party who has instituted proceedings from withdrawing them without the permission of the Tribunal or, in specified circumstances, the President or the Registrar;

    (b)   for the Tribunal to grant permission to withdraw proceedings on such conditions as it considers appropriate;

    (c)   enabling the Tribunal to publish any decision which it would have made in any proceedings, had the proceedings not been withdrawn;

    (d)   as to the effect of withdrawal of proceedings; and

    (e)   as to the procedure to be followed if parties to proceedings agree to settle.

(2) Tribunal rules may make, in relation to a claim included in proceedings under section 47B of the 1998 Act, any provision which may be made under sub-paragraph (1) in relation to the whole proceedings.

Interim orders

22

(1) Tribunal rules may provide for the Tribunal to make an order, on an interim basis –

    (a)   suspending the effect of any decision which is the subject matter of proceedings before it;

    (b)   in the case of an appeal under section 46 or 47 of the 1998 Act, varying the conditions or obligations attached to an exemption;

    (c)   granting any remedy which the Tribunal would have had power to grant in its final decision.

(2) Tribunal rules may also make provision giving the Tribunal powers similar to those given to the OFT by section 35 of the 1998 Act.

Miscellaneous

23

(1) Tribunal rules may make provision enabling the Tribunal to decide where to sit for the purposes of, or of any part of, any proceedings before it.

(2) Tribunal rules may make provision enabling the Tribunal to decide that any proceedings before it are to be treated, for purposes connected with –

(a)   any appeal from a decision of the Tribunal made in those proceedings; and

(b)   any other matter connected with those proceedings,

as proceedings in England and Wales, Scotland or Northern Ireland (regardless of the decision made for the purposes of sub-paragraph (1)).

(3) For the purposes of sub-paragraph (2), Tribunal rules may provide for each claim made or continued on behalf of an individual in proceedings under section 47B of the 1998 Act to be treated as separate proceedings.

24

Tribunal rules may make provision –

(a)   for a person who is not a party to be joined in any proceedings;

(b)   for hearing a person who is not a party where, in any proceedings, it is proposed to make an order or give a direction in relation to that person;

(c)   for proceedings to be consolidated on such terms as the Tribunal thinks appropriate in such circumstances as may be specified.

25

Tribunal rules may make provision for the Tribunal to transfer a claim made in proceedings under section 47A of the 1998 Act to –

(a)   the High Court or a county court in England and Wales or Northern Ireland; or

(b)   the Court of Session or a sheriff court in Scotland.

26

Tribunal rules may make provision in connection with the transfer of any proceedings from a court mentioned in paragraph 25 to the Tribunal under section 16.

SCHEDULE 5
PROCEEDINGS UNDER PART 1 OF THE 1998 ACT

Section 21

1

Part 1 of the 1998 Act is amended as follows.

2

In section 46 (appealable decisions) –

(a)   in subsections (1) and (2), for 'the Competition Commission' there is substituted 'the Tribunal';

(b)   in subsection (3) (in the full-out words), after 'other decision' there is inserted 'under this Part';

(c)   subsection (3)(h) shall cease to have effect.

3

Section 48 (appeal tribunals) shall cease to have effect.

4

For section 49 there is substituted –

'49   Further appeals

(1) An appeal lies to the appropriate court –

(a)   from a decision of the Tribunal as to the amount of a penalty under section 36;

(b)   from a decision of the Tribunal as to the award of damages or other sum in respect of a claim made in proceedings under section 47A or included in proceedings under section 47B (other than a decision on costs or expenses) or as to the amount of any such damages or other sum; and

(c)   on a point of law arising from any other decision of the Tribunal on an appeal under section 46 or 47.

(2) An appeal under this section –

(a)   may be brought by a party to the proceedings before the Tribunal or by a person who has a sufficient interest in the matter; and

(b)   requires the permission of the Tribunal or the appropriate court.

(3) In this section "the appropriate court" means the Court of Appeal or, in the case of an appeal from Tribunal proceedings in Scotland, the Court of Session.'

5

In section 58(1) (findings of fact by director) –

(a)   in paragraph (a), after 'appeal' there is inserted 'under section 46 or 47'; and

(b)   in paragraph (b), for 'an appeal tribunal' there is substituted 'the Tribunal'.

6

In section 59(1) (interpretation of Part 1) –

(a)   the definition of 'appeal tribunal' shall cease to have effect;

(b)   after the definition of 'the Treaty' there is inserted –

'"the Tribunal" means the Competition Appeal Tribunal;
"Tribunal rules" means rules under section 15 of the Enterprise Act 2002.'

7

(1) Schedule 7 (the Competition Commission) is amended as follows.

(2) In paragraph 1 (interpretation) –

(a)   the definitions of 'appeal panel member' and 'the President' shall cease to have effect; and

(b)   in the definition of 'general functions', paragraph (a) and the word 'or' after it shall cease to have effect.

(3) In paragraph 2 (membership), sub-paragraphs (1)(a), (3)(a) and (4) shall cease to have effect.

(4) Paragraph 4 (the President) shall cease to have effect.

(5) In paragraph 5 (the Council) –

(a)   sub-paragraph (2)(b), and

(b)   in sub-paragraph (3), the words 'and paragraph 5 of Schedule 8',

shall cease to have effect.

(6) Part 3 (appeals) shall cease to have effect.

8

(1) Schedule 8 (appeals) is amended as follows.

(2) Paragraph 1 shall cease to have effect.

(3) In paragraph 2 (general procedure for appeals under Part 1) –

(a)   in sub-paragraph (1), for the words from 'Competition' to 'Commission' (in the second place it appears) there is substituted 'Tribunal under section 46 or 47 must be made by sending a notice of appeal to it';

(b)   in sub-paragraph (3), for 'tribunal' there is substituted 'Tribunal'; and

(c)   after sub-paragraph (3) there is inserted –

'(4) In this paragraph references to the Tribunal are to the Tribunal as constituted (in accordance with section 14 of the Enterprise Act 2002) for the purposes of the proceedings in question.

(5) Nothing in this paragraph restricts the power under section 15 of the Enterprise Act 2002 (Tribunal rules) to make provision as to the manner of instituting proceedings before the Tribunal.'

(4) In paragraph 3, for 'tribunal' (in each place) there is substituted 'Tribunal'.

(5) Paragraphs 4 to 14 shall cease to have effect.

SCHEDULE 6
SCHEDULE TO BE INSERTED IN THE WATER INDUSTRY ACT 1991

Section 70

'SCHEDULE 4ZA
APPLICATION OF PROVISIONS OF ENTERPRISE ACT 2002 TO MERGERS OF WATER ENTERPRISES

Section 34

1

Part 3 of the 2002 Act (and any other provisions of that Act so far as relating to that Part) shall apply, with such prescribed modifications as the Secretary of State considers to be necessary or expedient, in relation to water mergers and merger references under section 32 of this Act as it applies in relation to relevant merger situations and references under Part 3 of that Act.

2

The modifications made by virtue of paragraph 1 above shall include modifications to give effect to paragraphs 3 to 6 below.

3

(1) The first questions to be decided by the Competition Commission on a merger reference under section 32(a) of this Act shall be –

    (a)   whether arrangements are in progress which, if carried into effect, will result in a water merger; and

    (b)   if so, whether that merger may be expected to prejudice the ability of the Director, in carrying out his functions by virtue of this Act, to make comparisons between different water enterprises.

(2) The first questions to be decided by the Competition Commission on a merger reference under section 32(b) of this Act shall be –

    (a)   whether a water merger has taken place; and

    (b)   if so, whether that merger has prejudiced, or may be expected to prejudice, the ability of the Director, in carrying out his functions by virtue of this Act, to make comparisons between different water enterprises.

(3) Any decision of the Competition Commission on a merger reference under section 32(a) of this Act that arrangements are in progress which, if carried into effect, will result in a water merger shall be treated as a decision that no arrangements are in progress which, if carried into effect, will result in a water merger if the decision is not that of at least two-thirds of the members of the group constituted in connection with the reference in pursuance of paragraph 15 of Schedule 7 to the Competition Act 1998.

(4) Any decision of the Competition Commission on a merger reference under section 32(a) of this Act that a water merger may be expected to prejudice the ability of the Director, in carrying out his functions by virtue of this Act, to make comparisons between different water enterprises shall be treated as a decision that the water merger may be expected not to prejudice that ability of the Director if the decision is not that of at least two-thirds of the members of the group constituted in connection with the reference in pursuance of paragraph 15 of Schedule 7 to the Competition Act 1998.

(5) Any decision of the Competition Commission on a merger reference under section 32(b) of this Act that a water merger has taken place shall be treated as a decision that no water merger has taken place if the decision is not that of at least two-thirds of the members of the group constituted in connection with the reference in pursuance of paragraph 15 of Schedule 7 to the Competition Act 1998.

(6) Any decision of the Competition Commission on a merger reference under section 32(b) of this Act that a water merger has prejudiced, or may be expected to prejudice, the ability of the Director, in carrying out his functions by virtue of this Act, to make comparisons between different water enterprises shall be treated as a decision that the water merger has not prejudiced, or may be expected not to prejudice, that ability of the Director if the decision is not that of at least two-thirds of the members of the group constituted in connection with the reference in pursuance of paragraph 15 of Schedule 7 to the Competition Act 1998.

4

(1) In deciding, on a merger reference under section 32(a) of this Act whether to take action for the purpose of remedying, mitigating or preventing the prejudice to the Director or any adverse effect which may be expected to result from the prejudice to the Director and, if so, what action should be taken, the Competition Commission may, in particular, have regard to the effect of any such action on any relevant customer benefits in relation to the merger concerned provided that –

(a)   a consideration of those benefits would not prevent a solution to the prejudice concerned; or

(b)   the benefits which may be expected to accrue are substantially more important than the prejudice concerned.

(2) In deciding, on a merger reference under section 32(b) of this Act whether to take action for the purpose of remedying, mitigating or preventing the prejudice to the Director or any adverse effect which has resulted from, or may be expected to result from, the prejudice to the Director and, if so, what action should be taken, the Competition Commission may, in particular, have regard to the effect of any such action on any relevant customer benefits in relation to the merger concerned provided that –

(a)   a consideration of those benefits would not prevent a solution to the prejudice concerned; or

(b)   the benefits which have accrued, or may be expected to accrue, are substantially more important than the prejudice concerned.

(3) This paragraph is without prejudice to the power of the Secretary of State to provide in regulations made under paragraph 1 above for other matters to which the Competition Commission may or must have regard in deciding the questions as mentioned in sub-paragraph (1) or (2) above (including matters which are to take priority over the effect of action on relevant customer benefits).

5

(1) No enforcement action shall be taken on a merger reference under section 32(b) of this Act in respect of an actual merger unless the reference was made within the period of four months beginning with whichever is the later of –

    (a)   the day on which the merger took place; and

    (b)   the day on which the material facts about the transactions which resulted in the merger first came to the attention of the OFT or were made public (within the meaning given by section 24(3) of the 2002 Act).

(2) This paragraph is without prejudice to the power of the Secretary of State to provide in regulations made under paragraph 1 above for extensions of the four month period; and, if any such provision is made in such regulations, the provision which is to be made in regulations under paragraph 1 above by virtue of sub-paragraph (1) above or paragraph 6 below may be adjusted accordingly.

6

If, on a merger reference under section 32(b) of this Act, the Competition Commission are satisfied that the reference was not made within the period of four months mentioned in paragraph 5 above, its report on the reference shall state that fact.

7

(1) For the purposes of this Schedule a benefit is a relevant customer benefit if –

    (a)   it is a benefit to relevant customers in the form of –

        (i)   lower prices, higher quality or greater choice of goods or services in any market in the United Kingdom; or

        (ii)   greater innovation in relation to such goods or services; and

    (b)   the Competition Commission believes –

        (i)   in the case of a merger reference under section 32(a) of this Act, as mentioned in sub-paragraph (2) below; and

        (ii)   in the case of a merger reference under section 32(b) of this Act, as mentioned in sub-paragraph (3) below.

(2) The belief, in the case of a merger reference under section 32(a) of this Act, is that –

    (a)   the benefit may be expected to accrue within a reasonable period as a result of the merger concerned; and

(b)   the benefit is unlikely to accrue without the merger concerned or a similar prejudice to the Director.

(3) The belief, in the case of a merger reference under section 32(b) of this Act is that –

    (a)   the benefit has accrued as a result of the merger concerned or may be expected to accrue within a reasonable period as a result of the merger concerned; and

    (b)   the benefit was, or is, unlikely to accrue without the merger concerned or a similar prejudice to the Director.

(4) In sub-paragraph (1) above "relevant customers" means –

    (a)   customers of any person carrying on an enterprise which, in the merger concerned, has ceased to be, or (as the case may be) will cease to be, a distinct enterprise;

    (b)   customers of such customers; and

    (c)   any other customers in a chain of customers beginning with the customers mentioned in paragraph (a);

and in this sub-paragraph "customers" includes future customers.

8

In this Schedule –

    "customers", "goods", "market in the United Kingdom", "services" and "relevant merger situation" have the same meanings as in Part 3 of the 2002 Act; and

    "water merger" means a merger of any two or more water enterprises.'

SCHEDULE 7
ENFORCEMENT REGIME FOR PUBLIC INTEREST AND SPECIAL PUBLIC INTEREST CASES

Section 85

Pre-emptive undertakings and orders

1

(1) Sub-paragraph (2) applies where an intervention notice or special intervention notice is in force.

(2) The Secretary of State may, for the purpose of preventing pre-emptive action, accept from such of the parties concerned as he considers appropriate undertakings to take such action as he considers appropriate.

(3) Sub-paragraph (4) applies where an intervention notice is in force.

(4) The Secretary of State may, for the purpose of preventing pre-emptive action, adopt an undertaking accepted by the OFT under section 71 if the undertaking is still in force when the Secretary of State adopts it.

(5) An undertaking adopted under sub-paragraph (4) –

(a)   shall continue in force, in accordance with its terms, when adopted;

(b)   may be varied or superseded by an undertaking under this paragraph; and

(c)   may be released by the Secretary of State.

(6) Any other undertaking under this paragraph –

(a)   shall come into force when accepted;

(b)   may be varied or superseded by another undertaking; and

(c)   may be released by the Secretary of State.

(7) References in this Part to undertakings under this paragraph shall, unless the context otherwise requires, include references to undertakings adopted under this paragraph; and references to the acceptance or giving of undertakings under this paragraph shall be construed accordingly.

(8) An undertaking which is in force under this paragraph in relation to a reference or possible reference under section 45 or (as the case may be) 62 shall cease to be in force if an order under paragraph 2 or an undertaking under paragraph 3 comes into force in relation to that reference.

(9) An undertaking under this paragraph shall, if it has not previously ceased to be in force, cease to be in force when the intervention notice concerned or (as the case may be) special intervention notice concerned ceases to be in force.

(10) No undertaking shall be accepted by the Secretary of State under this paragraph before the making of a reference under section 45 or (as the case may be) 62 unless the undertaking relates to a relevant merger situation which has been, or may have been, created or (as the case may be) a special merger situation which has been, or may have been, created.

(11) The Secretary of State shall, as soon as reasonably practicable, consider any representations received by him in relation to varying or releasing an undertaking under this paragraph.

(12) In this paragraph and paragraph 2 'pre-emptive action' means action which might prejudice the reference or possible reference concerned under section 45 or (as the case may be) 62 or impede the taking of any action under this Part which may be justified by the Secretary of State's decisions on the reference.

2

(1) Sub-paragraph (2) applies where an intervention notice or special intervention notice is in force.

(2) The Secretary of State or the OFT may by order, for the purpose of preventing pre-emptive action –

(a)   prohibit or restrict the doing of things which the Secretary of State or (as the case may be) the OFT considers would constitute pre-emptive action;

(b)   impose on any person concerned obligations as to the carrying on of any activities or the safeguarding of any assets;

(c) provide for the carrying on of any activities or the safeguarding of any assets either by the appointment of a person to conduct or supervise the conduct of any activities (on such terms and with such powers as may be specified or described in the order) or in any other manner;

(d) do anything which may be done by virtue of paragraph 19 of Schedule 8.

(3) Sub-paragraph (4) applies where an intervention notice is in force.

(4) The Secretary of State or the OFT may, for the purpose of preventing pre-emptive action, adopt an order made by the OFT under section 72 if the order is still in force when the Secretary of State or (as the case may be) the OFT adopts it.

(5) An order adopted under sub-paragraph (4) –

(a) shall continue in force, in accordance with its terms, when adopted; and

(b) may be varied or revoked by an order under this paragraph.

(6) Any other order under this paragraph –

(a) shall come into force at such time as is determined by or under the order; and

(b) may be varied or revoked by another order.

(7) References in this Part to orders under this paragraph shall, unless the context otherwise requires, include references to orders adopted under this paragraph; and references to the making of orders under this paragraph shall be construed accordingly.

(8) An order which is in force under this paragraph in relation to a reference or possible reference under section 45 or (as the case may be) 62 shall cease to be in force if an undertaking under paragraph 1 or 3 comes into force in relation to that reference.

(9) An order under this paragraph shall, if it has not previously ceased to be in force, cease to be in force when the intervention notice concerned or (as the case may be) special intervention notice concerned ceases to be in force.

(10) No order shall be made by the Secretary of State or the OFT under this paragraph before the making of a reference under section 45 or (as the case may be) 62 unless the order relates to a relevant merger situation which has been, or may have been, created or (as the case may be) a special merger situation which has been, or may have been, created.

(11) The Secretary of State or (as the case may be) the OFT shall, as soon as reasonably practicable, consider any representations received by that person in relation to varying or revoking an order under this paragraph.

Undertakings in lieu of reference under section 45 or 62

3

(1) Sub-paragraph (2) applies if the Secretary of State has power to make a reference to the Commission under section 45 or 62 and otherwise intends to make such a reference.

(2) The Secretary of State may, instead of making such a reference and for the purpose of remedying, mitigating or preventing any of the effects adverse to the public interest which have or may have resulted, or which may be expected to result, from the creation of the relevant merger situation concerned or (as the case may be) the special merger situation concerned, accept from such of the parties concerned as he considers appropriate undertakings to take such action as he considers appropriate.

(3) In proceeding under sub-paragraph (2), the Secretary of State shall, in particular –

(a)   accept the decisions of the OFT included in its report under section 44 so far as they relate to the matters mentioned in subsections (4) and (5) of that section; or

(b)   (as the case may be) accept the decisions of the OFT included in its report under section 61 so far as they relate to the matters mentioned in subsections (3)(a) and (4) of that section.

(4) In proceeding under sub-paragraph (2) in relation to an anti-competitive outcome, the Secretary of State may, in particular, have regard to the effect of any action on any relevant customer benefits in relation to the creation of the relevant merger situation concerned.

(5) No undertaking shall be accepted by the Secretary of State under this paragraph in connection with a possible reference under section 45 if a public interest consideration mentioned in the intervention notice concerned has not been finalised and the period of 24 weeks beginning with the giving of that notice has not expired.

(6) The Secretary of State may delay making a decision as to whether to accept any such undertaking (and any related decision as to whether to make a reference under section 45) if he considers that there is a realistic prospect of the public interest consideration being finalised within the period of 24 weeks beginning with the giving of the intervention notice concerned.

(7) A delay under sub-paragraph (6) shall not extend beyond –

(a)   the time when the public interest consideration is finalised; or

(b)   if earlier, the expiry of the period of 24 weeks mentioned in that sub-paragraph.

(8) An undertaking under this paragraph –

(a)   shall come into force when accepted;

(b)   may be varied or superseded by another undertaking; or

(c)   may be released by the Secretary of State.

(9) An undertaking under this paragraph which is in force in relation to a relevant merger situation or (as the case may be) a special merger situation shall cease to be in force if an order comes into force under paragraph 5 or 6 in relation to that undertaking.

(10) The Secretary of State shall, as soon as reasonably practicable, consider any representations received by him in relation to varying or releasing an undertaking under this section.

4

(1) The relevant authority shall not make a reference under section 22, 33 or 45 in relation to the creation of a relevant merger situation or (as the case may be) a reference under section 62 in relation to the creation of a special merger situation if –

    (a)   the Secretary of State has accepted an undertaking or group of undertakings under paragraph 3; and

    (b)   the relevant merger situation or (as the case may be) the special merger situation is the situation by reference to which the undertaking or group of undertakings was accepted.

(2) In sub-paragraph (1) 'the relevant authority' means –

    (a)   in relation to a possible reference under section 22 or 33, the OFT; and

    (b)   in relation to a possible reference under section 45 or 62, the Secretary of State.

(3) Sub-paragraph (1) does not prevent the making of a reference if material facts about relevant arrangements or transactions, or relevant proposed arrangements or transactions, were not notified (whether in writing or otherwise) to the Secretary of State or the OFT or made public before any undertaking concerned was accepted.

(4) For the purposes of sub-paragraph (3) arrangements or transactions, or proposed arrangements or transactions, are relevant if they are the ones in consequence of which the enterprises concerned ceased or may have ceased, or may cease, to be distinct enterprises.

(5) In sub-paragraph (3) 'made public' means so publicised as to be generally known or readily ascertainable.

5

(1) Sub-paragraph (2) applies where the Secretary of State considers that –

    (a)   an undertaking accepted by him under paragraph 3 has not been, is not being or will not be fulfilled; or

    (b)   in relation to an undertaking accepted by him under that paragraph, information which was false or misleading in a material respect was given to him or the OFT by the person giving the undertaking before he decided to accept the undertaking.

(2) The Secretary of State may, for any of the purposes mentioned in paragraph 3(2), make an order under this paragraph.

(3) Sub-paragraphs (3) and (4) of paragraph 3 shall apply for the purposes of sub-paragraph (2) above as they apply for the purposes of sub-paragraph (2) of that paragraph.

(4) An order under this paragraph may contain –

    (a)   anything permitted by Schedule 8; and

    (b)   such supplementary, consequential or incidental provision as the Secretary of State considers appropriate.

(5) An order under this paragraph –

(a)   shall come into force at such time as is determined by or under the order; and

(b)   may contain provision which is different from the provision contained in the undertaking concerned.

(6) No order shall be varied or revoked under this paragraph unless the OFT advises that such a variation or revocation is appropriate by reason of a change of circumstances.

6

(1) Sub-paragraph (2) applies where –

(a)   the Secretary of State has the power to make an order under paragraph 5 in relation to a particular undertaking and intends to make such an order; or

(b)   the Secretary of State has the power to make an order under paragraph 10 in relation to a particular undertaking and intends to make such an order.

(2) The Secretary of State may, for the purpose of preventing any action which might prejudice the making of that order, make an order under this paragraph.

(3) No order shall be made under sub-paragraph (2) unless the Secretary of State has reasonable grounds for suspecting that it is or may be the case that action which might prejudice the making of the order under paragraph 5 or (as the case may be) 10 is in progress or in contemplation.

(4) An order under sub-paragraph (2) may –

(a)   prohibit or restrict the doing of things which the Secretary of State considers would prejudice the making of the order under paragraph 5 or 10;

(b)   impose on any person concerned obligations as to the carrying on of any activities or the safeguarding of any assets;

(c)   provide for the carrying on of any activities or the safeguarding of any assets either by the appointment of a person to conduct or supervise the conduct of any activities (on such terms and with such powers as may be specified or described in the order) or in any other manner;

(d)   do anything which may be done by virtue of paragraph 19 of Schedule 8.

(5) An order under this paragraph shall come into force at such time as is determined by or under the order.

(6) An order under this paragraph shall, if it has not previously ceased to be in force, cease to be in force on –

(a)   the coming into force of an order under paragraph 5 or (as the case may be) 10 in relation to the undertaking concerned; or

(b)   the making of the decision not to proceed with such an order.

(7) The Secretary of State shall, as soon as reasonably practicable, consider any representations received by him in relation to varying or revoking an order under this paragraph.

Statutory restrictions following reference under section 45 or 62

7

(1) Sub-paragraphs (2) and (3) apply where –

    (a)   a reference has been made under section 45(2) or (3) or 62(2) but not finally determined; and

    (b)   no undertakings under paragraph 1 are in force in relation to the relevant merger situation concerned or (as the case may be) the special merger situation concerned and no orders under paragraph 2 are in force in relation to that situation.

(2) No relevant person shall, without the consent of the Secretary of State –

    (a)   complete any outstanding matters in connection with any arrangements which have resulted in the enterprises concerned ceasing to be distinct enterprises;

    (b)   make any further arrangements in consequence of that result (other than arrangements which reverse that result); or

    (c)   transfer the ownership or control of any enterprises to which the reference relates.

(3) No relevant person shall, without the consent of the Secretary of State, assist in any of the activities mentioned in paragraphs (a) to (c) of sub-paragraph (2).

(4) The prohibitions in sub-paragraphs (2) and (3) do not apply in relation to anything which the person concerned is required to do by virtue of any enactment.

(5) The consent of the Secretary of State under sub-paragraph (2) or (3) –

    (a)   may be general or specific;

    (b)   may be revoked by the Secretary of State; and

    (c)   shall be published in such manner as the Secretary of State considers appropriate for bringing it to the attention of any person entitled to the benefit of it.

(6) Paragraph (c) of sub-paragraph (5) shall not apply if the Secretary of State considers that publication is not necessary for the purpose mentioned in that paragraph.

(7) Sub-paragraphs (2) and (3) shall apply to a person's conduct outside the United Kingdom if (and only if) he is –

    (a)   a United Kingdom national;

    (b)   a body incorporated under the law of the United Kingdom or of any part of the United Kingdom; or

    (c)   a person carrying on business in the United Kingdom.

(8) For the purpose of this paragraph a reference under section 45(2) or (3) is finally determined if –

(a)   the time within which the Commission is to prepare a report under section 50 in relation to the reference and give it to the Secretary of State has expired and no such report has been so prepared and given;

(b)   the Commission decides to cancel the reference under section 53(1);

(c)   the time within which the Secretary of State is to make and publish a decision under section 54(2) has expired and no such decision has been made and published;

(d)   the Secretary of State decides under section 54(2) to make no finding at all in the matter;

(e)   the Secretary of State otherwise decides under section 54(2) not to make an adverse public interest finding;

(f)   the Secretary of State decides under section 54(2) to make an adverse public interest finding but decides neither to accept an undertaking under paragraph 9 of this Schedule nor to make an order under paragraph 11 of this Schedule; or

(g)   the Secretary of State decides under section 54(2) to make an adverse public interest finding and accepts an undertaking under paragraph 9 of this Schedule or makes an order under paragraph 11 of this Schedule.

(9) For the purpose of this paragraph a reference under section 62(2) is finally determined if –

(a)   the time within which the Commission is to prepare a report under section 65 in relation to the reference and give it to the Secretary of State has expired and no such report has been so prepared and given;

(b)   the time within which the Secretary of State is to make and publish a decision under section 66(2) has expired and no such decision has been made and published;

(c)   the Secretary of State decides under subsection (2) of section 66 otherwise than as mentioned in subsection (5) of that section;

(d)   the Secretary of State decides under subsection (2) of section 66 as mentioned in subsection (5) of that section but decides neither to accept an undertaking under paragraph 9 of this Schedule nor to make an order under paragraph 11 of this Schedule; or

(e)   the Secretary of State decides under subsection (2) of section 66 as mentioned in subsection (5) of that section and accepts an undertaking under paragraph 9 of this Schedule or makes an order under paragraph 11 of this Schedule.

(10) For the purposes of this paragraph the time when a reference under section 45(2) or (3) or (as the case may be) 62(2) is finally determined is –

(a)   in a case falling within sub-paragraph (8)(a) or (c) or (as the case may be) (9)(a) or (b), the expiry of the time concerned;

(b)   in a case falling within sub-paragraph (8)(b), (d) or (e) or (as the case may be) (9)(c), the making of the decision concerned;

(c)   in a case falling within sub-paragraph (8)(f) or (as the case may be) (9)(d), the making of the decision neither to accept an undertaking under paragraph 9 of this Schedule nor to make an order under paragraph 11 of this Schedule; and

(d)   in a case falling within sub-paragraph (8)(g) or (as the case may be) (9)(e), the acceptance of the undertaking concerned or (as the case may be) the making of the order concerned.

(11) In this paragraph 'relevant person' means –

(a)   any person who carries on any enterprise to which the reference relates or who has control of any such enterprise;

(b)   any subsidiary of any person falling within paragraph (a); or

(c)   any person associated with any person falling within paragraph (a) or any subsidiary of any person so associated.

8

(1) Sub-paragraph (2) applies where –

(a)   a reference has been made under section 45(4) or (5) or 62(3); and

(b)   no undertakings under paragraph 1 are in force in relation to the relevant merger situation concerned or (as the case may be) special merger situation concerned and no orders under paragraph 2 are in force in relation to that situation.

(2) No relevant person shall, without the consent of the Secretary of State, directly or indirectly acquire during the relevant period an interest in shares in a company if any enterprise to which the reference relates is carried on by or under the control of that company.

(3) The consent of the Secretary of State under sub-paragraph (2) –

(a)   may be general or specific;

(b)   may be revoked by the Secretary of State; and

(c)   shall be published in such manner as the Secretary of State considers appropriate for bringing it to the attention of any person entitled to the benefit of it.

(4) Paragraph (c) of sub-paragraph (3) shall not apply if the Secretary of State considers that publication is not necessary for the purpose mentioned in that paragraph.

(5) Sub-paragraph (2) shall apply to a person's conduct outside the United Kingdom if (and only if) he is –

(a)   a United Kingdom national;

(b)   a body incorporated under the law of the United Kingdom or of any part of the United Kingdom; or

(c)   a person carrying on business in the United Kingdom.

(6) In this paragraph –

'company' includes any body corporate;

'relevant period' means the period beginning with the publication of the decision of the Secretary of State to make the reference concerned and ending when the reference is finally determined;

'relevant person' means –

(a)   any person who carries on any enterprise to which the reference relates or who has control of any such enterprise;

(b)   any subsidiary of any person falling within paragraph (a); or

(c)   any person associated with any person falling within paragraph (a) or any subsidiary of any person so associated; and

'share' means share in the capital of a company, and includes stock.

(7) For the purposes of the definition of 'relevant period' in sub-paragraph (6), a reference under section 45(4) or (5) is finally determined if –

(a)   the Commission cancels the reference under section 48(1) or 53(1);

(b)   the time within which the Commission is to prepare a report under section 50 in relation to the reference and give it to the Secretary of State has expired and no such report has been so prepared and given;

(c)   the time within which the Secretary of State is to make and publish a decision under section 54(2) has expired and no such decision has been made and published;

(d)   the Secretary of State decides under section 54(2) to make no finding at all in the matter;

(e)   the Secretary of State otherwise decides under section 54(2) not to make an adverse public interest finding;

(f)   the Secretary of State decides under section 54(2) to make an adverse public interest finding but decides neither to accept an undertaking under paragraph 9 of this Schedule nor to make an order under paragraph 11 of this Schedule; or

(g)   the Secretary of State decides under section 54(2) to make an adverse public interest finding and accepts an undertaking under paragraph 9 of this Schedule or makes an order under paragraph 11 of this Schedule.

(8) For the purposes of the definition of 'relevant period' in sub-paragraph (6), a reference under section 62(3) is finally determined if –

(a)   the Commission cancels the reference under section 64(1);

(b)   the time within which the Commission is to prepare a report under section 65 in relation to the reference and give it to the Secretary of State has expired and no such report has been so prepared and given;

(c)   the time within which the Secretary of State is to make and publish a decision under section 66(2) has expired and no such decision has been made and published;

(d)   the Secretary of State decides under subsection (2) of section 66 otherwise than as mentioned in subsection (5) of that section;

(e)   the Secretary of State decides under subsection (2) of section 66 as mentioned in subsection (5) of that section but decides neither to accept an undertaking under paragraph 9 of this Schedule nor to make an order under paragraph 11 of this Schedule; or

(f)   the Secretary of State decides under subsection (2) of section 66 as mentioned in subsection (5) of that section and accepts an undertaking under paragraph 9 of this Schedule or makes an order under paragraph 11 of this Schedule.

(9) For the purposes of the definition of 'relevant period' in sub-paragraph (6) above, the time when a reference under section 45(4) or (5) or (as the case may be) 62(3) is finally determined is –

(a) in a case falling within sub-paragraph (7)(a), (d) or (e) or (as the case may be) (8)(a) or (d), the making of the decision concerned;

(b) in a case falling within sub-paragraph (7)(b) or (c) or (as the case may be) (8)(b) or (c), the expiry of the time concerned;

(c) in a case falling within sub-paragraph (7)(f) or (as the case may be) (8)(e), the making of the decision neither to accept an undertaking under paragraph 9 of this Schedule nor to make an order under paragraph 11 of this Schedule; and

(d) in a case falling within sub-paragraph (7)(g) or (as the case may be) (8)(f), the acceptance of the undertaking concerned or (as the case may be) the making of the order concerned.

(10) Section 79 shall apply for the purposes of paragraph 7 and this paragraph in relation to a reference under section 45 or 62 as it applies for the purposes of sections 77 and 78 in relation to a reference under section 22 or 33.

(11) In its application by virtue of sub-paragraph (10) section 79 shall have effect as if –

(a) subsections (1) and (2) were omitted; and

(b) for the reference in subsection (4) to the OFT there were substituted a reference to the Secretary of State.

Final undertakings and orders

9

(1) The Secretary of State may, in accordance with section 55 or (as the case may be) 66(5) to (7), accept, from such persons as he considers appropriate, undertakings to take action specified or described in the undertakings.

(2) An undertaking under this paragraph –

(a) shall come into force when accepted;

(b) may be varied or superseded by another undertaking; and

(c) may be released by the Secretary of State.

(3) An undertaking which is in force under this paragraph in relation to a reference under section 45 or 62 shall cease to be in force if an order under paragraph 6(1)(b) or 10 comes into force in relation to the subject-matter of the undertaking.

(4) No undertaking shall be accepted under this paragraph in relation to a reference under section 45 or 62 if an order has been made under –

(a) paragraph 6(1)(b) or 10 in relation to the subject-matter of the undertaking; or

(b) paragraph 11 in relation to that reference.

(5) The Secretary of State shall, as soon as reasonably practicable, consider any representations received by him in relation to varying or releasing an undertaking under this section.

10

(1) Sub-paragraph (2) applies where the Secretary of State considers that –

    (a)   an undertaking accepted by him under paragraph 9 has not been, is not being or will not be fulfilled; or

    (b)   in relation to an undertaking accepted by him under that paragraph, information which was false or misleading in a material respect was given to him or the OFT by the person giving the undertaking before he decided to accept the undertaking.

(2) The Secretary of State may, for any purpose mentioned in section 55(2) or (as the case may be) 66(6), make an order under this paragraph.

(3) Subsections (3) and (4) of section 55 or (as the case may be) subsection (7) of section 66 shall apply for the purposes of sub-paragraph (2) above as they or it applies for the purposes of section 55(2) or (as the case may be) 66(6).

(4) An order under this paragraph may contain –

    (a)   anything permitted by Schedule 8; and

    (b)   such supplementary, consequential or incidental provision as the Secretary of State considers appropriate.

(5) An order under this paragraph –

    (a)   shall come into force at such time as is determined by or under the order; and

    (b)   may contain provision which is different from the provision contained in the undertaking concerned.

(6) No order shall be varied or revoked under this paragraph unless the OFT advises that such a variation or revocation is appropriate by reason of a change of circumstances.

11

(1) The Secretary of State may, in accordance with section 55 or (as the case may be) 66(5) to (7), make an order under this paragraph.

(2) An order under this paragraph may contain –

    (a)   anything permitted by Schedule 8; and

    (b)   such supplementary, consequential or incidental provision as the Secretary of State considers appropriate.

(3) An order under this paragraph shall come into force at such time as is determined by or under the order.

(4) No order shall be made under this paragraph in relation to a reference under section 45 or (as the case may be) 62 if an undertaking has been accepted under paragraph 9 in relation to that reference.

(5) No order shall be varied or revoked under this paragraph unless the OFT advises that such a variation or revocation is appropriate by reason of a change of circumstances.

SCHEDULE 8
PROVISION THAT MAY BE CONTAINED IN CERTAIN ENFORCEMENT ORDERS

Section 86(4)

Introductory

1

This Schedule applies in relation to such orders, and to such extent, as is provided by this Part and Part 4 and any other enactment; and references in this Schedule to an order shall be construed accordingly.

General restrictions on conduct

2

(1) An order may –

    (a)   prohibit the making or performance of an agreement;

    (b)   require any party to an agreement to terminate the agreement.

(2) An order made by virtue of sub-paragraph (1) shall not –

    (a)   prohibit the making or performance of; or

    (b)   require any person to terminate,

an agreement so far as, if made, the agreement would relate, or (as the case may be) so far as the agreement relates, to the terms and conditions of employment of any workers or to the physical conditions in which any workers are required to work.

3

(1) An order may prohibit the withholding from any person of –

    (a)   any goods or services;

    (b)   any orders for any such goods or services.

(2) References in sub-paragraph (1) to withholding include references to –

    (a)   agreeing or threatening to withhold; and

    (b)   procuring others to withhold or to agree or threaten to withhold.

4

An order may prohibit requiring as a condition of the supply of goods or services to any person –

    (a)   the buying of any goods;

    (b)   the making of any payment in respect of services other than the goods or services supplied;

    (c)   the doing of any other such matter or the refraining from doing anything mentioned in paragraph (a) or (b) or any other such matter.

5

An order may prohibit –

(a)   discrimination between persons in the prices charged for goods or services;

(b)   anything which the relevant authority considers to be such discrimination;

(c)   procuring others to do anything which is such discrimination or which the relevant authority considers to be such discrimination.

6

An order may prohibit –

(a)   giving, or agreeing to give in other ways, any preference in respect of the supply of goods or services or in respect of the giving of orders for goods or services;

(b)   giving, or agreeing to give in other ways, anything which the relevant authority considers to be a preference in respect of the supply of goods or services or in respect of the giving of orders for goods or services;

(c)   procuring others to do anything mentioned in paragraph (a) or (b).

7

An order may prohibit –

(a)   charging, for goods or services supplied, prices differing from those in any published list or notification;

(b)   doing anything which the relevant authority considers to be charging such prices.

8

(1) An order may regulate the prices to be charged for any goods or services.

(2) No order shall be made by virtue of sub-paragraph (1) unless the relevant report in relation to the matter concerned identifies the prices charged for the goods or services as requiring remedial action.

(3) In this paragraph 'the relevant report' means the report of the Commission which is required by the enactment concerned before an order can be made under this Schedule.

9

An order may prohibit the exercise of any right to vote exercisable by virtue of the holding of any shares, stock or securities.

General obligations to be performed

10

(1) An order may require a person to supply goods or services or to do anything which the relevant authority considers appropriate to facilitate the provision of goods or services.

(2) An order may require a person who is supplying, or is to supply, goods or services to supply such goods or services to a particular standard or in a particular manner or to do anything which the relevant authority considers appropriate to facilitate the provision of such goods or services to that standard or in that manner.

11

An order may require any activities to be carried on separately from any other activities.

Acquisitions and divisions

12

(1) An order may prohibit or restrict –

   (a)   the acquisition by any person of the whole or part of the undertaking or assets of another person's business;

   (b)   the doing of anything which will or may result in two or more bodies corporate becoming interconnected bodies corporate.

(2) An order may require that if –

   (a)   an acquisition of the kind mentioned in sub-paragraph (1)(a) is made; or

   (b)   anything is done which results in two or more bodies corporate becoming interconnected bodies corporate;

the persons concerned or any of them shall observe any prohibitions or restrictions imposed by or under the order.

(3) This paragraph shall also apply to any result consisting in two or more enterprises ceasing to be distinct enterprises (other than any result consisting in two or more bodies corporate becoming interconnected bodies corporate).

13

(1) An order may provide for –

   (a)   the division of any business (whether by the sale of any part of the undertaking or assets or otherwise);

   (b)   the division of any group of interconnected bodies corporate.

(2) For the purposes of sub-paragraph (1)(a) all the activities carried on by way of business by any one person or by any two or more interconnected bodies corporate may be treated as a single business.

(3) An order made by virtue of this paragraph may contain such provision as the relevant authority considers appropriate to effect or take account of the division, including, in particular, provision as to –

(a)   the transfer or creation of property, rights, liabilities or obligations;

(b)   the number of persons to whom the property, rights, liabilities or obligations are to be transferred or in whom they are to be vested;

(c)   the time within which the property, rights, liabilities or obligations are to be transferred or vested;

(d)   the adjustment of contracts (whether by discharge or reduction of any liability or obligation or otherwise);

(e)   the creation, allotment, surrender or cancellation of any shares, stock or securities;

(f)   the formation or winding up of any company or other body of persons corporate or unincorporate;

(g)   the amendment of the memorandum and articles or other instruments regulating any such company or other body of persons;

(h)   the extent to which, and the circumstances in which, provisions of the order affecting a company or other body of persons corporate or unincorporate in its share capital, constitution or other matters may be altered by the company or other body of persons concerned;

(i)   the registration of the order under any enactment by a company or other body of persons corporate or unincorporate which is affected by it as mentioned in paragraph (h);

(j)   the continuation, with any necessary change of parties, of any legal proceedings;

(k)   the approval by the relevant authority or another person of anything required by virtue of the order to be done or of any person to whom anything is to be transferred, or in whom anything is to be vested, by virtue of the order; or

(l)   the appointment of trustees or other persons to do anything on behalf of another person which is required of that person by virtue of the order or to monitor the doing by that person of any such thing.

14

The references in paragraph 13 to the division of a business as mentioned in sub-paragraph (1)(a) of that paragraph shall, in the case of an order under section 75, 83, 84, 160 or 161, or an order under paragraph 5, 10 or 11 of Schedule 7, be construed as including references to the separation, by the sale of any part of any undertaking or assets concerned or other means, of enterprises which are under common control (within the meaning of section 26) otherwise than by reason of their being enterprises of interconnected bodies corporate.

Supply and publication of information

15

(1) An order may require a person supplying goods or services to publish a list of prices or otherwise notify prices.

(2) An order made by virtue of this paragraph may also require or prohibit the publication or other notification of further information.

16

An order may prohibit any person from notifying (whether by publication or otherwise) to persons supplying goods or services prices recommended or suggested as appropriate to be charged by those persons for those goods or services.

17

(1) An order may require a person supplying goods or services to publish –

(a)   accounting information in relation to the supply of the goods or services;

(b)   information in relation to the quantities of goods or services supplied;

(c)   information in relation to the geographical areas in which they are supplied.

(2) In sub-paragraph (1) 'accounting information', in relation to a supply of goods or services, means information as to –

(a)   the costs of the supply, including fixed costs and overheads;

(b)   the manner in which fixed costs and overheads are calculated and apportioned for accounting purposes of the supplier; and

(c)   the income attributable to the supply.

18

An order made by virtue of paragraph 15 or 17 may provide for the manner in which information is to be published or otherwise notified.

19

An order may –

(a)   require any person to supply information to the relevant authority;

(b)   where the OFT is not the relevant authority, require any person to supply information to the OFT;

(c)   provide for the publication, by the person who has received information by virtue of paragraph (a) or (b), of that information.

National security

20

(1) An order may make such provision as the person making the order considers to be appropriate in the interests of national security (within the meaning of section 58(1)).

(2) Such provision may, in particular, include provision requiring a person to do, or not to do, particular things.

Supplementary

21

(1) An order, as well as making provision in relation to all cases to which it may extend, may make provision in relation to –

    (a)   those cases subject to specified exceptions; or

    (b)   any particular case or class of case.

(2) An order may, in relation to the cases in relation to which it applies, make the full provision which may be made by it or any less provision (whether by way of exception or otherwise).

(3) An order may make provision for matters to be determined under the order.

(4) An order may –

    (a)   make different provision for different cases or classes of case or different purposes;

    (b)   make such transitional, transitory or saving provision as the person making it considers appropriate.

22

(1) An order which may prohibit the doing of anything (or the refraining from doing anything) may in particular by virtue of paragraph 21(2) prohibit the doing of that thing (or the refraining from doing of it) except to such extent and in such circumstances as may be provided by or under the order.

(2) Any such order may, in particular, prohibit the doing of that thing (or the refraining from doing of it) –

    (a)   without the agreement of the relevant authority or another person; or

    (b)   by or in relation to a person who has not been approved by the relevant authority or another person.

Interpretation

23

References in this Schedule to the notification of prices or other information are not limited to the notification in writing of prices or other information.

24

In this Schedule 'the relevant authority' means –

    (a)   in the case of an order to be made by the OFT, the OFT;

    (b)   in the case of an order to be made by the Commission, the Commission; and

    (c)   in the case of an order to be made by the Secretary of State, the Secretary of State.

SCHEDULE 9
CERTAIN AMENDMENTS OF SECTORAL ENACTMENTS
Sections 86(5), 164(2) and 168(9)

PART 1
POWER OF ENFORCEMENT ORDERS TO AMEND LICENCE CONDITIONS ETC

Telecommunications Act 1984

1

(1) Section 95 of the Telecommunications Act 1984 (modification of licence conditions by order) shall be amended as follows.

(2) For subsections (1) and (2) there shall be substituted –

'(1) Where the Office of Fair Trading, the Commission or (as the case may be) the Secretary of State (in this section "the relevant authority") makes a relevant order, the order may also provide for the revocation or modification of licences granted under section 7 above to such extent as may appear to the relevant authority to be requisite or expedient for the purpose of giving effect to, or taking account of, any provision made by the order.

(2) In subsection (1) above, "relevant order" means –

(a)   an order under section 75, 83 or 84 of, or paragraph 5, 10 or 11 of Schedule 7 to, the Enterprise Act 2002 where –
(i)   one or more than one of the enterprises which have, or may have, ceased to be distinct enterprises was engaged in the carrying on of a commercial activity connected with telecommunications; or
(ii)   one or more than one of the enterprises which will or may cease to be distinct enterprises is engaged in the carrying on of a commercial activity connected with telecommunications; or

(b)   an order under section 160 or 161 of that Act where the feature, or combination of features, of the market in the United Kingdom for goods or services which prevents, restricts or distorts competition relates to commercial activities connected with telecommunications.'

(3) For subsection (3) there shall be substituted –

'(3) Expressions used in subsection (2) above and in Part 3 or (as the case may be) Part 4 of the Enterprise Act 2002 have the same meanings in that subsection as in that Part.'

Airports Act 1986

2

(1) Section 54 of the Airports Act 1986 (modification of certain conditions in force under Part 4 of that Act) shall be amended as follows.

(2) For subsection (1) there shall be substituted –

'(1) Where the Office of Fair Trading, the Competition Commission or (as the case may be) the Secretary of State (in this section "the relevant authority") makes a relevant order, the order may also provide for the revocation or modification of any relevant conditions to such extent as may appear to the relevant authority to be requisite or expedient for the purpose of giving effect to, or taking account of, any provision made by the order.

(1A) In subsection (1) "relevant order" means –

    (a)   an order under section 75, 83 or 84 of, or paragraph 5, 10 or 11 of Schedule 7 to, the Enterprise Act 2002 where –
        (i)   one or more than one of the enterprises which have, or may have, ceased to be distinct enterprises was carried on by an airport operator; or
        (ii)   one or more than one of the enterprises which will or may cease to be distinct enterprises is carried on by an airport operator; or

    (b)   an order under section 160 or 161 of that Act where the feature, or combination of features, of the market in the United Kingdom for goods or services which prevents, restricts or distorts competition relates to the carrying on of any operational activities relating to one or more than one airport.'

(3) Subsection (3) shall cease to have effect.

(4) For subsection (4) there shall be substituted –

'(4) Expressions used in subsection (1A) and in Part 3 or (as the case may be) Part 4 of the Enterprise Act 2002 have the same meanings in that subsection as in that Part.'

3

In paragraph 13 of Schedule 1 to that Act –

    (a)   for 'section 54(3)(b)' there shall be substituted 'section 54(1A)';
    (b)   for 'the reference' there shall be substituted 'references'; and
    (c)   for 'a reference' there shall be substituted 'references'.

Gas Act 1986

4

(1) Section 27 of the Gas Act 1986 (modification of licence conditions by order) shall be amended as follows.

(2) For subsection (1) there shall be substituted –

'(1) Where the Office of Fair Trading, the Competition Commission or (as the case may be) the Secretary of State (in this section "the relevant authority") makes a relevant order, the order may also provide for the modification of –

    (a)   the conditions of a particular licence; or

    (b)   the standard conditions of licences under section 7 above, licences under subsection (1) of section 7A above or licences under subsection (2) of that section,

to such extent as may appear to the relevant authority to be requisite or expedient for the purpose of giving effect to, or taking account of, any provision made by the order.

(1ZA) In subsection (1) above "relevant order" means –

    (a)   an order under section 75, 83 or 84 of, or paragraph 5, 10 or 11 of Schedule 7 to, the Enterprise Act 2002 where –

        (i)   one or more than one of the enterprises which have, or may have, ceased to be distinct enterprises was engaged in the carrying on of activities authorised or regulated by a licence; or

        (ii)   one or more than one of the enterprises which will or may cease to be distinct enterprises is engaged in the carrying on of activities authorised or regulated by a licence; or

    (b)   an order under section 160 or 161 of that Act where the feature, or combination of features, of the market in the United Kingdom for goods or services which prevents, restricts or distorts competition relates to –

        (i)   activities authorised or regulated by a licence; or

        (ii)   the storage of gas on terms which have been determined by the holder of a licence under section 7 above, or could have been determined by the holder if he had thought fit or had been required to determine them by or under a condition of the licence.'

(3) In subsection (2) –

    (a)   for the words 'Secretary of State' there shall be substituted 'relevant authority';

    (b)   for the words 'section, he' there shall be substituted 'section, the relevant authority'; and

    (c)   for the words 'as he considers' there shall be substituted 'as the relevant authority considers'.

(4) Subsections (3) and (4) shall cease to have effect.

(5) In subsection (5) –

    (a)   for the words 'Secretary of State' there shall be substituted 'relevant authority'; and

    (b)   for the words 'he', in both places where they appear, there shall be substituted 'the relevant authority'.

(6) For subsection (6) there shall be substituted –

'(6) Expressions used in subsection (1ZA) above and in Part 3 or (as the case may be) Part 4 of the Enterprise Act 2002 have the same meanings in that subsection as in that Part.'

Electricity Act 1989

5

(1) Section 15 of the Electricity Act 1989 (modification of licence conditions by order) shall be amended as follows.

(2) For subsections (1) and (2) there shall be substituted –

'(1) Where the Office of Fair Trading, the Competition Commission or (as the case may be) the Secretary of State (in this section "the relevant authority") makes a relevant order, the order may also provide for the modification of the conditions of a particular licence, or the standard conditions of licences of any type mentioned in section 6(1), to such extent as may appear to the relevant authority to be requisite or expedient for the purpose of giving effect to, or taking account of, any provision made by the order.

(2) In subsection (1) above "relevant order" means –

(a)   an order under section 75, 83 or 84 of, or paragraph 5, 10 or 11 of Schedule 7 to, the Enterprise Act 2002 where –
(i)   one or more than one of the enterprises which have, or may have, ceased to be distinct enterprises was engaged in the carrying on of activities authorised or regulated by a licence; or
(ii)   one or more than one of the enterprises which will or may cease to be distinct enterprises is engaged in the carrying on of activities authorised or regulated by a licence; or

(b)   an order under section 160 or 161 of that Act where the feature, or combination of features, of the market in the United Kingdom for goods or services which prevents, restricts or distorts competition relates to the generation, transmission, distribution or supply of electricity.'

(3) For subsection (2B) there shall be substituted –

'(2B) Where the relevant authority modifies under subsection (1) the standard conditions of licences of any type, the relevant authority –

(a)   shall also make (as nearly as may be) the same modifications of those conditions for the purposes of their incorporation in licences of that type granted after that time; and

(b)   may, after consultation with the Authority, make such incidental or consequential modifications as the relevant authority considers necessary or expedient of any conditions of any licence of that type granted before that time.'

(4) In subsection (2C) –

(a)   for the words 'Secretary of State' there shall be substituted 'relevant authority'; and

(b)   for the words 'he', in both places where they appear, there shall be substituted 'the relevant authority'.

(5) For subsection (3) there shall be substituted –

'(3) Expressions used in subsection (2) above and in Part 3 or (as the case may be) Part 4 of the Enterprise Act 2002 have the same meanings in that subsection as in that Part.'

Broadcasting Act 1990

6

For section 193 of the Broadcasting Act 1990 (modification of networking arrangements in consequence of reports under competition legislation) there shall be substituted –

'193 Modification of networking arrangements in consequence of competition legislation

(1) Where the Office of Fair Trading, the Competition Commission or (as the case may be) the Secretary of State (in this section "the relevant authority") makes a relevant order, the order may also provide for the modification of any networking arrangements to such extent as may appear to the relevant authority to be requisite or expedient for the purpose of giving effect to, or taking account of, any provision made by the order.

(2) In subsection (1) "relevant order" means –

(a)   an order under section 75, 83 or 84 of, or paragraph 5, 10 or 11 of Schedule 7 to, the Enterprise Act 2002 where –
   (i)   one or more than one of the enterprises which have, or may have, ceased to be distinct enterprises was engaged in the provision of programmes for broadcasting in regional Channel 3 services; or
   (ii) one or more than one of the enterprises which will or may cease to be distinct enterprises is engaged in the provision of such programmes; or
(b)   an order under section 160 or 161 of that Act where the feature, or combination of features, of the market in the United Kingdom for goods or services which prevents, restricts or distorts competition relates to the provision of programmes for broadcasting in regional Channel 3 services.

(3) Expressions used in subsection (2) and in Part 3 or (as the case may be) Part 4 of the Enterprise Act 2002 have the same meanings in that subsection as in that Part.

(4) In this section –

"networking arrangements" means any such arrangements as are mentioned in section 39(1) above; and
"regional Channel 3 service" has the meaning given by section 14(6) above.'

Water Industry Act 1991

7

(1) Section 17 of the Water Industry Act 1991 (modification of conditions of appointment by order) shall be amended as follows.

(2) For subsections (1) and (2) there shall be substituted –

'(1) Where the OFT, the Competition Commission or (as the case may be) the Secretary of State (in this section "the relevant authority") makes a relevant order, the order may, subject to subsection (3), also provide for the modification of the conditions of a company's appointment under this Chapter to such extent as may appear to the relevant authority to be requisite or expedient for the purpose of giving effect to, or taking account of, any provision made by the order.

(2) In subsection (1) above "relevant order" means –

    (a)   an order under section 75, 83 or 84 of, or paragraph 5, 10 or 11 of Schedule 7 to, the 2002 Act where –

        (i)   one or more than one of the enterprises which have, or may have, ceased to be distinct enterprises was carried on by a relevant undertaker; or

        (ii)   one or more than one of the enterprises which will or may cease to be distinct enterprises is carried on by a relevant undertaker; or

    (b)   an order under section 160 or 161 of the 2002 Act where the feature, or combination of features, of the market in the United Kingdom for goods or services which prevents, restricts or distorts competition is –

        (i)   the structure or an aspect of the structure of a market for the supply of goods or services by a relevant undertaker; or

        (ii)   the conduct of a relevant undertaker or of customers of a relevant undertaker.'

(3) For subsection (4) there shall be substituted –

'(4) Expressions used in subsection (2) above and in Part 3 or (as the case may be) Part 4 of the 2002 Act have the same meanings in that subsection as in that Part.'

8

In section 36(1) of that Act (interpretation of Part 2 of that Act) –

    (a)   the definition of 'the 1973 Act', and the word 'and' at the end of the definition, shall cease to have effect; and

    (b)   at the end of the subsection there shall be inserted –

        '"the 2002 Act" means the Enterprise Act 2002;'.

Electricity (Northern Ireland) Order 1992 (SI 1992/231 (NI 1))

9

For article 18 of the Electricity (Northern Ireland) Order 1992 (modification of licence conditions by order) there shall be substituted –

'18 Modification by order under other statutory provisions

(1) Where the Office of Fair Trading, the Competition Commission or (as the case may be) the Secretary of State (in this Article "the relevant authority") makes a relevant order, the order may also provide for the modification of the conditions of a licence to such extent as may appear to the relevant authority to be requisite or expedient for the purpose of giving effect to, or taking account of, any provision made by the order.

(2) In paragraph (1) "relevant order" means –

 (a) an order under section 75, 83 or 84 of, or paragraph 5, 10 or 11 of Schedule 7 to, the Enterprise Act 2002 where –

  (i) one or more than one of the enterprises which have, or may have, ceased to be distinct enterprises was engaged in the carrying on of activities authorised or regulated by a licence; or

  (ii) one or more than one of the enterprises which will or may cease to be distinct enterprises is engaged in the carrying on of activities authorised or regulated by a licence; or

 (b) an order under section 160 or 161 of that Act where the feature, or combination of features, of the market in the United Kingdom for goods or services which prevents, restricts or distorts competition relates to the generation, transmission or supply of electricity.

(3) In paragraph (2) expressions which are also used in Part 3 or, as the case may be, Part 4 of the Enterprise Act 2002 have the same meanings as in that Part of that Act.'

Railways Act 1993

10

(1) Section 16 of the Railways Act 1993 (modification of licence conditions by order) shall be amended as follows.

(2) For subsections (1) and (2) there shall be substituted –

'(1) Where the OFT, the Competition Commission or (as the case may be) the Secretary of State (in this section "the relevant authority") makes a relevant order, the order may also provide for the modification of the conditions of a licence to such extent as may appear to the relevant authority to be requisite or expedient for the purpose of giving effect to, or taking account of, any provision made by the order.

(2) In subsection (1) above "relevant order" means –

(a) an order under section 75, 83 or 84 of, or paragraph 5, 10 or 11 of Schedule 7 to, the Enterprise Act 2002 where –

(i) one or more than one of the enterprises which have, or may have, ceased to be distinct enterprises was engaged in the supply of services relating to railways; or

(ii) one or more than one of the enterprises which will or may cease to be distinct enterprises is engaged in the supply of services relating to railways; or

(b) an order under section 160 or 161 of that Act where the feature, or combination of features, of the market in the United Kingdom for goods or services which prevents, restricts or distorts competition relates to the supply of services relating to railways.'

(3) In subsection (3) for the words 'Secretary of State' there shall be substituted 'relevant authority'.

(4) For subsection (5) there shall be substituted –

'(5) Expressions used in subsection (2) above and in Part 3 or (as the case may be) Part 4 of the Enterprise Act 2002 have the same meanings in that subsection as in that Part; and in subsection (2) above "services relating to railways" has the same meaning as in section 67(2A) of this Act.'

Airports (Northern Ireland) Order 1994 (SI 1994/426 (NI 1))

11

(1) Article 45 of the Airports (Northern Ireland) Order 1994 (modification of certain conditions in force under Part 4 of that Order) shall be amended as follows.

(2) For paragraph (1) there shall be substituted –

'(1) Where the Office of Fair Trading, the Competition Commission or (as the case may be) the Secretary of State (in this Article "the relevant authority") makes a relevant order, the order may also provide for the revocation or modification of any relevant conditions to such extent as may appear to the relevant authority to be requisite or expedient for the purpose of giving effect to, or taking account of, any provision made by the order.

(1A) In paragraph (1) "relevant order" means –

(a) an order under section 75, 83 or 84 of, or paragraph 5, 10 or 11 of Schedule 7 to, the Enterprise Act 2002 where –

(i) one or more than one of the enterprises which have, or may have, ceased to be distinct enterprises was carried on by an airport operator; or

(ii) one or more than one of the enterprises which will or may cease to be distinct enterprises is carried on by an airport operator; or

(b) an order under section 160 or 161 of that Act where the feature, or combination of features, of the market in the United Kingdom for goods or services which prevents, restricts or distorts competition relates to the carrying on of any operational activities relating to one or more than one airport.'

(3) Paragraph (3) shall cease to have effect.

(4) For paragraph (4) there shall be substituted –

'(4) Expressions used in paragraph (1A) and in Part 3 or (as the case may be) Part 4 of the Enterprise Act 2002 have the same meanings in that paragraph as in that Part.'

12

In paragraph 13 of Schedule 6 to that Order –

    (a)   for 'Article 45(3)(b)' there shall be substituted 'Article 45(1A)';

    (b)   for 'the reference' there shall be substituted 'references'; and

    (c)   for 'a reference' there shall be substituted 'references'.

Gas (Northern Ireland) Order 1996 (SI 1996/275 (NI 2))

13

(1) Article 18 of the Gas (Northern Ireland) Order 1996 (modification of licence conditions by order) shall be amended as follows.

(2) For paragraph (1) there shall be substituted –

'(1) Where the Office of Fair Trading, the Competition Commission or (as the case may be) the Secretary of State (in this Article "the relevant authority") makes a relevant order, the order may also provide for the modification of –

    (a)   the conditions of a particular licence; or

    (b)   the standard conditions of licences under sub-paragraph (a), (b) or (c) of Article 8(1),

to such extent as may appear to the relevant authority to be requisite or expedient for the purpose of giving effect to, or taking account of, any provision made by the order.

(1A) In paragraph (1) '"relevant order" means –

    (a)   an order under section 75, 83 or 84 of, or paragraph 5, 10 or 11 of Schedule 7 to, the Enterprise Act 2002 where –

        (i)   one or more than one of the enterprises which have, or may have, ceased to be distinct enterprises was engaged in the carrying on of activities authorised or regulated by a licence; or

        (ii)   one or more than one of the enterprises which will or may cease to be distinct enterprises is engaged in the carrying on of activities authorised or regulated by a licence; or

    (b)   an order under section 160 or 161 of that Act where the feature, or combination of features, of the market in the United Kingdom for goods or services which prevents, restricts or distorts competition relates to activities authorised or regulated by a licence.'

(3) In paragraph (2) –

    (a)   for the words 'Secretary of State modifies under paragraph (1)(ii)' there shall be substituted 'relevant authority modifies under paragraph (1)(b)'; and

    (b)   for the word 'he', in both places where it appears, there shall be substituted 'the relevant authority'.

(4) Paragraph (3) shall cease to have effect.

(5) In paragraph (4) –

    (a)   for the words 'Secretary of State' there shall be substituted 'relevant authority'; and

    (b)   for the word 'he', in both places where it appears, there shall be substituted 'the relevant authority'.

(6) For paragraph (5) there shall be substituted –

'(5) Expressions used in paragraph (1A) above and in Part 3 or (as the case may be) Part 4 of the Enterprise Act 2002 have the same meanings in that paragraph as in that Part.'

Postal Services Act 2000

14

(1) Section 21 of the Postal Services Act 2000 (modification of licence conditions by order) shall be amended as follows.

(2) For subsections (1) to (4) there shall be substituted –

'(1) Where the Office of Fair Trading, the Competition Commission or (as the case may be) the Secretary of State (in this section "the relevant authority") makes a relevant order, the order may also provide for the modification of the conditions of a licence to such extent as may appear to the relevant authority to be requisite or expedient for the purpose of giving effect to, or taking account of, any provision made by the order.

(2) In subsection (1) above "relevant order" means –

    (a)   an order under section 75, 83 or 84 of, or paragraph 5, 10 or 11 of Schedule 7 to, the Enterprise Act 2002 where –

        (i)   one or more than one of the enterprises which have, or may have, ceased to be distinct enterprises was engaged in the provision of postal services; or

        (ii)   one or more than one of the enterprises which will or may cease to be distinct enterprises is engaged in the provision of postal services; or

    (b)   an order under section 160 or 161 of that Act where the feature, or combination of features, of the market in the United Kingdom for goods or services which prevents, restricts or distorts competition relates to the provision of postal services.'

(3) In subsection (5) for the words 'Secretary of State' there shall be substituted 'relevant authority'.

(4) For subsection (6) there shall be substituted –

'(6) Expressions used in subsection (2) above and in Part 3 or (as the case may be) Part 4 of the Enterprise Act 2002 have the same meanings in that subsection as in that Part.'

Transport Act 2000

15

(1) Section 19 of the Transport Act 2000 (modification of licence conditions by order) shall be amended as follows.

(2) For subsections (1) to (4) there shall be substituted –

'(1) Where the Office of Fair Trading, the Competition Commission or (as the case may be) the Secretary of State (in this section "the relevant authority") makes a relevant order, the order may also provide for the modification of the conditions of a licence to such extent as may appear to the relevant authority to be requisite or expedient for the purpose of giving effect to, or taking account of, any provision made by the order.

(2) In subsection (1) above "relevant order" means –

　　(a)　an order under section 75, 83 or 84 of, or paragraph 5, 10 or 11 of Schedule 7 to, the 2002 Act where –
　　　　(i)　one or more than one of the enterprises which have, or may have, ceased to be distinct enterprises was engaged in the provision of air traffic services; or
　　　　(ii)　one or more than one of the enterprises which will or may cease to be distinct enterprises is engaged in the provision of air traffic services; or
　　(b)　an order under section 160 or 161 of that Act where the feature, or combination of features, of the market in the United Kingdom for goods or services which prevents, restricts or distorts competition relates to the provision of air traffic services.'

(3) In subsection (5) for the words 'Secretary of State' there shall be substituted 'relevant authority'.

(4) For subsection (6) there shall be substituted –

'(6) Expressions used in subsection (2) above and in Part 3 or (as the case may be) Part 4 of the 2002 Act have the same meanings in that subsection as in that Part.'

(5) In subsection (7) for the words '1973 Act is the Fair Trading Act 1973' there shall be substituted '2002 Act is the Enterprise Act 2002'.

PART 2
APPLICATION OF PART 4 OF THIS ACT TO SECTORAL REGULATORS

Telecommunications Act 1984

16

(1) Section 50 of the Telecommunications Act 1984 (application of monopoly provisions etc to the Director General of Telecommunications) shall be amended as follows.

(2) For subsection (2) (monopoly functions to be exercisable concurrently by the Director General of Telecommunications) there shall be substituted –

> '(2) The functions to which subsection (2A) below applies shall be concurrent functions of the Director and the Office of Fair Trading.

> (2A) This subsection applies to the functions of the Office of Fair Trading under Part 4 of the Enterprise Act 2002 (other than sections 166 and 171) so far as relating to commercial activities connected with telecommunications.

> (2B) So far as necessary for the purposes of, or in connection with, subsections (2) and (2A) above, references in Part 4 of the Act of 2002 to the Office of Fair Trading (including references in provisions of that Act applied by that Part) shall be construed as including references to the Director (except in sections 166 and 171 of that Act and in any other provision of that Act where the context otherwise requires).'

(3) For subsection (4) there shall be substituted –

> '(4) Before the Office of Fair Trading or the Director first exercises in relation to any matter functions which are exercisable concurrently by virtue of subsection (2) above, that person shall consult the other.

> (4A) Neither the Office of Fair Trading nor the Director shall exercise in relation to any matter functions which are exercisable concurrently by virtue of subsection (2) above if functions which are so exercisable have been exercised in relation to that matter by the other.'

(4) In subsection (6) –

(a)   for the words 'subsection (2)' there shall be substituted 'subsection (2A)';

(b)   the words from 'or paragraph' to 'Act 1994' shall cease to have effect; and

(c)   for the words 'Part IV or section 86 or 88 of the 1973 Act' there shall be substituted 'Part 4 of the Enterprise Act 2002'.

(5) For subsection (6A) there shall be substituted –

> '(6A) Section 117 of the Enterprise Act 2002 (offences of supplying false or misleading information) as applied by section 180 of that Act shall have effect so far as relating to functions exercisable by the Director by virtue of

subsection (2) above as if the references in section 117(1)(a) and (2) to the Office of Fair Trading included references to the Director.'

(6) Subsection (7) shall cease to have effect.

Gas Act 1986

17

(1) Section 36A of the Gas Act 1986 (application of monopoly provisions etc to the Gas and Electricity Markets Authority) shall be amended as follows.

(2) For subsection (2) (monopoly functions to be exercisable concurrently by the Gas and Electricity Markets Authority) there shall be substituted –

'(2) The functions to which subsection (2A) below applies shall be concurrent functions of the Authority and the Office of Fair Trading.

(2A) This subsection applies to the functions of the Office of Fair Trading under Part 4 of the Enterprise Act 2002 (other than sections 166 and 171) so far as relating to commercial activities connected with the carrying on of activities to which this subsection applies.

(2B) So far as necessary for the purposes of, or in connection with, subsections (2) and (2A) above, references in Part 4 of the Act of 2002 to the Office of Fair Trading (including references in provisions of that Act applied by that Part) shall be construed as including references to the Authority (except in sections 166 and 171 of that Act and in any other provision of that Act where the context otherwise requires).'

(3) In subsection (4) for the word '(2)' there shall be substituted '(2A)'.

(4) For subsection (5) there shall be substituted –

'(5) Before the Office of Fair Trading or the Authority first exercises in relation to any matter functions which are exercisable concurrently by virtue of subsection (2) above, it shall consult the other.

(5A) Neither the Office of Fair Trading nor the Authority shall exercise in relation to any matter functions which are exercisable concurrently by virtue of subsection (2) above if functions which are so exercisable have been exercised in relation to that matter by the other.'

(5) In subsection (7) for the words 'Part IV or section 86 or 88 of the 1973 Act' there shall be substituted 'Part 4 of the Enterprise Act 2002'.

(6) For subsection (8) there shall be substituted –

'(8) Section 117 of the Enterprise Act 2002 (offences of supplying false or misleading information) as applied by section 180 of that Act shall have effect so far as relating to functions exercisable by the Authority by virtue of subsection (2) above as if the references in section 117(1)(a) and (2) to the Office of Fair Trading included references to the Authority.'

(7) Subsection (9) shall cease to have effect.

(8) In subsection (10) for the words 'mentioned in subsection (2) or (3) above' there shall be substituted 'exercisable by the Authority by virtue of subsection (2) or (3) above'.

Electricity Act 1989

18

(1) Section 43 of the Electricity Act 1989 (application of monopoly provisions etc to the Gas and Electricity Markets Authority) shall be amended as follows.

(2) For subsection (2) (monopoly functions to be exercisable concurrently by the Gas and Electricity Markets Authority) there shall be substituted –

'(2) The functions to which subsection (2A) below applies shall be concurrent functions of the Authority and the Office of Fair Trading.

(2A) This subsection applies to the functions of the Office of Fair Trading under Part 4 of the Enterprise Act 2002 (other than sections 166 and 171) so far as relating to commercial activities connected with the generation, transmission or supply of electricity.

(2B) So far as necessary for the purposes of, or in connection with, subsections (2) and (2A) above, references in Part 4 of the Act of 2002 to the Office of Fair Trading (including references in provisions of that Act applied by that Part) shall be construed as including references to the Authority (except in sections 166 and 171 of that Act and in any other provision of that Act where the context otherwise requires).'

(3) For subsection (4) there shall be substituted –

'(4) Before the Office of Fair Trading or the Authority first exercises in relation to any matter functions which are exercisable concurrently by virtue of subsection (2) above, it shall consult the other.

(4A) Neither the Office of Fair Trading nor the Authority shall exercise in relation to any matter functions which are exercisable concurrently by virtue of subsection (2) above if functions which are so exercisable have been exercised in relation to that matter by the other.'

(4) In subsection (6) –

    (a)   for the word '(2)' there shall be substituted '(2A)';

    (b)   the words from 'or paragraph' to 'Act 1994' shall cease to have effect; and

    (c)   for the words 'Part IV or section 86 or 88 of the 1973 Act' there shall be substituted 'Part 4 of the Enterprise Act 2002'.

(5) For subsection (6A) there shall be substituted –

'(6A) Section 117 of the Enterprise Act 2002 (offences of supplying false or misleading information) as applied by section 180 of that Act shall have effect so far as relating to functions exercisable by the Authority by virtue of subsection (2) above as if the references in section 117(1)(a) and (2) to the Office of Fair Trading included references to the Authority.'

(6) Subsection (7) shall cease to have effect.

Water Industry Act 1991

19

(1) Section 31 of the Water Industry Act 1991 (application of monopoly provisions etc to the Director General of Water Services) shall be amended as follows.

(2) For subsection (2) (monopoly functions to be exercisable concurrently by the Director General of Water Services) there shall be substituted –

'(2) The functions to which subsection (2A) below applies shall be concurrent functions of the Director and the OFT.

(2A) This subsection applies to the functions of the OFT under Part 4 of the 2002 Act (other than sections 166 and 171) so far as relating to commercial activities connected with the supply of water or the provision of sewerage services.'

(3) For subsection (4) there shall be substituted –

'(4) So far as necessary for the purposes of, or in connection with, subsections (2) and (2A) above, references in Part 4 of the 2002 Act to the OFT (including references in provisions of that Act applied by that Part) shall be construed as including references to the Director (except in sections 166 and 171 of that Act and in any other provision of that Act where the context otherwise requires).'

(4) For subsections (5) and (6) there shall be substituted –

'(5) Before the OFT or the Director first exercises in relation to any matter functions which are exercisable concurrently by virtue of subsection (2) above, that person shall consult the other.

(6) Neither the OFT nor the Director shall exercise in relation to any matter functions which are exercisable concurrently by virtue of subsection (2) above if functions which are so exercisable have been exercised in relation to that matter by the other.'

(5) In subsection (8) –

    (a)   the words from 'or paragraph' to 'Act 1994' shall cease to have effect; and

    (b)   for the words 'Part IV or section 86 or 88 of the 1973 Act' there shall be substituted 'Part 4 of the 2002 Act'.

(6) For subsection (8A) there shall be substituted –

'(8A) Section 117 of the 2002 Act (offences of supplying false or misleading information) as applied by section 180 of that Act shall have effect so far as relating to functions exercisable by the Director by virtue of subsection (2) above as if the references in section 117(1)(a) and (2) to the OFT included references to the Director.'

(7) Subsection (9) shall cease to have effect.

Electricity (Northern Ireland) Order 1992 (SI 1992/231 (NI 1))

20

(1) Article 46 of the Electricity (Northern Ireland) Order 1992 (application of monopoly provisions etc to the Director General of Electricity Supply for Northern Ireland) shall be amended as follows.

(2) For paragraph (2) (monopoly functions to be exercisable concurrently by the Director) there shall be substituted –

> '(2) The functions to which paragraph (2A) applies shall be concurrent functions of the Director and the Office of Fair Trading.
>
> (2A) This paragraph applies to the functions of the Office of Fair Trading under Part 4 of the Enterprise Act 2002 (other than sections 166 and 171) so far as relating to commercial activities connected with the generation, transmission or supply of electricity.
>
> (2B) So far as necessary for the purposes of, or in connection with, paragraphs (2) and (2A), references in Part 4 of the Act of 2002 to the Office of Fair Trading (including references in provisions of that Act applied by that Part) shall be construed as including references to the Director (except in sections 166 and 171 of that Act and in any other provision of that Act where the context otherwise requires).'

(3) For paragraph (4) there shall be substituted –

> '(4) Before the Office of Fair Trading or the Director first exercises in relation to any matter functions which are exercisable concurrently by virtue of paragraph (2), it or he shall consult the other.
>
> (4A) Neither the Office of Fair Trading nor the Director shall exercise in relation to any matter functions which are exercisable concurrently by virtue of paragraph (2) if functions which are so exercisable have been exercised in relation to that matter by the other.'

(4) In paragraph (6) –

(a)   for the words 'paragraph (2)' there shall be substituted 'paragraph (2A)';

(b)   the words from 'or paragraph' to 'Act 1994' shall cease to have effect; and

(c)   for the words 'Part IV or section 86 or 88 of the 1973 Act' there shall be substituted 'Part 4 of the Enterprise Act 2002'.

(5) For paragraph (6A) there shall be substituted –

> '(6A) Section 117 of the Enterprise Act 2002 (offences of supplying false or misleading information) as applied by section 180 of that Act shall have effect so far as relating to functions exercisable by the Director by virtue of paragraph (2) as if the references in section 117(1)(a) and (2) to the Office of Fair Trading included references to the Director.'

(6) Paragraph (7) shall cease to have effect.

Railways Act 1993

21

(1) Section 67 of the Railways Act 1993 (application of monopoly provisions etc to the Rail Regulator) shall be amended as follows.

(2) For subsection (2) (monopoly functions to be exercisable concurrently by the Rail Regulator) there shall be substituted –

'(2) The functions to which subsection (2A) below applies shall be concurrent functions of the Regulator and the OFT.

(2A) This subsection applies to the functions of the OFT under Part 4 of the Enterprise Act 2002 (other than sections 166 and 171) so far as relating to the supply of services relating to railways.

(2B) So far as necessary for the purposes of, or in connection with, subsections (2) and (2A) above, references in Part 4 of the Act of 2002 to the OFT (including references in provisions of that Act applied by that Part) shall be construed as including references to the Regulator (except in sections 166 and 171 of that Act and in any other provision of that Act where the context otherwise requires).'

(3) In subsection (3ZA) for the words 'subsection (3)' there shall be substituted 'subsections (2A) and (3)'.

(4) For subsection (4) there shall be substituted –

'(4) Before the OFT or the Regulator first exercises in relation to any matter functions which are exercisable concurrently by virtue of subsection (2) above, that person shall consult the other.

(4A) Neither the OFT nor the Regulator shall exercise in relation to any matter functions which are exercisable concurrently by virtue of subsection (2) above if functions which are so exercisable have been exercised in relation to that matter by the other.'

(5) In subsection (7) –

(a) for the words 'on a monopoly reference' there shall be substituted 'under section 136 or 142 of the Enterprise Act 2002';
(b) the words from 'was made' to 'that it' shall cease to have effect; and
(c) for the word 'him' there shall be substituted 'the Regulator'.

(6) In subsection (8) –

(a) for the word '(2)' there shall be substituted '(2A)';
(b) the words from 'or paragraph' to 'Act 1994' shall cease to have effect; and
(c) for the words 'Part IV or section 86 or 88 of the 1973 Act' there shall be substituted 'Part 4 of the Enterprise Act 2002'.

(7) For subsection (9) there shall be substituted –

'(9) Section 117 of the Enterprise Act 2002 (offences of supplying false or misleading information) as applied by section 180 of that Act shall have effect so far as relating to functions exercisable by the Regulator by virtue of subsection (2) above as if the references in section 117(1)(a) and (2) to the OFT included references to the Regulator.'

(8) Subsection (10) shall cease to have effect.

Gas (Northern Ireland) Order 1996 (SI 1996/275 (NI 2))

22

(1) Article 23 of the Gas (Northern Ireland) Order 1996 (application of monopoly provisions etc to the Director General of Gas for Northern Ireland) shall be amended as follows.

(2) For paragraph (2) (monopoly functions to be exercisable concurrently by the Director) there shall be substituted –

'(2) The functions to which paragraph (2A) applies shall be concurrent functions of the Director and the Office of Fair Trading.

(2A) This paragraph applies to the functions of the Office of Fair Trading under Part 4 of the Enterprise Act 2002 (other than sections 166 and 171) so far as relating to commercial activities connected with the conveyance, storage or supply of gas.

(2B) So far as necessary for the purposes of, or in connection with, paragraphs (2) and (2A), references in Part 4 of the Act of 2002 to the Office of Fair Trading (including references in provisions of that Act applied by that Part) shall be construed as including references to the Director (except in sections 166 and 171 of that Act and in any other provision of that Act where the context otherwise requires).'

(3) For paragraph (4) there shall be substituted –

'(4) Before the Office of Fair Trading or the Director first exercises in relation to any matter functions which are exercisable concurrently by virtue of paragraph (2), it or he shall consult the other.

(4A) Neither the Office of Fair Trading nor the Director shall exercise in relation to any matter functions which are exercisable concurrently by virtue of paragraph (2) if functions which are so exercisable have been exercised in relation to that matter by the other.'

(4) In paragraph (6) for the words 'Part IV or section 86 or 88 of the 1973 Act' there shall be substituted 'Part 4 of the Enterprise Act 2002'.

(5) For paragraph (7) there shall be substituted –

'(7) Section 117 of the Enterprise Act 2002 (offences of supplying false or misleading information) as applied by section 180 of that Act shall have effect so far as relating to functions exercisable by the Director by virtue of paragraph (2) as if the references in section 117(1)(a) and (2) to the Office of Fair Trading included references to the Director.'

(6) Paragraph (8) shall cease to have effect.

(7) In paragraph (9) for the words 'mentioned in paragraph (2) or (3)' there shall be substituted 'exercisable by the Director by virtue of paragraph (2) or (3)'.

Transport Act 2000

23

(1) Section 85 of the Transport Act 2000 (interpretation of Chapter V) shall be amended as follows.

(2) In subsection (1) for paragraph (a) there shall be substituted –

> '(a)   the 2002 Act is the Enterprise Act 2002;'.

(3) In subsection (3) –

> (a)   the words 'the 1973 Act or' shall cease to have effect; and
> (b)   for the words 'Act concerned' there shall be substituted '1998 Act'.

24

(1) Section 86 of that Act (functions exercisable by the CAA and the Director) shall be amended as follows.

(2) For subsection (2) there shall be substituted –

> '(2) This subsection applies to the OFT's functions under Part 4 of the 2002 Act (other than sections 166 and 171) so far as they relate to the supply of air traffic services.'

(3) In subsection (4)(a) for the words from the beginning to 'Act' there shall be substituted 'Part 4 of the 2002 Act (except for sections 166 and 171 but including provisions of that Act applied by that Part)'.

(4) In subsection (7)(a) for the words from the beginning to 'Act' there shall be substituted 'Part 4 of the 2002 Act'.

25

In section 87 of that Act (CAA's 1973 Act functions) for the word '1973', wherever it appears, there shall be substituted '2002'.

26

In section 89 of that Act (carrying out functions) for the word '1973', wherever it appears, there shall be substituted '2002'.

SCHEDULE 10
PROCEDURAL REQUIREMENTS FOR CERTAIN ENFORCEMENT UNDERTAKINGS AND ORDERS

Section 90

Requirements for accepting undertakings and making orders

1

Paragraph 2 applies in relation to –

(a)   any undertaking under section 73 or 82 or paragraph 3 or 9 of Schedule 7 (other than an undertaking under the enactment concerned which varies an undertaking under that enactment but not in any material respect); and

(b)   any order under section 75, 83 or 84 or paragraph 5, 10 or 11 of Schedule 7 (other than an order under the enactment concerned which is a revoking order of the kind dealt with by paragraphs 6 to 8 below).

2

(1) Before accepting an undertaking to which this paragraph applies or making an order to which this paragraph applies, the OFT, the Commission or (as the case may be) the Secretary of State (in this Schedule 'the relevant authority') shall –

(a)   give notice of the proposed undertaking or (as the case may be) order; and

(b)   consider any representations made in accordance with the notice and not withdrawn.

(2) A notice under sub-paragraph (1) shall state –

(a)   that the relevant authority proposes to accept the undertaking or (as the case may be) make the order;

(b)   the purpose and effect of the undertaking or (as the case may be) order;

(c)   the situation that the undertaking or (as the case may be) order is seeking to deal with;

(d)   any other facts which the relevant authority considers justify the acceptance of the undertaking or (as the case may be) the making of the order;

(e)   a means of gaining access to an accurate version of the proposed undertaking or (as the case may be) order at all reasonable times; and

(f)   the period (not less than 15 days starting with the date of publication of the notice in the case of an undertaking and not less than 30 days starting with that date in the case of an order) within which representations may be made in relation to the proposed undertaking or (as the case may be) order.

(3) A notice under sub-paragraph (1) shall be given by –

(a)   in the case of a proposed order, serving on any person identified in the order as a person on whom a copy of the order should be served a copy of the notice and a copy of the proposed order; and

(b)   in every case, publishing the notice.

(4) The relevant authority shall not accept the undertaking with modifications or (as the case may be) make the order with modifications unless the relevant authority –

(a)   gives notice of the proposed modifications; and

(b)   considers any representations made in accordance with the notice and not withdrawn.

(5) A notice under sub-paragraph (4) shall state –

(a)   the proposed modifications;

(b)   the reasons for them; and

(c)   the period (not less than 7 days starting with the date of the publication of the notice under sub-paragraph (4)) within which representations may be made in relation to the proposed modifications.

(6) A notice under sub-paragraph (4) shall be given by –

(a)   in the case of a proposed order, serving a copy of the notice on any person identified in the order as a person on whom a copy of the order should be served; and

(b)   in every case, publishing the notice.

3

(1) If, after giving notice under paragraph 2(1) or (4), the relevant authority decides –

(a)   not to accept the undertaking concerned or (as the case may be) make the order concerned; and

(b)   not to proceed by virtue of paragraph 5;

the relevant authority shall give notice of that decision.

(2) A notice under sub-paragraph (1) shall be given by –

(a)   in the case of a proposed order, serving a copy of the notice on any person identified in the order as a person on whom a copy of the order should be served; and

(b)   in every case, publishing the notice.

4

As soon as practicable after accepting an undertaking to which paragraph 2 applies or (as the case may be) making an order to which that paragraph applies, the relevant authority shall (except in the case of an order which is a statutory instrument) –

(a)   serve a copy of the undertaking on any person by whom it is given or (as the case may be) serve a copy of the order on any person identified in the order as a person on whom a copy of the order should be served; and

(b)   publish the undertaking or (as the case may be) the order.

5

(1) The requirements of paragraph 2(4) (and those of paragraph 2(1)) shall not apply if the relevant authority –

(a)   has already given notice under paragraph 2(1) but not paragraph 2(4) in relation to the proposed undertaking or order; and

(b)   considers that the modifications which are now being proposed are not material in any respect.

(2) The requirements of paragraph 2(4) (and those of paragraph 2(1)) shall not apply if the relevant authority –

(a)   has already given notice under paragraphs 2(1) and (4) in relation to the matter concerned; and

(b)   considers that the further modifications which are now being proposed do not differ in any material respect from the modifications in relation to which notice was last given under paragraph 2(4).

Termination of undertakings and orders

6

Paragraph 7 applies where the relevant authority is proposing to –

(a)   release any undertaking under section 73 or 82 or paragraph 3 or 9 of Schedule 7 (other than in connection with accepting an undertaking under the enactment concerned which varies or supersedes an undertaking under that enactment); or

(b)   revoke any order under section 75, 83 or 84 or paragraph 5, 10 or 11 of Schedule 7 (other than in connection with making an order under the enactment concerned which varies or supersedes an order under that enactment).

7

(1) Before releasing an undertaking to which this paragraph applies or (as the case may be) revoking an order to which this paragraph applies, the relevant authority shall –

(a)   give notice of the proposed release or (as the case may be) revocation; and

(b)   consider any representations made in accordance with the notice and not withdrawn.

(2) A notice under sub-paragraph (1) shall state –

(a)   the fact that a release or (as the case may be) revocation is proposed;

(b)   the reasons for it; and

(c)   the period (not less than 15 days starting with the date of publication of the notice in the case of an undertaking and not less than 30 days starting with that date in the case of an order) within which representations may be made in relation to the proposed release or (as the case may be) revocation.

(3) If after giving notice under sub-paragraph (1) the relevant authority decides not to proceed with the release or (as the case may be) the revocation, the relevant authority shall give notice of that decision.

(4) A notice under sub-paragraph (1) or (3) shall be given by –

(a)   serving a copy of the notice on the person who gave the undertaking which is being released or (as the case may be) on any person identified in the order being revoked as a person on whom a copy of the order should be served; and

(b)   publishing the notice.

8

As soon as practicable after releasing the undertaking or making the revoking order, the relevant authority shall (except in the case of an order which is a statutory instrument) –

(a)   serve a copy of the release of the undertaking on the person who gave the undertaking or (as the case may be) serve a copy of the revoking order on any person identified in the order being revoked as a person on whom a copy of that order should be served; and

(b)   publish the release or (as the case may be) the revoking order.

Power to dispense with the requirements of the Schedule

9

The relevant authority may dispense with any or all of the requirements of this Schedule if the relevant authority considers that the relevant authority has special reasons for doing so.

SCHEDULE 11
THE COMPETITION COMMISSION

Section 185

1

Schedule 7 to the 1998 Act is amended as follows.

2

In paragraph 1 (interpretation), after the definition of 'newspaper merger reference' there is inserted –

> '"newspaper panel member" means a member of the panel maintained under paragraph 22;'.

3

In paragraph 2 (appointment of members) –

(a)   in sub-paragraph (1)(c), for the words from the beginning to 'from' there is substituted 'the members of';

(b)   in sub-paragraph (1), after paragraph (d) there is inserted –

         '(e)   one or more members appointed by the Secretary of State to serve on the Council.';

(c)   after sub-paragraph (1) there is inserted –

      '(1A) A person may not be, at the same time, a member of the Commission and a member of the Tribunal.';

(d)   in sub-paragraph (2), for '(a)' there is substituted '(aa)'; and

(e)   in sub-paragraph (3), before paragraph (b) there is inserted –

         '(aa)   a newspaper panel member;'.

4

In paragraph 5 (the Council) –

(a)   in sub-paragraph (1), the word 'management' shall cease to have effect;

(b)   in sub-paragraph (2)(a), after 'Chairman' there is inserted 'and any deputy chairmen of the Commission';

(c)   in sub-paragraph (2), before paragraph (c) there is inserted –

         '(bb)   the member or members appointed under paragraph 2(1)(e);'; and

(d)   after sub-paragraph (3) there is inserted –

      '(3A) Without prejudice to the question whether any other functions of the Commission are to be so discharged, the functions of the Commission under sections 106, 116, and 171 of the Enterprise Act 2002 (and under section 116 as applied for the purposes of references under Part 4 of that Act by section 176 of that Act) are to be discharged by the Council.'

5

In paragraph 6 (terms of appointment) –

(a)   in sub-paragraph (2), for 'five years at a time' there is substituted 'eight years (but this does not prevent a re-appointment for the purpose only of continuing to act as a member of a group selected under paragraph 15 before the end of his term of office)'; and

(b)   sub-paragraph (5) shall cease to have effect.

6

Paragraph 7(4) (approval of Treasury) shall cease to have effect.

7

Before paragraph 8 there is inserted –

'7A

The Commission may publish advice and information in relation to any matter connected with the exercise of its functions.'

8

In paragraph 9 (staff) –

    (a)   sub-paragraph (2), and in sub-paragraph (3) the words 'and the President', shall cease to have effect;

    (b)   in sub-paragraph (4), for paragraphs (a) and (b) there is substituted 'the Secretary of State as to numbers and terms and conditions of service'.

9

Paragraph 10 (procedure) shall cease to have effect.

10

(1) Paragraph 15 (discharge of certain functions by groups) is amended as follows.

(2) In sub-paragraph (1), after 'sub-paragraph (7)' there is inserted 'or (8)'.

(3) For sub-paragraph (5) (members of newspaper panel) there is substituted –

'(5) The Chairman must select one or more newspaper panel members to be members of the group dealing with functions relating to a newspaper merger reference and, if he selects at least three such members, the group may consist entirely of those members.'

(4) In sub-paragraph (7) (Chairman's role in setting aside merger references), paragraph (b) (and the word 'or' before it) shall cease to have effect.

(5) After sub-paragraph (7) there is inserted –

'(8) The Chairman may exercise the power conferred by section 37(1), 48(1) or 64(1) of the Enterprise Act 2002 while a group is being constituted to perform a relevant general function of the Commission or, when it has been so constituted, before it has held its first meeting.'

11

(1) Paragraph 20 (requirement for two-thirds majority on reports) is amended as follows.

(2) In sub-paragraph (1), for 'sub-paragraph (2)' there is substituted 'sub-paragraphs (2) to (9)'.

(3) For sub-paragraph (2) there is substituted –

'(2) For the purposes of Part 3 of the Enterprise Act 2002 (mergers) any decision of a group under section 35(1) or 36(1) of that Act (questions to be decided on non-public interest merger references) that there is an anti-competitive outcome is to be treated as a decision under that section that there is not an anti-competitive outcome if the decision is not that of at least two-thirds of the members of the group.

(3) For the purposes of Part 3 of the Act of 2002, if the decision is not that of at least two-thirds of the members of the group –

    (a)   any decision of a group under section 47 of that Act (questions to be decided on public interest merger references) that a relevant merger situation has been created is to be treated as a decision under that section that no such situation has been created;

    (b)   any decision of a group under section 47 of that Act that the creation of a relevant merger situation has resulted, or may be expected to result, in a substantial lessening of competition within any market or markets in the United Kingdom for goods or services is to be treated as a decision under that section that the creation of that situation has not resulted, or may be expected not to result, in such a substantial lessening of competition;

    (c)   any decision of a group under section 47 of that Act that arrangements are in progress or in contemplation which, if carried into effect, will result in the creation of a relevant merger situation is to be treated as a decision under that section that no such arrangements are in progress or in contemplation; and

    (d)   any decision of a group under section 47 of that Act that the creation of such a situation as is mentioned in paragraph (c) may be expected to result in a substantial lessening of competition within any market or markets in the United Kingdom for goods or services is to be treated as a decision under that section that the creation of that situation may be expected not to result in such a substantial lessening of competition.

(4) For the purposes of Part 3 of the Act of 2002, if the decision is not that of at least two-thirds of the members of the group –

    (a)   any decision of a group under section 63 of that Act (questions to be decided on special public interest merger references) that a special merger situation has been created is to be treated as a decision under that section that no such situation has been created; and

    (b)   any decision of a group under section 63 of that Act that arrangements are in progress or in contemplation which, if carried into effect, will result in the creation of a special merger situation is to be treated as a decision under that section that no such arrangements are in progress or in contemplation.

(5) For the purposes of Part 4 of the Act of 2002 (market investigations), if the decision is not that of at least two-thirds of the members of the group, any decision of a group under section 134 or 141 (questions to be decided on market investigation references) that a feature, or combination of features, of a relevant market prevents, restricts or distorts competition in connection with the supply or acquisition of any goods or services in the United Kingdom or a part of the United Kingdom is to be treated as a decision that the feature or (as the case may be) combination of features does not prevent, restrict or distort such competition.

(6) Accordingly, for the purposes of Part 4 of the Act of 2002, a group is to be treated as having decided under section 134 or 141 that there is no adverse effect on competition if –

(a) one or more than one decision of the group is to be treated as mentioned in sub-paragraph (5); and

(b) there is no other relevant decision of the group.

(7) In sub-paragraph (6) 'relevant decision' means a decision which is not to be treated as mentioned in sub-paragraph (5) and which is that a feature, or combination of features, of a relevant market prevents, restricts or distorts competition in connection with the supply or acquisition of any goods or services in the United Kingdom or a part of the United Kingdom.

(8) Expressions used in sub-paragraphs (2) to (7) shall be construed in accordance with Part 3 or (as the case may be) 4 of the Act of 2002.

(9) Sub-paragraph (1) is also subject to specific provision made by or under other enactments about decisions which are not decisions of at least two-thirds of the members of a group.'

12

In paragraph 22 (panel of persons to act in newspaper merger references), for the words from the beginning to 'suitable' there is substituted 'There are to be members of the Commission appointed by the Secretary of State to form a panel of persons available'.

SCHEDULE 12
COMPETITION COMMISSION: CERTAIN PROCEDURAL RULES

Section 187

'SCHEDULE 7A
THE COMPETITION COMMISSION: PROCEDURAL RULES FOR MERGERS AND MARKET REFERENCES ETC

1

In this Schedule –

"market investigation" means an investigation carried out by a market reference group in connection with a reference under section 131 or 132 of the Enterprise Act 2002 (including that section as it has effect by virtue of another enactment);

"market reference group" has the meaning given by paragraph 19A(9) of Schedule 7 to this Act;

"merger investigation" means an investigation carried out by a merger reference group in connection with a reference under section 59 of the Fair Trading Act 1973, section 32 of the Water Industry Act 1991 or section 22, 33, 45 or 62 of the Act of 2002;

"merger reference group" has the meaning given by paragraph 19A(9) of Schedule 7 to this Act;

"relevant group" means a market reference group, merger reference group or special reference group;

"special investigation" means an investigation carried out by a special reference group –

    (a)   in connection with a reference under a provision mentioned in any of paragraphs (a) to (l) and (n) of the definition of 'special reference group' in paragraph 19A(9) of Schedule 7 to this Act; or

    (b)   under a provision mentioned in paragraph (m) of that definition; and

"special reference group" has the meaning given by paragraph 19A(9) of Schedule 7 to this Act.

2

Rules may make provision –

    (a)   for particular stages of a merger investigation, a market investigation or a special investigation to be dealt with in accordance with a timetable and for the revision of that timetable;

    (b)   as to the documents and information which must be given to a relevant group in connection with a merger investigation, a market investigation or a special investigation;

    (c)   as to the documents or information which a relevant group must give to other persons in connection with such an investigation.

3

Rules made by virtue of paragraph 2(a) and (b) may, in particular, enable or require a relevant group to disregard documents or information given after a particular date.

4

Rules made by virtue of paragraph 2(c) may, in particular, make provision for the notification or publication of, and for consultation about, provisional findings of a relevant group.

5

Rules may make provision as to the quorum of relevant groups.

6

Rules may make provision –

    (a)   as to the extent (if any) to which persons interested or claiming to be interested in a matter under consideration which is specified or described in the rules are allowed –

          (i)   to be (either by themselves or by their representatives) present before a relevant group or heard by that group;

          (ii)   to cross-examine witnesses; or

          (iii)   otherwise to take part;

(b)   as to the extent (if any) to which sittings of a relevant group are to be held in public; and

(c)   generally in connection with any matters permitted by rules made under paragraph (a) or (b) (including, in particular, provision for a record of any hearings).

7

Rules may make provision for –

(a)   the notification or publication of information in relation to merger investigations, market investigations or special investigations;

(b)   consultation about such investigations.'

* * * *

SCHEDULE 24
TRANSITIONAL AND TRANSITORY PROVISIONS AND SAVINGS

Section 276

Operation of references to OFT before commencement of section 2(3)

1

(1) This paragraph applies to any provision contained in this Act, or made by virtue of this Act, which contains a reference to the OFT but comes into force before the time at which section 2(3) comes into force.

(2) Until that time any reference to the OFT is to be taken as a reference to the Director.

Pensions etc of former Directors

2

In the case of any such person who has held the office of the Director as may be determined by the Secretary of State with the approval of the Minister for the Civil Service –

(a)   such pension, allowance or gratuity shall be paid to or in respect of him on his retirement or death, or

(b)   such contributions or payments shall be paid towards provision for such a pension, allowance or gratuity,

as may be so determined.

First financial year of the OFT

3

(1) If the period beginning with the day on which the OFT is established and ending with the next 31st March is six months or more, the first financial year of the OFT is that period.

(2) Otherwise the first financial year of the OFT is the period beginning with the day on which it is established and ending with 31st March in the following year.

First annual plan of the OFT

4

(1) The OFT's first annual plan (as required by section 3(1)) shall be published within the period of three months beginning with the day on which it is established.

(2) Subject to sub-paragraph (3), that annual plan shall relate to the period beginning with the date of publication and ending with the next 31st March.

(3) If the period mentioned in sub-paragraph (2) is three months or less, that annual plan shall relate to the period beginning with the date of publication and ending with the 31st March in the following year.

Last annual report of the Director General of Fair Trading

5

(1) After the abolition of the office of the Director, any duty of his to make an annual report, in relation to any calendar year for which such a report has not been made, shall be performed by the OFT.

(2) The period between the abolition of that office and the end of the preceding calendar year (if less than 12 months) shall be treated as the calendar year for which the last annual report is required.

(3) If that period is nine months or more, the OFT shall make the last annual report as soon as practicable after the end of that period.

(4) Otherwise the OFT shall make the last annual report no later than the making of its first report under section 4(1).

(5) In this paragraph 'annual report' means a report required by section 125(1) of the 1973 Act.

Effect of transfers under section 2

6

(1) In this paragraph –

'commencement' means the commencement of section 2(1);

'transferred' means transferred by section 2(1).

(2) Anything which –

    (a)   has been done by or in relation to the Director for the purposes of or in connection with anything transferred; and

    (b)   is in effect immediately before commencement,

shall be treated as if done by or in relation to the OFT.

(3) Anything (including legal proceedings) which –

    (a)   relates to anything transferred; and

    (b)   is in the process of being done by or in relation to the Director immediately before it is transferred,

may be continued by or in relation to the OFT.

(4) Nothing in section 2 or this paragraph affects the validity of anything done by or in relation to the Director before commencement.

First President and Registrar of the Competition Appeal Tribunal

7

The person who is President of the Competition Commission Appeal Tribunals (under paragraph 4 of Schedule 7 to the 1998 Act) immediately before the commencement of section 12 is on that date to become the President of the Competition Appeal Tribunal as if duly appointed under that section, on the same terms.

8

The person who is Registrar of Appeal Tribunals (under paragraph 5 of Schedule 8 to the 1998 Act) immediately before the commencement of section 12 is on that date to become the Registrar of the Competition Appeal Tribunal as if duly appointed under that section, on the same terms.

9

Any person who is a member of the Competition Commission appeal panel (but not a member of the panel of chairmen) immediately before the commencement of section 12 is on that date to become a member of the Competition Appeal Tribunal, on such terms and for such a period as the Secretary of State may determine.

10

Any member of the Competition Commission appeal panel who is, immediately before the commencement of section 12, a member of the panel of chairmen under paragraph 26 of Schedule 7 to the 1998 Act is on that date to become a chairman of the Competition Appeal Tribunal, on such terms and for such a period as the Lord Chancellor may determine.

11

Nothing in paragraph 7, 8, 9 or 10 applies to any person who, before the commencement of section 12, gives notice to the Secretary of State stating that he does not wish that paragraph to apply to him.

Tribunal rules

12

(1) Any rules made under section 48 of the 1998 Act which are in force immediately before the commencement of section 15 above shall be treated after that commencement as having been made under section 15.

(2) The Secretary of State may treat any consultation carried out with the President of the Competition Commission Appeal Tribunals (before the appointment of the President of the Competition Appeal Tribunal) as being as effective for the purposes of section 15(1) as if it had been carried out with the President of the Competition Appeal Tribunal.

Merger references

13

(1) Subject to paragraphs 15 to 18, the old law shall continue to apply where –

    (a)   two or more enterprises have ceased to be distinct enterprises (within the meaning of Part 5 of the 1973 Act); and

    (b)   the cessation has occurred before the appointed day.

(2) Subject to sub-paragraphs (3), (4) and (5) and paragraphs 15 to 18, the old law shall continue to apply in relation to any relevant arrangements which were in progress or in contemplation before the appointed day and are in progress or in contemplation on that day and (if events so require) the actual results of those arrangements where, before the appointed day –

    (a)   a merger notice was given, and not rejected under section 75B(7) of the 1973 Act or withdrawn, in relation to the arrangements;

    (b)   no merger notice was so given but, in relation to the arrangements –

        (i)   a reference was made under section 75 of the 1973 Act;

        (ii)   undertakings were accepted under section 75G of that Act; or

        (iii)   a decision was made by the Secretary of State neither to make a reference under section 75 of that Act nor to accept undertakings under section 75G of that Act; or

    (c)   a merger notice was so given, was rejected under section 75B(7) of the 1973 Act or withdrawn, paragraph (a) does not apply in relation to a different merger notice given in relation to the arrangements and, in relation to the arrangements, paragraph (b)(i), (ii) or (iii) applies.

(3) Subject to sub-paragraph (8), the new law shall, in a case of the kind mentioned in sub-paragraph (2)(a), apply in relation to any relevant arrangements and (if events so require) the actual results of those arrangements if, on or after the appointed day, a

merger notice is rejected under section 75B(7) of the 1973 Act or withdrawn in relation to the arrangements.

(4) Subject to sub-paragraph (8), the new law shall, in a case of the kind mentioned in sub-paragraph (2)(a), apply in relation to any relevant arrangements and (if events so require) the actual results of those arrangements if –

 (a) the making of a reference under section 64 or 75 of the 1973 Act in relation to those arrangements and (if events so require) the actual results of those arrangements was, immediately before the appointed day and by virtue of section 75C(1)(c), (e) or (g) of that Act, not prevented;

 (b) the period for considering the merger notice has expired (whether before, on or after the appointed day); and

 (c) no reference has been made under section 64 or 75 of the 1973 Act and no undertakings have been accepted under section 75G of that Act.

(5) Subject to sub-paragraph (8), the new law shall, in a case of the kind mentioned in sub-paragraph (2)(a), apply in relation to any relevant arrangements and (if events so require) the actual results of those arrangements if –

 (a) the making of a reference under section 64 or 75 of the 1973 Act in relation to those arrangements and (if events so require) the actual results of those arrangements becomes, on or after the appointed day and by virtue of section 75C(1)(b), (c), (d), (e) or (g) of that Act, not prevented;

 (b) the period for considering the merger notice has expired (whether before, on or after the appointed day); and

 (c) no reference has been made under section 64 or 75 of the 1973 Act and no undertakings have been accepted under section 75G of that Act.

(6) Subject to sub-paragraph (8), the new law shall apply in relation to relevant arrangements and (if events so require) the actual results of those arrangements if –

 (a) the arrangements were in progress or in contemplation before the appointed day and are in progress or in contemplation on that day;

 (b) before the appointed day and in relation to the arrangements –

  (i) no reference was made under section 75 of the 1973 Act;

  (ii) no undertakings were accepted under section 75G of that Act; and

  (iii) a decision neither to make a reference under section 75 of that Act nor to accept undertakings under section 75G of that Act was not made by the Secretary of State; and

 (c) no merger notice was given to the Director or the OFT before that day in relation to the arrangements.

(7) Subject to sub-paragraph (8), the new law shall, in a case of the kind mentioned in sub-paragraph (2)(c) (excluding the words from 'and' to the end), apply in relation to any relevant arrangements and (if events so require) the actual results of those arrangements if, in relation to the arrangements, sub-paragraph (2)(b)(i), (ii) and (iii) do not apply.

(8) Subject to paragraphs 15 to 18, the old law shall continue to apply in relation to concentrations with a Community dimension (within the meaning of the European Merger Regulations) notified before the appointed day to the European Commission under article 4 of those Regulations.

(9) In this paragraph references to relevant arrangements which are in progress or in contemplation on the appointed day include references to the actual results of those arrangements if the arrangements were in progress or in contemplation immediately before the appointed day and have, at the beginning of the appointed day, resulted in two or more enterprises ceasing to be distinct enterprises (within the meaning of Part 5 of the 1973 Act).

(10) In this paragraph –

'the European Merger Regulations' has the meaning given by section 129(1);
'merger notice' means a notice under section 75A(1) of the 1973 Act;
'the new law' means Part 3 of this Act and any related provision of law (including, in particular, any modification made under section 276(2) to that Part or any such provision);
'the old law' means sections 64 to 75K of the 1973 Act and any related provision of law (including, in particular, any modification made under section 276(2) to those sections or any such provision); and
'relevant arrangements' means arrangements which might result in two or more enterprises ceasing to be distinct enterprises (within the meaning of Part 5 of the 1973 Act).

Monopoly references

14

(1) Subject to paragraphs 15 to 18, the old law shall continue to apply in relation to any monopoly reference made before the appointed day under section 50 or 51 of the 1973 Act.

(2) No person has to comply on or after the appointed day with a requirement imposed before that day under section 44 of the 1973 Act.

(3) In this paragraph –

'monopoly reference' has the meaning given by section 5(3) of the 1973 Act; and
'the old law' means Part 4 of the 1973 Act and any related provision of law (including, in particular, any modification made under section 276(2) to that Part or any such provision).

Enforcement undertakings and orders

15

(1) Section 94(1) to (6) shall apply in relation to any undertaking –

(a)   accepted (whether before, on or after the appointed day) by a Minister of the Crown –

   (i) in pursuance of a proposal under section 56A of the 1973 Act; or

   (ii) under section 56F, 75G or 88 of that Act; and

 (b) of a description specified in an order made by the Secretary of State under this paragraph;

as it applies in relation to enforcement undertakings under Part 3.

(2) Section 94(1) to (6) shall apply in relation to any order made by a Minister of the Crown under section 56, 73, 74, 75K or 89 of the 1973 Act (whether before, on or after the appointed day) and of a description specified in an order made by the Secretary of State under this paragraph as it applies in relation to enforcement orders under Part 3.

(3) Compliance with –

 (a) an undertaking accepted by a Minister of the Crown under section 88 of the 1973 Act (whether before, on or after the appointed day) and of a description specified in an order made by the Secretary of State under this paragraph; or

 (b) an order made by a Minister of the Crown under section 56, 73, 74 or 89 of the 1973 Act (whether before, on or after the appointed day) and of a description specified in an order made by the Secretary of State under this paragraph;

shall also be enforceable by civil proceedings brought by the Commission for an injunction or for interdict or for any other appropriate relief or remedy.

(4) Sub-paragraph (3) and section 94(6) as applied by virtue of sub-paragraph (1) or (2) shall not prejudice any right that a person may have by virtue of section 94(4) as so applied to bring civil proceedings for contravention or apprehended contravention of an undertaking or order.

(5) Sections 93 and 93A of the 1973 Act shall accordingly cease to apply in relation to undertakings and orders to which sub-paragraphs (1) to (3) above apply.

16

(1) Sub-paragraph (2) applies to any undertaking –

 (a) accepted (whether before, on or after the appointed day) by a Minister of the Crown –

   (i) in pursuance of a proposal under section 56A of the 1973 Act; or

   (ii) under section 56F, 75G or 88 of that Act; and

 (b) of a description specified in an order made by the Secretary of State under this paragraph.

(2) An undertaking to which this sub-paragraph applies may be –

 (a) superseded by a new undertaking accepted by the relevant authority under this paragraph;

 (b) varied by an undertaking accepted by the relevant authority under this paragraph; or

 (c) released by the relevant authority.

(3) Subject to sub-paragraph (4) and any provision made under section 276(2), the power of the relevant authority under this paragraph to supersede, vary or release an undertaking is exercisable in the same circumstances, and on the same terms and conditions, as the power of the Minister concerned to supersede, vary or release the undertaking would be exercisable under the 1973 Act.

(4) The duty under section 75J(b) of the 1973 Act to give advice shall be a duty of the OFT to consider what action (if any) it should take.

(5) Where the relevant authority has the power by virtue of this paragraph to supersede, vary or release an undertaking accepted by a Minister of the Crown –

(a)   in pursuance of a proposal under section 56A of the 1973 Act; or
(b)   under section 56F, 75G or 88 of that Act;

the Minister concerned shall accordingly cease to have the power under that Act to supersede, vary or release the undertaking.

(6) In this paragraph 'the relevant authority' means –

(a)   in the case of an undertaking accepted in pursuance of a proposal under section 56A of the 1973 Act or an undertaking under section 56F or 75G of that Act, the OFT; and
(b)   in the case of an undertaking accepted under section 88 of that Act, the Commission.

17

(1) Any order made by a Minister of the Crown under section 56, 73, 74 or 89 of the 1973 Act (whether before, on or after the appointed day) and of a description specified in an order made by the Secretary of State under this paragraph may be varied or revoked by an order made by the Commission under this paragraph.

(2) Any order made by a Minister of the Crown under section 75K of the 1973 Act (whether before, on or after the appointed day) and of a description specified in an order made by the Secretary of State under this paragraph may be varied or revoked by an order made by the OFT under this paragraph.

(3) Subject to sub-paragraph (4) and any provision made under section 276(2), the power of the Commission to make an order under sub-paragraph (1), and the power of the OFT to make an order under sub-paragraph (2), is exercisable in the same circumstances, and on the same terms and conditions, as the power of the Minister concerned to make a corresponding varying or revoking order under the 1973 Act would be exercisable.

(4) The power of the Commission to make an order under sub-paragraph (1), and the power of the OFT to make an order under sub-paragraph (2), shall not be exercisable by statutory instrument and shall not be subject to the requirements of section 134(1) of the 1973 Act.

(5) Where the Commission or the OFT has the power by virtue of this paragraph to vary or revoke an order made by a Minister of the Crown under section 56, 73, 74, 75K or 89 of the 1973 Act, the Minister concerned shall accordingly cease to have the power to do so under that Act.

18

(1) Section 94(1) to (6) shall apply in relation to undertakings accepted under paragraph 16 and orders made under paragraph 17 as it applies in relation to enforcement undertakings and enforcement orders under Part 3.

(2) Compliance with an undertaking accepted by the Commission under paragraph 16 or an order made by it under paragraph 17 shall also be enforceable by civil proceedings brought by the Commission for an injunction or for interdict or for any other appropriate relief or remedy.

(3) Sub-paragraph (2) and section 94(6) as applied by virtue of sub-paragraph (1) shall not prejudice any right that a person may have by virtue of section 94(4) as so applied to bring civil proceedings for contravention or apprehended contravention of an undertaking or order.

Paragraphs 13 to 18: supplementary provision

19

(1) In paragraphs 13 to 18 'the appointed day' means such day as the Secretary of State may by order made by statutory instrument appoint; and different days may be appointed for different purposes.

(2) An order made by the Secretary of State under paragraph 15, 16 or 17 –

    (a)   may make different provision for different purposes; and

    (b)   shall be made by statutory instrument which shall be subject to annulment in pursuance of a resolution of either House of Parliament.

Designation orders under Schedule 4 to the 1998 Act

20

(1) Subject to sub-paragraph (2), the repeals made by section 207 do not affect –

    (a)   the operation of Schedule 4 to the 1998 Act in relation to any application for designation of a professional rule which is made before the commencement date;

    (b)   the operation of section 3(1)(d) of and Schedule 4 to the 1998 Act in relation to any designation effected by an order made before the commencement date or on an application mentioned in paragraph (a).

(2) No designation order (whenever made) shall have any effect in relation to any period of time after the end of the transitional period.

(3) Subject to sub-paragraph (2) a designation order may be made after the end of the transitional period on an application mentioned in sub-paragraph (1)(a).

(4) For the purposes of this paragraph –

    'commencement date' means the day on which section 207 comes into force;
    'designation' means designation under paragraph 2 of Schedule 4 to the 1998 Act; and

'the transitional period' means the period of three months beginning with the commencement date.

Proceedings under Part 3 of the 1973 Act

21

The repeal of section 133(3) of the 1973 Act does not affect any right to disclose information for the purposes of any proceedings before the Restrictive Practices Court to which paragraph 42 of Schedule 13 to the 1998 Act applies.

Supplementary

22

Any provision made by any of paragraphs 1 to 21 shall not apply if, and to the extent that, an order under section 276(2) makes alternative provision or provides for it not to apply.

SCHEDULE 26
REPEALS AND REVOCATIONS

Section 278

Reference	Extent of repeal or revocation
Registered Designs Act 1949	In section 11A(1), paragraphs (a) and (b).
Agricultural Marketing Act 1958	In section 19A(2), the words from the beginning of the subsection to 'this section'.
Public Records Act 1958	In Schedule 1, in Part 2, the entry relating to the Office of the Director General of Fair Trading.
Parliamentary Commissioner Act 1967	In Schedule 2, the entry relating to the Office of the Director General of Fair Trading.
Trade Descriptions Act 1968	Section 28(5) and (5A).
Local Government Act 1972	Section 81(1) and (2).
Fair Trading Act 1973	Sections 1 to 3. In section 5 – in subsection (1), paragraph (a) and the word 'or' at the end of it, and paragraph (c) and the word 'or' before it; subsection (3). Sections 6 to 22. In section 30, subsection (3) and, in subsection (5), the words ', subsection (3)'. Sections 34 to 42. Sections 44 to 56G. Sections 63 to 76.

Reference	Extent of repeal or revocation
	In section 77 –
	subsection (1)(b) and (c);
	in subsection (2), paragraph (b) and the word 'or' before it;
	subsection (3);
	in subsection (5), paragraph (b) and the word 'and' before it.
	Sections 78 to 81.
	In section 82 –
	in subsection (1), the words 'the Advisory Committee or', and, in paragraph (b), the words 'the Advisory Committee or of' and the words ', as the case may be,';
	in subsection (2), the words 'the Advisory Committee or of';
	subsection (3);
	in subsection (4), the words 'other than a monopoly reference limited to the facts'.
	In section 83 –
	in subsection (1), the words from 'any report of the Advisory Committee' to 'applies, or';
	in subsections (3) and (4), the words 'of the Advisory Committee or'.
	Section 84.
	Section 86.
	Sections 88 to 93A.
	In section 93B(1), the words 'or under the Competition Act 1980'.
	Sections 124 and 125.
	In section 129(4), the words 'or 46(2)'.
	Sections 130 and 131.
	In section 132(1), the words 'section 46,'.
	Section 133.
	In section 137(2), the definitions of 'the Advisory Committee' and 'the Director'.
	In section 138, the words 'Parts II and III,'.
	Schedules 1, 2 and 4 to 9.
	In Schedule 12, the entry relating to the Public Records Act 1958.
Prices Act 1974	In the Schedule, paragraph 12.
Consumer Credit Act 1974	Section 5.
	Section 161(2).
	Section 174.

Reference	Extent of repeal or revocation
	In section 189(1), the definition of 'Director'.
	In Schedule 4, paragraph 28.
House of Commons Disqualification Act 1975	In Schedule 1, in Part 3, the entry relating to the Director General of Fair Trading.
Northern Ireland Assembly Disqualification Act 1975	In Schedule 1, in Part 3, the entry relating to the Director General of Fair Trading.
Patents Act 1977	In section 51(1), paragraphs (a) and (b).
	In Schedule 5, paragraph 7.
Estate Agents Act 1979	Section 9(5).
	Section 10.
	Section 26(2).
	In section 33(1), the definition of 'Director'.
Competition Act 1980	In section 11, in subsection (1), paragraph (c) and the word 'or' before it, and subsections (2), (9) and (9A).
	Section 13.
	In section 16, subsection (1) and, in subsection (2), the words 'or of the Director'.
	In section 17, in subsections (1), (3) and (4), the words 'or 13(5)'.
	Section 18.
	In section 19, subsections (1) to (3), (4)(c), (d) and (f) and (5) and (6).
	Sections 20, 21 and 24.
	In section 31, in subsection (1), the words 'or regulations', in subsection (3), the words 'regulations under this Act or', and subsection (4).
Telecommunications Act 1984	In section 13, subsections (9) and (9A).
	In section 50 –
	subsection (1);
	in subsection (6), the words from 'or paragraph' to 'Act 1994';
	subsection (7).
	In Schedule 4, paragraphs 57, 60(2), 72 and 73.
Dentists Act 1984	In Schedule 5, paragraph 6.
Companies Consolidation (Consequential Provisions) Act 1985	In Schedule 2, the entry relating to section 92 of the Fair Trading Act 1973.
Administration of Justice Act 1985	In section 60(6), the words 'in paragraph 10A of Schedule 4 to the Fair Trading Act 1973 and'.
Insolvency Act 1985	In Schedule 8, paragraph 22.
Bankruptcy (Scotland) Act 1985	In Schedule 3, paragraphs 1 to 3 and 8 to 8C.
Weights and Measures Act 1985	In Schedule 12, paragraph 6.

Reference	Extent of repeal or revocation
Airports Act 1986	In section 44, subsections (3) and (3A).
	In section 54, subsection (3).
	In Schedule 4, paragraphs 3, 4, 6 and 7.
Gas Act 1986	In section 24, subsections (7) and (7A).
	In section 26A, subsections (12) and (13).
	Section 27(3) and (4).
	In section 36A, subsections (1) and (9).
	In section 41E, subsections (7) and (8).
	In Schedule 7, paragraphs 15, 19, 27 and 28.
Insolvency Act 1986	In section 212 –
	in subsection (1)(b), the word ', administrator';
	in subsection (2), in each place, the words 'or administrator';
	in subsection (4), the words 'or administrator'.
	Section 230(1).
	In section 231, in each place, the word 'administrator,'.
	In section 232, the word 'administrator,'.
	In section 240(1), the word 'and' before paragraph (c).
	In section 245(3), the word 'or' before paragraph (c).
	Section 275.
	Section 282(5).
	In section 292(1)(a), the words 'except at a time when a certificate for the summary administration of the bankrupt's estate is in force,'.
	In section 293(1), the words 'and no certificate for the summary administration of the bankrupt's estate has been issued,'.
	In section 294(1), paragraph (b) and the word 'and' before it.
	In section 297 –
	subsections (2) and (3);
	in subsection (4), the words 'but no certificate for the summary administration of the estate is issued'.
	Section 298(3).
	In section 300 –
	subsection (5);
	in subsections (6) and (7), the words 'or (5)'.
	In section 310(1), the words ', on the application of the trustee,'.

Reference	Extent of repeal or revocation
	Sections 361 and 362.
	Section 405.
	In section 427 –
	in subsection (1), the words 'England and Wales or';
	subsection (7).
	In Schedule 6, paragraphs 1 to 7.
	In Schedule 10 –
	the entry for section 12(2);
	the entry for section 15(8);
	the entry for section 18(5);
	the entry for section 21(3);
	the entry for section 22(6);
	the entry for section 23(3);
	the entry for section 24(7);
	the entry for section 27(6);
	in the entry for section 31, the word 'Undischarged';
	the entries for sections 361 and 362.
Consumer Protection Act 1987	Section 38.
	In Schedule 4, paragraphs 2(2), 3, 4 and 7.
Consumer Protection (Northern Ireland) Order 1987 (SI 1987/2049 (NI 20))	In Schedule 3, paragraphs 2 and 4.
Income and Corporation Taxes Act 1988	In Schedule 29, in paragraph 32, in the Table, the references relating to the Insolvency Act 1986.
Criminal Justice Act 1988	Section 62(2)(a).
Copyright, Designs and Patents Act 1988	In Schedule 7, paragraph 15.
Control of Misleading Advertisements Regulations 1988 (SI 1988/915)	Regulation 7(6)(a), (b), (d) and (e).
Water Act 1989	In Schedule 25, paragraphs 45(3), 47, 57 and 59(2).
Electricity Act 1989	In section 12, subsections (8) and (8A).
	In section 14A, subsections (12) and (13).
	In section 43 –
	subsection (1);
	in subsection (6), the words from 'or paragraph' to 'Act 1994';
	subsection (7).

Reference	Extent of repeal or revocation
	In section 56C, subsections (7) and (8).
	In Schedule 16, paragraphs 16, 17(2), 24, 25 and 36.
Companies Act 1989	Sections 146 to 150.
	Section 152.
	In Schedule 14, paragraphs 4(5) and 8.
	In Schedule 20, paragraphs 3 to 11, 14 to 16 and 19.
Courts and Legal Services Act 1990	Section 46(3).
	In section 119(1), the definition of 'the Director'.
	In Schedule 18, paragraphs 4, 6, 22 and 23.
Broadcasting Act 1990	Section 187(3).
	Section 192.
	In section 194A(9), the definition of 'Director'.
	In Schedule 4, in paragraph 4, sub-paragraphs (7) and (7A), in paragraph 5, sub-paragraph (5), in paragraph 8, sub-paragraphs (3) and (4) and, in paragraph 10, the definition of 'the Director'.
	In Schedule 20, paragraphs 20 and 28.
EEC Merger Control (Consequential Provisions) Regulations 1990 (SI 1990/ 1563)	Regulation 2.
Property Misdescriptions Act 1991	In the Schedule, paragraphs 2 and 7.
Finance Act 1991	In Schedule 2, paragraphs 21A and 22.
Water Industry Act 1991	In section 14, subsections (7) and (7A) .
	In section 31 –
	subsection (1);
	in subsection (8), the words from 'or paragraph' to 'Act 1994';
	subsection (9).
	In section 36(1), the definition of 'the 1973 Act' and the word 'and' at the end of it.
Water Consolidation (Consequential Provisions) Act 1991	In Schedule 1, paragraphs 24, 26, 33, 34 and 52.
Social Security (Consequential Provisions) Act 1992	In Schedule 2, paragraph 73.
Timeshare Act 1992	In Schedule 2, paragraphs 2(1) and 5.
Electricity (Northern Ireland) Order 1992 (SI 1992/ 231 (NI 1))	Article 15(8) and (8A).
	In Article 46, paragraph (1), in paragraph (6), the words from 'or paragraph' to 'Act 1994', and paragraph (7).

Reference	Extent of repeal or revocation
	In Schedule 12, paragraphs 9, 10, 14, 20, 21 and 31.
Finance Act 1993	Section 36(1) to (3).
Railways Act 1993	In section 4, in subsection (2)(a), the words from 'in cases where' to 'market', and subsection (8).
	Section 13(8) and (8A).
	Section 66(1) and (2).
	In section 67 –
	subsection (1);
	in subsection (7), the words from 'was made' to 'that it';
	in subsection (8), the words from 'or paragraph' to 'Act 1994';
	subsection (10).
	In section 83(1), the definition of 'the Director'.
	In Schedule 12, paragraphs 7, 8, 11, 12(2) and (3) and 26.
Finance Act 1994	In Schedule 6, paragraph 13(1) and (2).
	In Schedule 7, paragraph 7(2).
Coal Industry Act 1994	In Schedule 9, paragraphs 14, 15, 21 and 23.
Value Added Tax Act 1994	In Schedule 14, paragraph 8.
Deregulation and Contracting Out Act 1994	Section 7(1).
	Section 9.
	Schedule 2.
	In Schedule 4, paragraph 2.
	In Schedule 11, paragraphs 2(3) and (4) and 4(6).
Airports (Northern Ireland) Order 1994 (SI 1994/426)	Article 35(3) and (3A).
	In Article 45, paragraph (3).
	In Schedule 9, paragraphs 2, 4, 7 and 8.
Finance Act 1995	In section 17, the words 'section 386(1) of the Insolvency Act 1986) (categories of preferential debts) and'.
Finance Act 1996	In Schedule 5, paragraph 12(1) and (2).
Employment Rights Act 1996	In sections 166(7)(a) and 183(3)(a), the words 'or an administration order.'
	Section 189(4).
Channel Tunnel Rail Link Act 1996	Section 22(1).
Gas (Northern Ireland) Order 1996 (SI 1996/ 275 (NI 2))	Article 15(9) and (9A).
	Article 18(3).
	Article 23(1) and (8).

Reference	Extent of repeal or revocation
	In Schedule 6, the entries relating to sections 16 and 133 of the Fair Trading Act 1973, the entry relating to the Estate Agents Act 1979, the entry relating to the Competition Act 1980 and the entries relating to section 38 of the Consumer Protection Act 1987.
Deregulation (Fair Trading Act 1973)(Amendment)(Merger Reference Time Limits) Order 1996 (SI 1996/345)	The whole Order.
Finance Act 1997	In Schedule 2, paragraph 6.
Justices of the Peace Act 1997	Section 65.

Competition Act 1998	In section 3(1), paragraph (d) and the word 'or' before it.
	
	Section 46(3)(h).
	
	Section 48.
	
	Sections 55 and 56.
	
	In section 59(1), the definitions of 'appeal tribunal' and 'the Director'.
	
	In section 61(1), the definition of 'the Director'.
	
	Sections 66 and 67.
	
	Schedule 4.
	
	In Schedule 5, in paragraph 5(2), the words 'for him'.
	
	In Schedule 6, in paragraph 5(2), the words 'for him'.
	
	In Schedule 7 –
	
	in paragraph 1, the definitions of 'appeal panel member' and 'President' and, in the definition of 'general functions', paragraph (a) and the word 'or' at the end of it;
	
	paragraph 2(1)(a), (3)(a) and (4);
	
	paragraph 4;
	
	in paragraph 5, in sub-paragraph (1), the word 'management', sub-paragraph (2)(b) and, in sub-paragraph (3), the words 'and paragraph 5 of Schedule 8';
	
	paragraph 6(5);
	
	paragraph 7(4);
	
	in paragraph 9, sub-paragraph (2) and in sub-paragraph (3), the words 'and the President'.
	
	paragraph 10;
	
	in paragraph 15(7), paragraph (b) and the word 'or' before it;
	
	paragraphs 23 to 27.

Reference	Extent of repeal or revocation
	In Schedule 8, paragraphs 1 and 4 to 14.
	In Schedule 10 –
	paragraph 1;
	paragraph 2(7) and (10);
	paragraph 3(6) and (9) to (11);
	paragraph 4(6) and (9);
	paragraph 5(7), (9), (10) and (13);
	paragraph 6(6) and (9);
	paragraph 7(6) and (9);
	paragraph 8(6) and (9) to (11);
	paragraph 9(5);
	paragraph 10(4);
	paragraph 12(4) and (6);
	paragraph 13(8);
	paragraph 15(4);
	paragraph 17(6).
	Schedule 11.
	In Schedule 12 –
	paragraph 1(4) to (7) and (14);
	paragraph 3;
	paragraph 4(3), (4), (9), (10), (12) and (15)(a);
	paragraph 10.
Competition Act 1998 (Competition Commission) Transitional, Consequential and Supplemental Provisions Order 1999 (SI 1999/ 506)	Article 22.
Financial Services and Markets Act 2000	Section 351(1) to (3) and (7).
	In Schedule 14, paragraph 3.
	Schedule 19.
Finance Act 2000	In Schedule 7, paragraphs 2 and 3.
Regulation of Investigatory Powers Act 2000	In section 32(6), the word 'and' at the end of paragraph (l).
	In section 35(10), the word 'or' at the end of paragraph (b).
	In section 36 –
	in subsection (1), the word 'or' at the end of paragraph (c);
	in subsection (6), the word 'and' at the end of paragraph (f).
	In section 37(1), the word 'or' at the end of paragraph (c).
Postal Services Act 2000	Section 20.

Reference	Extent of repeal or revocation
Utilities Act 2000	Section 40(2), (4) and (5). In Schedule 6, paragraph 9.
Transport Act 2000	Section 12(9), (10) and (11). In section 85(3), the words 'the 1973 Act or'. Section 90(8). Section 91(5). In Schedule 8, paragraphs 11 and 12. In Schedule 10, in paragraph 4(3), the words 'for him'.
Insolvency Act 2000	Section 9. In Schedule 4, paragraph 13(3).
Competition Act 1998 (Transitional, Consequential and Supplemental Provisions) Order 2000 (SI 2000/311)	Article 9(5).
Finance Act 2001	In Schedule 5, paragraphs 17(1) and (2) and 18.
Anti-terrorism, Crime and Security Act 2001	In Schedule 4, paragraphs 5, 9, 10, 11, 17, 27, 30 and 33.
Stop Now Orders (E.C. Directive) Regulations 2001 (SI 2001/1422)	The whole Regulations.
EC Competition Law (Articles 84 and 85) Enforcement Regulations 2001 (SI 2001/2916)	Regulation 35(1) and (2).

Index

References are to paragraph numbers.